POLITICAL ECONOMY IN NINETEENTH-CENTURY AMERICA

Selected and Introduced by
Morgen Witzel

Volume 4

History of American Thought

Political Economy in Nineteenth-Century America
Selected and Introduced by **Morgen Witzel**

Volume 1
Mathew Carey
Essays on Political Economy, 1822

Volume 2
Francis Wayland
The Elements of Political Economy, 1837

Volume 3
George Tucker
Political Economy for the People, 1859

Volume 4
Amasa Walker
The Science of Wealth: A Manual of Political Economy, 1866

Volume 5
William Graham Sumner
Problems in Political Economy, 1884 and
Essays on Political Economy, 1885

Volume 6
Francis A. Walker
Political Economy, 1892

Printed in England by Antony Rowe Ltd, Chippenham

THE SCIENCE OF WEALTH: A MANUAL OF POLITICAL ECONOMY

Amasa Walker

THOEMMES PRESS

Published by Thoemmes Press, 2003

Thoemmes Press
11 Great George Street
Bristol BS1 5RR, England

http://www.thoemmes.com

Political Economy in Nineteenth-Century America
6 Volumes : ISBN 1 84371 048 X

British Library Cataloguing-in-Publication Data
A CIP record of this title is available from the British Library

This book is printed on acid-free paper, sewn, and
cased in a durable buckram.

THE

SCIENCE OF WEALTH:

A MANUAL OF POLITICAL ECONOMY.

EMBRACING

THE LAWS OF TRADE, CURRENCY, AND FINANCE.

BY AMASA WALKER,

LECTURER ON PUBLIC ECONOMY IN AMHERST COLLEGE.

BOSTON:

LITTLE, BROWN, AND COMPANY.

1866.

CAMBRIDGE:

STEREOTYPED AND PRINTED BY JOHN WILSON AND SON.

PREFACE.

IN the preparation of the following work, it has been my hope, while furnishing a Manual of Political Economy, which should present clearly and intelligibly the leading principles of the science, to afford a full and thorough analysis and description of the different *currencies* used in the commerce of the world, especially to exhibit the nature and effects of the mixed-currency system of the United States.

Regarding the instruments of exchange as essential, not only to the largest production, but to an equitable distribution and advantageous consumption, of wealth, I have long felt that a work was needed which should give more prominence to the subject of money and currency than it has heretofore received. I have searched in vain for any work on Political Economy, domestic or foreign, which even attempted such a complete view of the monetary question, in all its bearings, as it appears to me to demand. Especially does such a work seem to be called for at the present time, when there are more conflicting views and wider differences of opinion among professors of economic science on this subject, and more popular ignorance and misconception, than on any other. To pass lightly over a matter so important, so interwoven with all the great interests of society, has seemed to me a great wrong to those who, as scholars, are expected to prepare themselves for active duties and responsible positions, and, as citizens, are to decide by their votes the financial policy of the country.

In 1857, I endeavored, in a series of articles upon Political Economy, in the (New York) "Merchants' Magazine," to show the nature and effects of mixed currency, and its practical influence upon trade and industry. This, so far as I know, was the first attempt of the kind. These articles, in connection with other matter appertaining to the same subject, were published in pamphlet form in December of that year.* In 1859, a small but excellent work on Political Economy appeared, from the pen of Professor Bascom, of Williams College, presenting the currency question with great correctness, but with such brevity as not, in my view, fully to meet the wants of the public. Within the present year, and since this work has been mostly in manuscript, a manual has been published by Professor Perry, also of Williams College. It is a work of great merit; the chapter on Foreign Trade being the most able essay upon that subject which has fallen under my observation. The work contains sound views in regard to currency, and a more extended discussion than any that has preceded it; yet it does not give so full analysis as I had already prepared, such as it seems to me *one work, at least*, should contain.

* Walker on Money and Mixed Currency, 83 pp.

And here I would recognize the earnest and efficient labors of William M. George, of Philadelphia, who published in 1841–2 "A Journal of Banking," and subsequently "A Short History of Paper Money," in both of which he presented an immense array of facts, statistics, and arguments, calculated to awaken inquiry. He was the pioneer in the great work of calling public attention to the effects of such a substitute for money; and his labors are appreciated in this country and Europe, by those acquainted with his writings.

Nor would I fail to acknowledge the valuable services rendered to this department of the science by a profound student and able writer in our public journals, over the signature of "Bullionist," whose untiring efforts have done very much to diffuse correct ideas in regard to the nature of money and currency.

I presume many persons will feel that a larger space has been given to currency than properly belongs to it. To this I can only reply, that nothing is inserted not deemed relevant and essential to a complete understanding of the question at issue, in all its relations. Statistics, facts, and diagrams have been introduced to substantiate the principles announced, and impress their truthfulness.

It may be thought, that too many and too minute details have been given in regard to trade and business affairs; but experience has shown me, that we cannot safely assume that the students of a college, or the masses of the people, are so well informed in regard to these matters as to make such explanations and illustrations unnecessary.

Another motive that has influenced my mind in the

preparation of this volume has been the desire to produce a work especially accessible and useful to business men, merchants, manufacturers, &c. They have a deep and immediate personal interest in all economical questions, and need particularly to be fully informed of the character of that instrumentality by which exchanges are made, and obligations discharged. They are not prepared for the responsibilities and hazards of their several callings, unless they fully comprehend the causes which operate to increase or depress trade, to assure or endanger credit, to expand or contract currency. Political Economy may be considered as emphatically *a business science.*

But, while a knowledge of the laws of wealth is especially desirable and useful for particular classes and professions, it is obvious that the masses of the people should have an intelligent understanding of its principles. In a country where suffrage is universal, every man is virtually a law-giver. His opinions will influence his action in his choice of those who are to decide the policy of the government, which will be but the general expression of the popular will. Every man has his ideas of currency, trade, and finance; and, however imperfect or mistaken, they influence his political action. Hence the great desirableness of a general diffusion of sound views upon all questions appertaining to the economical interests of the country.

That Political Economy is a science having nothing to do with morals or religion, nor in any way appertaining to human welfare, except so far as relates to the production and accumulation of wealth, is a common opinion; but it may be fearlessly asserted, that no other science is so intimately connected with the destiny of the human race, in its highest and most enduring interests. Such has been the uniform testimony of those in the clerical profession who have given special attention to its teachings. Dr. Chalmers, while he held the chair of Divinity in the University of Edinburgh, gave lectures upon Political Economy. In the preface to the volume he published upon the subject, he says, "We cannot bid adieu to Political Economy without an earnest recommendation of its lessons to all who enter upon the ecclesiastical profession." Rev. Dr. Bethune, in his address before the Literary Society of Yale College, 1845, spoke of Political Economy "as that philanthropic science, which, next to the gospel, whose legitimate offspring it is, will do more than any thing else for the elevation and fraternization of our race." Bishop Whately was heard to remark, a short time before his death, that "no theological seminary should be without its chair of Political Economy." Agreeing fully with the opinions expressed by these eminent men, I have felt desirous, throughout the following work, to show how perfectly the laws of wealth accord with all those moral and social laws which appertain to the higher nature and aspirations of man.

TAXATION in all its forms, as imposed by national, state, or municipal authority, has received a large share of attention in this work. The great change that has taken place in the fiscal condition of the country, by which the different modes of raising revenue have become matters of the first importance to every citizen, has been an inducement to enter more fully into details than usual with writers on the general science of public economy. The American system of taxation is more complex, perhaps, than any other, from the fact of its triple character; that on the part of the general government being both direct and indirect, while that by State and municipal authorities is, in the main, direct, upon property and polls. The National Debt and Public Finances occupy that position in the present work which their importance seems to require. The subject may almost be regarded as a new one in this country.

References are made in this work to the writings of the late M. Frederick Bastiat. No author of the present age has done more to dispel popular delusions, and expose popular sophisms, — especially in his own country, France. It would be well if his writings were more extensively read in this country; and the republication of his "Harmonies of Political Economy" here would be a great benefaction to the public.

We are already furnished with the valuable work of John Stuart Mill, who is undoubtedly the ablest of living writers. Though more especially adapted to European than American use in the application of economic principles, it is extensively read in this country. While the science of wealth is always and everywhere the same, it is equally true that certain subjects of which it treats have a more practical interest in one country than another; and, of course, the importance attached to different topics will be determined by that consideration. Pauperism, and the economy of the poor-laws, may be a matter of deep concern where a frightful proportion of the people are dependent upon public charity, but of little consequence where very few, as in this country, are found in that condition. It is for this reason, that each community, while recognizing precisely the same economic laws, finds that the subjects to which they may be applied vary greatly in importance.

I cannot claim for myself any peculiar qualifications for the work I have undertaken. Some twenty years of my early life were devoted to pursuits connected with the trade and manufacturing industry of the country, while a longer period has since been devoted to the study of the laws of wealth. A practical knowledge of business and banking affairs generally, and a most earnest and persistent search for the truth in all matters appertaining to my favorite science, are the only claims I have to the attention of the public.

I should do injustice to my own feelings, if I did not acknowledge the valuable assistance of my son, Colonel Francis A. Walker, late of the volunteer service of the United States, without whose aid it would have been nearly impossible, amid other avocations, to complete this work.

A. W.

NORTH BROOKFIELD, MASS., 1866.

TABLE OF CONTENTS.

BOOK I.—DEFINITIONS.

BOOK II.—PRODUCTION.

BOOK III.—EXCHANGE.

Part I.—Trade.

BOOK III.

Part II. — Instruments of Exchange

BOOK IV.—DISTRIBUTION.

THE SCIENCE OF WEALTH:

A MANUAL OF POLITICAL ECONOMY.

POLITICAL ECONOMY.

BOOK I.

DEFINITIONS.

CHAPTER I.

CHARACTER OF THE SCIENCE.

Political Economy is the Science of Wealth, and professes to teach the laws by which the production and consumption of wealth are governed.

The term, "political economy," is not a fortunate one, since it leads the popular mind to a misapprehension of what the science actually teaches, and confounds it with politics, or the science of government, from which it is distinct.

The relations into which these sciences enter are voluntary, and for the supposed advantage of both, not from any logical necessity to complete either. A just and efficient government of the state is important to realize the largest development of wealth, but only as a condition under which the laws of wealth, already complete and harmonious, may have their own proper sway.

Government cannot furnish a new power in man, or a new agency in nature. It can, to a certain extent, control the exercise of existing power, and the use of existing agencies; but it can control only by limiting them. Nothing is added through legislation. The science of wealth is complete in its own principles, though the statesman may think it policy to contravene them for a supposed good. Political economy is, then, silent before the law.

The science of wealth would be no less complete and certain, should the action of government render the creation or possession of wealth impossible. The science would vindicate itself by saying, that, when wealth is created, it must be as my laws determine. The independence of these sciences does not imply that they are indifferent to each other. The statesman must consult the economist at every step, if he would use the powers of government to national advantage, and legislate in accordance with the natural laws of wealth, and to the advancement of the national industry. It is not intended here to enforce this as a duty, but to show, by these remarks, the relation of the statesman to the science we are to investigate.

Political economy teaches the relation of man to those objects of his desire which he can obtain only by his efforts. He has wants: he needs food, clothing, and shelter; he wishes many things not vital to him. Together, these constitute his wants, in the view of political economy. This is the first fact of the science. It is the foundation of all. These wants can only be satisfied by efforts. This is the second fact. By it, man builds on the foundation laid in his wants. The objects or satisfactions obtained by these efforts are collectively called wealth, or those things which contribute to the welfare of man. This is the third fact to be noticed. The circle of political economy is here completed. It may hereafter appear that there is a perpetual progress, an unceasing self-multiplication; that each satisfaction creates a new want, which in turn seeks its object through an effort.

Let us make a formal statement of what we have obtained: —

WANTS, EFFORTS, SATISFACTIONS; *or,*
DESIRES, LABOR, WEALTH.

The wants of man, in which are all the springs of wealth, are various, and change their place and form with times and circumstances. But they arise from his nature. They are a certain and constantly operating force. They commence with man's existence, and terminate only with his life: and, when all the desires of the individual are satisfied in the grave, and his labor paralyzed, the wealth he lays down in death becomes the possession of other men, with full strength and fresh desires; and so the creation of wealth goes on in ever-increasing circles, expanded by the central force,—the wants of man. While the individual awakens but slowly to the consciousness of his needs, gradually exhausts his activity in supplying them, and finally resigns all as he passes from life, we find that the sum of such wants and energies experiences no diminution by an atom, no suspension for an instant. Differing as these do in the individual, they are, in the world, as well ascertained and determinate as the facts on which any other science rests.

While the one element of wants or desires is secured in the constitution of man's being, the other element—viz., the relation of effort or labor to them—is fixed in the constancy of nature, and the permanence we attribute to the created world,—a foundation sure enough to build upon.

If, on the one hand, man's being were so constituted that his wants should cease, or be intermitted without any reason at the time, and without any assurance of return, or prove too weak to move the activities towards their satisfaction; or, on the other, nature were so disposed that labor had no guaranty of reward, resulting indifferently in good to the laborer, or in nothingness, or in positive injury to him who performs it,—we could have no science of political economy.

But, as man's being and nature's laws are found in experience, political economy is to be regarded as a positive science. Nothing in its fundamental principles is hypothetical or problematic. None of its methods are whimsical or accidental. Each thing is susceptible of clear demonstration. All its parts are calculable.

"Political economy plainly belongs to the same class of sciences with mechanics, astronomy, optics, chemistry, electricity, and, in general, all those physical sciences which have reached the inductive stage. Its premises are not arbitrary figments of the mind, formed without reference to concrete existences, like those of mathematics; nor are its conclusions mere generalized statements of observed facts, like those of the purely inductive natural sciences."*

In his efforts to supply his wants, we have said, man avails himself of the powers of nature, the fertility of the earth, the stimulating quality of the sun's rays, the agencies of wind, water, and steam,—all the dynamical forces and mechanical supports at his hand. He must, therefore, recognize these, and know the laws by which they are governed. But such inquiries do not come within the field of the political economist. He takes them from the hands of the physical philosopher, furnished to his own use.

Let us say, then, that human nature in its wants, the physical laws which supply them, and the statistics of human industry in all its manifestations, are the material of our science.

Political economy is a science whose laws may be disturbed in their operation, or made perplexing to observation, by the legislation of the state. No enactment could affect the movements of the planets, nor could the utmost tyranny of his age obscure the eye of the philosopher who looked on the revolution of the earth. So far as political economy, as a science, is physical, depending on the forces and agencies of nature, it is above legislation. So far as it is moral, depending on human nature, it can be hindered or deflected by laws not its own. The desires of man may be influenced by enactments, not made to cease, not brought into being; for they are all in his nature: they have been

* Logical Method of Political Economy, by Professor Cairnes, p. 38.

created, and they are indestructible. But the force of the state, while it is impotent to present man with a single new motive, or to erase one from his mind, can yet modify and control what already exist. Practically, this is the great disturbing force which political economy has encountered in all the past. Wealth is the constant subject of legislation often in direct antagonism to its own laws.

The express purpose of much legislation has been to reform human morals by an external pressure on man's desires, or, at least, to reform human manners by denying all gratification of such desires; and this, not in the interest of religion, or for the safety of the state, but in matters of dress and equipage. Other legislation has sought to supply supposed deficiencies in human intelligence, and has substituted blind laws for the keen sight of personal interest and business experience. Institutions have been created, or have grown up, whose actual effect at the present time, if not their avowed design, is to counteract the operation of the natural laws of wealth; and with these institutions vast interests have become allied in such a manner as to influence the material welfare of a great portion of the people. Hence the laws of political economy are not only contravened by direct legislation, but are obstructed or perverted in many ways by false social and political opinions.

It will be easily recognized as a part of that human nature of which we have spoken, that the promulgation of principles whose legitimate operation threatens the overthrow of long-established abuses, or which interfere with existing customs, should excite prejudice and opposition. This is one of the chief difficulties the science has had to encounter from the first. Here we have the reason why it has made comparatively little progress, and is the only science that cannot obtain a candid and impartial examination from the mass of mankind. It is a long time since chemistry was considered a diabolical art, since geology and archæology were excommunicated as infidel, since the doctrine of gravitation was an offence in the nostrils of the Church; but prejudices and ignorance and partial interests never opposed economical truths more vehemently than to-day.

"A science that comes in contact with the interests of men, which lies in the region of daily action and desire, will find its theories more frequently questioned, and its proofs more severely tried, than one which has to do with the relations of abstract ideas, or the facts of the external world. Political economy is not a science varying with climate and country. There is not an English and an American political economy distinct from each other, and, in a measure, the reverse of each other. The forces of human nature, the agents of production, the arithmetic of gains, are the same everywhere, and lead to the same principles of economic action."—*Bascom's Political Economy.*

Of the advantage of a knowledge of political economy, the same writer thus speaks: "The knowledge which it imparts is of an important and—if we choose to make that the test —of a most practical character. Wealth underlies all civilization, and ultimately, therefore, in a large measure, both knowledge and religion. It is among the lowest, but also the first, steps to social worth and national strength. We are not to value wealth for that which it is in itself, but for that to which it can be made to minister. In its retinue come, or rather may come, all intellectual, social, and religious advantages."

CHAPTER II.

DEFINITION OF WEALTH.

Having now given the three great facts on which the science is founded, it becomes necessary to fix precisely the terms to be used in the further development of these inquiries. Political economy is unlike all other sciences in this, that it has not the option of making or choosing its own terms. From the nature of the case, it is obliged to adopt words in common use. It is encumbered with all the notions, false or loose, which may have been attached to these. It has to speak of wealth; of value and utility; of labor and capital; of production, exchange, distribution, and consumption. These are common phrases. Each has a variety of meanings in popular language; yet, when used in the discussion of this science, it must have one meaning as definite, exclusive, and precise as the terms of natural history. The liability to confusion from this source can only be guarded against by being kept constantly in mind. Until the proper definitions become instinctive, so that they arise freely in their own shapes on the mention of such terms, there will be a constant slipping back, as it were, to their habitual meanings in common life. At the best, the laborious reference of the mind to formal definitions will tend to diminish the force of all representations and arguments where they appear. The greatest obstacle, however, encountered by writers, is not that arising through popular prepossessions in regard to words; but it is their own misapplication of language, confounding things essentially distinct, and clothing exact principles in expressions so vague and indeterminate as to make science impossible.

We have said that political economy treats of wealth; but what is wealth? In popular language, it is houses, lands, ships, merchandise, with a general "and so forth,"—all that we call property. In science, the term "wealth" includes all objects of VALUE, and no other.

A discussion of its principles will be satisfactory only so far as the explicitness and exclusiveness of this term is held in view. No apology is to be given for the definition, and no substitute offered. The least deviation from this line will lead to ceaseless entanglements and perplexities.

The principle is cardinal. The science turns on it.

Political economy has been called the "science of values."

No definition could be more strictly accurate; but we shall retain that already given, as being more popular, and as nearer to the customary use of the words. It is, then, the science of wealth, understanding that wealth consists of objects of value only.

CHAPTER III.

DEFINITION OF VALUE.

WHAT, then, is value? When does an article or commodity possess value?

When it is an object of man's desire, and can be obtained only by man's efforts. Any thing upon which these two conditions unite will have value; that is, a power in exchange. Value is the exchange power which one commodity or service has in relation to another.

That such a power does exist, is not a matter of dispute. Its influence is felt and acknowledged in every country, civilized or savage. This it is which excites to industry, creates commerce, and supports governments. This power obeys laws as certain and immutable as those which appertain to any of the great forces of nature. Just as man is sure to feel wants, to put forth efforts, to realize satisfactions; so he is sure to be found exchanging an excess for a novelty, a home product for that which comes from abroad, the work of his mind for the work of another's body.

Again let us remark, that the term "value" always expresses precisely power in exchange, and no other power or fact. Desirableness is not value. Utility is not value. No objects are more useful and desirable than atmospheric air, the light of day, the heat of the sun; yet these have no value. They will exchange for nothing, because any one may have all he wishes without effort.

An object, to possess value, must be desired by some one who is willing to render a service or equivalent in order to obtain it, for the reason that he cannot have it without. It is what a man gets, what another will give, that determines value. The use of this term, in its strictest sense, is of the utmost importance. If confounded with any thing, or taken into any partnership, the whole science is thrown into confusion.

It has been common for writers to speak of exchangeable value, intrinsic value, value in use, &c.; but all these terms are inappropriate. The adjectives are superfluous: they have no significance whatever. To speak of exchangeable value is to speak of exchangeable exchangeability. The term "value," in the science of values, always implies power in exchange, and nothing else.

Of all the writers on the subject, no one seems to have been more full and clear in the definition and illustration of value than M. Bastiat, in his "Harmonies of Political Economy:" —

"Theorists have set out, in the first instance, by confounding value with utility. This was their first error; and, when they perceived the consequences of it, they thought to obviate the difficulty by imagining a difference between value in use and value in exchange, — an unwieldy tautology, which had the fault of attaching the same word 'value' to two opposite phenomena" (p. 161).

"The theory of value," he further says, "is to political economy what numeration is to arithmetic. Value is the RELATION OF TWO SERVICES. The idea of value entered into the world for the first time when a man said to his brother, 'Do this for me, and I will do this for you;' they had come to an agreement: then, for the first time, we could say the two services exchanged, — *were worth each other*."

The case of the blind man and the paralytic is given in illustration. The blind man says, "I have limbs: you have eyes. I will carry you: you shall be my guide." Each receives a benefit; their services are exchanged, — *valued* by each other. Here we have value appearing, not in material wealth, but in *services;* yet the principle is just the same as when the hatter says to the bootmaker, "I will give you a hat for a pair of boots," and they change accordingly. They really exchange their mutual services, which have been put into the form of material objects.

Another illustration is given: —

"I wish for water to quench my thirst; I go two miles to the spring, and get it. My neighbor goes on the same errand. I say to him, 'Bring me water, and I will do something in the mean time for you; I will teach your child to spell.' Here is the exchange of two services: one is worth the other. Presently, I say to my neighbor, 'Instead of teaching your child while you are gone for the water, I will pay you twopence each time.' If the proposal is accepted, we say the service is worth twopence. If others in the neighborhood employ the same man to bring water, he becomes a water-merchant; and the value of water is as fully recognized as the value of wheat. The water, at first valueless, is now an article of wealth. It has not changed its chemical qualities, but services have become materialized, or incorporated with it. If the well, in the case supposed, were brought nearer to the village, the value of the water would be reduced, because less labor or service would be required to obtain it."

Suppose an aqueduct built by the joint labor of the community. The business of the human water-carrier has ceased; but not the less is the value of the water, delivered at the door, the product of labor. The labor has been invested with a permanent form, as pipes, walls of masonry, gates, &c. Labor has been *accumulated* for the purpose, instead of using the hourly labor of the water-carrier. The industry of the bricklayer and the plumber carries water years after they ceased to work on the aqueduct.

We have said that it was not the properties of the water that gave value; no more does the value reside in the mere delivery of the same. The water-works of some regions furnish them water on the ground, at the rate of a million and a half square feet a day to each square league. Yet the water has no value there; for the agencies employed are not the labor of man, but the currents of air, — Nature's pipes and conduits.

The diamond, as M. Bastiat observes, makes a great figure in works on political economy. It is adduced as an illustration of the laws of value, or of the supposed disturbance of those laws; and, as he gives a more full and satisfactory explanation of the cause of value in a diamond than any other writer, we shall quote his words: —

"I take a walk along the sea-beach, and I find by chance a magnificent diamond. I am thus put in possession of great value. Why? Am I about to confer a great benefit on the human race? Have I devoted myself to a long and laborious work? Neither the one or the other. But, undoubtedly, because the person to whom I transfer it considers that I have rendered him a great service, — all the greater that many rich men desire it, and I alone can render it. The grounds of his judgment may be controverted. Be it so. It may be founded in pride or vanity. Granted again. But this judgment has nevertheless been formed by a man who is disposed to act upon it, and that is sufficient for my argument. Far from the judgment being based on a reasonable appreciation of utility, we may allow that the very reverse is the case. Ostentation makes great sacrifices for what is utterly useless. In this case, the value, far from bearing a necessary proportion to the labor performed by the person who renders the service, may be said rather to bear proportion to the labor saved to the person who receives it. This general law, which has not, so far as I know, been observed by theoretical writers, nevertheless prevails universally in practice.

"The transaction relative to the diamond may be supposed to give rise to the following dialogue: —

"'Give me your diamond, sir.'

"'With all my heart. Give me, in exchange, your labor for an entire year.'

"'Your acquisition has not cost you a minute's work.'

"'Very well, sir: find an equally lucky minute.'

"'Yes; but, in strict equity, the exchange ought to be one of equal labor.'

"'No: in strict equity, you put your value on your service, and I upon mine. I don't force you: why should you lay a constraint upon me? Give me a whole year's labor, or seek a diamond for yourself.'

"'But that might entail on me ten years' work, and would probably end in nothing. It would be wiser and more profitable to devote those ten years to another employment.'

"'It is precisely on that account I imagined I was rendering you a *service* in asking you only one year's work. I thus save you nine, and that is the reason why I attach great *value* to the *service*. If I appear to you exacting, it is only because you regard the labor which I have performed; but consider also the labor I save you, and you will find me reasonable in my demands.'

"'It is not less true that you profit by nature.'

"'And, if I were to give away what I have found, for little or nothing, it is you who would profit by it. Besides, if this diamond possesses great value, it is not because Nature has been elaborating it since the beginning of time. She does as much for a drop of dew.'

"'Yes; but, if diamonds were as common as dew-drops, you could no longer lay down the law to me, and make your conditions.'

"'Very true; and, in that case, you would not address yourself to me, or would you be disposed to recompense me highly for a service you could perform yourself.'

The result of this dialogue, M. Bastiat regards as proving that value no more resides in the diamond than in air or water.

"It resides exclusively in the services which we suppose to be rendered and received with reference to these things, and is determined by the free bargaining of the parties who make the exchange. The pretended value of commodities is only the value of services, real or imaginary, received and rendered in connection with them. Value does not reside in the commodities themselves, and is no more to be found in a loaf of bread than in a diamond, the water, or the air. No part of the remuneration goes to Nature. It proceeds from the final consumer of the article, and is distributed exclusively among men."

Again: —

"In order that a service should possess value in the economical sense of the word, it is not at all indispensable that it should be real, conscientious, and useful service. It is sufficient that it is accepted, and paid for by another service. It depends wholly on the judgment we form in each case; and this is the reason why MORALS will always be the best auxiliary of political economy. Economic science would be impossible if we admitted as values only values correctly and judiciously appreciated."

Value does not always exist in a visible form. The wealth of a nation is generally supposed to consist in the aggregate of its material objects having value,—in its lands, buildings, ships, merchandise, treasure, canals, railroads, &c.; but its potential wealth, or power of creating wealth, includes not only all these named, but the intelligence, skill, industry, and productive energy of its citizens. No inventory of a nation's effects will give an adequate idea of its economic condition, unless we hold in view its capacity of development, and the industrial genius of the people.

The main principle in the theory of value is expressed in the common phrase, "A thing is worth what it will fetch," — that is, what some one will give for it; the value depending on the will of the purchaser, as determined by his judgment.

Value is the appreciation of services.

The value of a thing is the service or labor which it will command in exchange.

If there is no resistance to the possession of an article, it can have no value. Labor alone does not always create value; but value never exists in an article, unless some one is willing to give labor, in some form or other, in exchange for it.

The ancients thus described the combinations of exchange:

Do ut des,	Commodity for commodity.
Do ut facias,	Commodity for service.
Facio ut des,	Service for commodity.
Facio ut facias,	Service for service.

This statement exhausts all the modifications of the principle.

CHAPTER IV.

DISTINCTION BETWEEN VALUE AND UTILITY.

WE have now gone over all the ground belonging to the theory of value: but we cannot leave it without dwelling a while on one part of it; without clearly marking the boundary which separates it from the domain of utility, — a most troublesome and intrusive neighbor.

There is between utility and value a distinction as real as between weight and color.

Suppose a farmer in Vermont has one thousand bushels of wheat; its value is two thousand dollars. Its utility is, that it will make forty thousand pounds of bread.

A farmer in Illinois has one thousand bushels of wheat, equally good; but its value is only one thousand dollars. Its utility is just the same. It will make as much bread, and as good, as the wheat of Vermont. The value, then, does not reside in the utility, but in the power in exchange. The wheat of Vermont commands a higher price than that of Illinois, because of its location nearer to the market. Here *location* means *labor;* that is, the labor required to overcome it. This will be still more apparent, if we suppose the farmer removed a thousand miles by land from any market. His wheat might then have no value; yet its natural, inherent utility would be as great as ever.

Take another illustration. A pound of small nails or tacks formerly had the value of twenty-five cents, equal to one-fourth of a day's labor. By the introduction of machinery, the value was reduced to ten, then to five cents, or the twentieth part of a day's labor; the utility remaining all the time as at first. The value of many articles, especially those called manufactures, are, in the ordinary progress of human effort, constantly diminishing, though never annihilated. This is because the labor or service to be appreciated in such values is constantly lessening, though it can never wholly disappear. In this is seen, not only the certain distinction between value and utility, but one of the most beneficent laws of the science, which may be stated as follows: Value moves, diminished constantly by the substitution of the gratuitous agencies of Nature, by the ingenuity and industry of man. Utility remains fast-anchored in the wants of man and the properties of matter. This is the primary fact. But value moves again, — not to increase, but to multiply. Values are no greater, but there are more of them. The factor that multiplies is the ever-growing wants of man. Now, utility begins to move, expanding with the enlargement of man's activities, and the increase of the fruits of labor. Here we have the promise that the human race is destined to a constant augmentation of utilities, bringing in a great amelioration of its condition. Man is relieved from part of his labor only to feel new wants, and so, through fresh efforts, to find greater satisfactions in life.

Political economy makes no inquiry whether the increase of material objects of desire is, in truth and on the whole, a good. It assumes this. It leaves to others the discussion whether the highest interests of society are attained by repelling the kindness of Nature, and by denying the instincts of man. This kindness, and those instincts, political economy accepts, and goes forward from them. It can never become stoic. It is not a science, unless wealth is a good.

It is a science; and it has no doubt that the healthful, honest increase of physical necessaries, comforts, luxuries, and refinements, with the opportunities which they bring for mental improvement and moral culture, with the safeguards they place upon social order and personal rights, and with the manifold strong and subtile motives which they contribute to the exertion of all the human faculties, and the full, friendly intercourse of all communities and peoples, — it has no doubt that this is desirable. But it does not labor to prove it so. It does not found itself on any supposed refutation of asceticism. It takes without inquiry the universal inclination to the accumulation of wealth, under the restraints of mutual duties and common rights.

We have said that *Nature* adds *value* to nothing. Though unceasingly at work for man, she receives no compensation. She creates utilities beyond computation, but does all gratuitously. Wind, water, and steam are most efficiently engaged in producing commodities necessary to the welfare of mankind; and the earth is unceasingly active to bring forth man's food in its many forms. Yet all is done without adding to the wealth of the world. The forces "work for nothing," and hence confer no value. The power of the wind, for example, in propelling vessels, adds no value to the articles transported. But, it may be objected, would it not cost a great deal more to transport that merchandise, if it had to be done by human hands working at the oar? Certainly; and, from the very illustration, it appears that the power of the wind has not increased the value, but rather diminished it. It has taken the slaves from the bench, and does the merchant's rowing for him. It is Nature's work, not man's labor; and hence value goes down, while utility stands fast.

Transportation does, indeed, add to the value, but only because man's vessels and man's labor are employed in effecting it. All the natural forces that come in take off from value. If a merchant were to make a charge for the use of his vessel, the payment of his hands, and the ordinary rate of profit on his voyage, and, besides these, for the use of the wind, it would not be allowed. Competition would correct his philosophy; and the eloquence of unsold merchandise would be his teacher in the theory of value. Take steam for an example in point. The services of this great agent in England are probably equal to the muscular effort of one hundred millions of men; but the whole of it is gratuitous. All that is required to secure these services is machinery and fuel, whose whole value has been given by labor.

If we look to the fertility of the land, by far the greatest of all the natural forces engaged in production, we shall find that it confers no value. Is it asked, "Why, then, do men pay for the use of it? Why buy it at a large price?" The answer at length to this question will be deferred till the discussion of rent; but it will be sufficient for the purpose of the present argument to say, that it is because appropriated or owned (whether rightly or wrongly) by individuals who can make a profitable use of it themselves.

There are many special products which have been presented, in discussion of this subject, as exceptions to the principle, that value comes only with and by labor; *e.g.*, precious stones, curiosities, the precious metals, monopolies, patents, &c., &c. The relations of the first two are fully defined in the extract already offered from the work of M. Bastiat. Of gold and silver, it is enough to say, that, whatever the theories of the past, it is now an abundantly recognized fact, that the mining of these metals proceeds strictly according to the laws of industry, with hardly its ordinary accidents and chances. It is estimated, that, when brought to market, these metals have cost sixty-six cents on the dollar. The remaining thirty-four cents constitute the remuneration of the laborer and the capitalist; which cannot be regarded as excessive when the privations, risks, and hardships of the occupation are kept in view. Monopolies and patents confer no value, but simply contravene its laws. This is their object. They are designed, by giving the exclusive right to produce or sell a given article, to reward the favored party for his skill in invention, or for a general good supposed to be conferred upon the community. They are compulsory contributions levied upon the public for the benefit of individuals.

CHAPTER V.

DEFINITION OF LABOR.

We have defined value at great length and with various illustrations, with the result, to our minds, that it arises from the union of desire and labor; but we have not defined the latter term.

What is labor?

The voluntary efforts of human beings to produce objects of desire.

Labor is always irksome. This is law. Men do not voluntarily put forth their exertions, except for a reward. By the beneficent provision of Nature, habit assists our activities; great desires overcome the sense of weariness and pain; the impetus of one movement carries us on into the next. Toil has its compensations. Its fruit is pleasant and wholesome. But not the less is it, of itself, against the drift of man's natural inclinations.* It is because men do not voluntarily put forth exertions, except for a reward, that every thing which costs labor will, as a general rule, command a corresponding amount of service or labor. Therefore it is that labor is the essential measure of value. Whatever disturbing causes there may be, it will, on the whole and in the long-run, be true that labor commands its equivalent in labor.

In this definition, we have spoken of *voluntary* efforts alone, because involuntary or uncompensated efforts are not to be classed as labor. They are merely the result of the use of a given amount of capital. Slaves are owned,

* "Labor is either bodily or mental, or, to express the distinction more comprehensively, either muscular or nervous; and it is necessary to include in the idea, not solely the exertion itself, but all feelings of a disagreeable kind, all bodily inconvenience or mental annoyance, connected with the employment of one's thoughts or muscles, or both, in a particular occupation." — J. Stuart Mill, Principles of Political Economy, p. 29, Am. ed., vol. i.

like horses or oxen; and what value they confer is from their employment as so much capital. This distinction is not unimportant, because we shall see that capital is controlled by other laws than those which govern labor.

Under a free-labor system, as will be shown, there are two proprietors of value,—the laborer and the capitalist. Under a slave-labor system, only the latter has any share in the product.

CHAPTER VI.

DEFINITION OF CAPITAL.

LABOR enters into production, or the creation of values, in two ways: —

First, As the labor of the present.

Second, As the labor of the past.

We call the first "labor" simply; the second, "capital," which is accumulated labor. In their nature, these are identical. They have assumed different forms, have acquired independent rights, and each obeys certain laws peculiar to itself. These two forms of labor may be, and often are, owned by different persons. One man has present labor at his command. This must be his own. Another has accumulated labor. This may be his own, or that of others, of which he has come into possession.

In practice, the two forms of labor must come together and help each other, if they would effect the barest subsistence of mankind. Even the naked savage goes hungry till he gets his bow and his fishing-hook by the labor of his hands. As society goes forward to plenty, comfort, luxury, civilization, the union and mutuality of the two become more intimate and vital. By such a connection alone is wealth produced.

The growth of capital, and the steps by which it comes to its proper position in the creation of values, may be best shown by a familiar illustration. An able-bodied workman presents himself to you, having the full disposal of his own powers, fully representing the labor of the present, and that only. We will, however, compromise so far with his necessities as to allow him to be clothed; though each article he wears has come from the labor of the past, and, in this supposition, is capital. He has no tools; and, if you have no work that can be done without tools, you must deny him employment. His chances, then, of labor, are hardly as one to a hundred without tools. In the other ninety-nine, he starves for want of capital. But, by chance, you find work requiring no help from accumulated labor. You set him to clearing a field by throwing the stones into heaps. He has secured subsistence for the day without capital. It was uncertain whether he would obtain it. It is certain the employment cannot last long, since need of such assistance closes, perhaps, with the first evening; and you send him away helpless in the midst of civilization. His livelihood to-morrow is still more precarious. But no: he carries away his earnings for the day. He chooses to lay them out in an axe, rather than on any object of comfort or pleasure. He has practised a self-denial. He appears the next morning with his axe. He has enlarged the sphere of his activity, perhaps, fifty-fold. He has now fifty chances of employment. He has secured work for fifty days. Before the close of this period, he can, by thrift, provide for his immediate bodily wants; pay for his clothes, for which we gave him credit more in charity than logic; and become the possessor of a pick and shovel, scythe and rake. He is now a full farm-laborer, able to do any part of the strictly necessary work of agriculture with such tools as he has, and may rightfully expect employment every day of the year. So it is, in the grand field of the world's industry, that capital — the accumulation of labor — helps the labor of the present, not only to its immediate sustenance, but to permanent occupation, to increase, and to the highest economic civilization.

CHAPTER VII.

RELATION OF CAPITAL AND LABOR.

But this union creates the competing interests of labor and capital, since they are generally found in different hands. An interest is, in scientific meaning, a share. Each has now only a share. Before, each had the whole of its own product, but a most melancholy whole. They are competitors; for those shares are not determined absolutely in the nature of the union to which they have consented. It is by the earnestness and persistency of competition alone that either can secure its remuneration, or maintain its existence.

But they are not antagonists. All their effort, even in the severest assertion of their individual claims, goes to the increase of the common property, and the advancement of their mutual service. Antagonism tends to destroy. Its purpose is, so far as it proceeds, to remove one or the other of the parties. The competition of labor and capital never ceases; but it respects the bond of union in which only each has its own full development.

Here we see the folly of the supposed antagonism. They are partners, and should divide the results of industry in good faith and good feeling. False philosophy, or unprincipled politics, may alienate their interests, and set them at discord. Capitalists may encroach on labor. Laborers may, in their madness, destroy capital. Such is the work of ignorance and evil passions. It is the surpassing folly of the members that combined to cut off supplies from the stomach.

However far such a strife may be carried, it must result in mutual injuries; and health can only be restored by obtaining the recognition of the full rights and obligations of each. The condition of well-being is peace. A false philosophy has set the world at war for ages, proclaiming that what one nation may gain another must lose. Such a philosophy has had its trial, extending over centuries of waste and terror; and is now, fortunately, dishonored through the whole civilized world.

Akin to it is the belief that hatred and retaliation are the normal relations of capital and labor, and that mutual distrust and hurtfulness are inevitable in all the developments of industry. Such a belief blasphemes against the harmonies of Providence, — is sightless before the glorious order of man and nature. It was the popular faith in such a principle of hurt, not help, between the two great divisions of industrial power, that effected the Revolution in France. The cruel, shallow selfishness of capital has robbed labor by means of law. Labor, impoverished, ignorant, degraded, has often turned upon its tyrant, and laid in a common waste church and state, letters and wealth.

CHAPTER VIII.

THE GENERAL DIVISIONS OF THE SCIENCE.

1st, It being admitted that man has wants which he can satisfy from the world around him, and which he desires to satisfy as fully and easily as possible, we are first led to inquire in what manner this can be done most effectively, — how the forces at his command may be most advantageously employed; in other words, what are the laws which govern the PRODUCTION OF WEALTH.

2d, Since men have different capacities and tastes, — since they are placed in a variety of circumstances as to soil, climate, and civilization, — their products will be various; and yet, since all men desire nearly the same objects, an interchange of their respective commodities will become a necessity. Hence arises that department of industry called EXCHANGE, the laws of which it is the province of political economy to investigate.

3d, Almost all objects which men desire are produced by the joint efforts of several individuals. One contributes strength; another, skill; another, capital: yet the product must be distributed among them all, and in just proportions. As this division, it is quite clear, should not be left to the caprice of individuals, but be determined by natural laws, it becomes one of the departments of inquiry upon which the political economist must enter. It is here his duty to ascertain what those laws are, and under what circumstances and conditions they will effect an equitable DISTRIBUTION of the WEALTH which has been produced.

4th, As all commodities created by human exertion are designed for use, and as such use implies consumption more or less rapid, and as upon this depends the power and disposition for reproduction, the question of CONSUMPTION has a scientific place among the objects of our inquiry, and will be found to possess a practical importance second only to that of production.

These are the four great questions which suggest the general divisions of our subject; viz., production, exchange, distribution, and consumption of wealth.

Exchange might not improperly be regarded as belonging to the first general division, since it contributes largely in the actual production of wealth: yet, as it also greatly facilitates and increases consumption, and has influence throughout the whole domain of human industry, it seems desirable to regard it as a separate department; and it has often been treated as such by writers on the general subject.

BOOK II.

PRODUCTION.

CHAPTER I.

FORMS OF PRODUCTION.

ALL values are created by modifications of existing matter. Man cannot create one particle; but he can modify what he finds, or change its condition, in three ways; viz.:—

By TRANSMUTATION, *by* TRANSFORMATION, *by* TRANSPORTATION.

First, by *transmutation*.

This is eminently the work of the agriculturist, who, availing himself of the chemical agencies of the earth and air, transmutes seeds into vegetables, fruits, and grains; and these again, by the aid of animal organizations, into butter, beef, hides, &c. This is the most extensive branch of industry, and employs probably four-fifths of the human race from generation to generation. It is the base of the great pyramid of production. It furnishes the material and the support of all other forms of labor; and not this only, but it renews and restores their waste with an unceasing supply of fresh bodily and mental power. The air of trade and of the mill heats and rises, and cold currents rush in from the prairie and the mountain. The foot of the rustic is ever turned to the marts of commerce, and the busy gatherings of men. He comes with clumsy tread and homespun dress; but he takes the first place in the market and the synagogue. Basil enters Constantinople as night is falling, stares about on the magnificence of the city, and falls asleep on the steps of the Church of St. Diomede. He is tired of Macedon. He has business on the throne of the world. He who restored the laws of the Eastern empire, and reclaimed the lands deluged by the barbarian floods, is the exemplar of the countryman, in all times, gazing rudely around on the luxury his homely virtues are to appropriate. The millionnaire dashes by in his splendid turnout: a raw, tall lad, with a bundle on a stick, looks on with wonder, — the employer of that man's children.

Just as agriculture sends to the markets and the mills of the world their materials, so it sends them their workmen. Strength and even life go fast in the eager competitions of manufactures and trade. Cool air, fresh blood, flows in from the country, to supply the waste. The bare, bleak hills, where Nature grudges every morsel of food, and stabs cruelly through every chink in the wall, every rent in the clothes, feed the busy cities with men. The streams of vigorous life run off from them to refresh the plains below.

Agriculture has no need to receive back, in any form, her contributions to the other occupations. The power to give without exhaustion lies in the liberal, healthful *reproduction* of man, when living in intimate relations with Nature. Here, after all its hurts, humanity comes for healing. War and pestilence, the fierce contest of the mart, the stifling atmosphere of the mill, may waste our kind in quick or lingering deaths; but still, by the side of the brooks, men will be born to hold up the frame of industry and social order when their supporters faint and fail. Yet agriculture does get back a certain share of what it gives. Because it is not a labor of ambition, because honors are not to be gathered in the fields it cultivates, because the excitements of machinery and association are not to be found in its work or play, because quick wealth is not to be realized in its slow increase, the rustic turns himself to the city; and because it is not a labor of ambition, and for each of the other reasons given, the *citizen*, weary with all, goes back to the open fields and fresh air of the country. The cabbages of Diocletian, the eggs of John Ducas Vataces, the apples of Sir William Temple, are the return made to agriculture for Basils, Astors, and Lawrences.

But the department of agriculture is not confined to the popular view of it. When grain is produced, the seed must be planted in prepared ground, the long interval of growth to maturity must be filled with care and labor; and, at last, the work of harvesting completes the round of duties that go to the production of the grain. But there are great industries in the department of agriculture, where harvesting alone is performed by man. Nature has done all the rest. Man's part is to find and to take of her bounty. Such an industry is mining, — whether of iron or coal, whether of diamonds underground in Golconda, or sponge under water in the Archipelago. Such an industry is the fisheries, — whether of whales off Greenland, of cod off Newfoundland, or of pearl-oyster off Ceylon. So great, indeed, is the scientific extension of the department of agriculture, that even the smelting of the ore, and the transportation from the fishing-grounds to the port from which the venture began, are included in it, because these first put the products in the possession of the capitalist in an available form. Any further change, whether to make the metal up into forms for use, or carry the fish or oil or pearls to market, would come under the other forms of production, to which we now proceed.

Man modifies matter and exchanges its condition, —

Secondly, by *transformation.*

This is the business of the manufacturer and the mechanic. These create values by changing the forms of matter, as cotton and wool into cloth, iron into tools and implements. This is the second great department of human industry. Its ramifications extend throughout the world, yet not everywhere of the same vigor and extent. Since manufactures, as a whole, do not meet wants so primitive and absolute as does agriculture, they are, by a law evident in all industry, found not to be so equally diffused. Those needs which are peremptory and instant will, from that reason, tend to obtain their supply from the immediate neighborhood in which they arise. The nearer objects of desire approach to being luxuries, the more cosmopolitan they become. Other reasons, which will appear in our progress, will further account for the unequal growth of manufactures, which have yet more uniformity than is exhibited in statistical tables, or in general estimation, since the staple articles of manufacture attract more attention than those multiform smaller products which far outweigh them in value.

The distribution of manufactures is governed by a variety of conditions, among which may be briefly stated the following: —

1. The industrial genius of a people. Without plunging into the deep questions of ethnical differences, or compensations in the whole of character, it is yet evident beyond discussion, that the active powers of every people have something of their own which they do not fully share with others. Were all the nations of the earth possessed of mental, moral, and physical qualities which could be positively estimated to be, in the sum of them, *equal*, it is quite certain that they would be far from *similar:* their energies would develop in different lines towards different objects. Patience and a kind of business faith distinguish some peoples, mark their features, and are impressed distinctly in the results of industry. Activity and daring speculation no less characterize others. To a class of minds thoroughly representative of more than one nation, mechanical contrivance gives the same glow of pleasure that rewards the painter for his years of toil. A distrustful, reserved, secretive disposition may be observed through the entire industry of another country, tending to individualize efforts and discourage combination. The catalogue of

traits has been extended sufficiently to account for much of the inequality which exists in the distribution of manufactures among the nations of the civilized world.

2. The territorial advantages of a people, which are both positive and negative in their nature,—positive, as a people is endowed with water-power, and with the collocation of necessary materials, as of ore, coal, and lime for making iron; negative, as a people is not attracted to other branches of production by superior facilities. It is estimated that Holland has not agricultural capacities to supply a third of its population. With some peoples, this niggardliness of soil would have been a reason for emigration or starvation; but there, uniting with the peculiar genius of the inhabitants, this necessity has produced a wealthy and flourishing state. It has ever been held by moral writers, that such unkindness of Nature develops the industrial energies of a people, where it is not so extreme as to destroy even the conditions of production. But the inquiry is too abstruse for our purpose.

3. Great accidents, belonging neither to the essential genius of the people, or its territorial endowments. Such are the transcendent discoveries in the sciences and the arts. Such are wars which exhaust nations, leaving them weak for generations. Such are persecutions, like that which scattered over the continent six hundred thousand Huguenots,—the cunning artisans of France; like that which wrought devastation still greater in the "reconciled" provinces of Spain.* Such was the windfall of the Indies in the lap of Europe. The desirableness of such a distribution of manufactures will be discussed elsewhere. Our purpose here is only to show by what means it comes about so unequally.

Passing now from this question, and looking only to the aggregate of such industries, we find it to be small, if we

* "Our manufactures were the growth of the persecutions in the Low Countries."—EDMUND BURKE, in his speech to the electors of Bristol.

consider only the number of those employed. But labor here acts in connection with a greater amount of capital than in agriculture, and avails itself of more and mightier agencies of Nature. The factor into which labor is multiplied is vastly increased when we enter the workshop and the mill.

But man modifies matter or changes its condition,—

Thirdly, by *transportation.*

The merchant does not primarily create value in objects, but enhances that already existing by transporting such objects from one locality to another.

The characteristic illustration is of the most familiar kind. Cotton bought at New Orleans, in 1860, for twelve cents per pound, transported to Liverpool, would have sold, say, for fifteen cents. By his capital and skill, the merchant has added twenty-five per cent to the value or exchangeability of the cotton. He has increased the wealth of the world so much. He, therefore, has produced value. Such transactions are useful alike to the producer and to the consumer of the articles transported.

In so far as the transportation of products gives them value, it belongs to the present general division of the subject; but its methods and agencies are so unlike those of the other forms of production, it is governed by laws so peculiar and complete in themselves, it composes so large and easily separate a department of inquiry, that it is, for the discussion of its principles, placed as a general division of the science under the title of "Exchange." To complete the sphere of production, we recognize here the share it has in creating values; but the means by which this is effected, and the impressive phenomena exhibited in the operation of this agency throughout the entire world, are set apart for special consideration.

We have thus gone through the three forms in which man modifies matter to create values,—transmutation, transformation, and transportation. The inquiry will at once occur, whether these exhaust all possible efforts in production. The answer may come out more clearly if we proceed by an illustration.

The chemist, — what is his position in the world of values? He has been ranked, by some scientific writers, among the agricultural class, because he so aids and directs the processes of Nature as to produce objects of value by changing the elementary powers of acids and alkalies into salts, &c. That is, he transmutes. It seems more accurate to say, that he belongs among producers just so far as he assists in any one of the three forms defined. He works by the side of the agriculturist, helping how best to direct the labor of the farm. Here the chemist produces value. He works by the side of the manufacturer, with lubricants and solvents, removing obstacles which no muscular strength could shake; and here, again, he produces values. He may, also, labor by the side of the merchant, making much cunning use of Nature; and here, again, he produces values, in the form of transportation. From each he receives remuneration in proportion as he renders service.

The division we have made of production into three modes seems to afford the best view attainable of the subject. It will be observed, that these are not distinct forms in which labor appears, as in so many moulds; but that they result from an arbitrary classification of individual efforts, according to the best reason of the case. The whole authority of such a classification consists in this, — that it is more complete and definite than any other which is offered.

All these forms of productive effort may be united in a single commodity; and, indeed, there are but few products which do not contain them all. To the agriculturist has been attributed the work of transmutation. Yet, practically, he performs every function of human labor; and, directly or indirectly, uses nearly every known agency of Art or Nature. The manufacturer has the work of transformation; but he can only create values by mingling his labor with that of the agriculturist and the merchant, and thus the final product is the property of all. By what principle, and through what force, the remuneration of each is determined, will appear under the title of "Distribution." Such, then, are the general forms in which man puts forth his efforts for the satisfaction of his desires.

CHAPTER II.

CONDITIONS OF THE HIGHEST PRODUCTION.

IF labor, through some form, produces all wealth, we are led to inquire into the circumstances and conditions that increase or diminish the efficiency of this great force. That there are mighty variations as it appears in different countries, and even in adjacent communities, is so manifest as hardly to require mention or illustration.

If the wealth of any nation cannot be determined merely by the proportion of its population to that of the world, or of its territory to the general mass of the globe, — as it clearly cannot, — the question, Why? introduces us to the discussion of all those influences which directly or indirectly, immediately or remotely, make one to differ from another. These may be classed as follows: —

DIVISION OF LABOR.
CO-OPERATION OF CAPITAL.
ECONOMIC CULTURE.

CHAPTER III.

DIVISION OF LABOR.

In some countries, a man wishing for a chair goes into the forest, fells a tree, carries the timber to his workshop, forms the parts, and puts them together into a chair. It is a rude and imperfect article, but it has cost him the labor of two days.

In other communities, we find a chair, equally serviceable and far more elegant, produced by the labor of half a day. Here one man cuts the timber, another transports to the mill, another saws it into suitable dimensions, another forms the legs, another the seat, another the back, another puts the parts together, while still another paints it. A great many chairs are produced by the combined labor of many individuals; and the result is, that one chair has the value of only half a day's labor. Three-fourths of the labor employed in the making of chairs is, then, liberated, to rest in idleness, or to apply itself to further production with still increasing results, as the desires which control efforts shall determine. We cannot be ignorant, that, in some communities, labor, when set free, does waste itself in idleness and frolic. But this is true chiefly of those in which leisure is bestowed, not by man's contrivance, but by the generosity of Nature. Here the power of labor is too often corrupted by the very luxuriance of growth, which gives it great opportunities, and opens a world to its easy conquest.

But it may safely be assumed, that such an industrial genius in a people, as seeks to lessen present labor by the distribution of its several offices, will find fresh objects of desire. The very thoughtfulness and care, the social confidence, and mutuality of service, which are required to effect a division of labor, insure such a susceptibility to new industrial wants as shall necessitate the employment of all the labor so relieved.

The savage who can provide himself with clothing, shelter, and food in twenty days of the year, may be willing to spend the rest of the time in doing nothing. But it was never heard that men came together to do any thing, and remain content to do nothing more. The full discussion and illustration of this principle, which governs the use of labor saved, belongs to the third inquiry; viz., that of "Economic Culture." We have here, strictly, to show only how labor *is* saved by the division of employments. This forms the great fact of modern industrial civilization. We shall find it the most important condition of production, multiplying all its powers faster than the soil multiplies the seed. Here is more of the explanation of wealth than can be found in all other inquiries. This force is being rapidly introduced into every department of industry, and will finally become as general as the nature of the different employments will admit. We do not find that it has yet reached its ultimate limit in any sphere of human activity. We shall give its phenomena and its principles special attention; for the greatest interests of society, moral as well as economical, connect themselves with it.

What is the significance of division of labor, as expressed in the fewest words? It is, that each workman confine himself to a single operation.

In this way, all great and successful manufactures are carried on.

Take, for illustration, that of boots. One person cuts the fronts; one crimps; one cuts in; one cuts out the backs, one the linings; one pastes together; one strips out the sole leather; one cuts the soles; one makes the heels; one stiches the backs; one sides up; one binds; one bottoms; one buffs; one trees; one packs, marks, &c. Here are sixteen persons employed in the production of a single boot. In many cases, a still further division of the parts is made with success. In passing, it may be remarked, that, of those operations, seven are performed by the aid of machines, as distinguished in popular acceptation from tools, which latter are controlled by the hand, and have all their motive power in the muscular force of man.

As long ago as Adam Smith wrote, it took sixteen persons to make a pin.

Such, in description, is division of labor. Let us consider its advantages, limitations, and disadvantages.

CHAPTER IV.

THE ADVANTAGES OF DIVISION OF LABOR.

1st, It gives increased dexterity. All common observation testifies how rapid and accurate our motions become, when confined to a single operation. The juggler is not more remarkable for the nice use of his muscles, than is an accomplished mechanic at his bench. The powers of his body are in perfect discipline. They have learned their parts, and obey instantaneously and harmoniously. The more simple the movement assigned, the greater will be the efficiency of performance.

2d, It allows the workman a better knowledge of his business. This is to the mental powers what the first is to the bodily. It gives intellectual dexterity. The man has a mastery of his special operation. He knows more about it than if he had two things to think of and care for. He becomes shrewd in every motion. He adapts his labor to the material; he discriminates between the qualities of that material. He meets the little difficulties of his work with more skill and less waste. These two advantages of the division of labor are shown in the different wages which skilled mechanics obtain as compared with unskilled, able seamen with landsmen.

3d, It saves time, in passing from one work to another. In the making of a chair after the primitive fashion, we have supposed a great deal of time will be spent in passing from one part of it to another, from the place of one operation to that of another. And, even where we suppose a laborer to be engaged in two operations only, there is still a loss inflicted, just as often as he has occasion to leave one for another. It is not a loss alone of the time physically necessary in effecting the transition, but each operation will leave something to harass the mind in the other. During the first part, the attention will be distracted by what has just been left. During the last part, the attention will run on, anticipating what is to come. The shadow is cast both ways upon the mind.

4th, It facilitates the invention of tools and machines. If a treasure of gold or iron or oil is hid under the ground, the discoverer is more apt, other things being equal, to be the man who owns the land, and resides and works on it, than a casual visitor. So, if there is a possibility of adapting foreign forces to the production of values, the inventor will, on the same condition, more probably be the workman than any one else; he is constantly engaged upon the operation; he desires, of course, to simplify it, since it is a law of mind to do as little work as possible for a certain result; he knows the wants of the subject; he knows all the capabilities of his material; he thinks about it all the time, and can try an experiment without changing his place. Therefore, by the logic of Nature, he invents. And, in fact, few of the great aids to industry have been discovered by disinterested science. They came from the laboring brain of the mechanic. Where the work was almost too delicate for human eyes, a thousand iron fingers go around to do it, never losing their nimbleness, nor ever getting weary; where the work was too great for human strength, monster arms swing the hammer, or toss the load in air.

The history of American manufactures expounds the

phrase, "Necessity is the mother of invention." Even the slaves of the South have been directed to important mechanical discoveries, in the way we have described. One simple operation, constantly employing the attention, must, in time, lose all its secrets.

5th, It secures the better adaptation of physical and mental abilities. No consideration is more vital than this. The work which man finds to do, the efforts he has to make for satisfactions, however high his wants may rise, will be of the most various character, and require the most diverse powers. There are operations which demand great strength; others, rapid motion; others, good judgment; others, a mechanical eye; others, fidelity and trust; others, high intelligence and education. Such qualities, even those purely physical, are not found equally in all; nay, by the compensations of Nature, they are generally, though not necessarily, found apart. Therefore, unless work were divided according to the several qualities required, a deficiency in one would neutralize all the others, and exclude the workman from employment, or compel him to work at great disadvantage.

The extensive applications of this principle will occur to every mind. Each man finds the sphere of his highest usefulness as he is endowed by Nature. Those who are gifted with education and ingenuity devote all their time and energy to duties appropriate to such powers. They thus confer on others the advantage of their own gifts, and are themselves spared from drudgery and uncongenial labor. The poorest in qualifications, also, find a place in which they can produce within the great partnership of society. Women are enabled to undertake business of the most delicate and important character, to which their strength is sufficient; while children of all ages take parts that would otherwise occupy men. The power saved or gained, by such an adaptation of talents to special branches of industry, is incalculable. Without it, a great part of the human race would be helpless paupers, and the remainder would earn a scanty and miserable livelihood. Man working by himself is a poacher on the domain of Nature; men, in industrial society, found empires, build cities, and establish commerce.

And not merely do all find in a proper division of labor their full occupation and fair reward, but the work of each is just as truly productive as that of any other. The boy who watches crows does as much at that business as the bravest and greatest of earth. He takes the place of some one who goes away to do a larger work. In anthropology, this is only a boy; in political economy, he is a man. He and the other make together two men.

6th, It increases the power of capital in production, tends to concentrate manufactures in large establishments, and reduce profits.

Supposing all men equally capable of carrying on independent business, which is not the case, — if we compare seven men each with a capital of $1,000 and one man with a capital of $7,000, we shall find the economical advantage greatly in favor of the latter. The former must do business on a small scale, and purchase materials in small quantities. The latter can buy at wholesale prices, can afford to go often to market, and to keep himself well informed, and will sell as well as buy to great advantage.

In addition to this, the large manufacturer can afford to work for a smaller rate of profit.

A single hatter, for example, who makes only $2,000 worth of hats, must secure 25 per cent, in order to have a net income of $500; while the man who can make $20,000 worth of hats will, if he realize only 12½ per cent, have an income of $2,500. A cotton manufacturer, who makes 3,000 yards per day, or 900,000 per annum, if he gets but half a cent per yard profit, has an income of $4,500; the man who makes but 300 yards per day, at one cent per yard, or double the profit, gets but $900.

We see from these illustrations why the great establishments drive smaller ones out of the market. A tendency to a reduction of profits is a natural consequence of this. Therefore, other things being equal, it is desirable that manufacturing establishments should be sufficiently large to secure all the advantages of concentrated capital, and effect the complete division of labor.

7th, It shortens apprenticeship.

Every art, trade, or profession must be preceded by an apprenticeship, more or less extended, according to what is necessary to be learned. A trade, which, in order to be perfectly understood in all its parts, requires an apprenticeship of seven years, — if it be subdivided into seven different operations, may, it is evident, be obtained with as great a degree of perfection by an average, in each branch, of one year's service. Some of the parts may require more than one year, others less.

Now, we find this to be practically true; and the result is a great saving of time, and time is money.

For example: —

Seven men serve seven years each to learn to make hats, — in all, a service of	49 years
Seven men serve one year each to learn to make a seventh of a hat, equal to	7 „
Saving of	42 years

in the mechanical education of every seven men employed in this manner.

Apply this principle to the manufacturers of Massachusetts, which has at least 75,000 skilled workmen, and suppose the apprenticeship to be seven years, we have —

75,000 at 7 years each	525,000 years
75,000 at 1 year each	75,000 „
Saving of	450,000 years

in one generation of skilled workmen.

It will be observed that these are years of apprenticeship,

not of labor. In considering what is the saving to the wealth of the country, we must estimate the amount of values created by these workmen during the apprenticeship under the first system supposed. *Per contra*, we must take into account the greater amount of material destroyed in teaching each man to do all the parts, and the greater interruption of the employer or journeyman.

If we suppose these years, saved from apprenticeship, to have an average value of $200, we have a saving of $90,000,000 *for each generation* of skilled workmen in Massachusetts.

The principle, under which this saving of time is made, cannot be disputed.

8th, It gives opportunity for greater social development, and increases the social power of labor.

This is immediately of moral interest; but it has important economic bearings. The principle itself is indisputable. Not only is the workman brought near his fellows, and, by such contact, stimulated to industry, to acquisition, to taste; not only does such association of purposes and means afford more of the instruments of intellectual advancement, — schools, lectures, churches, journals; not only does the close neighborhood of mind quicken and brighten all the faculties, teaching by example, and firing by controversy; but, by such association, workmen are brought nearer their employers, have a greater sympathy and cooperation, act intelligently and harmoniously as to their rights, and form a public opinion among themselves which has often been found a great power, economically and civilly. Such an association, moreover, brings the workman nearer the government and the public force; sometimes for evil, but often for good. A population thus concentrated is capable of prodigious impulses. All the artisans of the empire are not equal to the mob of the capital. Government knows and respects the power of this class, no matter how fully disfranchised it may be in the law.

CHAPTER V.

THE LIMITATIONS TO THE DIVISION OF LABOR.

But the great principle of division of labor, so very beneficial in its operations, is yet limited by certain conditions, which it cannot disregard.

1st, When the principle has been so far applied that each operation has been made as simple and fully a unit as human ingenuity can devise. Beyond this, there is no division, but only *repetition*. Any attempt to refine the process so far as to give the workman less than one naturally complete motion of the body, will only embarrass and delay industry.

2d, When the concentration of capital has become so great that interested personal supervision cannot be brought to bear upon each department, and upon the whole enterprise, with sufficient intensity to insure efficiency and fidelity on the part of those employed, and harmony in the general conduct of the business. Beyond this point, the advantages derived from the power of concentration are neutralized. It may even become mischievous. It is well that there should be limitations, because they prevent such aggregations of capital as would swallow up the whole industry of a state. Experience shows that the greatest establishments are not always or generally the most profitable. Those which are large enough to secure all the real advantages of concentrated capital and combined effort, yet are small enough to be brought under direct, personal, interested supervision, are the most beneficial to their owners and the public.

3d, Where the industry consists of an indefinite number of parts, yet the special circumstances will not allow each workman profitable employment in a single operation, — for example, agriculture in most of its branches: first, from the fact that its operations cannot be sufficiently localized;

and, second, from the necessities of the seasons. No department is capable of so much subdivision as this; yet, in practice, none experiences so little. In mining, the fisheries, and many incidental matters, it is effected to a considerable extent; but, in most of the parts of pure agriculture, it has very limited range. Boys and women are indeed made useful in it, but they have not the same continuous and profitable employment as in manufactures. Nor does their work correspond precisely with what is required in our definition of the division of labor. They are occupied, generally, not in one operation so much as in a miscellaneous class of light duties, too variable to realize the dexterity and thoroughness obtained elsewhere.

There are other instances which seem to approach near to the conditions of the highest efficiency. Some persons are employed for an entire community to plant, to graft, or to team; but not only does the extent of territory limit their application to a single pursuit, but the change of the seasons drives them from one to another almost every month. Stock-raising, and gardening for large markets, afford the best American example in agriculture; yet each of these is not only a considerable department in itself, but whoever engages in either of them must do much not directly connected with it.

The culture of the grape realizes, perhaps, as fully the mechanical advantage of division of labor as any in agriculture.

But, generally speaking, the farmer is a laborer of a thousand duties.

This fact alone does not account for the different productiveness of the manufacturing and the agricultural interests. In the nature of their objects, it is found that machinery must be applied to them in far different proportions. The mechanic arts, which can be localized to the highest degree of concentration, and made general to all seasons of the year, admit also of prodigious multiplication by artificial agents. From these considerations, we deduce the principle, that the value of agricultural products, as a class, — that is, their power in exchange for products other than agricultural, — will be constantly increasing. A bushel of corn, in 1820, would purchase only four yards of cotton cloth. In 1860, it would purchase ten yards of the same or better quality. This difference will continue to grow wider and wider as the mechanic arts advance; but not indefinitely, inasmuch as the materials of manufactures are always themselves of agricultural origin, and hence the depreciation of the price is limited.

We have thus far spoken of the division of labor as applied only to direct, material production, affecting the laboring classes, and those immediately superintending them; but the principle has been extended to mental labor, as well as that which is simply muscular.

The professions known as the learned, and others which have an important though indirect agency in production (for, unless they have some agency in production, we have nothing to do with them here), naturally divide themselves into branches more or less numerous and special, as occasion offers. The recognition of professions and industrial classes is itself a tribute to the great principle of the division of labor; but it proceeds still further, to assign special functions, within those professions and classes, to individual members.

Thus the law, when a sufficient concentration of legal labor is secured, branches into the departments of titles and conveyances, of insurance, of marine losses, forfeiture and salvage, of patents, of criminal jurisprudence, &c. In medicine, the eye, the ear, the skin, consumption, fevers, cancers, have each their own practitioners.

That science and skill are promoted by such subdivision, and that the immediate efficiency of professional labor is greatly increased thereby, cannot be intelligently questioned.

As any community advances to a higher civilization, specialties are more and more resorted to. Individuals, finding themselves peculiarly adapted by their talents and tastes to a particular calling, or having unusual advantages for the pursuit of it, give themselves up to that object. They concentrate upon it their thoughts, their time, and their resources. They excel. They know more, and can do better, in their chosen line than those about them. This gives them position and power. They are sought for, are looked to, because they have something that is wanted. No matter how humble his station, or how minute his field of investigation, if a man understands something perfectly, his world — whether a hamlet or an empire or the race — will resort to him. He becomes a benefactor of society. He receives its honors and rewards. There is no person in any position in life, however exalted or lowly, who may not advantageously cultivate a specialty.

CHAPTER VI.

THE DISADVANTAGES OF THE DIVISION OF LABOR.

1st, It tends to enervate the laborer, because it does not, as a general fact, give full activity and development to all the functions of the body.

We shall proceed to show that this is true of those classes who perform what we have designated as material labor, while the very distinction of mental labor implies such a separation between the natural functions as seems not to consist with the best physical condition of those engaged. Common observation will affirm that this is strikingly true. It is not necessary, but the tendency exists.

In the material occupations, it is found that confinement to a single operation is often highly injurious. There are forms of labor which sufficiently exercise the several parts of the body. The mere fact of uniformity of motion brings no objection to such as these. But there are those which require the constant fatiguing use of some member, to the injury of the rest of the body; others require a cramping posture that oppresses and disorders the vital organs; others still require the workman to poison his blood with unwholesome gases. In the great centres of capital and labor,—whether we regard the mill, or that larger mill, the city itself,—it is notorious that distortion, paralysis, and organic feebleness, are more common than where labor is diffused, and the laborer changes his work and his place frequently.

That this will occur in the course of all manufacturing industry is probable. That it is inevitable does not so clearly appear. The sanitary arts keep even pace with the advance of machinery. The civil war in America developed astonishingly the resources, which are at the command of government, to suppress malaria, and reform the habitations of disease. The growth of manly sports, and the cultivation of gymnastics for health's sake, are likely to work a great change for the better in the sanitary conditions of our people. The intelligent precaution of operatives in every country, where their remuneration is any thing less than robbery, can guard against all excessive derangement of the bodily functions.

It is perhaps significant to the question whether the application of the bodily powers to a single continuous action is really in practice injurious, that we find in the statistics of Massachusetts, ranging over sixteen years, the average life of "laborers having no special trades" to be less by two years than that of "active mechanics in shops."

Mechanical operations were formerly considered as disqualifying for military service; and even our modern philosophy has found in them a reason for the employment of mercenaries, and the maintenance of standing armies. But the great civil war just referred to exhibited the novel fact, that, beyond all dispute, the troops raised in agricultural districts are not so hardy in the privations and exposures of camp and field as those coming from the towns. This does not, however, imply a better state of health at home. It may be, that the latter class find, in the constant exercise and the out-door employment, just that *change* of habit and condition which they needed. All that is different from their usual course of life is in the direction of more air and light and motion; while the agricultural laborers find no change except for the worse. They have been accustomed to active employment; but the harsh necessities of the service come to them fresh and strong. It is perhaps the *direction* of influences more than the degree of them which determines these matters of health; or it may be, that mechanical occupations, contrary to general opinion and in spite of some plain drawbacks, do tend to compact the frame and the sinew, and lend force and vitality to the organs. Whatever the explanation, we will rest with the fact, that, in the severe trial of strength and endurance made by the war, the mechanical occupations have not been discredited.

2d, This system, in some of its applications and in certain degrees of extension, does not give that full employment and expansion to all the powers of the mind which its normal development requires. This is obvious. The mind, if intensely devoted for a whole life to a single effort, and that perhaps of the most simple kind, cannot but be unfavorably affected. Unless counteracting influences are resorted to, it will undoubtedly be contracted and enervated.

To this liability are opposed three compensations: —

a. The great communicativeness observable in such circumstances, the eager discussions, the free inquiry, the school, and the lyceum.

b. The saving principle that the employment of one member is, to a certain extent, the employment of all. The human faculties, mental and physical, are a knot. They interpenetrate so completely that it is impossible to move one without affecting the rest. If we compare the mind to a reservoir, we may say that the individual powers and dispositions flow out of it as so many streams; but there is nothing to prevent them from flowing back, if the level is sufficiently disturbed. The special use of one may develop it greatly; make it more strong and active than the others. But such a predominance is not distortion. Few minds are capable of even and temperate growth. In this principle resides the variety of human character. It may be questioned whether any but the most gifted can be educated in any other way so thoroughly and efficiently as by interested application to some single matter. Generalization and broad philosophy rouse the full powers of but few intellects. In the majority of cases, it will remain true that intense, spirited, persistent labor directed to one point is better than the languid, nerveless, unspurred, rambling play of all the faculties. Mind, to be energetic, must not be republican. The powers must be centralized. Some must be despotic.

Indeed, the argument against division of labor on this score would be better expressed by saying, that the constant repetition of single acts so far dispenses with thought, and even with consciousness, in the operation, that it makes man, in some sense, a machine. This is, to a considerable extent, true; the compensation being that it affords a greater opportunity for discussion and reflection, if the workman chooses to avail himself of the kind of mental leisure which is afforded by the monotony of his occupation. It is, therefore, not the excessive use, but the disuse, of the intellectual faculties, that is to be feared in those arts to which labor has been carried to its fullest division.

c. The laborer is not all workman. While his special occupation provides for his subsistence, and endows him with energy, industry, and concentrativeness of mind and character, he has other hours and other duties, ample, if reasonably used, to compensate for all the evil mental effects of his continuous toil.

It will be observed, that it is only to the division of labor *beyond a certain point*, that the objections we have discussed have any application. A more ill-developed society, with more ill-developed members, could not be conceived than where this principle was not applied at all. In fact, there could be neither members nor society; but here and there a savage would bask in the summer sun, or hide himself in the storms of winter, in hopeless, helpless barbarism.

However we may speculate, *a priori*, on the consequences of dividing minutely the parts of labor, we may perhaps get a stronger light and a better view by observing the mightiest experiment of industry ever known in the world, — that of England to-day. Nowhere are the natural advantages of agriculture more apparant; nowhere has manufacturing been more elaborated. Yet no person can be cognizant of the condition of the English population, without being assured that the manufacturing, laboring class is almost immeasurably above the agricultural in intelligence, in independence of character, and obedience to law. Probably the most conservative nobleman of the realm would admit that the former class is far better qualified for the franchise than the latter.

3d, It will follow, from what has been already urged, that division of labor, in its greatest extension, has a tendency, or at least there is found in it a liability, to lower the average of health, to shorten life, and prevent the natural increase of population.

All these results are found, on examination, more or less, but still above the general facts of the country, in all the great centres of manufacturing industry, where the full possibilities of the mechanic arts are realized by the intense subdivision of labor. This result can only be partially and confusedly shown by statistics: still enough can be extracted to assure us that there is a great loss of vital energy, whether or not it is necessary to such a state of industry.

The American average of life may be expressed nearly as follows: * —

Cultivators of the earth	64 years.
Active mechanics out of shops	50 „
Active mechanics in shops	47½ „
Inactive mechanics in shops	41¾ „
Laborers, no special trades	45½ „

These statistics, accurately gathered and showing the results of many years, require "correction" in several particulars, if the real lesson of them is to be obtained. In the first place, two-thirds of the class of mechanics as presented here are engaged in such occupations as do not allow any very extended subdivision of the parts, so that the average of the great manufacturing establishments and their dependent cities would be found still more striking. In the second place, the agricultural occupations are continually making contribution to manufacturers of their best blood and bone, renewing the natural waste of the mill and shop, and so interfering with the statistics of the subject. This element can neither be eliminated nor determined. We shall rest satisfied with knowing it is there. So important is it at times, that Lowell appears on the tables as one of the healthiest cities of America. It is unquestionably true that much of the historical feebleness and mortality of such places has been avoided by more humane and intelligent precautions, by gymnastic sports and out-door games, and by a better adaptation of all the conditions of production to the necessities of life and well-being. But the great fact which accounts for this seeming healthfulness of a manufacturing city is the constant infusion of the fresh, vigorous, young blood of the country.

* Massachusetts Registration of Births, Deaths, and Marriages.

It is not necessarily a disadvantage in this respect, that manufactures, in their greatest centralization, prevent the full natural increase of population. Indeed, it is a beneficent provision of Nature which checks propagation in precisely those circumstances where the offspring is less likely to receive that nourishment and care and exercise which shall secure its best development. Far from being a misfortune, it is well that those who are to live in the cities should be born in the country, and get size and strength on the hills and in the open air. This tendency does not go so far as to deprive the dwellers in the cities, and the workers in brass and wool, of the cares and the pleasures and the culture of paternity. Yet the law that men shall be born upon the land is as clear in history, and in our common observation, as any fiat of Nature.

4th, The division of labor lessens the number of those who do business on their own account. This is a natural consequence of what has been shown. We have said that capital has a tendency toward concentration; and, if it be aggregated, labor must also be. The result of this, in agriculture, is to absorb the yeomanry into the class of those who labor by the day or month, with no interest in the land. The result in manufacturing is to subordinate hundreds of operatives to the control of a single will. This has a threefold relation: *a*. To the formation of character. Something of independence and self-respect is unquestionably lost, so far as these depend on external conditions. Position and responsibility do foster and strengthen manliness and self-mastery. By the division of labor, the independence of each is sacrificed to the good of all. It will not be doubted, that, on the whole, it is desirable that it should be so; nor can it be denied that there are partial drawbacks, even in this plain tendency of civilization. It is the sacrifice man has to make in society, in industry, in government. *b*. To the fairness of remuneration. A very few now participate in the profits. The great bulk of workmen receive only wages, and that on temporary engagements. This disproportion may be excessive, and is likely to be where laws or institutions check enterprise, and discourage individual effort. In such cases, laborers are practically a herd of cattle, driven about from place to place, receiving bare subsistence, and unable to mend their condition. This is a lamentable state of things; an abuse of a good principle. No one can deny, however, that the worst-treated operatives of the civilized world receive infinitely more than if the efforts of men were all individual and independent, and each was left to satisfy his wants from the primitive resources of Nature. But, even if we come forward from the barbarous state to that in which the work of man has divided itself into numerous trades, each of these, however, yet remaining distinct, and compare this with the present state, in which trades have been repeatedly subdivided, — capital aggregate and labor subordinate, — we shall yet find that the share of the poorest laborer in the mighty product of our industry of to-day is greater than ever before. Augustus, says Arbuthnot, had neither glass to his windows nor a shirt to his back.

Thus much could be urged of the wretchedest operatives on the earth; but, when we regard the condition of labor as it exists in nearly all the countries of the world, we shall quickly confess, that, though the laborer has given up his share of profits, he receives back, as wages, far more objects of desire than he could have obtained in the old way. *c.* To the steadiness of employment. By the attraction of labor to great centres, the fate of many laborers is made dependent on that of a few capitalists. This is a great fact, scientifically and historically. It must continue. It has issued, in the past, in the form of great industrial distresses, of a general suspension of *mechanical* labor from causes affecting only the *mercantile* credit of the employers, of frantic appeals for support, of laws in which government assumes the duty of providing work for its whole population, of riots and revolution. So far as this will occur in spite of prudence and careful management, it is the condition on which we have the advantages of division of labor. Men cannot cross the great ocean alone. They must go together, have help of each other, and embark their fortunes on a common bottom. More of them would perhaps be safe if each was on a ship of his own; but that cannot well be.

Even in regard to steadiness of employment, the aggregation of capital and consequent division of labor assist the workman *up to a certain point.* That point is the great catastrophe which no structure can withstand. Then, the greater the structure, the more completely it crushes the laborer.

Where capital is concentrated, it is stronger, protects itself better; and, of course, the workman shares in this power and immunity. Where the industry of thousands is controlled by the mind of one, it will be more intelligently and harmoniously administered, and with a larger view of the business. By such superiority of union in production (for that is synonymous with division of labor), the industry of a country is lifted clean over obstacles which individual enterprise could not pass,—is preserved amid storms that would shatter the feeble fabric of single hands. Industry in masses, when it receives a shock, can hold on to the accumulations of the past and to the credit of the future, and so stands firm.

But when the blow becomes so heavy as to shatter even the great workshops of modern industry, and they come down, then truly the fall is great. The ruin is more complete than if the storm had prostrated a village of huts. The reservoir of gathered power has burst; the springs have long since been broken down; the wells been filled up; and there is no supply for immediate wants. Such a loss is repaired slowly. The trampled grass raises itself, and looks up again; but the oak lies as it falls. Independent has been discouraged by collective industry; the shop has been abandoned for the mill; each workman has learned only the fraction of a trade; no one can buy, make, and sell; no one dares to undertake any business, foreseeing that the corporation must rise again. For a while, all is distress. It is only when the stately fabric of associated industry is reared again, that plenty is known in the land.

We have discussed, somewhat at length, the relations which division of labor holds to the condition of the laborer, by depriving him of the opportunity to do business on his own account. Until recently, it has been supposed that the advantages of the principle could not practically be obtained without this defect; that capital could not be concentrated, and the trades perfected, without diminishing the independence and self-reliance of labor. But recent developments seem to be anticipating the objection. It is now a matter of common practice to admit the laborer to an interest in business, — a share in profits. This is done by merchants to their salesmen, by master mechanics to their workmen, by ship-owners to their hands. All stock-companies, of whatever character, admit of this principle. Mutual industrial associations for trade, mining, and insurance, furnish its most significant and hopeful applications. There is no reason why these should not be extended much further by a gradual growth, as they are found convenient and profitable. Just so far as a sufficient spring of self-interest can be maintained in the effort, both of the employer, or manager, and of the operative, so far may mutuality of profits be applied to all departments with the most beneficial results.

CHAPTER VII.

THE DIVISION OF LABOR (*concluded*).

We have passed through the discussion of the advantages, the limitations, and the disadvantages of the division of labor.

If, now, we inquire on which side the balance lies, there will be no question that it is in favor of the application and extension of the law. It appears as the great multiplying power of modern industry; it has made the difference between barbarism and civilization; it resides in man's being as the principle of help; it is the only name that savage nature fears.

If we could personify the forces of matter and the treasures of the earth, holding council how they might escape being enslaved or plundered by rapacious man, we should hear them say: "Let us spread disunion among our foes; let us convince them that their interests are separate, and lie apart; let us excite among them suspicion and hatred. Then the summer sun shall make them languid, and winter shall bring torpor on them. The waves shall overwhelm them, struggling singly with the ocean; the drought shall starve, the snow shall freeze them. So will we conquer, and be safe."

And indeed, as if they had so talked, like the councillors of a state invaded by a powerful foe, and had so planned, we find them for ages deceiving the hearts of men, sowing dissension, and enkindling strife by treacherous bounties of gold and precious stones, like bribes sent into an enemy's camp. Nations fell to quarrelling about the accidental and trivial treasures scattered, in fraud of their full rights, upon their paths. Great wars were waged to secure paltry balances in coin: wealth of continents was disregarded. Men stood over against each other, hunted for gold in the dust, neglecting the mighty riches that lay deep in the soil. They had no heart to say, Let us help each other, and see what we can do. Whole peoples acted, and look now in history just as we imagine miners to do when they suspect the presence of some great treasure among them; each hunting silent by himself, casting angry glances from under steadfast lids; each heart beating fast with fear and wrath that some other may find it first; hateful all, and hating one another.

That this sketch is not exaggerated, let it be said, to the shame of mankind, that the Mercantile theory was undoubted till the middle of the last century; proclaiming as truth, and pursuing as policy, the world over, the double lie that the only wealth is gold and silver, and that what one people gains in trade another must lose. So man had need of his fellow only to rob him; so man had need of Nature only to get her gold.

Palaces and warehouses floating safely on the waves; breakwaters along the sea; coast-lines of docks and wharves; arterial railroads to the length of the continents; canals connecting oceans; bridges leaping rivers; the genii of the woods groaning in the windmills; brook-nymphs grinding corn in the valleys; the spirit of the air hard at work pegging shoes; mountains of iron split open; precious crystals, forming for ten million years, strewn about the land, — these are the first fruits of man's confidence in his fellow.

CHAPTER VIII.

THE CO-OPERATION OF CAPITAL.

THIS is the second grand condition, through which the productiveness of labor is increased.

We have before spoken of capital: we now proceed to define it strictly.

It is that portion of wealth employed in reproduction.

The distinction involved is an important one. All capital is wealth, but all wealth is not capital. The very use of the term "reproduction" testifies to the feeling of man that the object of any thing is not fulfilled in its own creation or perfection, but that there is an endless series of propagations, with a constant view, and with increasing force, to some ulterior end. And we find that production does go forward, not by the increase alone of the laboring class, not by mere annual savings and gross accumulation, but by the employment of that which before was an object of desire in itself, as now a means to the gratification of new desires. Since it is recognized that human wants create others of their kind, and hence go on increasing in number and urgency, it is necessary that human efforts should find some force having a corresponding rate of increase, by which to assist themselves in supplying the growing demand. Such an agent is found in capital, which is taken out of wealth.

A man may have much wealth, and use little capital. Wealth is as it is *had;* capital, as it is *used.* For example, a man may live in a house worth thirty thousand dollars, and have ten thousand dollars invested in a ship, from which he derives all his support, and which forms his capital. It may be asked, Is not the house itself capital? It is so far as necessary to production, in sheltering the producer and his family, even with the style and comfort usual to such a degree of society. Beyond this, it ceases to be capital. It is devoted, not to the creation of values, but to personal enjoyment and culture; noble and worthy ends for wealth, but not for capital.

We may change the supposition. The man may have a house worth ten thousand dollars, and ships to the value of thirty thousand dollars. The difference to production will be apparent, inasmuch as his active capital now consists of three-fourths of his wealth, while before it was only one-fourth.

It will follow from this illustration, that there is much of the wealth of the world which it is difficult to classify whether as capital or not, much in which the two ends unite, much in which the share devoted to reproduction is doubtful. Still, this casts no discredit on the distinction itself, which stands manifest to all. There are many such principles in political economy, the general direction and character of which cannot be intelligently doubted, yet in whose particular applications we find difficulties and apparent contradictions; just as the mountain-ranges stretch across the continent, unmistakable in their great course, shedding the waters of one slope to the east and of the other to the west, making clear separation between the Flora and Fauna of the adjacent countries, and forming impassable boundaries of empire, yet are occasionally interrupted by one cause or twisted away by another, so that we find peaks here and there, which a little critic can take his stand upon, and deny the geography of the hemisphere.

How does capital arise?

From the net savings of labor. A person who earns five hundred dollars a year, and places one hundred dollars of it in a savings-bank, or invests it in land or machinery or railroad stock, or anywhere at work, has increased his own capital and the capital of the country by so much. It is not what he lays aside for use in his own occupation merely, but for use anywhere.

All capital comes in this way. A country increases in capital just in proportion to the increase of capital accumulated by its members. If the individuals of a nation apply none of their net income to reproduction, there is no increase of the national capital. If they withdraw any of their capital to meet personal consumption, the country becomes poorer.

Many of the considerations which pertain to the accumulation of capital, and the ultimate use of it, belong to the discussions of economic culture, or go further on, to the general division of "Consumption." We have simply to do with those principles which apply existing capital to the wants of present labor.

Capital is known as "fixed" or "circulating."

Fixed capital consists of every description of property employed in production, which, from its nature, cannot be advantageously changed to any other use than that for which it was originally designed. The land, buildings, and tools of the farmer, the ships and warehouses of the merchant, the machines and implements of the manufacturer, belong to this class. They must be used for the purposes to which they are particularly adapted, or they have little value. They are fixed. The ship cannot be used as a wagon, or the spinning-jenny as a locomotive.

Circulating capital, on the other hand, consists of those articles or commodities which can be readily changed from one purpose of production to another. Of this class are the stock and produce of the farmer, the money and wares of the merchant, the raw materials of the mechanic. These are easily transferred from one business to another, and indeed from one place to another, and may be used in a great variety of forms. Of all these, money is the most mobile, as it can be changed without delay or loss to any occupation or locality.

Fixed is, in its nature, more permanent than circulating capital, not merely in its adaptations, for its name implies that, but in its existence. The greater part of circulating capital — stock and materials, for example — is held only in the immediate view of transmuting or transferring or transporting it, so that it shall pass into fixed capital. There, on the contrary, it has taken its ultimate form. If it loses this, it is only by destruction. It does not intend to assume any higher condition.

It is in this way that fixed capital receives the mighty annual additions which astonish us on the page of the statistician. The products of last year form a part of the houses, ships, railroads, and machinery of the present. The farmer adds something to his stock, or his land, or his buildings. The mechanic widens his shop, and multiplies his tools. The merchant enlarges his business, and extends his connections. The laborer saves something out of his wages, beyond the demands of immediate subsistence. It is in this way that fixed capital is increased by the contributions of circulating capital. The products of labor are generally in this form; and it is enabled to pay its tribute without being itself impoverished.

In popular language, all wealth is divided into real estate and personal property. This distinction, if not scientific, is convenient for occasional use. We must bear in mind, however, that, while all real estate is fixed, all personal property is not circulating capital. Ships, machinery, and many other things not attached to the soil, are personal property, though standing in the category of fixed capital.

CHAPTER IX.

THE CO-OPERATION OF CAPITAL (*continued*).

Is the distinction between productive and unproductive capital real? It has been urged by many writers at considerable length. It is susceptible of much illustration. It involves many important considerations.

There is, however, no such thing as unproductive capital. There may be misapplied wealth, misused wealth, wasted wealth; but capital reproduces. If any discrimination is necessary between that portion of wealth which is applied successfully to reproduction, and that which is intended for such an end, but fails in attaining it, we may say that capital is that portion of wealth applied to reproduction, which secures a compensation to its owner. Whatever his intention, if he uses any part of his wealth without multiplying it, it remains wealth; he has not made it capital; it may, by unproductive use, cease even to be wealth. Wealth put into an enterprise which results in nothing is no more capital than wealth put into a house which burns down, and probably is wealth as little.

Nay, more: so far as wealth thus applied, while making some return, fails of securing the fair, average remuneration of capital, it so far ceases to be capital. It may be wealth merged for a time; it may be wealth lost for ever: it is not capital.

A complete illustration of this principle is found in common business. Suppose a man to be possessed of fifty shares of certain stock, par value one hundred dollars. The enterprise does not succeed; the stock does not pay adequate dividends; the value of the shares has sunk to fifty dollars. Would any one say that his capital, so far, was five thousand dollars? Clearly, it is but two thousand five hundred dollars. Half of his investment has been sunk; half is capital.

But it has been urged, that much capital is reproductive that does not afford a remuneration to its owner. For example: a railroad is projected and built, does not pay; its stock sinks to nothing; yet, though it does not pay dividends, it improves the industry of the country through which it passes.

We have nothing to do, in the discussion of production, with any such incidental advantages, even if they exist. It may be, that, in the consumption of wealth, we shall find principles explaining the effects of such an investment.

In the light of production, however, we can only say, that, in so far as the railroad does not remunerate its owner, it ceases to be capital. So far as it is supposed to promote agriculture or manufactures, and indirectly help the industry of the community, it is simply on the level of the gratuitous gifts of Nature, — the powers of the wind, rain, and sun, or the courses of streams and valleys; assisting man unquestionably, but having no value, being neither capital nor wealth.

A canal that does not pay for its building is no more capital than a river. Both may transport commodities with a great saving of labor, and with great encouragement to production. The world abounds in natural bridges, causeways, roads, mountain cuts, dikes, &c. If a man, with ill advice, constructs artificial works of this character, which prove failures, he adds just so much to what is gratuitous in the world. Economically speaking, it has ceased to be *property*: it has become *common*.

CHAPTER X.

THE CO-OPERATION OF CAPITAL (*continued*).

HAVING considered the two great agents by which all wealth is created, viz. capital and labor, we come to speak of their union, and to inquire under what circumstances it will be most effective.

1st, When a due proportion of each is found. Labor halts without capital; capital wastes without labor. Which shall govern the other? Which shall be the fixed quantity to which the other must conform? Labor, certainly, because it is less variable in amount. It can be diminished or increased but slowly, depending as it does on the propagation of the human race; an element that is determined positively, in the old countries, to a very gradual growth, and, in new countries, has never more than doubled itself in thirty or forty years. Capital, on the contrary, is liable to very rapid fluctuations; can be accumulated, under favorable circumstances, with great ease; and can be wasted or scattered just as fast under different conditions.

Labor, then, being that which is most restricted in quantity, capital must, in order to the highest production, conform to it. There must be as much capital as labor requires, not as much labor as capital needs. We do not put this on the ground of any superior rights of labor. Capital is the labor of the past, and has rights as perfect as that of the present.

What this proportion should be in any community, it would be impossible to declare beforehand, as it is even impossible to decide precisely what it is in fact. Still less could a proportion be determined which capital should bear to labor in all communities. It is plain that this will vary according to the occupation; as, for instance, we have seen that in agriculture there cannot be so general application of machinery as in manufactures; while, on the other hand, because its operations cannot be localized or made independent of the seasons, the number of tools is thereby greatly increased; each farmer requiring certain tools, yet not using them to their full capacity at any season, and letting them lie idle for months.

The mechanic, on the other hand, while he uses a greater share of tool-power, has it yet so arranged that the tools lie idle little of the time.

It is plain that the proportion will vary, also, according to the natural advantages a person or community enjoys. Expensive clothing and shelter are essential to the support of the laborer in some climates; in others, a piece of cotton cloth and a bamboo hut serve for protection the year round. In some countries, there is required an immense system of pipes and conduits to water the soil, barely to preserve animal life; in others, an equable moisture is preserved the whole twelve months without any application of capital. In some, strongly constructed and carefully connected dikes and levees, extending hundreds of miles, are essential to the use of the land; others were placed high and dry at first. In some, the soil is so generous with fruit, that, "if you tickle Nature with a hoe, she laughs with a harvest;" in others, the earth has to be carried in baskets up the sides of the mountains. That which, in one country, would be capital, acquired by labor and having value, is, in another, a free gift.

For these and other manifest reasons, the proportion that should exist between labor and capital cannot be determined with any considerable degree of assurance. It is plain that there should be as many tools as workmen needing to use them, else some will stand idle. It is equally plain that an excess of tools will not help at all in production. Capital is the instrument of labor; and the instrument should, of course, be adapted to the power of the laborer and the work to be done.

By the census of 1860, "the real and personal property of the Union was valued (slaves excluded) at $14,183,000,000."* A calculation made at the Treasury Department estimates the products of 1860 at 26.8 per cent of the wealth of the country at that time. Without intending to vouch at all for the correctness of this estimate, it is doubtless approximately true; and, if so, we shall be surprised, if we look at the large proportion of annual product to the accumulated wealth of the nation. If, for the sake of convenience, we call the annual product 25, instead of 26.8 per cent, we find that it amounts to $3,545,750,000 per annum. It certainly appears almost incredible that the total amount of wealth accumulated in the country since its first settlement should be only equal to four times the product in 1860; but such we understand to be the statement. If so, it shows what an immense proportion of all the wealth annually produced is annually consumed. From these figures, too, we may make an estimate of the proportion of the product which belongs to labor and capital. Allowing for the use of the latter ten per cent, in the shape of interest and rent, or use, the amount will then stand thus: —

* Report of the Secretary of the Treasury, 1865.

Aggregate national wealth, $14,183,000,000, at 10 per cent, is $1,418,300,000, which deducted from the whole product, as before, of $3,545,750,000, will leave us the share of labor, $2,127,450,000, or about two-thirds of the whole.

From these statistics, we find that the whole national wealth is only equal to about seven times the *gross earnings of labor* for a single year.

We have also an opportunity of comparing the wealth and production of the United States with Great Britain. The estimated wealth of the latter, according to Leone Levi (see his work on Taxation, page 6), is $30,000,000,000, or $1000 per capita; the estimated yearly production, $3,000,-000,000, or $100 per capita. The wealth of the United States, according to the foregoing figuring, and taking the whole population, as in 1860, at 31,443,321, is $451 each; while the amount of *product* per capita is $112 each: so that, while Great Britain has more than double the capital, she has less annual product per capita. This is a confirmation of the well-known fact, that capital and labor, interest and wages, are at least double in this country what they are in Great Britain. We must not confound the annual product with the annual accumulation; the latter being but a small fraction of the former.

Capital should, at least, increase in a degree corresponding to the increase of population. If it does not, labor is crippled, wages fall, and starvation eventually ensues. Ireland may be quoted as an illustration. Her soil, wrested from the people by conquest at different periods, from the reign of Henry II. to the Battle of the Boyne, has passed into the hands of foreigners, who draw away annually all her surplus products. Population increases from year to year; but capital does not increase correspondingly. Nay, even the waste of the soil and of implements is not fully and honestly supplied.

What is the necessary consequence? Increasing poverty, and ultimate starvation or emigration. We have said that capital is formed from the annual savings of labor. Four million pounds a year go from Ireland to absentee landlords, and eight million pounds are taken away every year in taxes. The Irish people can make no savings. There can be no increase of their capital. Starvation or emigration is their inevitable fate.

Is it possible that there should be a surplus of capital?

It is evident that there may become such a surplus, if we assume that production itself does not expand in the meantime. Given a certain industry, within defined limits, it may become full and overflowing with its accumulations. By economy and thrift, these multiply fast, and crowd their barriers. Common observation shows this to be often true, with the enterprises of individuals. The excess is transferred to other branches, or withdrawn for personal gratifications. A seamstress, who, by saving, obtains a sewing machine, has a wonderful help in her industry; but a second sewing machine would not assist her a single stitch.

The same is true of special occupations. The limit of profitable production being reached, the amount of capital employed cannot well be increased. The product, being generally in the form of circulating capital, now flows off to other business, or is turned to purposes of adornment and culture.

The same is also found true, though more rarely, of entire communities. States and cities sometimes reach the limits within which they desire to use capital in their traditional industries. They become bankers for the world, or direct their profits to sumptuous houses and works of art. Such were Genoa and Venice under the merchant princes, who, having reached the boundaries of known trade, and brought all its machinery to the perfection of existing art, began, wisely enough at first, that wonderful career of architecture, whose ultimate extravagance exhausted the industry that gave it rise, and passed the commerce of the world to traders who had not become gentlemen.

It is evident, then, that, within the bounds of present occupations, capital might easily attain a surplus, increasing as it can more rapidly than population. It is productive only as applied by labor; and therefore its production is limited by the capacities of labor.

But in fact, and on the whole of things, the limits of industry do not remain the same. Wants expand, as we have seen. Capital is relieved from its former employments, and goes on to new efforts. It can hardly multiply fast enough to meet the growing demand. Enterprises spring up over night. Capital hardly breathes, for the work it has to do.

We believe that the time when capital shall become excessive in the world is far beyond the occasions of reasonable calculation. It is so distant at the nearest, so doubtful every way, as not to be a question in a practical science, like political economy. We are not called on to provide for the day when all the continents shall be crowded with wealth that can find no room to work. When wealth ceases to be wanted for capital, it is pretty certain to be consumed in luxury. Yet we are not to anticipate the same rapid progress at all times and everywhere which we see in a new country like our own, full of wants, and stimulated to efforts. Capital has its checks, just as population has. Theoretically, steady increase is certain in both: practically, each meets obstacles; is lost here, and checked there. The forces which operate to stay it may be briefly summed up as follows: a certain disinclination of capital to emigrate; the lessening power of personal supervision from a distance; and a distrust in the administration of foreign laws.

Another constant force operating against the increase of capital is found in those wants of man which do not look to reproduction. The desire to spend is just as truly in human nature as the desire to earn, and can be as accurately calculated. Hence it follows, that, as the desire to earn loses power by capital becoming plenty and cheap, the desire to spend gains force. A man is not nearly as likely to use his money for personal gratification when he can get eight per cent for it, as when he can get only four.

Yet, for all these obstacles, capital, when it has supplied the demands of labor in its own vicinity, has gone abroad to colonize. It has carried on great wars in which it had no interest, has developed the resources of infant states, and saved old nations tottering to their fall. Capital has gone round the world in the same boat with the inspired discoverer. It watched with Columbus the weeds drifting from an unknown land; it "stared at the Pacific" by the side of stout Cortes; it debarked with the gallant Cook, nor was it frightened at the savage violence which took his life. Like Cæsar, it would not wait for the boat to come to land. It freighted vessels for countries not named; it sent fleets to ports never visited by civilized man.

CHAPTER XI.

THE CO-OPERATION OF CAPITAL (*concluded*).

2d, The union of capital and labor will be most effective, when each is sure of its just reward. If the rights of man as a holder of property are sacred, and his rights as laborer equally so, the greatest motive to production can be secured. If otherwise, the creation of wealth will be restricted. Men will not work or save, unless sure of their reward.

There cannot come, out of the earth or heaven, a blow that levels all industry in the dust so quickly and hopelessly as wrong done between labor and capital.* Pestilence, drouth,

* It will be recollected that production carried on by slaves is done wholly by capital: the producer being a chattel, the whole product is that of capital.

or floods do not so thoroughly and permanently prostrate the strength and hopes of a country as a breath of suspicion on the union of the two great agents of production. Then comes an antagonism, indeed, fatal to both. There is hardly any climate or soil so unpropitious that man will not struggle on, earning his livelihood with much endurance, and laying something by for the future. There is hardly any government so rigorous as wholly to suppress the energy of its people. There is hardly any taxation so exhaustive that something still cannot be got out of Nature for man. In all these difficulties, the motive to exertion is not destroyed. But if foul play or legal fraud comes between labor or capital and their reward, the very life of industry ceases at the thought. The spring of work is broken. Its admirable parts and its cunning mechanism are useless, motionless. The exactions and oppressions of the old regime had not so broken the spirit of France, but that her population and her wealth went on increasing, slowly, painfully, but constantly, certainly. The Revolution came; the Convention questioned the rights of property, confiscated the estates of nobles, and sequestered the entire endowment of the Church. Half this would have been enough for ruin. The industry of France dropped where it stood. In a few months, the Convention was devising schemes by which work should be provided by the State for all its citizens. Capital had fled to the dark places of the kingdom. Labor was helpless, crippled, starving. What had wrought all this? The violation of rights. Property was discredited; capital outlawed; labor prostrate.

Labor is the first to suffer. Its wants are instant, immediate, vital. Capital, in such economical convulsions, has the privilege of leviathan. It can dive down to the depths, and give up breathing for a while. If labor goes under, it dies.

It is familiar to every reader of history how the brutal rapacity of the Spanish conquerors terrified the nations of

Peru and the Antilles, and shut up the treasures of the New World in a secrecy that even torture could not break. The wisdom of the man that owned the hen that laid the golden egg has been embodied a thousand times in the acts of government. The result is never the enriching of one; it is ever the ruin of all. Wealth itself becomes valueless, since it has no security in possession, and only excites the cupidity of the common tyrant.

If such is admitted to be the effect of occasional invasions of property rights, either in labor or capital, we shall be prepared to explain the barrenness of many countries the oldest and best endowed of the world.

The dreariness of Asia rises in eloquent vindication of the harmonies of natural law. A perfidious and cruel despotism has there made property undesirable. Man finds safety only in poverty and degradation. The Jewish is perhaps the only people that has pursued wealth steadily and unremittingly, in spite of injustice and robbery.

3d, The union of labor and capital is most effective when the latter is appropriately distributed. Capital creates no values by its own powers. It must be joined with labor. Somebody must use it, bring his personal energies to bear upon it, set it in motion, watch its operations, work with it. The farmer, the merchant, the manufacturer, must each bestow constant attention on the capital he employs, or no good will come of it. The more intense and vigilant the application, the more certain the return, the larger the profits. This is a well-known practical principle; and from it follows that the point will be reached where an individual has so much capital under his control that his entire efforts, by himself and those working under his direction, are not sufficient to secure its greatest effectiveness. Of course, in such a case, it is economically right that the excess of capital should be transferred to some other position, where its full productiveness can be obtained.

Such limitations are highly beneficial to society; for, were there no restrictions of this kind, were capital in vast aggregations equally efficient as in smaller bodies, the business of the world might be controlled, and the profits appropriated, by a very few persons.

The point is of great importance. Such a concentration of capital as effects the highest division of labor, and the fittest application of machinery, is desirable for the interest of all; and for those purposes, and up to such a degree, capital so concentrated has a wonderful power in production. But its aggregation, merely, is a hinderance rather than a help. After the two advantages spoken of above are once secured, capital becomes potent and beneficial just in proportion as it is distributed. By such distribution, it comes closer to labor and natural advantages. It makes use of various powers; it defends itself better in emergencies; it adapts itself more shrewdly to peculiarities of circumstance; it has a keener intelligence of the public wants; it commands a greater amount of executive talent; it superintends its *employés* with more accuracy; it saves the pieces, keeps machinery oiled, looks after tools.

The man who is to gain by the work is brought nearer to it. He is well served, because he serves himself.

For a long time, it was a favorite belief with the American people, that corporations were the most efficient agents of production, even where the work was not so great as to be beyond individual enterprise. The older wisdom of the country turns more and more to the smaller establishments, which secure full, interested personal supervision of labor. The English economy has always preferred these, except where the operations were beyond the reach of ordinary capital.

4th, The union of capital and labor is most effective where there is the greatest freedom of industry.

Whenever a population is sufficiently intelligent to understand its own interests, it should be left to direct its own labors. Its industry should never be interfered with by government. In all countries which may be considered as enlightened or civilized, like the European and Anglo-American, the people have no occasion to look to government for direction as to the business they shall engage in, or the manner in which they shall conduct it. Every branch of industry, in a normal state of society, grows spontaneously out of the wants and capacities of the people. Tillage, manufacturers, commerce, fisheries, spring up in the places to which they are best adapted. They can never be advantageously forced into being, or maintained by governmental authority and patronage. Every plant will thrive best in its own soil. Soils and climates vary: productions will differ in consequence.

But our immediate topic relates, not to acts of government, based on a distinct purpose to change the general course of national industry, — which will be more appropriately discussed elsewhere, — but rather to those which impose minor restrictions; directing the modes of labor, moulding the forms of capital, and prescribing the conditions of their union. All limitations of the rights and powers of capital or labor, not required by the public morality or security, are useless and mischievous.

No lawmaker can gather and express the desires of his people so accurately and seasonably as they are shown in the market demand; or set in train and carry on their efforts, with myriad instrumentalities, to that end, so savingly and earnestly as is done by interested, educated capitalists; or present satisfactions so fully and happily as is done by the merchant whose fortune is to answer for his appreciation of the public wants.

The work of the politician in this behalf is gratuitous and impertinent. It is an indignity to industry which will be revenged upon the people. Capital and labor should be mobilized as far as possible; free to collect or divide, to turn to the right or to the left; free in gift, purchase, and heritage. On the contrary, the effort of legislation has generally been to impose checks and limitations and hinderances everywhere.

We have thus discussed at length the union of capital and labor; passing close by the great practical questions of protection and entail, but reserving them, the one to the division of "Exchange," the other to that of "Distribution."

CHAPTER XII.

ECONOMIC CULTURE.

We shall best define the field of this agency by discussing one of the most severely contested questions of political economy, viz.: —

What is the distinction between productive and unproductive labor?

The form of this question is unfortunate, and has caused the greater part of the confusion prevailing on the subject. In itself, it is of slight importance; but, in the course of the discussion, a very grave matter has become involved with it, helping the understanding of neither.

Dr. Adam Smith insisted strongly on the distinction between productive and unproductive laborers. In the former class he embraced all those who produce material objects, which are generally admitted to be of use and benefit to mankind. Such, clearly, are farmers, mechanics, and merchants, in the general application of their industry. Of unproductive laborers, he says, "In this class must be ranked some of the greatest and most important, and some of the most frivolous professions, — churchmen, lawyers, physicians, men of letters of all kinds, players, buffoons, musicians, opera-singers, opera-dancers, &c." This somewhat extended list by Dr. Smith has suffered curtailment by almost all writers since. The distinction between physical and mental labor, between direct and indirect agency in production, could not long be permitted to remain as founding a distinction between productive and unproductive labor. It is clear that the physician who preserves the life and strength of the workman on the farm or in the shop is equally productive with him; and that the lawyer by whom transfers of property are effected, and personal safety secured, is equally productive with the owner or the overseer.

One occupation after another, "important or frivolous," was withdrawn from the unproductive class, as prejudices disappeared in the light of a better philosophy, and as the part of each in the great economy became manifest; so that now little is left of that sweeping condemnation of unproductiveness passed by the father of the science upon the learned and artistic professions. Yet there is a residuum, which it is our business to clear away.

All labor, in the economic sense, is productive. The only office of labor is production. We do not, in either popular or scientific language, call by that name the efforts a man makes to do mischief, to dig away a dam or girdle trees, though he may devote his utmost energies to such destruction. Nor do we call that labor which does not seek a reward, whether it be play, though of the hardest kind, or gratuitous service, however useful to the recipient. No more should we call by the name of labor that misdirected or mistaken effort which fails of its reward.

Labor is defined as the efforts of man directed to the satisfaction of his desires. Every effort that is not so directed is a shot thrown away. It is wasted power, not labor. If I spend a twelvemonth in the invention of a machine, which, when completed, is of no sort of use to any one, and for which I can get nothing, my exertions have been unproductive. I have worked enough for a reward; but, as it proved, my work was not directed to the satisfaction of human desires. So of expenditures to improve land, which in no way enhance its fertility. There is a great deal of this kind of effort: perhaps much is inevitable. It is waste, not labor.

But it may be urged, Suppose a man works for months preparing ground, planting, and cultivating till his crop is nearly ready; but a flood comes, and carries all off from before his eyes, and leaves him nothing to show for what he has done. Was there not labor bestowed? Certainly; and the labor was productive, and it had its reward, not the less that each individual effort did not carry off its result in a complete form at the time, but waited for the harvest. Value was produced at every stroke of the shovel — palpable, appreciable, marketable value — just as truly as if it had been taken home at the close of each day. Labor had been there, and received its recompense; but the flood made a robbery of it all. Not the less was there labor, not the less was there production, not the less was there value.

In this view, we see that all labor is productive.

But it may be asked, Does it make no difference to the community what objects of labor are selected, and by what means these objects are attained? Certainly; and, in this inquiry, we reach the field of economic culture, which is that education of the desires, that instruction of efforts, and that use of satisfactions, which will unite to bring out desires, efforts, and satisfactions in ever-increasing circles of industry. Here arise, properly, all the important questions which were formerly discussed under the head of productive or unproductive labor.

Now it can be asked with effect, whether the opera-dancer, the physician, and the churchman are useful; whether they expand the desires, instruct the efforts, and dispose the satisfactions of men to a constantly enlarging industry.

Let us inquire closely. It will be readily granted, that these and other similar classes may have influence upon, or power in, production in two forms, either primary or secondary.

Primary, where a direct part is taken, an active agency maintained, in the creation of values.

Secondary, when an effect is produced, which, by modifying human capacities or desires, however indirectly and in whatever degree, brings about ultimately a greater creation of values.

For example: that great class which, in various offices, maintains civil justice and order, has indisputably a primary influence or power by rendering possible the present creation of values, and by watching over their keeping and transfer. Government and the law are great agencies of production. Without them, however desirous people might be of wealth, and however capable of effort, little or nothing could be produced. Robbery and violence would scatter and destroy what already exists, and a universal waste would speedily follow. But they have, also, a secondary power or influence; for it is found that the maintenance of peace and property rights awakens new and increasing desires, widens the horizon of ambition, and stimulates everywhere to honest industry. Civil security is an education for wealth, an economic culture.

Then that great class which teaches has both a primary and a secondary power and influence, — primary, in that it gives instruction to present labor, as it is struggling to-day with the difficulties of production; explains chemical and mechanical laws; and establishes the alphabet, the written letter, electric communication, the rules of book-keeping, and the art of navigation: secondary, in that the progress of mind brings it infallibly to higher stations of aspiration and activity.

The work of the physician is almost entirely of the primary character. He saves the lives of producers, and preserves their strength to labor. This secondary power or influence of his profession, if such exists, is distant and trivial.

On the other hand, we shall add nothing to the dignity of

the churchman or priest or minister, by attributing to him any direct power in production. Yet his part may be no less important because secondary. The influence of religion is hardly less marked than that of race, in the creation of values. If its influence tend to improve the morals, and thus aid in the preservation of public order; to elevate the mind, and thus give it nobler and higher aspirations, and a better appreciation of the right uses of wealth, — it must be a great auxiliary to its production.

That class of agencies which we have designated as primary comes within the view of production. The class of secondary agencies belongs to the department of consumption, which treats of the use of wealth, so that it may bring forth more wealth.

Here, in economic culture, is the point at which production, passing by exchange and distribution, comes into relation with consumption. In pure theory, production and consumption complete the economic good, which is reproduction. The harvest which is gained in production is sown or wasted, as the case may be, in consumption, to re-appear in a more abounding harvest, or in barrenness, in reproduction. Practically, however, we have to introduce the laws of exchange and distribution, as the agencies by which production is finished, and consumption made possible.

We have used metaphors drawn from the chemistry of agriculture to express the significance of economic culture. To illustrate from mechanics, we should say that it treats of the re-action of labor. No force can re-act except from something external. Labor is a force directed to an object. The energy with which it is to move in a new direction will depend on the temper and shape of the body on which it impinges. Reproduction, then, is the rebound of production from consumption.

If labor expends itself on objects that do not stimulate to further efforts or serve as instruments to further production, but rather debauch the energies and corrupt the faculties, it is evident that reproduction will be lessened and debased, and the whole course of industry be downward.

If, on the contrary, labor expends itself on objects that present fresh and urgent desires, and excite to renewed activities, it is evident that the course of production is upward; and the people will rise economically, with a rapidity and force, such as signalized the career, in the fourteenth century, of Florence; in the seventeenth, of Holland; in the eighteenth, of England; in the nineteenth, of the United States.

BOOK III.

EXCHANGE.

PART FIRST.—TRADE.

CHAPTER I.

THE PRINCIPLES OF TRADE.

EXCHANGE has its origin from the division of labor; and the further that division is carried, the greater extension is given to exchange. If each man supplied his own wants by his own work, trade could not exist. But, so far from this being the rule of industrial society, the article to which a man devotes all his labor may be such as he never used, perhaps never saw used.

Exchange is that agency which brings a man what he wants for what he does not want, which furnishes gratification for his desires out of objects which are adapted to gratify few or none of his desires.

As the division of labor begins in the most savage state, so exchange is known there. One goes into the woods for venison; another, to the river for fish. At night, they divide. Half the fish is given for half the meat. Perhaps other parties are introduced. Instead of exchanging the whole of their fish or venison, each of the two gives a portion for a trinket, and another portion to the medicine man for herbs which he alone knows how to collect. We have here brought in exchange, not only in regard to the plain necessaries of life, but to the services of science and to luxuries. Yet all this occurs in the daily life of the savage.

Only one went for venison: four have venison now. Only one went fishing: four have fish to eat. The hunter and the fisherman have trinkets and medicine they know not how to get. The doctor and the cripple who made the trinket have fish and venison they could not procure for themselves.

This is the idea of exchange. It extends first to the industry of a hamlet; it enlarges to take in the entire community; it remains through all the successive modifications and refinements of labor and accumulations of capital. It goes abroad; it crosses rivers, then narrow seas, then the broad ocean; hunting out everywhere what the seller wants, carrying everywhere what the buyer wants. The word "exchange" expresses the economical principle of all this: its office is the creation and apportionment of wealth.

"Trade" is a technical term for the sum of all actual exchanges. It is exchange realized.

There are several kinds of trade: —

1st, Domestic or home trade, which includes what is commonly known as the coasting trade.

2d, Carrying trade, in which the carriers have no interest in the commodities beyond their transportation.

3d, Foreign or international trade, to which the word "commerce" is generally applied.

These kinds of trade are subdivided into the wholesale, retail, and jobbing trades; and specialized indefinitely as the iron, cotton, shoe trades, &c.

Whence does trade arise?

From the desire which individuals and communities have for each other's products. It is evident that this is essential to trade; since, if men or peoples produced by themselves all they wished for, there could, as we have said, be no occasion for an exchange. It is evident, also, that this is sufficient for trade, since it supplies all the motive that can exist for an exchange.

To what extent can trade be carried?

To the extent of the surplus production of each individual or nation. Given the aggregate surplus products of all the people of a country *severally*, and we have the amount of its *entire* trade. Given the aggregate surplus products of the people *collectively*, and we have the amount of its *foreign* trade.

Illustration: Suppose a community of one hundred individuals, each producing three hundred dollars' worth a year, — aggregate revenue, thirty thousand dollars. If each person desires to consume only one hundred dollars' worth of his own articles, he will have left for trade two hundred dollars' worth, — aggregate in the community, twenty thousand dollars. But if, after exchanging around with his neighbors, it is found that each member of the community has one hundred dollars which he does not wish to part with for any thing he can get at home, we have the aggregate surplus available for foreign trade, ten thousand dollars.

Ordinarily, individuals or peoples do not wish to part with all their products. Ohio, for example, does not wish to dispose of all her wheat. A share must be kept for home consumption. The surplus will be exchanged for other commodities abroad.

Exactly the amount to be so retained will depend, within certain limits, on the degree of disposability. The more the wheat is in demand, — that is, the more of desirable things are offered for it, — the less will the producers be inclined to retain it; the greater effort will they make to dispense with its use themselves, or substitute other things for it at home. But this result will be limited by the necessities of the people. It cannot be calculated on to increase very largely the amount available for trade.

It will, of course, be remarked, that the amount of surplus, in particular countries, will vary with the character of their products. We can suppose an entire people engaged in industry, of which they make no use themselves. In such a case, their trade would be to the amount of their whole production and their whole consumption. In fact, this condition of things is never realized. The nearer it is approached, the more general the trade. The more vital and primitive the articles produced, the greater will be the share consumed at home. Ohio has no such trade, proportionately, as Rhode Island; not necessarily because the latter produces more, but that she produces more of what she does not want. The people of Birmingham consume but an infinitesimal part of the articles they produce.

We have here the principle that the wealth of a people is not determined by the extent of its trade.

We have said that the trade of a community, whose whole production was exchanged, would be equal to its production and consumption. It would be so, but that would be *determined* by its production only. It would be this alone which it would carry in its hands into the markets of the world, and on this would depend what it should get there.

What persons or communities will trade most largely with each other?

Other things equal, those whose productions differ most.

Two tailors will not traffic much together. Both will trade with the shoemaker and hatter. Indiana will not trade extensively with Illinois; but both will trade largely with Louisiana and Massachusetts. Russia and Sweden will make very few exchanges, because their productions are as much alike. Both will deal largely with the West Indies.

What determines the character and kind of products each country will afford?

1st, Soil and physical conformation. One will be a wheat-raising, another a wool-growing country. Each will spontaneously turn its industry in that direction where it will produce the greatest values with the least outlay of labor and capital. This must be where the natural adaptations of the land are followed. This operates, in respect to nations, precisely as we see it in smaller communities, where one farm is especially fitted for grazing, another for tillage, another for timber.

2d, Climate. From the Arctic regions to the tropics, from Siberia to Hindostan, is infinite variety, both of heat and moisture. Some countries are deluged with twenty-five feet of water in a season;* others parch the year round with ten inches. Some are locked with frost eight months in twelve; others are open the year round. It is evident that the conditions which are admitted to have given rise to the differing species of fruits and grains and vegetables will control their increase.

3d, Social condition. Take, for examples, England and Brazil,—one distinguished for the high moral and mental endowments of its citizens; the other having a heterogeneous population, in a poor and semi-barbarous condition. The latter would, plainly, seek to enrich themselves from the spontaneous yield of the soil, from the wild wealth of the pampas and the forests, from the precious ores and stones along their streams and in natural caves, rather than till the ground to the fertility of a garden, sink shafts into the solid rock, cast up highways upon the rivers, and work iron into the needle and lancet.

4th, Difference of race.

This is additional to differences of social condition, and looks to those peculiarities of industrial character in the races of man, which are no less distinguishable than their peculiarities of stature, complexion, and feature. These do not affect the degree of production only, as greater or less, but multiply the fashions, and complete the varieties of wealth.

All the causes here enumerated conspire to give a great extent and activity to trade. It is in the commerce of the world that we have illustrated —

THE TERRITORIAL DIVISION OF LABOR.

The Chinese raise tea and silk. This is their specialty,

* The mountains south of Bombay receive three hundred and twenty inches of water a year, mostly in three months.

the form of industry to them most profitable. The Cubans produce sugar; and the Sicilians, oranges, for the same reason. England excels all nations in useful manufactures; France, in those of taste and beauty; while the United States has its great industrial power in cotton and wheat.

Under the operation of natural laws, each country employs and disposes of its labor, without any arbitrary enactments, in just the way most congenial and profitable; in other words, in that way which develops its greatest industrial power, and secures the largest possible production.

Suppose, on the contrary, that we of the United States should determine to raise our own oranges. We could do so, and create a supply equal to the demand. The cost of one orange would probably be equal to the cost of raising a bushel of wheat, which would procure for us abroad one hundred oranges. The loss would be equal to ninety-nine out of every hundred oranges. We should force a certain part of the labor engaged in other pursuits into the business of raising oranges. The supply would be fully equal to the demand; for, at the rate of a bushel of wheat for each orange, few oranges would be wanted. The people would lose the enjoyment of ninety-nine out of every hundred oranges they would otherwise consume, and could just as well have, if allowed to pay for them in wheat.

If we turn to the advantages alleged * of the division of labor *individually*, we shall find that each one of them holds good in the application of the principle *territorially*. Indeed, it may be assumed that it is here more active and efficient, since the differences of communities range higher than those of individuals. On the other hand, the limitations prescribed are indefinitely removed when we come to the field of national industry; and the disadvantages disappear altogether. That would be a bold philosophy that should declare a people one-sided which does not produce every thing it consumes. So far from being considered a defect,

* See Production, ch. iv. *et seq.*

that races or nationalities should develop very strongly in special directions, it is highly desirable. While it takes nothing from the individual excellence, each contributes with a greater generosity to the completeness of the whole.

From these general considerations of trade, we deduce the following principles: —

1st, That individuals must produce a surplus of their own commodities to have an opportunity to trade, and must trade to make it an object to produce a surplus. Wants create wealth, and wealth creates wants.

2d, That every nation is interested in the production of every other nation. Any thing which impedes the production of any individual or community injures the trade of the world. Such causes, for example, are pestilence, as the cholera, yellow-fever, and plague; the convulsions of nature, as earthquakes and inundations; war, as in the case of the late war in India, which sensibly affected the trade of the world, and, still more striking and recent, in the case of the great Rebellion in the United States, which was felt, it may almost be said, by every human being on the globe. Not a consumer of cotton, high or low, civilized or savage, but suffered in consequence.

3d, That this mutual interest exists between any two nations, whether they have direct commercial intercourse or not. For example: there may be a German principality that purchases nothing of the United States, yet it may purchase largely of the cotton yarn of England. That causes a demand for American cotton; that benefits the Southern States; that, in turn, helps the trade of the North; and that, again, the producers of the West, on whom the North depends for agricultural supplies.

By such ramifications, exchange extends itself through the world.

4th, Since, by the laws of trade, those countries which lie most remote from each other, and are most unlike in soil, climate, civilization, and ethnical characteristics, are most nearly united by commerce, it is shown, that, by this territorial division of labor, the most extended production and the most beneficent distribution of all the commodities of the earth are secured; and that, if any nation creates an article of peculiar desirableness, it is placed within the reach of all. Every invention or improvement becomes, in this way, the common property of mankind.

5th, That commerce harmonizes all differences in the industry of the world.

"All Nature's difference makes all Nature's peace."

Any natural impediment or artificial obstruction to the intercourse of nations, in fact, so far injures the production and trade of all.

"A commercial nation," says Sir James Mackintosh, "has the same interest in the wealth of her neighbors that a tradesman has in the wealth of his customers. . . . Not an acre of land has been brought into cultivation in the wilds of Siberia, or on the shores of the Mississippi, which has not widened the market for English industry."

6th, That commerce diminishes the number of wars, and shortens their duration.

There may have been a time when the galleons of Spain and the Indiaman of England bringing home the stored treasures of barbarism influenced the cupidity of governments to the point of war. But as commerce abandoned the spoils of conquest for the honest industry of the world, as its field became widened, its connections more intimate, its benefits more popular, the temptation to plunder and violence died away. The advantages of a peaceful participation in trade are greater to every people, even those least maritime, than all that could be hoped from the ravages of a Drake or a Doria. The whole interest of commerce is now the inalienable ally of peace. It has not been found sufficient, thus far, to prevent all wars. But it enters into negotiations, tempers grievances, and delays violence. And when, in spite of its admonitions, war is declared and waged, it remains still an argument for peace more impressive and influential by reason of the distresses and inconveniences attending the loss of accustomed traffic.

CHAPTER II.

OBSTRUCTIONS TO TRADE.

THESE are of three kinds: —

First, physical, which are natural; *second*, social, which are incidental; *third*, legal, which are conventional.

Looking at these in the light of what has gone before, we shall be inclined to regard them as so much imposed as a burden on industry, shackling the movements of capital and labor.

But they have been presented in another aspect, as if there were compensations for this hinderance of spontaneous trade; and to this, also, we will attend.

Inasmuch, therefore, as these obstructions to trade have been regarded as the *protection of local industry*, and on that account have been received with favor by scientific men and rulers, we shall speak of them as different forms of PROTECTION. The propriety of the term "protection" we shall discuss at another point.

1st, Physical protection.

This results from obstacles which Nature interposes. They may all be expressed by the single term "location." The wheat of Vermont has a protection in its own markets as against the wheat of Illinois, to the extent of all the cost of transportation from the latter to the former State. If the cost of transportation and attendant charges are fifty cents per bushel, then the farmers of Vermont can, as far as competition from Illinois is concerned, continue to sell their wheat until they reach a price fifty cents per bushel greater than they could obtain but for this. All this may not much enrich the farmer; for the greater price may be rendered necessary by the additional labor required. But, at any rate, it assists him in selling just so much. On the other hand, the mechanic of Vermont must pay more, up to fifty cents, for a bushel of wheat. The protection of the farmer, though a natural one, is at the expense of the consumer. The mechanic, in so far as his bread is concerned, is placed at a disadvantage in production, in competition with those who can purchase their wheat at the prices of Illinois. It costs him more to live: he must, therefore, charge more for his wares, and, of course, sell less.

If, now, the introduction of railroads reduces the cost of transportation to twenty-five cents, the Vermont farmers have lost half their protection. The consequence of this will naturally be, that some of that class in Vermont will become mechanics, because the latter class has gained what the former has lost, by the reduction in the cost of transportation. Any thing which reduces the price of agricultural products has a tendency to increase all other branches of production.

This protection amounts generally to an entire prohibition of the foreign article in the case of certain manufactures, such as houses, barns, stores, &c., which might often be erected more conveniently and cheaply than in the country where they are to be occupied; but the cost of transportation puts it out of the question, except in cases where the local facilities are very crude and insufficient. There have been great numbers of houses sent out by ship to California and Australia; and there are, even now, remaining in the eastern portion of the United States, houses which were framed in the old world, or which are made of brick imported from England.

Yet, looking to the whole of things, we find that this class of protection builds up, in every country, an amount of manufacturing and mining industry, often amounting to one-half of its consumption in that line.

Such a protection to industry being in the nature of things, and, in fact, being the very *condition* of material existence, we have no more call to inquire whether it is desirable than we have to ask the same concerning weight. It exists, and must continue. The effect of it may be lessened by man's contrivances, but can never be annihilated. Those very contrivances will be among the effects of it.

In a certain sense, and to a degree, such obstructions, even when apparently removed, still continue to exert a protection on local industry. Suppose, for example, a swamp, near a certain town, requires a detour of many miles for all passengers and freight. It is a natural protection on the industry of the place. If, now, a causeway is constructed or the swamp drained, so that the difficulty of travel is avoided, the protection is removed, unless, indeed, it exists in the form of the debt incurred for drainage. In either case, the people are relieved of a certain amount of labor once indispensable; and, though their "protection" has been removed, their industry has been greatly benefited.

In the prodigious enterprises undertaken by science and labor for removing, in every direction, obstacles to uninterrupted communication, do we not find the best practical commentary on all artificial and conventional arrangements for putting countries further apart by imposing restrictions on commerce? If the approach of foreign industry is undesirable, it is an economic curse, that the steamship and the Indiaman have replaced the galleys of Columbus or the triremes of Themistocles. Let the ocean be turned to quicksand, and the earth to mire; that so the mutual hurtfulness of nations may cease in an entire impossibility of reaching each other.

The second of the modes of protection is what we have termed social. We have also called it incidental, there being no original intention to affect the direction of labor. It arises from social obstructions or political disturbances. These increase the protection afforded the interests of particular localities. A most impressive illustration is found in the results of the war of the Rebellion in the United States. The production and sale of cotton was greatly hindered, and, for a time, almost annihilated. This operated as an immense protection to the cotton of India and Egypt, where, before, the culture was comparatively unprofitable. Yet, under the encouragement of the American war, it became more advantageous than any other branch of industry. Indeed, so largely was it raised in India, that the country increased in wealth at a rate quite astonishing, and a great industrial revolution, for the time at least, was effected. But it was at a heavy expense to all other peoples and countries. What India gained, Europe and America lost; the former as producer, the latter as consumer. The wealth of the world was not increased, but greatly diminished, and its natural and healthy commerce widely deranged.

Even India itself has not been permanently benefited by the extraordinary demand for her cotton. The return of peace in the United States, bringing down the price of her great staple, has caused extensive bankruptcy and great commercial distress. The season of artificial prosperity led to the wildest extravagance and speculation, to the neglect of the culture of rice and other needful crops, so that the event, which, for a while, brought unwonted prosperity, must, in the end, produce equal depression and suffering.

In some countries, the despotic rapacity of the government, and the violence and fraud that pervade society, serve as a great protection to the industry of others, by diminishing personal safety and business security in trade. Such an element affords the same encouragement to others as the introduction of a bear into one store would give to the sales of others. It plainly reduces the quantity or quality of inducements that can be held out to buyers in the community where the disturbance or disorder exists.

Suppose the Gulf of Mexico to be infested with pirates, so that the danger to life and risk of property should double the price of sugar brought from New Orleans to New York. This increase of price, caused by the cost of insurance against robbery and murder, so long as it lasted, would be a protection to that extent to the cultivation of maple sugar in the North.

War, under all circumstances, whatever the occasion or result, whether between different nations or parts of the same, always has the effect of disturbing trade, arresting all the healthful agencies of production, and disturbing the harmony of the economic world.

3d, The last of the modes of protection is what we have called legal. It is purely conventional, and arises with the direct purpose of affecting production, or, at least, with the expectation that such will be the result. This is effected, firstly, by the prohibition of imports from one or all nations; secondly, by a direct premium on the products of home industry; or, thirdly, by the imposition of duties on the foreign article.

The former method is so violent and extreme as to be entirely out of the sympathies of modern economy and statesmanship. In so far as it exists, it intends to destroy trade. It may arise during a state of war, or in greatly embittered controversies for purposes of injury or revenge; in which case its effects are to be regarded rather as belonging to a state of war, and as incidental to it, though brought in by specific enactment.

The second, though used at different times and in different countries, has never been a favorite with governments, although it is by far the most economical mode of giving encouragement to a particular branch of industry. An illustration of the great advantage of this mode of protection over that of laying duty on exports will be given in our chapter on national taxation.

We shall have to do, then, only with that kind of legal protection which is secured by the imposition of duties on imports. This has been the practice of nations generally, in a greater or less degree, and so with more or less effect. England formerly laid taxes on four hundred articles brought into her ports from France. The United States has always maintained a system of import duties of a varying character, sometimes directed to one object and sometimes to another, as the popular feeling went.

CHAPTER III.

PROTECTION.

LEGAL protection may be imposed from one or more of four general reasons: —

1st, To raise a revenue.

2d, To encourage the protection of certain commodities at home.

3d, To support existing forms of production.

4th, To secure commercial independence.

All these will be examined in detail.

1st, To raise a revenue. So far as this is the only convenient way in which the state can raise a certain sum of money which it must have, it is but a mode of taxation, with which we have no present concern. So far as it also affects industry, it becomes a species of protection. We have not called it *incidental*, because its bearing on industry is known and considered in its imposition. So far as the element of protection remains, it should be subject to the judgment which shall be pronounced on what follows. If the "protection" of certain domestic products be found a good, then the revenue duties should be so disposed as to afford them all possible assistance at the same time that it serves the public purse. If, on the other hand, it is decided to be mischievous to substitute man's law for Nature's, such revenue duties should, as far as may consist with the public safety, be imposed on articles where it will not mislead industry.

2d, To encourage the growth or manufacture of certain commodities at home. This is the field in which protection joins battle of choice with freedom of industry. In all the other particular reasons, its argument is, as we shall see, linked with some real or fancied necessity; but here protection takes ground freely and fairly, virtually making two propositions which it assumes to defend: —

First, that the desires of man, as an industrial being, are so blind, so passionate, or so weak, as to require correction by the public will, enlightening, chastening, or stimulating.

Second, that the efforts of man, as an industrial being, are not sufficient, of themselves, to achieve the satisfaction of desires, without the aid of law, coercing him to that which he would not voluntarily undertake.

What is industrially wanting, then, in man's nature, either individually or in voluntary association, is to be supplied by such enactments as are called protective.

We will inquire about the second of these propositions, with the view of reducing both to one.

Man's industrial efforts can never be assisted in production by any legal enactment. Deriving all value from labor, we have here an adamantine basis, which no sophistry can move. Laws may be supposed to stimulate desires, or to repress them; but they cannot lay hand on man's labor, except to hinder it. It is a power given by the Creator, to work upon the constant properties of matter. It has no fellow in its work; its only tools are capital, its own creature, and nature, whose forces are fixed by God. Labor has its commission and its reward in itself. Just as surely as man cannot add one cubit to his stature, so is law impotent to help man's labor, except through man's desires.

There is another reason, more abstract, for reducing these two propositions to one. It is, that the efforts men will make are included in their desires. Those efforts are those desires going out after their objects. Man's work is man's want *active.*

We have thus to consider only the first proposition in the theory of protection; namely, that the desires of man, in the economic sense, need government by law. Men, as consumers, are to be shut off from certain objects to which they naturally incline; and, as capitalists or laborers, are to be shut up to certain efforts, which, so far as the legislation has any influence, are not the direct, simple, and proper means to the satisfaction of existing wants. And all this not at all in the interests of morality or good government, but wholly with a view to the greater wealth and industrial prosperity of the community. This proposition has its only basis in a want of confidence in the intelligence of the people to direct their own desires, and of the competency of labor to gratify such desires. The proposition here reaches a point where there is no argument. Consciousness and experience must affirm or deny sharply and decisively. Such wisdom or power, we believe, has not been vouchsafed to legislators, whether absolute or representing the will of a people.

Economically, it will ever remain true, that the government is best which governs least. The wants of a people are the sole proper, the sole possible, motives for production. Nothing can be substituted for them. Any thing that seems to take their place is merely a debasement of them. The interests of producers, whether laborers or capitalists, secure, better than any other possible means, the gratification of such wants. Their intelligence is always superior on such points to that of any foreign body. These we believe to be absolute affirmations of universal experience, not dependent on reasoning, not condescending to argument.

General proposition: There is no sense so subtile as that

with which a man detects his own wants. There is no spur so sharp as that which urges him to satisfy them.

This is all the defence it seems necessary to make against the direct attack of the protection theory. It will be more troublesome when we meet it in alliance with other interests, on ground not its own, and displaying uncertain colors.

If, then, protection is founded on false economical principles, we should expect to find it working mischief in its application to national industry, perverting the desires, crippling the efforts, and plundering the satisfactions of society.

Since the subject is of great practical importance and of great popular interest, we will take an illustration at length from the history of American industry, exhibiting the principles thus far attained.

We choose the manufacture of iron, for six reasons: —

1st, Because it may be produced in great amount in our own country, and is found in almost all others. There is, therefore, nothing of the nature of a monopoly about it.

2d, Because it enjoys the largest natural protection arising from its weight and bulk.

3d, Because it is one of the most simple of all manufactures.

4th, Because it has been tried on a large scale, affording material for great inductions, and freeing the results from any imputation of accident.

5th, Because the public attention has been turned to it for a long time, and it is better understood than any other we could name.

6th, Because a stronger argument can be made in favor of its receiving governmental protection than any other.

What is the fact in regard to the manufacture so described? At present, iron cannot be so cheaply and extensively produced in the United States as to exclude the foreign article. Why is this? We answer negatively: —

1st, Not that we do not know how to make it. Being, as

has been said, the most simple of all manufactures, we have had, from the earliest settlement of the colonies, the necessary knowledge, and have produced it from our colonial days.

2d, Not that we have not sufficient capital. No branch of business is more accessible than iron-making, or requires less capital proportionally. As a matter of fact, the business was commenced with little difficulty, and we succeeded up to a certain point. Had it been as profitable as other branches of industry, it would, like the manufacture of boots and shoes, have been extended to the full demands of the country. Yet the latter industry has been carried nearly to the full demand. The former has stopped far short of it.

It is to be observed, in this connection, that a successful business, once started, creates its own capital. Labor no more seeks assistance from capital, than capital employment by labor. Every year of profitable enterprise affords a surplus, which can be applied to the increase of business more efficiently than twice the amount of raw capital, coming in the lump. The daily or monthly increments are applied with an aptness and a promptness that make them far more useful than wholesale, occasional accessions of capital from abroad.

3d, Not that we have not the best natural facilities for the manufacture.

Five great conditions of success are found most remarkably in the United States,—(*a*) Our ore is not only of excellent quality and most abundant, but (*b*) is found very generally on the surface and (*c*) in proximity to the best river navigation, and almost always in close juxtaposition to (*d*) coal for smelting, and (*e*) limestone for flux. Perhaps in no other country of the world are these requisites so fully secured. The absence of a single one of them might be sufficient to destroy the prospect of production.

The importance of this element will be seen in the following remarks from Dr. Allen's excellent work on "India, Ancient and Modern:" —

"India has valuable iron mines (the writer once heard a distinguished geologist, who had been inspecting them, say they contained iron enough to supply the world); and yet nearly all the iron used in the country is procured from Europe, because the iron mines are in one province, and the coal is in another."

4th, Not that the manufacture here lacks a good natural protection. America has been put at a great distance from Europe. The effects of such a protection we have already seen. The foreign product is, in this case, charged with freight and insurance for a voyage of three thousand miles. This, with articles having little bulk or weight for the value, might not serve as a great encouragement to the home product; but, with iron, it is a very considerable item.

Why, then, with all these facilities, do we not produce all our iron without governmental protection? There is but one reason.

WE CAN DO BETTER. We can obtain our iron with less labor than by making it.

How can this be? Because, though we have facilities for making iron, greater perhaps than any other people, we have *still greater* facilities for raising agricultural products.

We can raise forty bushels of wheat with, say, twenty days' labor that will purchase a ton of iron, to produce which would cost twenty-five days' labor: net saving, five days, or twenty per cent on all our iron.

What is the explanation of this state of things?

Land is an instrument, and the greatest of all, in producing agricultural values. Good arable land, on which wheat is raised in England, is worth, say, two hundred dollars an acre.

In this country, the same is worth, say, twenty dollars.*

* Often not a fourth part of that sum. The government holds the best wheat land at one dollar and twenty-five cents, and gives it away to actual settlers.

Then, with our price of land, we have the advantage, so far, over the European, in the production of crops, of nine-tenths, or ninety per cent. Our capital in land is ten times as productive as that of England. On the other hand, we have not an equal advantage over the European in making iron; for, although it costs him more labor (and labor is, as we have said, the chief item in making iron), that labor costs him much less per day than it costs us; say, at least, fifty per cent less. So that, if it is estimated to cost him twice as much labor to make iron, still labor costs him no more in money than ours costs us. In respect of labor, then, we are on a level.

So far as money, as capital is concerned, the European again has the advantage of us by fifty per cent, since money is as well worth eight per cent here as four per cent there.

Now, these facilities which the European has, from the cheapness of labor and capital, counterbalance to a great extent, if not fully, the advantages which we have from the ease with which we can get the materials of which iron is made.

If so, in getting our iron by raising wheat, we have the net advantage over the European of ninety per cent in the land, which is the great item of expense in such products; so much so, indeed, that the pure rent of farms in England is estimated to equal the entire wages of the agricultural laborers.

Thus it is that our unequalled natural advantages, arising from cheap virgin lands, render it unprofitable for us to make iron, or engage in many other kinds of manufactures.

Such is the situation. We will now apply protection. Government, in 1816, laid a duty of thirty dollars per ton on bar iron; equal to about fifty per cent on the cost of the foreign article. Let us inquire into the effect of this policy.

1st, Iron was produced. Labor and capital were at once withdrawn from other occupations, and invested in furnaces and iron-making. We undertook to make iron ourselves, under the belief, that, with a protection of thirty dollars per ton, the manufacture would be found very profitable. So far, the object of the duty was accomplished.

2d, A great loss was caused to the general production of the country. Labor and capital were withdrawn from pursuits of ordinary profitableness, and invested in business that required fifty per cent protection to make it profitable at all. If the duty was necessary to establish the manufacture in 1816, *as it was*, — for a still higher protection was called for, — does it not follow, that, on the whole amount made under the forced system of production, there was a loss to the country of thirty-three and one-third per cent; thirty-three and one-third per cent of ninety, the enhanced price, being fifty per cent on sixty, the original price?*

Is it possible that there can be any doubt of this? The production of wealth was decreased so much. The enhanced price, thirty dollars per ton, took the following form: —

* It should be understood that there can be no greater DISCOUNT than one hundred per cent, which takes the *whole* of any thing; yet there are men who profess to be learned and even well versed in financial matters, who speak very flippantly of two hundred or five hundred per cent discount. Professor Fawcett, in his "Manual of Political Economy," page 365, says, "Mr. Gladstone has been confident in his belief that a reduction of one hundred per cent, in the price of inferior French wines, will cause those wines to be purchased by classes of society in this country who have never before purchased them; and, therefore, the consumption will increase more than one hundred per cent." Certainly, Mr. Gladstone is right in supposing the *consumption* would be increased more than one hundred per cent, if the price were reduced one hundred per cent; but it seems almost incredible that the Chancellor of the Exchequer could have used the expression attributed to him. The fact that Professor Fawcett himself could write in this manner shows the importance of having the exact meaning of the term "discount" defined and determined. A writer in one of the most respectable magazines in New York lately stated that a certain commodity "had fallen six hundred per cent." Occurrences of this kind are frequent. The difficulty in the case seems to be, that discount and premium (or advance) are confounded. The first is limited to one hundred, the latter is illimitable.

Suppose the consumption of the United States at that time, 1816, to have been eighty thousand tons per annum, and that, under the system of protection, we made twenty thousand tons, importing the balance; there was, then, paid duty on sixty thousand tons, at thirty dollars	$1,800,000
Twenty thousand tons made, at a price enhanced by thirty dollars	600,000
Total enhanced cost to the people*	$2,400,000

Now, as the iron-masters did not get more than the average rate of profits, the entire six hundred thousand dollars was lost to the country, both to people and government. The sum of one million and eight hundred thousand dollars went to the national revenue. The protection of iron cost two million and four hundred thousand dollars, the people paying a tax not the less on the domestic than on the foreign product.

But the real loss to the country was much greater, because,—

3d, Many wasteful and disastrous experiments were made. When any branch of industry grows up naturally, it commences upon a small scale, and is cautiously extended, as found profitable. Under a forced system, it is quite otherwise. A duty of thirty dollars a ton is laid upon iron.

Pennsylvania is full of iron ore and coal. What prevents her from making a vast sum by it? Has she not a protection of fifty per cent? So everybody reasons; so everybody acts. Great establishments are started at once. There is no occasion longer to consult adaptations of character, experience in business, or local economy. Success and fortune are secured to all by omnipotent protection. Men plunge headlong into the work, if, indeed, they suppose it to be any thing so serious as work. Merchants, professional men, farmers, mechanics, all are seized with the mania of iron-making. Large iron works are hastily and ignorantly got up.

* Besides all the profits charged on the duties and enhanced cost of the iron.

Incompetent heads manage them.
Inexperienced hands work in them.
Imperfect iron comes out of them.
Inevitable loss attends them.
Insolvency is the end of them.

And the iron interest clamors loudly and successfully for more protection. Fifty per cent is not enough for the people to pay extra on iron. These are not accidental or peculiar results, but natural and certain, where the great laws of trade and the even course of production are disturbed.

We have seen these marked effects of protection in the *protected* country. How of the *excluded* country?

Just so far as the "protection" is adequate, England cannot send us iron. What then? So much of her iron trade is cut off; and her capital and industry must be directed to raising wheat, or to some other less profitable, productive, and natural employment. A part of it is forced into wheat-growing, and this reduces the quantity she would naturally require of American wheat. Her industry is made less advantageous; our market is correspondingly diminished. So far as her labor cannot find employment, it must emigrate, as it has done by crowded packet lines, to Australia, Canada, and the United States.

Which country will be most injured by this commercial warfare?

We answer, decidedly, the protected, because England would not have made, on the iron sent us, more, say, than ten per cent; while we make a clean loss, as we have seen, of some thirty or forty per cent; that is, all left of the fifty per cent enhancement of price, after the profits of the American manufacturer are deducted.

But it may be urged, that, if a part of the labor of the country had not been taken from agriculture, its products would have declined in value, and this would have counterbalanced what was lost by the manufacture of iron. This is a favorite view with a certain class of minds. There are many theorists who are continually foretelling the decline of prices, and general starvation; many business men, who are expecting daily to exhaust the market, and reach the limit of their industry; many householders, who dread the disappearance of fuel and light from the earth, with untold horrors beside. Such persons are much afraid of using nature up.

The markets of the world being open to us, all our surplus products would remain in demand. Provisions, especially, are a sort of "legal tender" the world over; and there seems to be no immediate occasion to anticipate their disuse. There is no market that keeps open so long and surely as this. The English ports were wrested from the monopolists of grain, by a power that government and society could not resist,—the power of indignant want. The misfortune of overdone agricultural products is one that statesmen may well leave to their successors.

But, if there were no other markets open but those at home, there would be a certain tendency, not at all frightful in its vehemence, to a decline of prices, in a country like ours; *because* an agricultural people, under favorable circumstances, always produces more than it consumes, and would, sooner or later, create such a surplus as to lower the price. Admitting, then, all that is claimed for such a possible glut, let us inquire into the results.

As soon as wheat, to take it as the exponent of all agricultural products, had fallen so low that it required as many days' work to get a ton of iron by raising wheat as by working the ore, the manufacture would be successfully introduced. That is precisely the point at which this branch of industry would legitimately begin. It would not spring up suddenly, at some arbitrary point, but grow up in those places where the natural protection was most felt, and facilities for production were greatest; for instance, in a region far from any considerable market, where iron could only be obtained by long and expensive transportation, where the land was not adapted to wheat, but where ore, coal, and lime were plentiful. It would extend to all parts of the country where it was as advantageous as wheat-growing. The business would be introduced without any disturbance of existing interests; without wild, extravagant, and wasteful experiments. It would be a natural development and growth, not an arbitrary creation. It would feel its way with a sense as subtile and secure as that with which the plant raises itself into a world of big trees and wild tornadoes, and fierce, rushing life.

CHAPTER IV.

THE FALLACIES OF THE PROTECTIVE THEORY.

We leave now the illustrations of the principles of protection, as exhibited in the manufacture of iron. We believe we have shown the unsoundness of all that political philosophy which proposes to substitute artificial for natural laws, in production. But there still remains some popular arguments, which we will notice.

1st, It is claimed as good policy to protect "an infant manufacture" until it is well established, because it will then take care of itself, and ultimately confer great wealth on the country. Of this it may be said: —

(*a*) There is no assurance, under a system which removes the sole test of usefulness and self-support from the production of a people, that enterprises will not spring up which never will come to maturity, which have no vital force of themselves, which exist solely by reason of the protection, and will never become remunerative. If good enterprises, why not bad, since the test of bad or good has been withdrawn? In such a rankness of unnatural growth, it is far more likely that weeds will be produced than useful plants. Thus the whole industry of a country may become perverted and falsified by removing the principle of competition. There will be no reason for healthful industries to spring up, which will not also give life to such as are weak, tardy, ephemeral; to such as are parasitic and exhausting.

(*b*) Other things aside, the desirableness of raising the "infant" will depend very much on the length of time and total cost required to bring it to full age and size. There have been nations that exposed sickly and unpromising children, holding it to be for the advantage of the state to rear none but such as promised to become vigorous and useful members of society. Religion and humanity have changed this, out of respect for the image of God found in every human creature; and now the cripple and the idiot are reared tenderly and patiently. But the protective policy extends the same kindness and forbearance to industry. No matter how plainly palsy, scrofula, or fatuity may appear in the form or features, the infant is sure of an affectionate solicitude, that only changes to become more anxious as the infant gets punier and weaker.

France protected one of these industrial infants; *i.e.*, the beet-sugar culture. Dr. Wayland said of it, in 1837, "The present protection costs one million and four hundred thousand pounds per annum. Suppose this to continue for twenty years, it will amount to two million eight hundred thousand pounds sterling; the interest of which, at five per cent, will bring, at two and a half pence per pound, one hundred and twenty-six million pounds of sugar, or nearly the whole annual amount of sugar now consumed in France." In 1865, we can say that this child, born in the early part of the great Napoleon's career, has not yet become strong enough to walk alone, or hardy enough to take the air. Supposing an equable annual consumption of any article, it requires but common school arithmetic to show that a protection to the extent of fifty per cent, continuing for eighteen years, would amount to a sum, which, at six per cent interest, would furnish the nation in that article to the end of time, without ever paying any thing more for it. A child that is so costly to bring up ought to make a very useful man; whereas it is generally true that such children have to be brought up three or four times over, and then live on the poor-rates. If such a protection, however, were to be continued only eighteen years, and the necessity for it then cease, the industry having become self-supporting, it would yet be true that every pound would have two prices, added to each other: one, the present cost of making; the other, interest on old protection equal to the present cost.

In fact, iron and sugar have been protected in this country since 1816, and the duties still continue. And all for what? Where is the advantage of making a great annual sacrifice, for a long time, to establish an industry that will grow up of itself as soon as it will pay, as was growing up slowly, but successfully, before there was any protection?

(*c*) Finally, no sound and healthful manufacture needs protection at all. The phrase "infancy" is entirely sophistical, as applied to any branch of legitimate industry. Each one comes full-grown and full-armed into life. We do not mean that it has no growth, as far as extension is concerned. It certainly does go on from town to town, from State to State, out of small beginnings. But there is no infancy, so far as completeness or robustness of life is concerned. Suppose, for example, that there was but one manufacturer of iron in the country, and he produced only to the amount of five thousand dollars a year. Yet, if he could bring to the market as good and cheap an article as the foreigner, he would be none the worse for being a solitary producer on some mountain in Pennsylvania. The security of any manufacture does not reside in the number of those engaged, but in its power to meet the public wants. However few may be employed, however humble their beginnings, they stand simply in their ability to sell a good article at a reasonable price, and are as strong in this as ever was the proudest guild of London.

Of course, there is a period in every enterprise when all is experiment and outlay. But capital is always ready and able to meet the necessity. It belongs to capital to do this; for it gets the remuneration of it when the yield begins.

There is a remarkable confirmation of the truth of these remarks in the history of the boot and shoe manufactures of the United States. They never asked for protection; never received any notice in all the conflicts for increased tariffs. The trade grew up naturally, steadily, and profitably, from the first; increasing gradually, with the growth of the country, until, at the present time, it is not only the largest, but one of the most profitable branches of manufacturing industry. In Massachusetts alone, this manufacture extends to over fifty millions of dollars annually, and is by far the most advantageous branch of industry in the State.

There is another popular argument for protection.

2d, It is claimed that we ought to protect our labor against the pauper labor of Europe.

Does a restrictive tariff do this? Does it prevent the laborers of Europe from entering into competition with ours? Does it not, in fact, bring them to our very doors?

For fifty years prior to the date of the first important tariff, viz. 1816, there was no immigration of any consequence. Soon after this, we began to attract skilled workmen. Some were expressly hired to come over to teach us how to spin, weave, &c. As we raised the tariff and increased manufactures, the current increased, until it has inundated the country. All Europe pours in its starved labor upon us.

What kind of labor naturally emigrates? The poorest, because the better by character and capacity can protect itself longer at home. An employer does not turn his good men off first.

Why so large a proportion of Irish? Because theirs is the cheapest labor; the first thrown out in any reduction. The tide, once turned upon us, kept swelling, till our nationality is almost in dispute. This immense immigration never came here in obedience to natural laws, but to the legislation of Congress. Instead of protecting American labor against the pauper labor of Europe, we have brought that labor here to meet the American citizen face to face, on a perfect level, with equal civil rights, and have given to him the advantage of our immense landed capital. Whether this is good state policy; whether a forced immigration, in such vast numbers as to prevent an easy and natural assimilation with the native population, is desirable or not,—it is not our province to discuss. That is a political question. It only belongs to us to show that no protection has been given to American labor.

3d, It has been gravely said, that the general average of all profits is raised by a protective policy.

If true, this is a valuable discovery. It affords the easiest known method of making everybody rich at once, and without effort. Government has only to place sufficient restrictions on trade to carry up profits to one hundred per cent; and, when all trade has ceased, everybody's profits will be immense!

The folly of such assertions is too apparent to justify any considerable notice.

Where are the enhanced profits to come from? Out of the diminished production? Is the whole lessened, and every part increased? So far as protection creates a monopoly at the expense of the public, it may, for a while, add to the profits of an individual or a class, but only by taxing other industries for the purpose.

4th, But it is urged, leaving mere argument, do we not *know* that protection especially develops manufactures? and are not manufacturing countries found to be, in fact, richer than those which are more exclusively agricultural? Both propositions are true in an isolated form.

Other things equal, in a normal state of things, manufacturing communities are older than agricultural, and, of course, have much greater accumulated wealth. England is older and richer than the United States; Massachusetts than Ohio. Manufactures arise *because* a people have a dense population, abundant capital, and great industrial activity. Under such circumstances, great wealth will be created, because these are the fit conditions of creating wealth. Such creations are natural.

It is, without question, true, that in an equal manufacturing population will be found a greater accumulation of wealth. One important reason of this is, that a larger share of the population are engaged in production, and a larger amount of capital is employed. Women and children, who could earn but little in agricultural labors, can earn much in manufacturing. This is one of the most striking results of a division of labor, as we have already shown. As we carry on agriculture, women and children do little, though in Continental Europe they do much. Agriculture, too, can be performed only in certain portions of the year. Manufacturing need never stop, summer or winter, cold or hot, fair or foul. This makes a wonderful difference.

All these, however, are economical advantages, which manufacturing communities have, when properly constituted and employed. These are reasons which may induce such industry; never reasons why it should be compelled. If, with so great a superiority, manufactures do not arise freely and support themselves fully, it becomes a double argument for not forcing them. If such advantage will not secure free manufacturing, it is certain that compulsory manufacturing will not secure these advantages, without the sacrifice of other interests.

But all this argument in favor of manufactures, and these anticipations of agricultural glut, come out of a false idea of what are the natural relations of these two great branches of labor. Granted, that manufactures are a desirable form of national industry, give a good market for the produce of the farm and the mine, and help build up the common wealth; yet it is not necessary to bring them on by a forcing process, for they come of themselves as soon as profitable. We have already shown (page 86) that certain large classes of manufactured products receive such a natural or local protection as insures their home growth. But there are other classes which have an encouragement even more liberal. There is a principle always operating to bring manufactures out, on every part of the earth's surface. It is the impossibility of carrying on certain branches anywhere but at the place where the article is wanted. The survey, grading, and construction of railroads and canals, forming as they do an immense portion of the public industry, cannot be brought within the purview of the custom-house. They are necessarily confined to the field in which these means of transport are to be used. These may stand as examples of a vast class of industry, which arises indifferently to protection. So all tinkering, patching, and repairing, great or small, must be done on the spot. A glance at any village, no matter how intimate its connection with some centre of trade, will show how large a share of its labor, other than agricultural, is employed in its local work; so that, one way and another, these classes of manufacturing interests, which inevitably come to the community without help of law, form a very considerable part of the whole.

The value of manufactured articles imported, for the four years preceding the war of the Rebellion, ranged from one hundred and fifty to two hundred millions a year; while the authorities of the treasury and of the census estimate the value of home manufactures at not less than one thousand millions a year, for the same period. Such comparisons are necessarily crude; but it would be far within bounds to say *that four-fifths of all the present consumption of manufactures would be supplied by our national industry, irrespective of protection.* All the matter, then, comes to this: Shall we impose heavy duties to force labor and capital into such channels as shall provide, at great expense, the remaining fifth of the manufactures we consume?

5th, Perhaps the most popular plea of all for protection looks to "the development of our natural resources." This does not propose to increase the gross or net product of national industry, does not assume or assert that the labor and capital of the country are not well employed at present; but it remembers the great mineral and metallic wealth we have yet hidden in the Middle States and the West, and it sighs for the thought of their uselessness. It regards as of no consequence the fact that digging or working the ores will not pay. It can only exclaim, "What a pity that such great advantage should be unimproved!" These reasoners would call labor off from the rich fields of agriculture, from no other motive than a desire to see our wonderful mineral treasures developed.

The answer to this species of patriotism may be very short. Since Nature has taken thousands of years to form these ores and store these mines, man can at least take time enough to wait till it will pay to dig them. It may seem to some a pity they should remain underground; but the true cause of the misfortune resides in the fact that we have not population enough to settle densely one-tenth of our territory. It is a misfortune that will cure itself as our numbers increase. We can certainly afford to leave for future generations what we cannot afford to take for ourselves.

CHAPTER V.

PROTECTION (*concluded*).

We have said that legal protection may be imposed from one or more of four general reasons.

We have discussed the first two; viz.,—

To raise a revenue.

To encourage the growth of certain commodities at home.

We now come to the remaining reasons, which will demand but little attention, as their principles have already been developed.

To support existing manufactures.

Here we leave the expediency of founding special industries by a system of protection, and confine ourselves to the question, whether, such industries having been begun and developed under high tariffs, capital having become so engaged, labor having become so employed, it is not necessary to continue the protection.

So far as this acknowledges a moral obligation on the government to save from loss those who have followed the guidance of its laws, it is a question for the statesman. But the economist can urge, that, if the burden of such bad investments must be borne by the public, it would be preferable to have it assumed in the shape of direct relief to the manufacturers, rather than by a system which is sure to multiply such unfortunate enterprises, and perpetuate their weakness. That great caution and forbearance are necessary, in removing even a false institution, is not a maxim which economy has to teach politics.

And here we come face to face with the great practical difficulty of protection in our country; that which, if all its principles were triumphantly proved in general reasoning, should still throw it out of our legislation. If it were proved harmless, if it were proved beneficial, there is a strong reason against ever attempting to realize it here. That difficulty resides in the varying politics of our country. Injurious as protection is to the best interests of the country, any system of it, however severe, would be preferable to the "open-and-shut" policy, absolutely unavoidable in a government like ours. It is not within the bounds of reason to suppose that the alternate successes of parties will not continue to convulse our national legislation; and therefore it is with emphasis true, that a consistent system of protection is only possible in a government with great conservative force and great central powers. A representative body, embracing the most opposite interests, swayed by such influences and intrigues as notoriously possess such an organization, and changed in all its parts every few years, is not the place in which to adjust accurately and dispassionately the economical parts of a nation, and distribute the agencies of production.

It is our felicity, that our well-being does not depend on such counsels, but that great Nature has fixed the forces of industry in perfect harmony, and to the most beneficent ends.

To secure commercial independence. True commercial independence is attained by any nation, when its natural resources are so developed and cultivated that it becomes a power in the world, can command the products of the industry of every clime, because it can furnish that which all others want. This is independence *in* commerce. Independence *of* commerce is the independence of the savage, or of undiscovered countries. To assume that such independence of all mutual helpfulness is desirable, outrages the earliest sense of humanity.

But it is claimed that such a separation from all offices of kindness is necessary to protect nations in war.

So far as the state urges the claims of its own safety, the principles of economic science must be silent. But this interference with the laws of value, for the preservation of the national life, must be strictly limited to the absolute necessities of war.

There are many reasons to suppose, that this interference is rarely, if ever, necessary. There are very few states which could not, on occasion, supply from their own soil the means of warfare. It would be much better that nations should, by anticipation, secure from abroad a sufficient amount of *material*, than by indirect efforts distort their industry to an extent many times greater than would be involved in obtaining beforehand, by commerce, whatever might be necessary.

But finally and decisively, if it is alleged, under any circumstances, to be essential that a nation should possess within itself the means of war, we answer that it should undertake the manufacture by a special government agency, not by changing the entire industry of a people to produce this as an incidental result. Such is, in fact, the procedure of most, if not all, civilized nations, and leaves no force in the plea for national independence. But the argument for protection from the necessities of war has almost disappeared in the intenser light of our growing civilization. The independence of each nation *in* commerce, existing harmoniously with its dependence *on* commerce, forms the best hope of peace and tranquillity for the future. It may be safely assumed, that the probabilities of war between any two peoples are inversely as their commercial relations. The great reason against war, in the present age, is not the expense of maintaining armies, nor the destruction of life, but the interruption of trade. This not only puts peacemakers in the councils at home, but makes all nations mediators between the parties at variance.

The intercourse between the United States and Austria is but trifling. A little fire would kindle great strife between these two peoples. There would be no great motive to forbear and adjust the occasions of dispute. The United States and England, on the other hand, have a yearly trade of four hundred and fifty millions of dollars, which interposes itself between the nations, however angry, a great standing policy of peace.

All general economic principles urge the extinction of war. All special economical interdependences postpone and weaken the provocations of war. Resting on this principle, we shall find nothing good in the scheme of making nations independent, that they may the better fight. We shall recognize commerce as the great bond of human brotherhood.

But, after all argument has been closed on the principles of protection, we still find one plea remaining. If freedom of intercourse, it is said, were only universal, it would be well; but, since it is not, each nation must protect itself, and do as it is done by.

Let us suppose that England refuses to take our wheat. Would that be a good reason why we should not take iron from her, if we get it so, cheaper than by making it? We have already shown that the protected suffers more than the excluded community. If England should exclude our wheat, whom would she injure? Ourselves somewhat, that is, to the extent of the profits we should have made; herself still more, that is, to the extent of the vastly enhanced cost of the grain. If, in retaliation, we exclude her iron, whom do we injure? Her somewhat; ourselves much more.

Let us examine more in detail the consequences of our exclusion from foreign ports. If partial, we could still, by selling our wheat, get iron cheaper than by making it.

If total, the closing of our markets for wheat could turn our industry towards other forms of production. This would constitute one of the conditions under which manufactures would legitimately arise; and it would be more sensible and healthful than if it came as the result of our own restrictive legislation.

The full consequences of the policy of retaliation would be, each people refusing to receive the products of others, trade annihilated, industry crippled, all nations isolated, with no mutual interest but robbery and plunder.

We have said, that England, by imposing a duty, say of fifty per cent, on our wheat, would injure us to the extent of our possible profits, and herself to the extent of the enhanced cost of the grain. On a closer inquiry, we shall see that the injury to ourselves is compensated in part; that to herself is aggravated.

The consequence of such a duty would be, that the consumption would fall off in some degree. Her poor would subsist more on potatoes, or other articles cheaper than flour. But, notwithstanding these shifts, it would be found that it cost her laboring population more to live, even though they lived more meanly. Their wages must be raised: this is certain. All taxes laid on commodities which the laborer must use have the effect to reduce the quantity or quality of his food to a certain point; but he must *live*, and his wages must be raised to enable him to do so with the enhanced price of wheat. This would make it more expensive for England to manufacture her goods, and would, in part, so far reduce her ability to compete in the markets of the world. By such a policy, she would weaken her own industry, and to a degree exclude herself from commerce. This would afford another condition under which manufactures would legitimately arise in this country, whose wheat was excluded.

That this is no impossible supposition, will be evidenced by the condition of England before the repeal of the corn laws. The movement in favor of that great measure *originated* in Manchester, and was carried, against the nobility and the landed interest, by the resolute efforts of the manufacturing class.

What advantage is there in refusing to buy of a nation because it refuses to buy of us? It is retaliation and revenge, not self-defence or self-vindication. The first historical instance of such retaliatory legislation is the establishment, by the Venetians, of customs duties, to deprive foreigners of the benefit of their trade; in return for which, Charles V. imposed twenty per cent duty on all Venetian merchandise. The most wise and useful economical act of this century was that by which, by the exertions of Mr. Cobden, England and France, so long contending only in exclusions and mutual injuries, threw open their ports to the free entry of hundreds of articles, to the common benefit of both, and to the advancement of good feeling and hearty alliance; *a measure*, that, between the years 1859 and 1863, increased by seventy-three per cent the trade of Great Britain with France, while proving no less beneficial to the labor of the latter country.

We infer, from all that has preceded, that "protection" is an unfortunate expression. To restrict industry, to put the bad on the level of the good, to remove from industry its only guaranty of a full reward, to contract trade and neutralize the gifts of Nature, is not protection, in any proper sense of the word.

In conclusion of the subject, it may be proper to allude to the great natural characteristics of our national industry. We see that the important fact of our condition is unequalled agricultural power. Possessing such an advantage, with an active, enlightened, and enterprising population, and an industry perfectly untrammelled, we should naturally become the granary of the world, and create, as a certain consequence, the most extensive and powerful commercial and naval marine on the globe. We should secure, by sea and land, a greater power to give help to friends, or hurt to foes, than any other people, and should rapidly attain our best national condition.

We should have, not only the most profitable, but the most salutary industry, as favorable to the acquisition of unlimited wealth as to a sound physical development and high moral culture. We should have manufactures, also, in their spontaneous growth. They would arise — they were arising previous to any tariff — as fast as the best interests of the country required them.

States and sections, like New England, would naturally and profitably undertake manufactures, because they have a thinner soil, a denser population, and a larger capital relatively, than others. Such regions would be the workshops of the nation, while the prairies of the West and the rich uplands of the Middle States would be the nation's farms.

What manufactures arise of themselves should be *welcomed*, for they come in obedience to natural laws; they are founded on extraordinary facilities, on high natural protection, on local necessities. But we bind the swelling thews of the youth when we endeavor to force on America the industry of Europe. We grow enough every year to cover some of the kingdoms of the old world. Every year's growth stretches over and appropriates some country, fertile as the plains of the Nile, and bearing every manner of precious or useful ore. Here is our destiny. This is our wealth.

It cannot be too often repeated, because it is the great fact in regard to manufactures, that they only need to be "let alone." When a distinguished French minister of finance called the manufacturers of that country to Paris, and asked what he could do for them, they made the well-known answer, "Laissez nous faire." It is within our personal knowledge, that, when the proposal was made to impose the protective tariff of 1816, the leading manufactures of Rhode Island, amongst whom was the late Mr. Slater, the father of cotton-spinning in this country, met at the counting-room of one of their number, and, after deliberate consultation upon the matter, came unanimously to the conclusion, that they had "rather be let alone." Their business had grown up naturally, and succeeded well; and they felt confident of its continued prosperity, if uninterfered with by government. On the other hand, they argued, that, by laying a protective tariff, the business would be thrown out of its natural channels, and become fluctuating and uncertain. How well founded were these anticipations subsequent events have fully shown.

It will, doubtless, be a matter of profound astonishment to the future historian, that a people who had a free and untrammelled industry, with natural advantages for the most productive agriculture in the world and for the legitimate growth of every kind of manufacture, should ever have asked for restrictions upon trade. But, in truth, they did not ask for protection at the outset. It was forced upon them by politicians, irrespective of their wishes, for the avowed purpose of securing a home market for *cotton.*

All New England was opposed to the policy, and protested against it; yet it was carried. Special forms of manufacturing were brought into existence; and, as these were sickly and needed all the help they could obtain from government, an interested party was formed which clamored incessantly for protection. Yet it was not until the third tariff, that of 1824, had gone into operation, that the Northern and Central States became the partisans of protection. As New England was the last to assent to restrictive legislation, so she will undoubtedly be the first to ask for its abandonment. No policy could be more adverse to her permanent interests. She has great natural advantages for manufacturing. With these, she can carry them on successfully. By high protective duties, other sections of the country, not having the same natural advantages, will be led to introduce the same branches of industry,* and she will find her severest competition at home; while all parts of the nation will be crippled by a false system, equally against the laws of nature and value; since protection, as previously shown, puts the bad on the level with the good, and destroys all natural tests of usefulness in production. It should always be borne in mind, that protective duties must be high enough to enable the home manufacturer to get, at least, average profits; that is, such profits as commodities in general afford. He will not make broadcloth unless it is as profitable as any other branch of trade, manufacture, or agriculture. Nothing short of this is protection; and the duties must be carried upwards, until they arrive at that point in which those who are manufacturing *to the greatest disadvantage* can make average profits; otherwise there will be a call for higher duties. This is one of the

* This is already becoming quite apparent.

practical difficulties of protection. The higher the duties imposed, the greater will be the rush into the protected branch of industry; and none will be satisfied until they make the business profitable, however imperfectly conducted. Hence there will be a constant call for increased duties. Witness the history of protection in the United States, — a tariff in 1816, a higher one in 1820, higher yet in 1824, still higher in 1828, with continued changes from that time to this.

CHAPTER VI.

BALANCE OF TRADE.

WHAT is meant by the balance of trade?

An actual balance of trade is the difference between the amount of values exported and the amount of values imported. This seems a very simple proposition; yet the question is one of great complexity, from the fact that it is difficult to determine with certainty whether the exports of a nation do or do not actually equal the imports. Superficial observers resort to the financial returns made to the government; and finding, for example, that the imports of 1854 amounted to $304,562,381, while the exports were but $278,241,064, leaving a difference of $24,321,317, they hastily conclude that the balance of trade was against this country to that amount. Such a conclusion would not have a sufficient foundation.

To understand this subject, we must notice that the exports are stated at their value at our own custom-houses, while the amount imported is stated at the value in foreign countries.* If we suppose the amount exported in 1854 was on American account, and paid a profit of only nine

* Besides, exports are estimated at currency prices; imports, in gold values, — a very wide difference under a depreciated currency.

per cent on the custom-house valuation, we shall find that it will amount to $26,321,317, a sum larger than the assumed balance; and, if so, the commodities exported actually paid for the amount imported, and the supposed unfavorable balance is annihilated. As the goods exported should sell for enough abroad, and as they do generally sell for enough to pay all charges of freight, insurance, &c., with reasonable commissions, say in all fifteen per cent, we may justly infer that there was, in fact, a balance in favor of this country in 1854. But the question whether there was or was not an actual balance that year can only be determined by ascertaining whether our exports generally sold for an advance sufficient to pay for the imports. This is known only to those engaged in or familiar with the results of the export trade of 1854. The balance might have been greater or less than what it appears from custom-house statistics.

On the other hand, in 1855, our exports exceeded our imports by $13,688,326. Does that show a balance in favor of the United States? Apparently; yet there might have been a loss upon our exports which would more than balance the $13,688,326.

Although the financial tables of the Secretary of the Treasury do by no means decide the balance of trade, and the custom-house returns are never conclusive evidence, yet there are cases in which there is no reasonable doubt on which side the balance is. In 1836, for example, we exported one hundred and twenty-eight millions, and imported one hundred and eighty-nine millions; an excess of sixty-one millions, making a difference of sixty per cent over exports. In this case, there could be no doubt there was a larger actual balance against the country, because the profits could not have been equal to the excess. So too, to go further back, in 1816, the exports were fifty-two millions; imports, one hundred and twelve millions; excess, sixty millions, or more than one hundred per cent. The unfavorable balance in both cases caused great distress by the necessary exportation of specie.

Balance of trade how adjusted.

We have heretofore said that an unfavorable balance must be liquidated with specie. This is the general fact; but it is not always disposed of in that way. For example, the balance against the United States in 1853, as per Financial Report, was thirty-seven millions. Now, if this were in fact an actual balance, a part of this might have been extended to the next year, and paid in cotton or wheat; or, what is more probable, several millions of railroad or other stocks might have been sent abroad and sold, and the balance settled from the proceeds.

If the commerce of a country is in a really prosperous condition, the value of its imports will, in the long-run, exceed its actual exports, because its export trade should pay a profit. No country is enriched by trade, unless its aggregate imports do exceed in value its exports. It is no matter whether the excess of imports over exports is brought into the country in specie or any other desirable commodity, provided its own currency be a true standard of value.

The trade of the United States for 1863 showed the following results: Exports (Financial Report, 1864), $350,-152,125; imports, $252,187,587; balance, $97,864,538. The returns also showed an export of gold to the amount of $82,364,482, an import of gold of $9,584,105, giving a balance of $72,780,377. A considerable part of this gold was, doubtless, sent abroad for safe keeping by timid capitalists, and not over-loyal citizens. The large balance of seventy-two millions in favor of the United States was no indication of a profitable trade that year; quite otherwise. The balance of gold exported in 1864 was ninety-one millions. Another fact, that throws additional conjecture upon the apparent balance of trade, is, that false invoices are used to an enormous extent at our American custom-houses.

Whenever duties are charged upon the cost of the commodities, it is an object to have them invoiced as low as possible. Fraudulent invoices are often made out *abroad* and sworn to by the importers *here*, and thus the actual value or amount paid for the foreign merchandise is not accurately exhibited. The Revenue Commissioners (see their Report to the Secretary of the Treasury, January 29, 1866, page 45) estimate that the frauds at the New-York Custom-House alone are from "twelve to twenty-five millions annually." The aggregate of these frauds throughout the country has been estimated as high as forty millions per annum; but, if they amount to only thirty millions, the "balance of trade" is seriously influenced by them.

There is still another consideration; viz., that the United States are much indebted abroad, and a large sum is required to pay the annual interest. This can only be *paid* by our exports of merchandise or specie; for both are alike reckoned in our list of "exports." We owed $500,000,000 abroad in 1860 (see Foreign and Domestic Commerce, 1863, page 42, Treasury Report). The Comptroller of the Currency, in his Report for 1865, page 7, estimates the amount of our securities sent abroad the *last five years* at $713,000,000,—in all, then, $1,213,000,000. The interest on this sum, at six per cent, will be $72,780,000; and this must be provided for in our exports.

Many considerations of this general character might be brought forward; but sufficient has already been said, we trust, to show what the real nature of a balance of trade is, and how difficult a matter it must always be to determine with accuracy upon which side it actually is, and what its amount.

PART SECOND.—INSTRUMENTS OF EXCHANGE.

CHAPTER I.

BARTER AND THE DIFFERENT FORMS OF CURRENCY.

We have discussed the principles upon which exchanges are made. We now come to consider the instruments by which they are effected.

These are of three kinds: —

1st, Barter.

2d, A common medium, or currency.

3d, Different forms of credit.

No person produces every thing he wishes to consume. Even in the savage state, men will obtain different products, as they have skill and opportunity. These they will exchange among themselves in kind.

As the civilized state appears, the necessity for interchange of commodities increases. Every mechanic must exchange his products with every other mechanic, and all these with the agriculturist and fisherman; so that exchange becomes one of the greatest departments of human industry. But, under these circumstances, barter, or exchange in kind, becomes a very inconvenient and clumsy mode of effecting the desired object. For example, the farmer may wish to exchange wheat for a hat; but the hatter is already supplied: what, then, will the hatter accept? A table. The farmer must then go to the cabinet-maker, and offer his wheat for a table. But the cabinet-maker is supplied with wheat. He would, however, accept a pair of boots. The farmer applies to the boot-maker, who happens to wish for wheat and accepts the offer. With the boots the farmer gets the table, and with the table gets the hat which he desired.

In such a state of things, this was the only process by which exchanges could be effected; circuitous, and expensive in time and labor, as it was.

We might have supposed a far more difficult case; but this is sufficient to illustrate the inconvenience of *barter*, or the direct exchange of commodities. But there is still another difficulty, of scarcely less magnitude. When articles to be exchanged became numerous, it would be found a very intricate matter to establish satisfactorily the relative value of each. For example, how many sheep shall be given for a cow? How many cows for a horse? How much corn for a bushel of wheat? How much butter for a gallon of molasses? How many eggs for a pound of tea, sugar, or coffee? How many of any or all of these for a cart, plough, spade, chair, table, &c., through an interminable series of exchanges?

Under such circumstances, there could be no such thing as *price*, because there would be no common standard, to which the value of all articles could be referred.

What, then, was wanted? Evidently, some article which all persons, either by common consent or the force of law, shall accept for whatever they have to sell, and by which they will measure the value of any thing sold.

That article would perform two important functions; viz., it would be an instrument of exchange, and a standard of value: in other words, it would be money.

We learn the true nature of money, then, from its origin and the functions it performs. These offices or functions we must examine in detail.

1st, As a medium of exchange. This may be wholly conventional. Any thing, which, by general consent or in obedience to law, all receive in exchange, will answer the purpose. So far as this function is concerned, it is of no consequence whether the article has value or not: safety and convenience are the only considerations of importance.

Money, in this respect, is simply a counter, token, or universal equivalent.

2d, As a standard of value. Value is not conventional. It attaches to all objects which are desired, but cannot be had without effort or labor. Since the value of any thing is its power in exchange, we say that nothing is valuable which will not command labor, or that which costs labor.

"Value implies comparison, appropriation, estimation, measure. In order that two things should measure each other, it is necessary that they be commensurable; and, in order to that, they must be of the same kind." — BASTIAT.

Therefore, if we would measure value, we must use an article that has value in it. The measure must evidently have the same quality as the thing to be measured, — weight to measure weight, length to measure length, volume to measure volume, value to measure value.

The standard must be as nearly invariable as possible. An absolutely invariable standard is unattainable, because the standard itself must be subject to the same laws as the objects to be measured; that is, cost of production, supply and demand, &c.

Hence we must take that for a standard, which, on the whole and in the long-run, is subject to the least fluctuation. Of all objects of this kind, we shall see that the precious metals are the least liable to great and violent changes in value.

In examining the principle of barter, we were forced, by its practical difficulties, to accept the resource of a universal equivalent for all commodities. This, in its original form, is money. But the course of civilized industry has introduced several forms of such an equivalent, of which the money, by which men first escaped from the difficulties of barter, is only one. All these forms are classed as currency; and therefore, in discussing the instruments of exchange, next after barter we come to the subject of —

CURRENCY.

This is a general term for all the contrivances by which society seeks to effect a general exchange of values, and discharge pecuniary obligations. There are four distinct kinds or species of currency, each differing from the others in important particulars.

1st, The first of these instruments is called MONEY. Any article, which, having a universally recognized value in itself, all persons accept as an equivalent, or medium of exchange, and which, consequently, becomes the standard by which all other values are measured or determined, and in which all pecuniary obligations are expressed and discharged, is money. Being composed generally of the precious metals, it is often known as "hard-money currency," but is more properly a *value currency*. Real money is simply value in a form the most available for commanding all other values, a service which all will accept for any other kind of service, which measures all other services or values most conveniently.

2d, The second kind of currency consists of written promises, made usually by governments, to pay money at a distant or indefinite period, which nevertheless, by force of law or other circumstances, are accepted as money, and perform its general functions. The notes issued by the treasury of the United States, and familiarly known as "greenbacks," now (1865) in circulation, are of this description.

They form a strictly credit currency, but, in common parlance, are called PAPER MONEY.

3d, A third description of currency is formed of written promises to pay specie on demand, issued in excess of the actual amount of specie, or money, in possession of the promisors absolutely held for the redemption thereof. These notes or promises are generally issued by corporations, called banking institutions, and circulate, while current, as money, performing all its functions. This is called a MIXED CURRENCY.

4th, A fourth kind of currency consists of written promises, payable on demand, issued by responsible parties, for the payment of which, in full, the specie is actually held in trust by the promisors. As such a currency is precisely adapted to all the wants of the trading and business classes, and fully combines convenience with safety, the two great desiderata, it is with great propriety called a MERCANTILE CURRENCY.

Of the four kinds of currency, it will be observed, that two, the first and fourth, are classed as value currency; the second, as credit; the third, as mixed, consisting of value and credit.

The following is a brief recapitulation of the different kinds of currency: —

I.	Money	*i.e.*	Specie.
II.	Credit currency	*i.e.*	Promises without specie.
III.	Mixed currency	*i.e.*	Promises with part specie.
IV.	Mercantile currency	*i.e.*	Promises with full specie.

After this statement and classification of the different kinds of currency, it is proposed to examine each in detail, and determine their several characteristics, and also the influence of each upon the industrial interests and general welfare of mankind.

No subject is more involved in mystery and uncertainty in the popular mind than that of currency. This arises, principally, from the fact, that the different kinds are confounded, and the whole matter thereby rendered incomprehensible. The general use of mixed-currency notes, which, to a superficial observer, seem to possess all the attributes of money, has a tendency to produce this result.

To obtain a clear and intelligent view of the subject, it is therefore quite necessary, that we divest it of all its usual environments and associations, and, for the time being, even of the forms and terms with which we are familiar, and regard the question as abstractly as possible.

CHAPTER II.

I. MONEY.

HAVING examined the nature and functions of currency, we shall now speak of the actual money of commerce, or the universally accepted equivalent.

In all ages and countries, this has consisted of the precious metals, gold and silver, with the baser metals or alloys for fractional purposes.

Local currencies have been various. Lacedæmon had iron money. The Romans are supposed by many to have used cattle and sheep in the early periods of their history; and their coins bear the images of those animals, as indicating their value.*

Tobacco was once currency, and a legal tender, in Virginia.

The first currency legally established in Massachusetts was bullets. The "General Courte ordered [March 4, 1635] that bulletts of a full boare shall passe currently for a farthing a peice, provided that noe man be compelled to take above 12ᵈ at a time." Again, it was enacted "that merchantable beaver shall pass at Xˢ the pound." In 1637, the "Courte ordered that Wampumpege should pass at six for a penny, for all sums under 12ᵈ." In 1640 and 1641, additional laws were enacted, making wampum a lawful tender.

Many expedients like these have, at different times and different countries, been adopted to secure a temporary and partial currency; but from the days of Abraham, who paid "four hundred shekels, current money with the merchants,

* Hence called *pecunia*, money, from *pecus*, a flock.

for the field of Ephron," to the present time, the money used in commerce has always been composed of gold and silver. These, and these only, have formed the universal medium of exchange and standard of value.

The use of these metals arises from nothing conventional. No international agreement was ever made respecting them; yet they are everywhere and at all times, without hesitation, received in exchange for whatever any one may wish to dispose of. They secure their currency simply by their peculiar adaptedness to the purpose.

What their peculiarities are we propose now to consider.

1st, *They possess value, that is, have power in exchange.* They cost labor, and are objects of desire. They cannot be had without labor, or an equivalent. We have already said that the article used as a standard of value must possess value in itself, since we can only compare value with value. Gold and silver have this indispensable requisite. They are subject to all the laws of value as truly as wheat or any other commodity.

2d, *These metals are stable in value;* that is, the most so of known commodities. They are subject to no violent changes, like flour or cotton: for example, wheat often varies from twenty-five to fifty per cent in a few months. They change in value, indeed, from age to age; but so gradually is this accomplished as to be quite imperceptible at the time.

The discovery of the Western Continent, which opened to the commercial world the accumulated treasures of Mexico and South America, caused the greatest change known to history; yet it is calculated, that from 1492 to 1650, a period of one hundred and fifty years, gold and silver fell only seventy-five per cent, equivalent to half of one per cent per annum; so that even this great change must have been so gradual as to have inflicted little injury on individuals, and could only have been appreciated by those holding long annuities or similar securities.

3d, They are *conveniently portable;* the most so, in fact, of all commodities existing in adequate quantity. One pound weight of gold will ordinarily command, in exchange, fifteen thousand pounds of wheat, thirty thousand pounds of Indian corn, five tons of rice, or a ton and a half of cotton.

4th, These metals are *malleable.* They can be wrought into any shape, will receive and retain any impression, may be divided into the minutest quantities, and again united, with the smallest possible loss. Hence they are admirably adapted for coinage, or a great variety of alternate uses.

5th, They are of *uniform quality.* Gold and silver are always and everywhere the same. Found in California, Australia, or Russia, gold is everywhere gold. The iron of different countries varies greatly. The copper of Siberia is better than that of Germany, while that of Sweden is better than that of Siberia, and that of Japan surpasses that of Sweden. It is not so with the precious metals.

6th, They may be readily *alloyed* or *refined.* By alloy they are made harder, and so adapted to use as money. However alloyed, they can easily be restored to their original purity without loss.

7th, They are *indestructible by accident.* Fire does not consume them; atmospheric influences cause no decomposition: so that the gold and silver in use in the time of the Ptolemies may form a part of the currency of the world to-day.

8th, They are *universally appreciated.* The precious metals are regarded as beautiful and desirable in all countries, and among all races, civilized or savage. The demand for them is without limit.

9th, They are *generally diffused.* These metals are found in every principal section of the globe, — Europe, Asia, Africa, North and South America, and Australia.

10th, They are *sufficiently plentiful.* Not more than two-thirds of the gold and silver now in the possession of man is believed to be used as money, the balance being in plate or other objects of utility and ornament.

11th, They are nearly *inconsumable by use.* The use of almost all other commodities causes their rapid destruction. Articles used as food or clothing, for example, disappear entirely in a comparatively short period. Even iron, as used for most purposes, — in railroads, agriculture, the mechanic arts, &c., — lasts only a few years.

With gold and silver it is quite different, though the exemption from waste is more remarkable in the case of gold. Indeed, its ordinary and principal use can scarcely be called consumption, it is so gradual.

It has been ascertained, from data carefully obtained in the Bank of England, that gold in coin loses only 4.16 per cent in one hundred years, or about one per cent in twenty-five years.

The following comparison exhibits approximately the great difference in this respect between gold and other commodities: —

Potatoes	consumed	within	. . . . . .	1 year.
Wheat	"	"	say	2 years.
Cotton	"	"	average, say . .	4 years.
Wool	"	"	" " . .	5 years.
Lead	"	"	" " . .	10 years.
Iron	"	"	" " . .	20 years.
Gold in coin	"	"	" " . .	2400 years.

Investigations made at the United States Mint, as by Report of 1862, showed that the wear and tear of gold was only as 1 to 2,400; that is, a gold dollar would be worn out by 2,400 years' service, or the loss annually of $\frac{1}{2400}$ of one per cent.

When used for gilding and similar purposes, it is much more rapidly consumed; but the amount so employed is very small, in comparison with the whole mass. When used in plate, the consumption is even less than in coin; and a larger part of that which goes into jewelry returns into bullion in the lapse of time. So that we must estimate the yearly consumption of gold, in all its uses, exceedingly small as compared with the annual production.

COINAGE.

Having seen how admirably adapted the precious metals are for use as money, we pass to a consideration of those artificial arrangements by which they are still further and more completely fitted for that purpose.

At first, these metals were used in ingots and bars, and passed by weight. Whenever a pecuniary transaction was made, scales were required to determine the quantity given in exchange.

This was a clumsy and imperfect mode of payment; for there would arise the question of quality as well as quantity, — of the pureness or fineness of the metal. This could only be ascertained by assay; and that could be accomplished only by persons having the necessary knowledge of metallurgy, with apparatus for conducting the process.

It was therefore natural, that, at an early period, a contrivance was hit upon which obviated all difficulties.

The bars, or ingots, designed for money, were first assayed, and made of one degree of fineness. This degree was called the *standard*. The metal thus assayed was then divided into pieces, and the weight carefully ascertained, and stamped upon each. These pieces were called coins; the process, coinage.

As this coinage involved great responsibility, it very properly became the duty and prerogative of the government. Each government established an institution for the purpose, called a mint. To these mints the people carried their gold and silver, and, by paying a very trifling seigniorage, had the whole amount returned to them in coin.

Such, at least, has been the general fact; but in the United States, and possibly some other countries, no seigniorage is charged, the whole being done at the expense of the government. The policy of this is quite doubtful. Government should retain a slight compensation for two reasons: first, a benefit has been conferred, for which the recipient should pay a fair equivalent: additional value, within the particular country, has been given by the additional labor; gold in the national coin being more useful than in bars. Second, because coin should be a slight fraction less valuable for mechanical purposes and for export than bullion; otherwise it will be wrought up into jewelry at home or shipped abroad, instead of bullion, and thus an unnecessary waste in coinage will be the consequence.

Such is the character of a currency composed entirely of money, or that which has value in itself. Of all subjects, this is one of the most simple, most free from all complexity and mystery. No one can fail to understand it. Government has not the slightest occasion to interfere with or regulate it. It obeys certain natural laws, which cannot be improved by man. All that government can usefully do is to certify to the weight and fineness of the coinage. It has no further concern with money.

The main point to be borne in mind, in relation to coinage, is, that government does not determine the value at all, but simply certifies to the weight and purity.

CHAPTER III.

II. CREDIT CURRENCY.

THIS we have already stated to consist of the promises of government to pay money, which, by force of law or the necessities of the people, are received as money. It is simply the credit of the nation, used as currency. The element of value does not enter into it at all. It is precisely the opposite of a value currency.

ITS CHARACTERISTICS.

Such a currency may *transfer* debts, but it cannot pay them. The creditor may accept the promises of the government in place of that of an individual, but he receives no value. So far as issued by the government and accepted for taxes and other public dues, such notes are mere *counters*, used for cancelling reciprocal obligations. If such notes are issued beyond the natural volume of the currency, they can never be kept at par with specie, or circulate at their nominal value. Gold, as compared with them, will bear a premium, the amount of which will indicate the excess and depreciation of the currency, and the want of confidence in the promisors.

This premium is the result of the operation of the laws of value; and no legislation of free government or edict of despotism can permanently change it. Governors might as well prescribe the height to which the tides of ocean shall rise, as to restrict or reduce the premium on gold.

Such legislation is not only futile, but injurious, producing an effect just opposite to that intended. It disturbs the market price of gold, destroys confidence in its actual price, and, by exciting distrust, drives the premium far up beyond its natural limit.

The experiment made by the Congress of the United States in 1864 showed most conclusively the utter folly of attempting to interfere with the laws of value. After the "gold bill," so called, became a law, the premium rose at once some fifty per cent above its previous rate. The unwise act was speedily repealed, and the excessive premium it had caused fell off.

EFFECT OF CREDIT CURRENCY ON PRICES AND INCOMES.

A general rise of prices follows the introduction of a credit currency, because it is always issued in excess of the natural volume of money; and consequently, as prices must, in the average, conform to the quantity of currency, they will advance as it is increased. It is quite idle to attempt to evade the operation of this law. When the Secretary of the United States Treasury endeavored to "float" his bonds by the issue of credit currency, he unfortunately "floated" all the merchandise of the country at the same time, so that the rise of prices compelled him to pay double for all the government needed; and hence he lost at least one-half of all the bonds that were thus sold.

The effect on fixed incomes is very marked. From whatever source, fixed incomes are depreciated in value just in proportion to the depreciation of the currency. But there is one exception in the practical operation of this principle. If the income received were to be expended entirely for food, clothing, and other ordinary articles of merchandise, the full depreciation of the currency would be felt. But if, as would usually be the case, a portion of it were used for the payment of rent, the depreciation, in so far, would be less operative. Neither the fee nor the use of real estate rises in proportion to other things.

The price of real estate, and its use, would, however, unquestionably advance to nearly the same extent as commodities in general, provided a credit currency were continued as the currency of the country for a long period, say from one generation to another. This, however, never has, and, in the nature of the case, is not likely to take place; credit currency being, necessarily, of limited duration.

Doubtless, investments have been made, especially in large cities, that would not have been made but for the great inflation in the currency of the United States during the Rebellion; but the price of such property has advanced slowly, as compared with flour, clothing, &c.*

* That real estate in some large cities has much advanced, we are well aware; but, take the whole country through, it is doubtful if there has been an advance of ten per cent. Indeed, none is visible in the country generally.

A house in New York, worth twenty thousand dollars in 1859, was not worth fifty thousand dollars in 1864; but twenty thousand dollars' worth of flour, at prices of 1859, would have brought fifty thousand dollars in 1864. Why is this? Because everybody believes that prices have not permanently advanced, but will before many years, perhaps before many months, decline. Therefore permanent investments will not be made at prices corresponding to those of ordinary merchandise. This difference between real estate and consumable commodities, as influenced by the expansions and contractions of the currency, should be borne in mind, as it will explain phenomena that will be presented in our further inquiries.

EFFECT ON CONTRACTS.

A credit currency, it may be safely assumed, is always redundant; and, as such, its effect on contracts is twofold. Obligations to pay money made with a specie standard, and paid with credit currency, will impose a loss of value on the creditor equal to the depreciation of the currency. Great injustice and suffering resulted from this cause during the progress of the American wars of the Revolution and of the Rebellion.

On the other hand, contracts made to pay money during the existence of a credit currency, but which mature and are discharged under a value currency, will subject the debtor to the loss of all the difference in the value of the two currencies. Great injustice and suffering resulted from this source, on the recognition of American independence, in the last century, among the first of which may be reckoned the Shay's Rebellion of Massachusetts. At what time, and with what results, the return to specie payments at the present period will next be made, it is yet impossible to predict.

Historically, it is found to be true, that a credit currency has never yet been kept within the natural limit of the value currency of the country in which it was established. The "continental money" of the American Revolution; the assignats of the French Revolution; the bank money of England during the Napoleonic wars; and, lastly, the greenbacks, or treasury notes, issued during the late Rebellion, and the present paper currency of Russia, are illustrations in point.

The French assignats were issued in such excess that their utter repudiation by the government became a necessity. So of the "mandates" which followed them. The "continental money" became entirely worthless. The notes of the British Bank, which depreciated during the great struggle with France, were finally restored to par at the cost of immense suffering and loss to the commercial and business classes.

The paper issues of the American government will, doubtless, be paid; but it will be at an incalculable amount of bankruptcy and ruin to those who are greatly indebted.

The treasury notes, now acting as currency, will be redeemed ultimately; that is, be taken in for taxes and other dues to government, and thus annihilated. They could not be paid in coin, but are sufficiently certain to be cancelled in the way just indicated.

A credit currency never has been regulated in such a manner as to keep it on a par with specie, and probably never will be. The necessities of government are so pressing that the temptation to increase the amount becomes too great for resistance. As prices rise in consequence, the currency becomes of less and less value, that is, has a decreasing power in exchange, so that the inducement to issue becomes continually stronger as the volume expands. Unless this course can be arrested, final bankruptcy is sure.

But the issue of a legal-tender credit currency is, under any circumstances, a great wrong, and can never be justified except in the most extreme cases of national peril;

and, even in those instances where it has been defended as an indispensable measure, events have generally proved it to have been a mistaken and short-sighted policy.

CREDIT CURRENCY A FORCED LOAN.

When a government issues its notes as currency, and makes them a legal tender, or authorizes other parties to do so, it creates a forced loan.

All creditors are compelled to receive these notes for whatever may be due to them, which is equivalent to making a loan to the government to the amount so received; and those who sell their property are obliged to take these promises, since there is no other currency in use, so that the whole amount thus put into circulation becomes a compulsory loan to the government.

CREDIT CURRENCY A DIRECT TAX.

As soon as legal-tender credit notes begin to depreciate in value, or, in other words, as soon as commodities rise in consequence, each person who receives them pays a tax equal to their depreciation while in his possession. For example, if he receives a ten-dollar note, which will bring him but eight dollars' worth of merchandise at the gold price, he has contributed two dollars to the government. So, of course, with all who receive notes in payment for debts contracted prior to the issue of such currency. When, as in the case of the "continental money," these notes become utterly worthless, those through whose hands they have passed have contributed, at least *nominally*, the whole amount. We say nominally; for the contribution thus forced from the people is not in fact to the full amount in actual *value*.

For illustration, the government issues one hundred millions of its notes at first; and for this, as prices have not been raised, it receives an equal amount in value. It issues a second hundred millions; but prices have advanced in consequence of the first issue, we will suppose, fifty per cent, so that the government gets but $66,666,666 in value. A third issue is made of one hundred millions; but prices have gone up one hundred per cent, and the government gets but fifty millions in value. Another issue of one hundred millions carries prices up to one hundred and fifty per cent, and only forty millions is realized in value. This is not intended as a statement of the precise fact, but to exhibit the natural operation of such issues. That it is not exaggerated, appears from what is well known, that the United States government sold many millions of its bonds for that which was equivalent to but forty per cent in gold. The result is shown in the following recapitulation: —

First $100,000,000, issued at par value, ...	$100,000,000
Second $100,000,000, issued at $33\frac{1}{3}$ per cent discount	66,666,666
Third $100,000,000, issued at 50 per cent discount	50,000,000
Fourth $100,000,000, issued at 60 per cent discount	40,000,000
Government receives in value for $400,000,000 issued	$256,666,666
Loss to the government, or people	143,333,334
	$400,000,000

The people must finally pay in taxes $143,333,334 more than the government received in value, if the debt is paid; but, if it should be repudiated, the loss of actual *value* to the people would be but $256,666,666, the balance being merely the enhanced prices they have received for commodities furnished. But, unfortunately, those who received the extra prices and those who will pay the taxes may not be the same identical persons.

The foregoing illustration shows the operation or general result upon the community of a credit currency as a direct tax: but the effects upon different individuals are diversified in every possible manner; one man losing, another gaining by it, according to the position in which the parties are found at the time they were compelled to accept such a currency instead of money. The laws of value having been violated, universal chaos in all monetary affairs is the inevitable consequence.

The final result of the issue of an inconvertible currency, then, is, that, if it is never redeemed, the taxation it imposes is most unequally and unjustly distributed; if it is finally paid, then the taxation is not only unfairly distributed, but the amount vastly increased, since the expenditures of the government have been largely enhanced by it. It does not admit of question that a large part of the debt of the United States represents expenditures made solely to meet the excessive prices caused by a credit currency, especially in the years 1863–5, when the premium on gold averaged nearly seventy per cent, and for a considerable period, when the heaviest expenditures were made, as high as one hundred and fifty. Of course, the taxation of the country will be correspondingly increased for the payment of this excess.

CHAPTER IV.

III. MIXED CURRENCY.

MIXED currency is a modern invention, as yet known only to a small part of the human race, and but partially understood even in those countries into which it has been introduced.

The Bank of England, the parent of all mixed-currency institutions throughout the world, was established in 1694; but its operations were so limited, and its influence so partially felt, during the first century of its existence, that the character of the currency it issued was hardly appreciated. This bank made a grand suspension in 1796, and continued in that state for over twenty-three years. This was the first occurrence* which demonstrated practically the true nature of this kind of currency.

If we carefully observe the composition of a mixed currency, we shall find it to consist of promissory notes issued by individuals or corporations legally authorized to do so, in excess of the actual specie held for their redemption. These notes form the circulation or currency, and consist wholly of paper; yet, as they profess to be convertible, they have the same power in exchange as the specie itself, so long as confidence in the ability and integrity of the promisors remains unimpaired.

This is rightfully called a *mixed currency*, because it is, in fact, composed in part of value and in part of credit. So far as specie is held for the payment of these notes, this kind of currency is actually convertible, and equivalent to money; but, in so far as the credit element exceeds the specie, it is only a promise to pay money, and is inconvertible. A mixed currency, therefore, can only be regarded as partially convertible; the degree of its convertibility depending upon the proportion the specie bears to the notes issued and the deposits. It is this proportion of specie, whatever it may be, which determines the *quality* of this kind of bank-note circulation. Its quality is the great question of interest to all who use this kind of currency; and of that we propose now to speak.

THE QUALITY OF A MIXED CURRENCY.

This is by far the most important matter in relation to a mixed currency. What is the proportion of specie held for its conversion? To ascertain this, we must know, on the one hand, the amount of notes in circulation, and the inscribed credits, that is, the deposits; and, on the other, the amount of specie in bank. We have naught to do with any other inquiry, so far as the quality of the currency is con-

* The bank suspended for two years, very shortly after its organization; but its capital and operations were then too limited to occasion much notice.

cerned. We have no occasion to make such an inquiry in regard to money, for that was value in itself, and needs no conversion; nor in relation to a purely credit currency, for that does not profess convertibility: but a mixed currency, to be reliable and beneficial to the public, must be what it proclaims itself to be; viz., *convertible on demand into coin;* and therefore a sufficiency of coin should be held to secure that object.

And here it is necessary to distinguish carefully between the convertibility and the redeemableness of a currency. The first may be uncertain or impossible, while the last may be sure. A bank may be perfectly solvent, while its currency is almost entirely inconvertible. By convertibility, then, we understand the power of the bank to exchange its promises for specie on demand; by redeemableness, its power to liquidate or discharge its obligations some time or other, by the resources it may possess for ultimate payment.

For example, a bank has promised to pay one hundred thousand dollars in specie, while it has only ten thousand dollars in specie to pay with. The same bank has demands against individuals, for their notes discounted, to the amount of two hundred thousand dollars. Now, it is certain that this bank can convert only ten thousand dollars of its bills; but it can, if sufficient time is allowed, redeem the whole amount, by taking in its own notes in exchange for those of its debtors. The power of the bank ultimately to redeem or cancel its notes is amply sufficient; though, for the conversion of them into specie, it has the ability only to the extent of one-tenth. This point needs to be well understood and remembered, because, as we shall have occasion to show, the difference between the *redemption* and *conversion* of a currency is a matter of the utmost importance to the business world, and the former cannot be made a sufficient substitute for the latter. This is evident from the following consideration.

A bank-note converted into coin, the money still exists

in circulation: a bank-note, redeemed by receiving it for indebtedness to the bank, is taken out of circulation; that is, it ceases to be currency, and, for the time being, is practically annihilated. The circulating medium of the country is diminished to that extent.

To illustrate this point, and show how much depends upon the quality or convertibility of a mixed currency, we propose to take that of the United States as an example.

In doing this, it will be indispensable that we refer to the statistics of banking institutions, and use the terms commonly employed by them; and therefore we now proceed to define them.

LIABILITIES OF A MIXED-CURRENCY BANK.

1. *Capital Stock.*—This is the sum total of all the amount paid into the bank, to constitute its means of doing business.

2. *Circulation.*—This consists of notes of the bank, of different denominations, payable on demand, signed by its officers, and issued to circulate as money.

3. *Deposits.*—These include all sums, from whatever source, that stand on the books of the banks to the credit of individuals. They are properly called *inscribed credits:* they are nothing more or less. They are all legally payable on demand, in specie, to those persons in whose names they stand.

A more full description of their nature and effects will be given hereafter.

Bank Balances.—"Due to other banks" and "due from other banks" are terms used in the official returns made to the Treasury Department of the United States.

They explain themselves. Banks, like individuals, have open accounts with each other. These, in the aggregate, must balance each other; but there is often a considerable apparent difference, arising from the fact that large sums are constantly *in transitu.*

As affecting the character of a mixed currency, these balances are an important item, because they form the most explosive and dangerous element. They are "deposits" in their nature, certain to be drawn in any sudden emergency. This was strikingly illustrated in the autumn of 1857. At that time, the banks in the city of New York owed some sixty millions of dollars which had been left with them by distant banks in order to meet their own liabilities. When the pressure came on, in September and October of the year mentioned, these banks began, of necessity, to call in their balances.

This placed the New-York banks in a position of great difficulty. To answer these calls would require a large part of all their means; while, at the same moment, the merchants and business men of the city needed all the resources they could command. But the banks must meet the drafts made for their balances, or suspend at once; and, accordingly, were compelled to cut off all discounts, or loans, to their regular customers. This state of things could not be long endured; and the merchants of the city, being soon driven to desperation, began to draw upon their own deposits for *specie;* and thus a general suspension took place, not only in the commercial metropolis, but through the country.

These balances, as they exist extensively in all great cities, form the train that ignites the magazine, and causes an instant and general explosion.

The Bank of England was compelled, in 1847, to obtain a suspension of the act of 1844, by the threat of the banking houses to withdraw their *balances*, and again in 1857.

Other Liabilities.—These consist of various obligations, which banks incur in the course of their transactions with the public and each other. They are not large in the aggregate, as compared with their aggregate liabilities, but must be taken into the account. They may be immediate or remote liabilities, but are mostly immediate.

RESOURCES OF A MIXED-CURRENCY BANK.

Loans. — This item includes the sum total due the bank from its customers for discount and advances, and for which the banks hold notes or other obligations, payable at some future time; say, from one day to four or six months, as the case may be.

Stocks. — Banks are large purchasers of the various State and national stocks, and also those of towns, cities, railroad companies, &c. The whole amount so held is included in the term "stocks."

Real Estate. — A place of business being indispensable to the operations of banking, buildings are erected for such purposes. These, being often beyond the needs of the bank, are rented in part.

Other Investments. — A general term that includes all kinds of property the bank may hold, from necessity or choice, not embraced in any preceding title.

Notes of other Banks. — As banks, in the course of business, are constantly receiving each other's notes, they must necessarily have, in the aggregate, a large amount, which appear among their assets. Notes thus held in no essential particular affect the general character of the currency: they only concern the relations of the banks to each other. In their nature, they do not differ from other notes in circulation: they are held by corporations, instead of individuals. They would not assist a bank in meeting immediate demands, as they are not legal tender.

Cash Items. — Many banks have the practice of reckoning certain assets they hold as equivalent to cash, and class them as "cash items" in their returns. For example, a bank may hold a check upon another bank for a given sum, which, in its account with that bank, and for many other purposes, may be equally available for the time being, with money actually in hand. Checks drawn by individuals on other banks, foreign exchange, sight drafts, and the like, are often reckoned among these items. But, whatever their origin or character, they add in no degree to the strength of the currency. They may help the individual bank that holds them, as compared with the debtor banks, but not the general mass.

Reserved Profits. — Although no such item appears in the returns published by the national government, it is one of some importance. In most banks, it is customary to reserve a certain sum from the profits of each year, to ensure against unexpected losses or contingencies. In some cases, this reserve is large; in others, small. In Massachusetts, in 1863, the amount so reserved was nearly five millions, equal to eight per cent on the capital. This, while it does not in any way change the character of the currency, gives the bank greater ability to make loans. It is, for the time being, an increase of banking capital. It adds nothing to the convertibility of current notes.

With this explanation of the terms employed, we proceed to give such statistics of the banks of the United States as shall exhibit the character of the currency they issue.

The first point to be noticed is the aggregate capital of these banks, which we find to be $421,880,095, on the 1st of January, 1860. We have selected that point of time, because the country was then undisturbed, and the currency in its natural condition. This capital, as we have already explained, is the amount which the banks have at their command, and which it is their business to loan out to the public; and, let it be recollected, this is *all* which they can loan, except their own CREDIT, issued in the form of bank-notes, or inscribed in their books as "deposits," in exchange for the notes of individuals or business firms and corporations.

The next point to be noticed is the aggregate of all the assets or property of these banks; and by ascertaining this, and subtracting therefrom the capital, as before stated, we shall find to what extent the banks *have* loaned their credit,

No. 1.

Fig. 1.

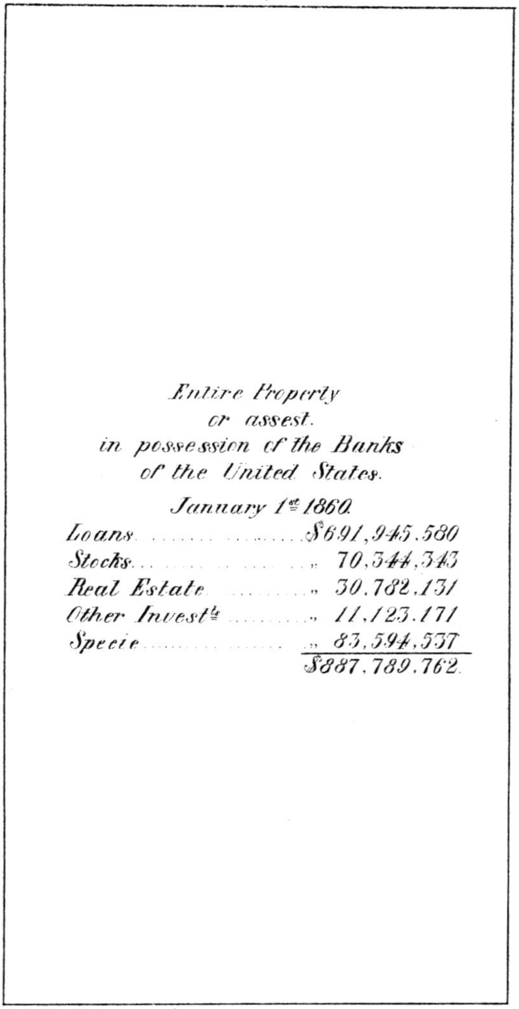

Fig. 2.

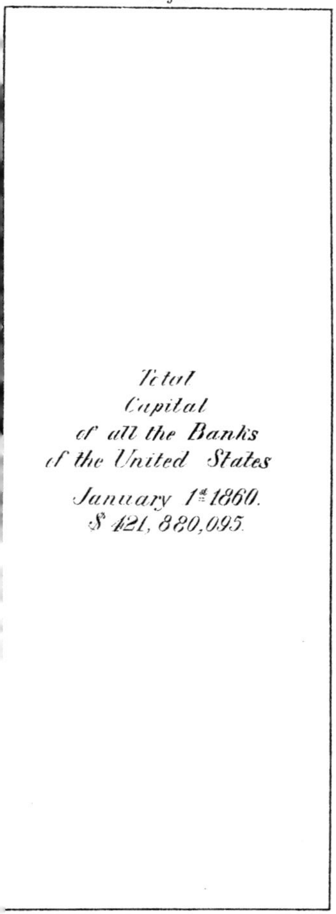

and, of course, to what extent credit enters into the currency. The statistics are presented in the form of a diagram, as annexed. See Diagram No. 1.

From the foregoing, it will be seen that the whole property in possession of the banks was (Fig. 1)	$887,789,762
From which deduct the aggregate capital (Fig. 2) .	421,880,095
Total credit issued by the banks	$465,909,867

On this amount the banks were receiving interest, or income beyond that received for their actual capital.

This "total credit" issued by the banks was —

Its circulation	$207,102,447
Deposits	253,802,129
Total currency	$460,904,576

It will be observed, that the "total credit" does not exactly correspond with the "total currency." This may be accounted for by the consideration that the item of "reserved profits," though given in the returns of some of the State banks, are not noticed in the returns made to the general government; so that, as those "profits" increase the actual capital of the banks, some unimportant discrepancies may be found in the accounts.

This remarkable difference, then, between the *capital* of the banks and their *property in possession*, is the first thing to be noticed in regard to the mixed-currency system, because it shows how it is that large profits may be made upon mixed-currency banking. Interest is obtained upon twice the amount of actual capital. This income, however, is not uniformly distributed among the banks acting under the system. Some obtain more; others, less.

We also see why it is that such banks must be constantly desirous of increasing their loans, by issuing their own credit in the shape of circulation and deposits. The more they can get out, the larger the income. This is the *motive power* that ensures the constant expansion of a mixed currency to its highest possible limit. The banks will always increase their indebtedness when they can, and only contract it when they must.

These facts show, too, why a mixed currency exists at all; viz., because those who create it make a profit both on their capital and credit, and as much on the latter as the former.

But still another view of the currency is necessary, to show the preponderance of the credit over the value element in the actual currency: —

1860.	Circulation, as before	$207,102,477
	Deposits	253,802,129
	Whole currency	$460,904,606
	Specie, or value	83,594,537
	Pure credit	$377,310,069

This will give eighteen cents and one mill on the dollar as the *value* element, and eighty-one cents and nine mills as the *credit* element, in the entire currency; credit being to value as more than five to one.

But yet another view of the system is necessary, if we would understand the true position of the banks in relation to each other, in case of an actual demand for specie, occasioned by want of confidence or demand for exportation.

Immediate liabilities of the banks of the United States, 1860: —

Circulation	$207,102,477	
Deposits	253,802,129	
Due other banks	55,932,918	
Other liabilities	14,661,815	$531,499,339

Immediate resources: —

Specie	$83,594,537	
Cash items	19,331,521	
Notes of other banks	25,502,567	
Due by other banks	67,235,457	195,664,082
Excess of immediate liabilities over immediate resources		$335,735,257

No 2.

Showing the immediate Liabilities and immediate Resources of the Banks of the United States in 1860.

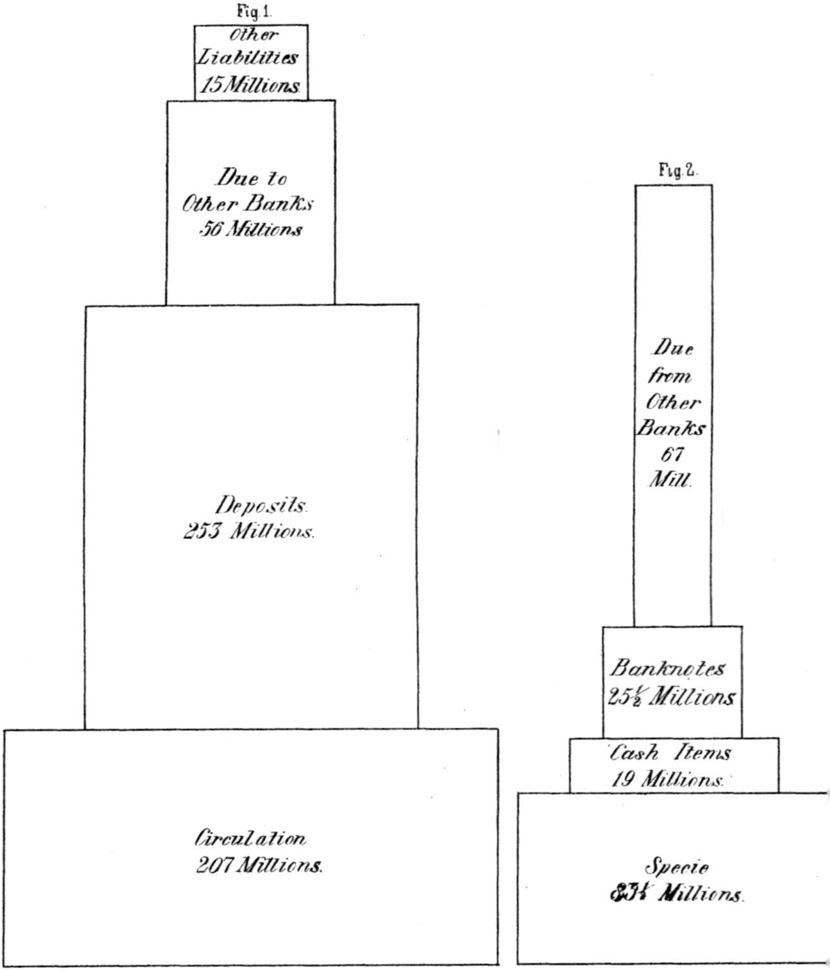

Total Immediate Liabilities 531 Millions.

Total Immediate Resources 195 Millions.

Excess 336 Millions.

No. 3

Fig. 1.

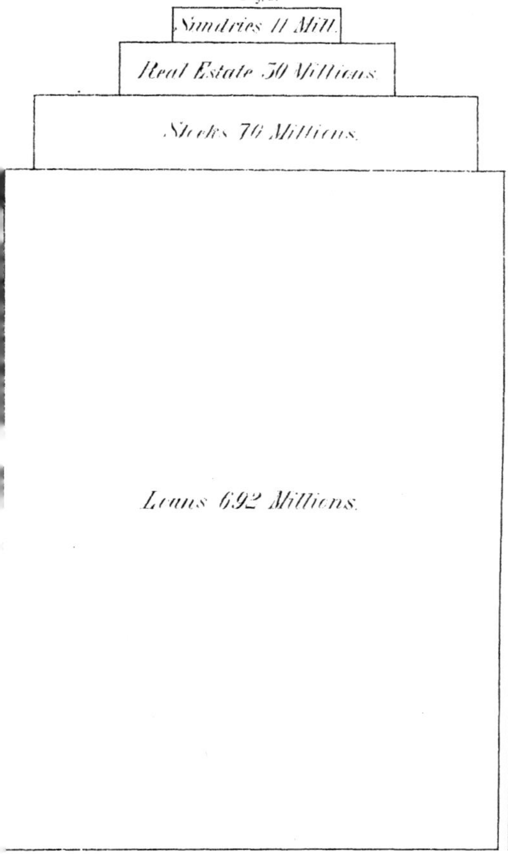

Total 804 Millions
Ultimate Resources.

Fig. 2

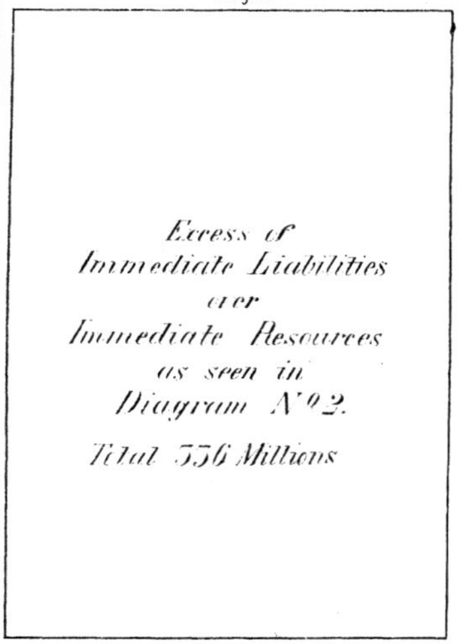

Total 336 Millions
to be provided for
out of the Ultimate Resources.

Diagram No. 2 presents to the eye the facts just stated, and shows the real position of the banks in reference to the convertibility of their currency.

It appears that the banks owed over three hundred and thirty-five millions on demand, which they had no means in their possession to discharge, but for which they held the following ultimate resources:—

Loans	$691,945,580
Stocks	70,344,343
Real estate	30,782,131
Other investments	11,123,171
	$804,195,225

This relation between the excess of immediate liabilities and the mass of ultimate resources, is exhibited in Currency Diagram No. 3.

From this view of the matter, we find that the banks had a surplus of four hundred and sixty-six millions for the payment, the *final* payment, of their *immediate* liabilities.

It is, therefore, quite clear that these notes and deposits are sufficiently secure, if the loans and other property of the bank prove to be reliable. But this is not the main point of interest.

The *grand problem* of mixed currency is to realize enough, at the necessary time, out of Fig. 1, to meet the demands of Fig. 2; that is, from eight hundred and four millions of stock, loans, &c., to meet the three hundred and thirty-five millions of instant obligations. The latter is all payable on demand. The former is, in part, a permanent investment; and, in part, falls due from one day to six months ahead.

The question, then, upon which the convertibility of the currency depends, is as follows: Will the obligations constituting the item of "loans" be paid in fast enough to meet the excess of immediate liabilities over immediate resources? That question we shall answer in the sequel.

CHAPTER V.

ANALYSIS OF DEPOSITS.

OUR analysis of mixed currency will be far from complete, if we do not give a full description of the origin and character of deposits, as forming an element most dangerous to such a currency, and generally very mysterious in the popular understanding.

In the currency of the United States, deposits constitute the largest item, considerably exceeding the circulation.

The nature of these deposits has, until within a very few years, been a matter of serious disagreement amongst those who ought to be well acquainted with their nature and effects. To present the subject in such a light that it shall be clearly understood, we must carefully examine it in all its details.

First, What are deposits? We have already defined them as credits given to individuals in the books of the banks, for which they are authorized by law to demand the specie.

Secondly, How do they arise? In various ways.

1. A customer may deposit coin, and have the amount passed to his credit. The proportion thus deposited is infinitesimally small, compared with the aggregate deposits.

2. He may deposit checks, drawn by himself or others, on other banks.

3. He may deposit the notes of the same or other banks.

4. He may deposit the notes of individuals, or bills of exchange running to maturity; and, when they are collected, the amount will be passed to his credit.

5. The customer may get his own notes, or the notes of others, discounted at the bank, and the amount is passed to his credit; and this last is the origin of the *greater part* of all deposits.

Of these different kinds of deposits, it will be observed that only one, and that a small one, was in specie; and yet the bank has promised to pay specie on demand alike for all. But it must be observed, that, while all these stand legally on the same basis, as a matter of fact they are practically held by the banks upon different conditions, expressed or implied. They may be divided into three kinds: —

First, Permanent or compulsory deposits, made by business men wishing for bank accommodations, in order to secure larger loans.

Second, Fiduciary or trust deposits, made wholly for temporary safe keeping, by executors, guardians, treasurers of corporations, &c., who are receiving funds to be paid out, or invested at a future period.

Third, Active deposits, made by business men, to be withdrawn to meet their current payments.

It will be necessary to explain these different deposits.

The permanent or compulsory deposits are not used at all by those who make them. They are made with the tacit understanding that they are to remain in the bank, and not be drawn upon. They are made to secure favors from the bank, and in order to show a "good account." No bank, perhaps, compels its customers, by any law or rule, to do this; but custom in such a case is as imperative as law. Banks are conducted wholly with reference to profit, and the most profitable accounts will secure the most liberal discounts.

These deposits constitute a permanent loan to the banks, without interest; and the banks can loan the same to their customers upon interest. It is one of the forms in which a bank may secure extra interest in a legal way; but it is done at the expense of those who make the deposits.

This kind of deposits forms a very dangerous element in the mixed-currency system, for the reason, that, when the merchants of any great city are driven to desperation, they may demand these deposits in specie, and then the banks must suspend. This was done in New York in October, 1857, as before stated. The merchants saw clearly, that, unless the banks would make discounts, they could not meet their engagements. The banks refused to do this, because they could not, and continue to pay specie. The merchants then, by concerted action, called for their deposits; and the banks themselves succumbed.

This will always be re-enacted in a time of great pressure, if the mixed-currency system is continued. It is the only remedy which the mercantile interest has within its power. It is properly used, because the banks have no right to make promises which they know perfectly well they cannot keep.

Another objectionable consideration is, that these deposits greatly and unnecessarily enlarge the immediate liabilities of the banks, and give them a frightful preponderance over the immediate means of payment. This injures the credit of the banks in times of pressure. All sagacious financiers look with suspicion on institutions owing ten or fifteen dollars on demand for every dollar they have in their possession. On the 29th of August, 1857, the banks of the city of New York owed for eighty-four millions for deposits and nine millions for circulation, — in all, ninety-three millions, — and had but nine millions of specie.

Here, perhaps, it is proper to remark, that this kind of deposits is probably unknown in any other country than the United States. In England, for example, the rate of interest is not arbitrarily fixed by government, but fluctuates from time to time, according to the laws of currency and the demands of trade. Consequently, there is no occasion for this indirect mode of obtaining extra interest, so common in some, if not all, the commercial cities of the American Union.

Compulsory deposits mean, simply, extra interest; but that interest is paid in a manner most burdensome to the depositors, and most dangerous to the banks. The former must lie out of a considerable part of capital which they need in their business; the latter must enlarge their deposits to a most unreasonable extent, and place themselves at the mercy of the depositors in any time of severe pressure or panic.

Of the second class of deposits, viz. those on trust or for safe keeping merely, it may be said, that they are perfectly legitimate, and may, to a certain extent, be loaned by the banks with safety. They should be so loaned for the advantage of the public, and thus no capital be left unemployed. An obvious benefit arises to all parties: the depositor has his money securely kept, the borrower has the use of it, and the bank rightfully gets interest upon so much of the sum as it has loaned.

The third class of deposits may be described as follows: —

(*a*) A business man, who is making sales each day, will receive, in payment, notes of all the different kinds in circulation. He will also receive checks on different banks. All these he will deposit in bank; and the amount is passed to his credit, and becomes a bank deposit.

(*b*) He will also receive notes of hand, drafts, and bills of exchange, in payment. All these, when nearly due, he will deposit in bank; and, when paid, they are passed to his credit.

(*c*) Or, if he desires to anticipate the payment of such notes, he may ask the bank to deduct the interest (and exchange, if there be any), and place the amount to his credit; and this the bank will, in ordinary circumstances, be ready to do; and the amount so passed to the credit of the customer will constitute a part of the deposits of the bank.

ARE BANK DEPOSITS CURRENCY?

Lord Overstone, one of the best authorities, has maintained the negative; but most writers* in this country take

* We do not know of any intelligent writer in this country who now denies that deposits are as truly currency as the circulation itself.

the affirmative side of the question: indeed, there are, at the present time, few, if any, who doubt that deposits are currency. The New-York Board of Currency has given its verdict unequivocally as follows: "*They constitute at this time five-sixths of the active currency of this city.*" See the official report of that association for November, 1858. No array of authorities, however, but an examination of facts, should determine the question.

Deposits are an *instrumentality* by which by far the greatest amount of values are transferred in commercial centres. They discharge debts, purchase commodities, and perform all the functions of currency.

For example, A has a deposit in the Merchants' Bank. He purchases of B a bill of sugars, amounting to ten thousand dollars, and pays for the same with a check on that bank, with which B either draws the notes or specie of the bank, or has the check passed to his credit by the bank. This transaction has been equivalent to the transfer of ten thousand dollars in value from one party to the other.

If A owed B a note of ten thousand dollars, he might pay it in the same way.

Now, what difference did it make to A whether he had ten thousand dollars of bank-notes in his till, or an equal amount to his credit in the bank? Clearly, not the slightest. One was as truly currency as the other. If A was pondering the question whether he should purchase the sugar for cash (*i.e.*, immediate payment), did not the consciousness that he had ten thousand dollars to his credit in bank operate on his decision precisely to the same extent as if he had ten thousand dollars of bank-notes in his pocket-book? Undoubtedly. Where, then, is the difference? And, if all this would be true in the case of A, then in the case of any one similarly situated; and therefore we must conclude, that deposits are, in their nature and influence, of the same character as bank-notes, and, of course, are currency.

All bankers and business men are well satisfied that deposits are even more active by far in transferring values than the bank circulation; that a much greater number of exchanges is made with deposits than with an equal amount of bank-notes.

A little reflection will satisfy any one that such is the fact. The sum of ten thousand dollars, for example, might easily pay in a single day, in ten different transfers by checks, a total of one hundred thousand dollars.

This would not be an extravagant supposition; but it would be quite improbable that bank-notes make ten payments in a single day.

The efficiency of money, or its substitutes, depends greatly upon the rapidity with which exchanges are made. John Stuart Mill recognizes this principle; and it is a very obvious one. It is on that principle that we see the propriety of admitting, that, although the *active* deposits in bank may be less than its notes, yet the greater rapidity with which they are used makes the whole amount equivalent in their effects to an equal amount of bank-notes.

The currency of any country is as its quantity multiplied by the rapidity of its circulation. This consideration will lead us to regard the whole amount of deposits as equal in effect to an equal amount of circulation.

STOCKS AS IMMEDIATE RESOURCES.

Here it may be proper to explain why we have not placed the item of "stocks" held by the banks amongst their immediate resources. Many persons seem disposed to regard them as such. But, so far as the quality and character of the currency are concerned, the stocks held by the banks do not essentially differ from any other securities. Suppose a severe pressure for specie comes on, what can they do with them? Force the sale, and realize the money for them? This cannot be done, of course, at such a time, except at a great sacrifice; besides, if they do this, what will the banks receive for the stocks sold? Their own notes and deposits. There is nothing else in which the stocks can be paid for. But if, after having received their notes in this way, they refuse again to loan them, they contract the currency by so much, and increase the pecuniary distress by all that amount; if they do reloan the notes, they have gained no relief to themselves by the operation. The great object desired is to relieve the pressure for money: the sale of the stocks will have the opposite effect. Hence they cannot be regarded as the immediate resources.

CHAPTER VI.

MIXED CURRENCY. — FLUCTUATIONS IN QUANTITY AND QUALITY.

We have explained the organization of mixed-currency institutions, the character of their operations, the quality and form of their issues. We pass now to consider this currency in its several relations to the public wealth. Such an inquiry will demand great carefulness and impartiality, and must necessarily be made in detail.

We have two grand questions which arise naturally at the start: —

1st, Does it perform satisfactorily the functions of money? If we answer this inquiry favorably, we have still to ask, —

2d, What, and how great, are its effects on public interests, beyond the proper effects of value currency?

These questions are so full of interest to all the departments of wealth, are so deeply obscured by prejudice and misapprehension, and are so especially important at the present time, that their discussion will be protracted through several chapters.

1st, DOES A MIXED CURRENCY SATISFACTORILY PERFORM THE FUNCTIONS OF MONEY?

Those functions are as already stated, — to act as a medium of exchange, and to be a standard of value.

Does a mixed currency perform them well? We answer, no. The essential quality of such a currency, which unfits it to act well as either a standard of value or a medium of exchange, is this: —

IT IS NOT GOVERNED BY THE LAWS OF VALUE.

It is subject to quite other laws. It varies as to its volume and character; but we do not find that it does this out of respect for value. The great principle of value is, demand creates supply; supply satisfies demand. They are measured against each other, and are found equal. There is no supply which demand does not call for: there is no supply which is not enough for demand. And the reason for this perfect equality is that value cannot exist without labor. The same cause that increases supply, expands demand to the same proportions: the same cause that restricts supply, reduces demand correspondingly.

A mixed currency is not regulated in this way. In so far as it has not value, it is not controlled by the laws of value.

It is put out or taken in by bank managers at their pleasure, and for their profit. It is not produced by labor. This last fact removes the gravitation which alone can secure a currency. It makes it a thing to be blown about by every breeze, carried up or carried down with the currents, or whirled around in the eddies of trade. It should be stable, and not sport for the winds. There should be a reason for the putting-out or taking-in of every dollar of money; and that reason should be found in the laws of value.

Now, this law controls the expansion or contraction of money, or a value currency. If it is increased, as it may be in the natural course of commercial transactions, it is because actual money has been brought into the country by the balance of trade; but a mixed currency is increased by the voluntary and interested action of bank managers, without regard to the laws of value, and without the addition of a dollar to the real money, or wealth, of the country. The increase of *money* by importation takes place in obedience to causes that are gradual and appreciable; and any one who watches the course of commerce can anticipate its arrival. If it comes in excess, from any unusual source, it easily and naturally passes off to other countries, till the balance is restored. Real money is like the water of the globe, rising and falling by natural laws, and keeping its level by its own mobility. If a redundance exists in one spot, there is, for that reason, a deficiency somewhere else. Where it is, it is less valued; where it is not, it is the more desired; and the equilibrium is soon restored. No artificial appliances or legal enactments are needed to keep true money at a level the world over.

We have found that the quantity of a mixed currency is not governed by the laws of value. Do we, then, find that it is controlled by accident? It would be better so, for there would be more chances of its coming right. But, on the contrary, we find laws positively mischievous substituted for the wholesome operation of supply and demand.

Firstly, Of expansion. The more that is issued of a mixed currency, the more will be wanted. The supply does not satisfy the demand: it excites it. Like an unnatural stimulus taken into the human system, it creates an increasing desire for more; and the more it is gratified, the more insatiable are its cravings.

There are two reasons for this: one, that, as the currency is expanded, prices are raised correspondingly, and more currency is demanded to effect the same exchanges; the other, that the speculation inevitably following the rise of prices leads to an enormous extension and repetition of indebtedness, which requires, for its discharge, a greatly increased amount of the circulating medium. Thus, by the action and interaction of these causes, the demand for the issue of this kind of currency is certain to be greatest when it is already redundant. All this, of course, is quickened and helped by the fact that the manufacturers of this currency are ready and eager to crowd upon the public all it will take, like a very earnest friend who thrusts his purse into your hand before you are quite decided that you wish to borrow.

Secondly, Of contraction. We have seen the forces that raise the currency higher and higher. We have not seen that it is done for the public good, or in obedience to a call of trade. We might suppose that there would be an unending progress in this direction, till any degree of expansion should be reached, inasmuch as the law of value does not govern a product into which the element of labor does not enter. It is not, therefore, the expense of multiplying it, nor is its increase limited by any consideration of utility. If every dollar of credit were *called* a million dollars, it would effect an exchange just as well. The only difference would be the work of adding six ciphers in accounting. No: the cause that limits the expansion, and finally produces contraction, is the liability of the notes to be presented for payment in money.

The occasion for this cause to operate may be almost any thing,—a political convulsion, an adverse balance of trade, a failure of some large trading or banking company, or an unaccountable mood of the popular mind.

We will take that one which is most common and sensible,—an adverse balance of trade. If it be large, the demand for specie which it occasions will create a profound sensation among the banks. With actual money, there is, under these circumstances, no reason for excitement or alarm: ten million dollars of the currency will discharge that amount of debt abroad, and the currency at home is reduced but so much. A mixed currency has, in itself, no power whatever to satisfy a foreign creditor. If ten million dollars are to be paid abroad, it must be taken from the specie of the banks; the basis of the currency is so much diminished, and the circulation must be curtailed accordingly; that is, notes must be brought in, and not put out again till the basis is restored. If the proportion of specie, as is the case on an average in this country, is only as one to five of notes, then the export of ten million dollars abroad must cause a contraction to the extent of fifty million dollars at home. The removal of so much currency, and of that very part which circulates most actively, causes stringency; and stringency causes suspicion. Let another ten millions be called for out of the specie basis, and affairs will become very critical. The legitimate effect of the export, so far, would be to contract the currency one hundred million dollars; but *another* cause is introduced now. Vague apprehensions abound, everybody gets prudent, many are scared. Here is another reason for contraction. With a value currency, the fact that it was especially wanted would be a reason why it should stay. Not so with credit money: it won't bear to be looked in the face.

It is hardly necessary to trace the course of contractions, they are so familiar to the American mind.

The banks know their own position better than any one else. They understand precisely what they must do. They act instantaneously. They curtail their loans. They know that trouble is at hand, and they propose to meet it in the best way for themselves. They know that their notes may now prove their ruin, and they propose to get them out of the way as fast as possible.

There are two classes of banks: —

1st, Those who transact all their business in an honorable manner, and, so far as the nature of the currency they issue will admit, on a secure basis. They are careful not to extend their loans beyond their means, and they keep a respectable amount of specie.

2d, Those who get out, and keep out, all they can, and carry their circulation, deposits, and loans as high as possible, without regard to the specie in their vaults. This class is numerous, especially among those of small capital. They rely on their baseless circulation for extraordinary profits.

In case of a demand for specie, the latter class are obliged to call for assistance from the former, who, willing or unwilling, are equally obliged to give it. The "feeble banks" must be sustained, or the whole system will be suspected. If these be allowed to dishonor their notes, a run will be made at once on all the rest; and, having as we see only one dollar in five to pay with, they must, of course, soon stop paying altogether.

It should be borne in mind that these contractions and expansions are not imaginary, not possible only, not merely occasional, nor at all local, but occur frequently and everywhere within the field of such a currency.

It is commonly said that the banks only increase their issues as demanded by the wants of trade; that they extend their credits, because the public require them as business facilities.

If this were true, it would be of no consequence in the discussion; because, the laws of value having been disturbed in this matter, the demand is no longer normal. We have no longer the assurance that trade will call into use just that amount of currency which it needs.

But it is not true. The movement always commences with the banks. When, by a monetary revulsion, their circulation and deposits have been reduced so low that they feel safe in commencing another expansion, the panic being over, the banks begin to offer extraordinary inducements to their customers to borrow money. They will discount all good paper offered, even if it has a long time to run. It is not uncommon, at such times, to solicit the privilege of making loans.* As soon as this state of things takes place, all business men begin speculative operations; for prices have begun to rise. Speculation will give a still greater rise to prices, and cause a still greater demand for currency. The expansive force is now in full operation, and is sure to increase in power till by revulsion the equilibrium is restored.

But it may be asked, are there not natural tides in business, irrespective of a mixed currency? Certainly; but they are never aggravated or intensified until they end in panic or ruin. They are calculable and healthful. They are tests of business character. They may go to the extent of exposing the emptiness of bad concerns, but never destroy those that are good. When they occur, money will be wanted to pay debts; but, when one debt is paid, there is just as much money as before with which to pay others. The pressure does not annihilate any part of the currency. The party who receives a payment does not put the money away in vaults, not to appear again till the crisis is past. The means of payment can be reduced only by the amount actually sent out of the country. Gold and silver are as little injured by panic as by fire.

CHAPTER VII.

TABLES AND DIAGRAMS OF MIXED-CURRENCY FLUCTUATIONS.

WE have shown, from the reason of the case, that a mixed currency is not governed by the laws of value; and that therefore its variations are controlled by other principles,

* This is within the personal knowledge of the writer as a bank director.

which give no guaranty to the public good, but, on the contrary, threaten great mischief to the community, both by expansion and contraction.

We now propose to show, by facts taken from official statistics, that such fluctuations are frequent and violent.

We introduce a diagram, carefully prepared, for the purpose of showing, in the most compact and striking form, these fluctuations of the currency, both in quantity and quality.

The following table exhibits the fluctuations in the *absolute* quantity of the mixed currency (circulation and deposit) of the United States from 1834 to 1859 inclusive, a period of twenty-six years.

TABLE I.

1834	170,000,000	1847	197,000,000
1835	186,000,000	1848	231,000,000
1836	255,000,000	1849	205,000,000
1837	276,000,000	1850	240,000,000
1838	200,000,000	1851	284,000,000
1839	225,000,000	1852	328,000,000
1840	182,000,000	1853	348,000,000
1841	172,000,000	1854	392,000,000
1842	146,000,000	1855	377,000,000
1843	114,000,000	1856	408,000,000
1844	159,000,000	1857	445,000,000
1845	177,000,000	1858	341,000,000
1846	202,000,000	1859	452,000,000

These facts are collected, as nearly as possible, from the returns made at the beginning of the years mentioned. Therefore the contractions or expansions made during a year do not appear till the return of the next year. For example, the great contractions of 1837 and 1857, beginning several months after January, do not exhibit their effects till the currency returns of the years 1838 and 1858.

Diagram No. 4 exhibits the fluctuations in the currency (circulation and deposits), and also the proportion of specie, from 1834 to 1859 inclusive, both reckoned per capita.

The upper line indicates the currency, the lower the specie, and show the fluctuations of both.

In the last diagram, we see distinctly the actual fluctuations in the currency, because its amount, at the several periods, is reckoned per capita. This is a far more correct mode of getting at the real changes than taking the absolute quantity.

The diagram is prepared from a table published by the Massachusetts Bank Commissioners, in their Report of 1861, furnished by J. V. Yatman, Esq., of New York, to whom the public are indebted for valuable contributions of a statistical character.

The upper line shows the fluctuations in the quantity of the currency: the lower line indicates its quality from time to time.

The following table shows the extreme fluctuations in the quantity of the currency of the United States per capita, at different times, with the corresponding variations per cent in its quality: —

TABLE II., *showing the Extreme Fluctuations in the Currency of the United States per Capita at different Times, with the Corresponding Variations in its Quality, or the Proportion of Specie held for its Redemption.*

Years.	Currency per capita.	Fluctuations.	Per cent.	Quality, or specie to circulation.	Variations in quality.	Per cent.
1834	11.82	. . . . . .	.	15½ to 100	. . . . . .	.
*1837	17.61	Expansion	50	13½ to 100	Depreciation	11½
1840	10.70	Contraction	39	18 to 100	Improvement	33
1843	6.18	"	42	29 to 100	"	61
1846	9.94	Expansion	61	21 to 100	Depreciation	36
1849	9 18	Contraction	7	21 to 100	Stationary	0
1852	13.31	Expansion	45	15½ to 100	Depreciation	27
1855	13.93	"	13	14 to 100	"	10
*1857	15.50	"	11	13 to 100	"	7
1858	11.55	Contraction	26	22½ to 100	Improvement	73
1859	14.90	Expansion	23	23 to 100	"	2

* Years when the banks suspended. Observe the great expansion between the years 1834 and 1837 of some fifty per cent; and between 1849 and 1857 of some seventy per cent.

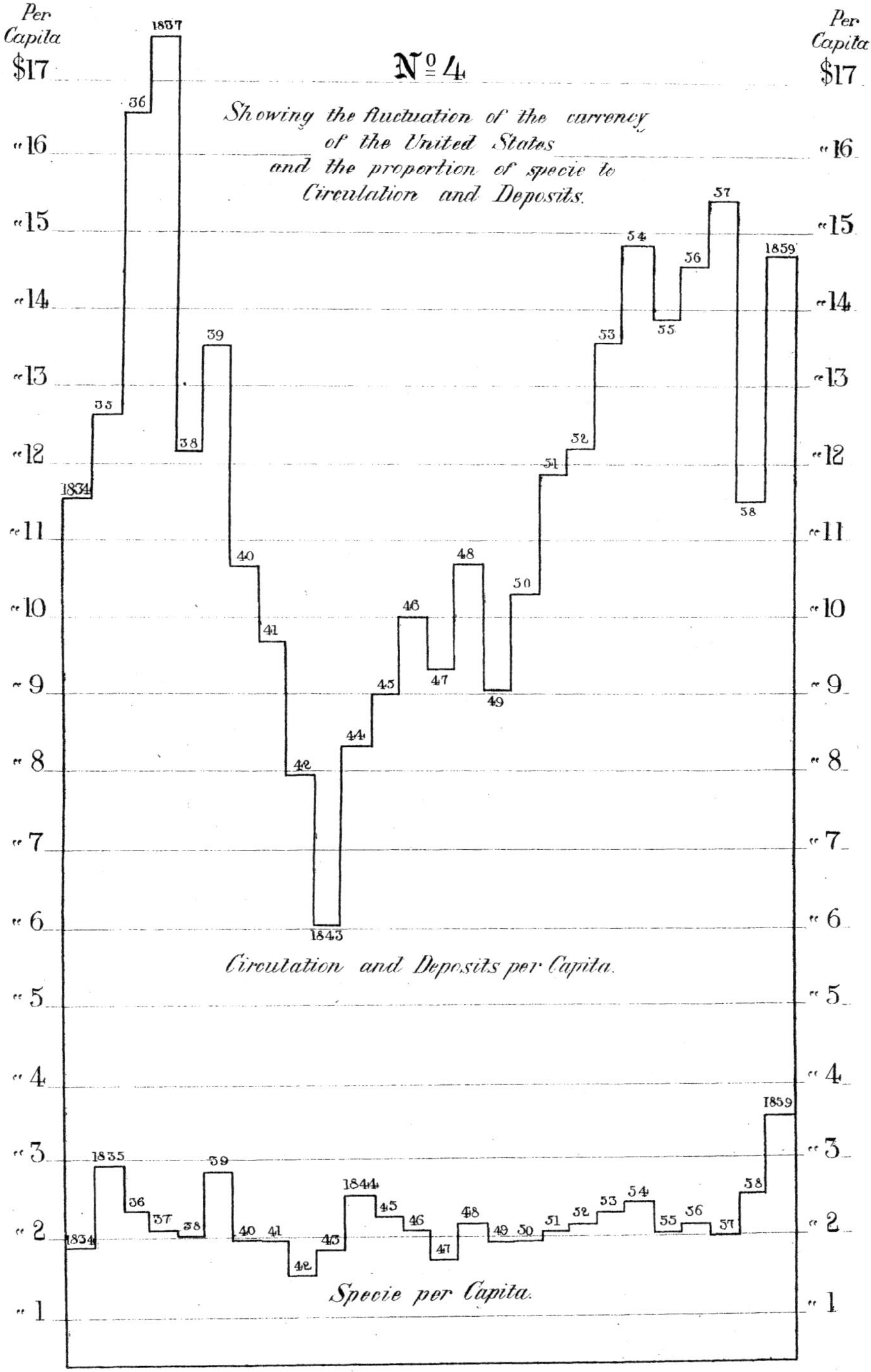
№ 4
Showing the fluctuation of the currency of the United States and the proportion of specie to Circulation and Deposits.
Per Capita
$17
" 16
" 15
" 14
" 13
" 12
" 11
" 10
" 9
" 8
" 7
" 6
" 5
" 4
" 3
" 2
" 1
Circulation and Deposits per Capita.
1834
35
36
1837
38
39
40
41
42
1843
44
45
46
47
48
49
50
51
52
53
54
55
56
57
58
1859
Specie per Capita.
1834
1835
36
37
38
39
40
41
42
43
1844
45
46
47
48
49
50
51
52
53
54
55
56
57
58
1859

TABLE III. — *The following Table exhibits the Composition of the Mixed Currencies of the several States of the Union, Jan.* 1, 1860; *that is, the Percentage of Specie to the Circulation and Deposits in the Currency of each State:* —

	Per cent.		Per cent.		Per cent.
Louisiana	38.6	Pennsylvania . .	21.3	Delaware	9.9
Missouri	37.	Iowa	20.	New Jersey . . .	8.9
Georgia	23.7	Virginia	16.7	Connecticut . . .	7.5
Kentucky	23.4	New York . . .	15.6	Rhode Island . .	6.3
Tennessee	23.	South Carolina . .	15.5	New Hampshire .	5.7
North Carolina . .	22.08	Ohio	15.2	Wisconsin . . .	5.5
Indiana	22.3	Massachusetts . .	15.1	Vermont	4.2
Alabama	22.2	Florida	10.5	Michigan	4.
Maryland	21.4	Maine	10.	Illinois	2.3

But there are variations, not only in the general currency of the United States, such as we have indicated, but also in the currency of each State, at different periods.

We take that of Massachusetts, in illustration: —

TABLE IV., *exhibiting the Quality of the Currency of Massachusetts.*

Year	1835.	1837.	1840.	1843.	1851.	1857.	1859.	1860.
Specie, per cent . .	7.1	8	18¾	44.1	7.5	8.9	14.6	15.1

From this it appears that the highest proportion of specie was in 1843, which year marked the termination of the great monetary convulsion that commenced with the failure of the banks in 1837, at which date the banks of Massachusetts had but eight per cent, as shown above. The severe pressure began in 1836, when the specie was seven.

By a law of that Commonwealth, passed in 1858, the banks are required to keep at least fifteen per cent of specie. This law has much increased the average amount of specie.

Another fact may be noticed in this connection; viz., that the banks of Massachusetts were, to a considerable extent, responsible for all the mixed-currency circulation in New England, because the banks of the neighboring States had all their bills redeemed in Boston. Those of Vermont, for example, whose average specie is only four or five per cent, kept bank balances (not actual specie, as often supposed) with certain banks which were under obligations to redeem all their bills as fast as presented. This, of course, greatly enhanced the responsibilities of the Massachusetts banks, and decreased the strength of their currency.

The currency of New England was thus made a complete unit. The system of redemption, first established by the Suffolk Bank of Boston about forty years ago, was so perfected, that, while the banks of each State might act independently, they were bound together by a common tie, and involved in a common fate. This was known as the "Suffolk-Bank system."

Volumes of statistics might be given of the same general character; but these, it is presumed, are sufficient to show the fluctuating character of the mixed currency of the United States, both in quantity and quality; and of course, in degree, of all other countries where such a currency exists: for it is, at all times and everywhere, the same in its general characteristics. The quality may and does vary greatly in different communities, as we have seen it in the different States of the American Union. But this is merely a question of degree.

CHAPTER VIII.

MIXED CURRENCY AS A MEDIUM OF EXCHANGE.

HAVING shown that a mixed currency is certain to expand and contract, without reference to the healthful and harmonious provisions of value, and to a degree more extreme and dangerous than a currency composed of real money, we are prepared to answer summarily the principal question.

Does a mixed currency perform satisfactorily the functions of money?

1st, Does it act efficiently as a medium of exchange?

Currency, regarded merely as a medium of exchange, may be said to perform two offices: (*a*) To transfer commodities from one person to another. For this purpose, a mixed currency, having a circulation wholly of paper, is found to be portable, readily counted, easily carried, safely kept, and is, consequently, as convenient as any agent that could reasonably be desired. (*b*) To discharge indebtedness between different parties. For this purpose, the thing to be desired is, that currency should be reliable; that is, that there should be nothing in its own nature, which disqualifies it to act *fully, at all times*, as a means of discharging obligations.

Coin is always perfectly reliable for the payment of debts. When one debt has been discharged by it, the coin is just as available and acceptable for the discharge of a second or any succeeding debt. If gold and silver are called for by foreign obligations, they retain their full power to discharge them.

There can never be a scarcity of them that an earnest demand will not create a supply for. If a community wants them very much, it will certainly get them.

They crowd to their best market, as truly as cotton or wheat.

We here make two principal statements: —

A foreign demand is the only cause that can take away the real money of a people. We have seen that an indefinite number of causes may take away a currency based, in any degree, on credit.

But, again, a foreign demand can only take away *its own amount* of real money. We have seen that such a cause takes away an amount of mixed currency of which the quantity required abroad is only one factor; the other factor being that number which represents the proportion between the bulk of the currency and the specie basis. In these two statements are clearly shown the entire unreliability of mixed currency to discharge indebtedness. The man who promises to pay money can never know what may be the demand for specie, arising from a want of confidence in the banks, or from a necessity of export; and, of course, can never be safe in giving his notes predicated upon the currency as it exists at the time.

So far as the fluctuations we have shown derange general plans of business, distort prices, work injustice to one party of every bargain, and tend, by such inequalities and uncertainties, to discourage steady enterprise, they do not present themselves here for examination. We shall meet them, when discussing a mixed currency as performing its function as a standard of value. We have to do here, not with the unfairness and injustice with which indebtedness is discharged under such a currency, but with the difficulty or impossibility of discharging it at all.

To falsify the standard of value is a serious, but not necessarily a ruinous error. It takes from one unjustly, and adds to another; but it destroys nothing directly. There *are* fluctuations in the currency, found in our national experience and depicted in the diagrams given, which proceed to an entire revulsion of the body of trade. Panic is not a century plant. It blossoms and bears fruit once or twice while a child is growing up; many times while a man remains in business.

How does a mixed currency perform the functions of money, so far as discharging indebtedness in such times?

Let us suppose the case of the best man in the community. He has, in the legitimate course of business, contracted obligations, all within the limit of his abilities, now coming due. The banks are withdrawing their circulation as largely as possible, and do not mean to let it out again. The fact of his own excellent standing is of no moment in securing discounts; for there is just as much danger to the banks in his having their notes as in their being anywhere else. It is the peculiar hardship of good men, in such times, that it is not *their* credit, but the credit (that is, the condition) of the banks, which is to decide the question of loans. With a value currency, on the other hand, the only matter of importance is the solvency of the applicant himself.

If he cannot get money, he cannot meet his obligations; for he cannot pay in merchandise or real estate. The money is not to be had; that is, if the banks would accomplish what they must do to save their credit.

Of course, there are individuals and institutions, who, in consideration of high premiums and full security, will grant accommodations to a limited amount. He may try to get along, sacrificing his property to save his name, and paying twenty-four or thirty-six per cent for loans. Perhaps, if others stood well, he might get through; but all are not so firm as himself. Most have less accumulation and less credit. His *debtors* fail to pay: how can he answer his *creditors?* If he tries to go through, the payments are all one way, like the tracks about the lion's den. He has to pay both sides of the ledger.

We have spoken of the credit element of a mixed currency. But panic, suspicion, apprehension, are the deadly enemies of credit: when these are aroused in the community, it cannot go abroad. Just as nearly as the object can be accomplished in the time given, all forms of credit will be withdrawn. But this will produce, in its several degrees, stringency, distress, panic, ruin.

Is it, then, too much to say that credit is not reliable for the discharge of indebtedness?

The element of credit introduces a direct hostility between the interests of those who control the currency and those who wish to use it. The interest of the one requires that the notes shall be withdrawn. The interest, nay, the life, of the other requires that they shall be kept in circulation. Is there any such hostility in a value currency? Not at all. No matter how intense the apprehension, how manifold the suspicion, how frenzied the panic, there is never a moment when it is not better for the owner that such money should be used than kept out of use.

We have said that a sudden and severe contraction is necessary whenever any cause threatens the specie basis of a mixed currency. Such a contraction deprives the community of the means of meeting obligations undertaken when the currency was redundant.

But this contraction, when it has become inevitable, does not take place without danger and loss to the banks themselves; danger and loss being the proper consequences of such operations. The banks make no more loans, or as few as possible. The *means* of discharging debts become less and less in the community each succeeding day, until the rate of interest goes up to two or three per cent a month, and money can hardly be had at all.

The banks now find themselves in this dilemma: if they make loans, they must keep paying out their specie. This will soon become exhausted, and they must suspend and be dishonored. If they do not continue to accommodate their customers with the *usual* means of paying debts, the latter must succumb. But, if their customers generally fail, the banks will lose their capital (it being chiefly in the form of notes given by individuals), and be permanently ruined. The history of the country shows on which horn of the dilemma they choose to be impaled. They suspend or stop specie payments, and then furnish the public with an abundance of their notes, such as they are.

After this has been accomplished, and after the credit of the banks has been exchanged for the credit of the individuals who owe them, and after the demand for specie has ceased, the banks can resume payments.

It may be said, at this point, that the result we have reached does not seem very formidable; that, let it but be understood the banks are to suspend in such circumstances, we can by this means still have the advantages of a mixed currency in favorable times, and relieve the distress when a contraction is threatened. The answer to this plea will be deferred to the chapter on "Fallacies," in preference to interrupting the present line of argument.

CHAPTER IX.

MIXED CURRENCY AS A STANDARD OF VALUE.

2d, DOES a mixed currency act justly as a standard of value?

This function of money is of a very important character. It lies at the foundation of all credit and all business calculations. If no man dealt with or trusted another, or waited a day to receive and consume the reward of his labor, there would be no great need of such a standard. It would then be only of *scientific* interest, to show what was the comparative wealth of different communities and ages, and what the fairness of their several systems of distributing the result of industry among the producing classes. If every act of labor received its own reward, in a distinct form, at the time, to be consumed then and there, a standard of value would be of less practical importance.

But whenever there is the slightest exchange of commodities or association of laborers; whenever one man trusts another for recompense of service, or applies wealth and toil to an enterprise in the faith of receiving a reward at a future time,—a standard of value must be had, so that all can be done safely, expeditiously, and justly. Unless something possessed the property of being a standard of value, all exchange would inevitably be confined to the gross and clumsy form of barter. It has already been included in the definition of money, that it performs this office. There is not a possibility of taking a scientific exception to this statement; yet a great deal of popular controversy has arisen, which we are obliged to stop here to notice. It has been said, that a dollar, for example, no more measures the value of wheat, than wheat does the value of the dollar; that "the dollar is wholly an arbitrary, conventional standard, forced on the people, unjustly, by legislative enactment."

Much confusion has undoubtedly been caused by mistaken views of what is really meant by a standard of value.

Suppose A sells B a tract of land, and agrees to take five hundred oxen in payment at a future day. The value of the land sold is, in this case, clearly measured by the oxen. These latter are the standard by which the value of the land is determined. They form the money, or currency, by which the debt is legally and rightfully to be discharged. The oxen here occupy precisely the position of the dollar in ordinary contracts; and, if we suppose a community in which they are altogether used as money, they become, without any necessary legal enactment, the universal standard, or that by which all other values are measured and expressed. Value must be determined in some way; and it can only be done by comparison, — by measuring the land against oxen, wheat, gold, or something else that has value.

As long as the land was measured, in the single instance, by the oxen, so long each measured the other alike; but, when the use of the oxen was extended to a comparison with each other commodity in the market, and all others together, *then* it became as improper to say that the land measured the oxen as to say that the wood or the cloth measure the yardstick by which their length and breadth are universally determined. The government does not insist that length or breadth shall be determined in all bargains by the yardstick. Men can and do take arms and fingers for the purpose, or any thing else they please: it is nothing to government, which only says *what* a yard shall be.

So, by universal consent, mankind have agreed to measure every thing by the precious metals. The laws of the United States, for example, enact that a certain coin, or *planchet*, of gold, nine-tenths fine, and weighing $25\frac{8}{10}$ grains, shall be called a dollar. That is all the government does, all it ought to do. It compels no one to receive the dollar for any thing, *unless he has agreed to do so*, any more than it compels him to receive hats or boots, wheat or cotton. But, the government having provided the coin, — that is, having certified to its weight and fineness, — the people, of their own choice, make use of it to measure every other thing. If they buy merchandise or land or cattle, they agree to take so many of these dollars in payment. They might say, so many oxen or horses, or any thing else; but they prefer dollars, merely because they have the most convenient form of value, and are universally acceptable. As society in general adopts this way of determining the worth of property, the dollar, not by law, but by the voluntary preference of the people, becomes the measure, or standard, of value, in all transactions.

So far as indebtedness between individuals is concerned, the government makes the dollar lawful tender; that is, if an individual has a just claim for a given number of *dollars*, the government enacts that the same number of *dollars* shall discharge the debt.

True it is, that every object, having value and used in exchange, is really, in so far, and for the time, a measure of value; but that which has been selected by mankind as the best adapted for a *universal* equivalent, and actually so used, is emphatically, and for all purposes, *the* measure or standard.

Some writers have insisted that people should not be compelled to pay so many dollars in coin; then they should not promise dollars merely, but any thing else.

The establishment of such a standard is no wrong to the people; for it can easily be seen that payments in any other specific product would be more likely to involve hardships; *e.g.*, an obligation to pay wheat or potatoes or cotton at any certain time, would bring infinitely more chances of distress resulting from a failure of the crop in that particular article.

Neither is it an arbitrary act on the part of the government. It is purely a favor, an accommodation, provided at great cost, for the benefit of the public. All objections, on the ground that it is arbitrary and unjust to compel men to discharge indebtedness in coin, are idle and absurd. Those who make them are bound to show, what has never yet been found, a better standard.

During the suspension of the Bank of England from 1796 to 1819, it was gravely argued, by some gentlemen in the House of Commons, that "the pound sterling was really an abstraction;" but the return to specie payments in the latter year showed that the pound sterling was really a concretion of 113.001 grains of fine gold, by which all debts, public and private, were to be discharged.

A mixed currency, wherever it exists, forms the standard of value for the community, just as certainly as the precious metals where they alone are used. That of the United States, to be sure, is not a legal tender,* like the Bank-of-England notes; but, as no other currency exists, as there is no other money of importance in circulation, it must be employed for all purposes, and so, to all practical intents, is the standard of value.

We are now prepared to inquire how a mixed currency performs this function.

We have seen its fluctuations, certain to occur, yet wholly uncertain as to direction and degree. These fluctuations make it plain enough, that, as a standard of value, a mixed currency must work injustice and mischief, both in expansion and contraction. Destructive as are the great occasional convulsions of trade, it is doubtful whether they produce as extensive evil as those minor disturbances which come every year, and, indeed, affect the entire transactions of the people. Arithmetic will hardly suffice to compute losses on a scale of such magnitude. Every bargain, in an industry of three thousand millions a year, is more or less vitiated by a harsh and unnatural change, one way or the other, of the currency.

* This whole discussion supposes this currency in the state it occupied before the war of the Rebellion.

In the mildest form of such a currency, fluctuations to the extent of fifteen per cent are shown by our diagrams to be as commonplace as yearly occurrence can make them. If the yardstick were stretched to 42 inches one year, and shrunk to 30 another, or both should happen the same year, without any possibility of anticipating the change, or any public proclamation of it, that fact would influence manufactures, and every branch of production, greatly; would not only cause injustice to individuals, buyers and sellers, but would have a bearing on the trade and public prosperity; would influence investments, and affect labor no less.

Yet, under the fluctuations of a mixed currency, buyers and sellers of all classes experience injustice as great and as distressing as would result to the dealers in cloth from the falsification of the yardstick. If the great changes are destructive, the more ordinary are constantly embarrassing. Arbitrary interference with currency produces mischief and injustice, just so far as it operates at all. The quantity cannot be artificially increased or diminished, but some one is wronged; either he who relied on obtaining it at ordinary rates to discharge his obligation, or he who trusted to get quite another value from what he does.

Enormous transfers of property take place under this system, without any desert in the party who receives what is another's, and without any fault in the party who gives up what is his own. This it is which makes business a very complicated kind of gambling. This it is which tosses up or pulls down prices enough to ruin the merchant and manufacturer or make their fortunes, while their goods are in their hands, before they can be turned.

Not to insist here that injustice between the parts is injury to the whole, or to dwell on the claims of public morals, if we turn to that large class especially entitled to social and governmental care and consideration, who put out money at interest or invest in stocks, or rely on permanent salaries or wages for support, we shall here find a mischief without relief, a wrong without a remedy. These receive no appreciable benefit from any of the changes of a mixed currency, but all its evils fall heavy and unbroken upon them.

This matter is so near our daily observation as scarcely to need enforcement, so plain as to be scarcely susceptible of illustration. The sad effects of such a currency are strongly set forth in the following extract from an article in the "North-American Review" of January, 1840, understood to have been written by one who has been long and intimately connected with the banking institutions of Massachusetts: —

"It is the standing reproach of our commercial life, that it involves more intellectual suffering from violent fluctuations than any other pursuit. With all our recuperative powers, there is a vast waste of life amongst us as a people, growing out of our financial disasters. Witness the fact, stated to be derived from accurate statistics, that, among one hundred merchants or traders, not over three ever acquire independence. Add to this the other fact, also deduced from trustworthy records, that commercial and financial revolutions produce excessive mortality amongst business men in maritime cities. Here we have the cause and effect. Meanwhile we have statistical data of the still severer calamities to widows and orphans."

PRICE.

Currency performs the function of a standard of value, by fixing the *price* of commodities. In order to examine the subject intelligently, we shall be called first to notice the import of the term "price." It expresses the relation of all objects to a common measure or standard. For example, if the standard were sheep, it might be said that an ox was worth twenty sheep; the price of the ox would be twenty sheep. If the standard were dollars,—that is, certain well-known coins,—we should say that the ox was worth twenty dollars, and that would be its price. And it would be the same, if by dollars we meant only certain pieces of paper, promising to pay these coins.

Price and value are often confounded together. The difference is this: value is the relation which all objects have to each other in exchange; while price is the relation of all commodities to one special object, viz. money or currency.

Price may be increased without increasing value. For example: the price of flour in 1859 was $5; in 1864 it was $10. Yet a barrel of flour had no more value at the latter date than before the war, because it would command no more of other value; that is, of broadcloth or tea, or other commodity.

This discrepancy is found, not only at different periods in the same country, but between different countries at the same time. If all commodities in all countries were always measured by the same standard, price and value would be synonymous; but if, as often happens, a standard is adopted in one country less valuable than that of others, commodities will adapt themselves to the currency, and the agreement between price and value is destroyed in the act of vitiating the standard.

"The value of a thing is its purchasing power: the price of any thing is its power to command gold, silver, or that which constitutes the currency of the country. Value may be expressed in any commodity whatever: price is expressed in one commodity only." — BASCOM, p. 22.

If an inventory of all the property belonging to the people of the United States had been made in 1864, at the then prevailing prices, it would have amounted to nearly double what it was two years before, even though the quantity of all commodities had been identically the same. This, because *prices* were measured not by gold, but by credit, or the promises of government and the banks; but the *value* of all these commodities in the commerce of the world, and among themselves, was no greater than two years before.

The difference between price and value was also strikingly exhibited in the history of the Confederate States during the Rebellion. In both sections of the country, the variations in 1864 were so great as to attract universal attention; but they always exist, in greater or less degree, under a mixed-currency system, because the standard of value, except at short intervals, is not sound. The difference begins to manifest itself whenever the currency is inflated beyond its natural volume, and increases with that inflation.

We here present a table, showing the historical variations in certain commodities, for a series of twenty-six years, under the undisturbed operation of a mixed-currency system.

We have selected, for the purpose, the period 1834–1859, inclusive, because it is the only one for which we have correct data, — that is, well-authenticated returns; and for the additional reason that the period was one of general peace, at home and abroad.

The articles we have selected for this comparison are the most common in use, whose prices are best known and least liable to variations, except from changes in the value of the currency, and therefore, it is supposed, most proper for our illustration.

TABLE V.—*Average Price of Ten Commodities in the New-York Market for Twenty-six Years** (1834–1859), *with the Amount of Currency per capita.*

YEARS	1834.	1835.	1836.	1837.	1838.	1839.	1840.	1841.	1842.	1843.	1844.	1845.	1846.
CURRENCY, PER CAPITA . .	11.82	12.58	16.73	17.61	12.44	13.58	10.70	9.82	8.10	6.18	8.34	9.00	9.94
Coffee	11½	11¾	11½	10½	10	11	10	10	8½	7¼	6½	6¾	7
Leather	16¼	17¼	18½	19	18¾	21½	18½	21	17	16¼	15½	14½	13
Molasses, Muscovado . . .	27	30	39¼	35½	34½	31¾	25½	23½	18¼	21½	27	27¼	29½
Mess Pork	13.71½	16.39	22.50	21.08	21.37	14.80	14.80½	11.12	8.41	9.90	9.28	12.46	10.78
Cheese	7	7¼	9	9½	8	9	7	6	7	5¼	4¾	6¾	7
Rice, ordinary	2.81	3.50	3.68	4.01	4.36	4.36	3.38	3.41	2.80	2.64½	3.03	3.81	3.65½
Salt, Liverpool	1.56	1.77	1.91	2.00	1.74	1.74	1.47½	1.59	1.67	1.46½	1.40½	1.37	1.34
Sugar, Muscovado	7	7¾	9	7	7	7	5¾	6	4½	6	6¼	6	6¾
Tobacco, Kentucky	6½	8	7¾	6½	13	13	8½	8¼	5	4¾	4	4½	4¾
Wool, common	30	33¾	42½	43½	38½	38½	32	27	32	20½	30	27	23½
	19.13¾	22.81¾	29.46½	28.40½	28.35¾	22.21¾	20.73¼	17.93¾	13.80¼	14.82½	14.65½	18.56½	16.69

* Financial Report, 1863.

TABLE V. (continued).—*Average Price of Ten Commodities in the New-York Market for Twenty-six Years* (1834–1859), *with the Amount of Currency per capita.*

YEARS	1847.	1848.	1849.	1850.	1851.	1852.	1853.	1854.	1855.	1856.	1857.	1858.	1859.
CURRENCY, PER CAPITA	9.38	10.67	9.18	10.39	11.86	13.31	13.65	14.95	13.93	14.64	15.50	11.55	14.90
Coffee	7	6	6¾	10½	9	8½	9¼	10	10	11¾	11	10½	11¼
Leather	15¾	13¾	15½	15¾	14½	15¼	18½	21	22½	25½	26½	23	24½
Molasses, Muscovado	27	24½	23½	24¼	25¾	22½	22½	22¼	30½	41½	45½	22½	26½
Mess Pork	14.42	11.11	10.78	10.62½	14.02	15.55	16.09½	13.77½	16.06	18.56	18.47½	17.01	16.38½
Cheese	7	7	6	6½	5¾	7	8½	9½	9½	8½	9½	6½	8½
Rice, ordinary	4.12½	3.17	3.46½	3.18½	3.02½	3.71	3.92½	4.39	4.51½	4.14½	4.34	3.26½	3.66½
Salt, Liverpool	1.35½	1.39	1.29	1.36½	1.34	1.20	1.34½	1.59½	1.03½	92½	80	65½	83
Sugar, Muscovado	6	4	4½	5	5	4¾	4⅛	4¾	5¾	7¾	8½	6	6
Tobacco, Kentucky	5	5¼	6	8¼	8½	6½	7	8	9½	11	14	10½	9
Wool, common	26½	26	29¼	32½	35½	32	41	32½	30	33½	37	30	38
	20.82¼	16.53½	16.45	16.20½	19.42½	21.42½	22.47¾	20.84	22.78¾	25.07½	25.13½	21.92	22.11½

Nº 5.

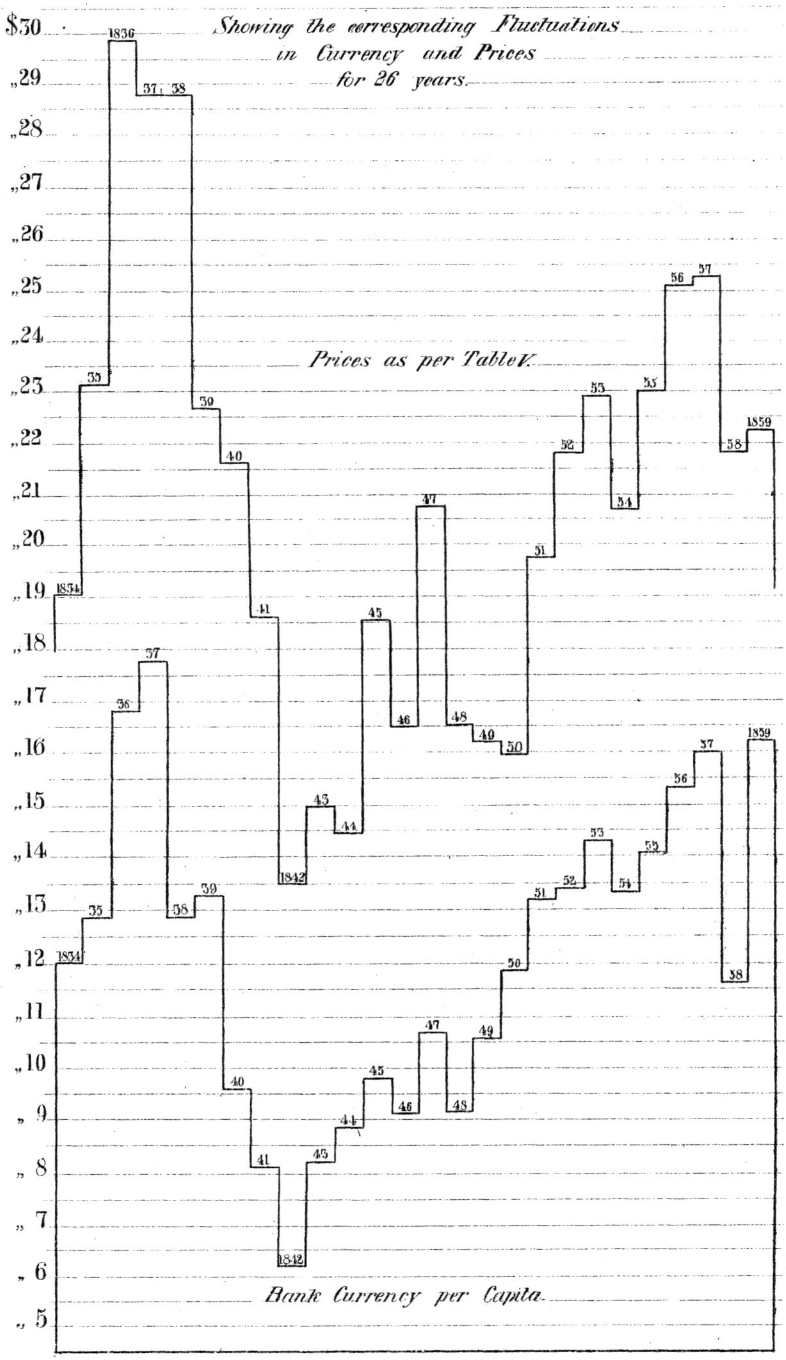
Showing the corresponding Fluctuations
in Currency and Prices
for 26 years.
Prices as per Table V.
Bank Currency per Capita.
$30
„29
„28
„27
„26
„25
„24
„23
„22
„21
„20
„19
„18
„17
„16
„15
„14
„13
„12
„11
„10
„ 9
„ 8
„ 7
„ 6
„ 5
1834
35
1836
37
38
39
40
41
1842
43
44
45
46
47
48
49
50
51
52
53
54
55
56
57
58
1859

These facts are shown geometrically in Diagram No. 5.

This Diagram may require some explanation. The upper line represents the variations in the prices of the ten commodities chosen, for each year, from 1834 to 1859 inclusive, as already given in the tables. The lower line represents the bank currency, per capita, for the corresponding years.

Several important facts appear in this figure. The first to be noticed is the remarkable correspondence between the first and second lines, rising and falling together; proving most conclusively, by their agreement through so long a series of years, that prices depend on the quantity of currency in circulation.

The average currency, per capita, from 1834 to 1859, 26 years, was	$11.99
Average prices during that time	20.80
Highest amount of currency (1837)	17.61
Highest prices (1836)	29.46
Next highest prices (1837)	28.40
Difference between lowest and highest currency	185 per cent.
Difference between lowest and highest prices	101 per cent.

It will be observed, that the difference in prices is not as great, *per cent*, as the difference in currency *per capita*. This is in accordance with what has been already laid down in regard to the unnatural extension of credits, caused by the expansion of the currency. These, of course, require a larger amount for their discharge. The currency has relation to credits as well as commodities.

The correspondence exhibited, in the foregoing tables and diagram, between the quantity of currency and the rate of prices, shows conclusively and impressively the effects of a mixed currency as a standard of value; viz., that as it expands or contracts from arbitrary but resistless causes, so prices are elevated or depressed, — variations which are often sudden and excessive.

In 1857, the highest point of expansion was attained, amounting to 103 per cent over 1849; and the price of commodities had advanced 69 per cent.

The list (see United-States Financial Report, 1863) from which the foregoing table of ten items was selected contains seventy articles, the prices of which correspond essentially to those we have presented.

Two important articles are omitted, viz. cotton and flour, from the list here given, because their prices are more affected by the foreign market than by our own, and may be noticed hereafter.

After making due allowance for those fluctuations which arise from supply and demand and from accidents, the evidence is most conclusive that the quantity of currency in existence does determine, essentially, the prices of commodities; and that, as a mixed currency must fluctuate greatly in amount from its inherent properties, it cannot perform satisfactorily its function as a standard of value.

The foregoing calculations, it will be observed, are made on the currency as estimated per capita. This is regarded as the most correct mode; since, as population increases, it is presumed that the industry and trade of the country is increased proportionally, and, if so, a larger amount of currency will be needed. If the increase of currency is greater than the increase of population, the *per-capita* calculation will show it.

It may be said, at this point, that the same effect on prices would be produced by an equal expansion or contraction of a value currency. Granted; but such rapid and violent changes could not take place. Specie cannot be increased like paper. It costs labor, like corn or cotton, and is subject to the same laws of supply and demand. It can only be brought in because it is wanted,—because some one wishes to give its price for it; but this desire to bring it in decreases regularly with the amount obtained. The more it is introduced into the country, the less, by the natural laws of trade, is it worth; the weaker the inducement to send for it. If, by any chance, it comes in till there is a redundancy, the prices of other things are raised, its own value is therefore lowered, and it flows off till the equilibrium is restored. Such an exportation would cause no more anxiety or alarm than the shipment of an equal value of flour. With a mixed currency, there is the embarrassing fact, that it cannot be exported. The foreign balances must be taken out of the specie basis. We have seen the course of contraction that must ensue.

To observe further the operation of mixed currency as a standard of value, and its effect, not on trade generally, but on ordinary production, let us take the case of the wheat-grower.

A farmer, we will suppose, has a crop of one thousand bushels of wheat, which he sells at ninety cents per bushel, which is thirty cents more than it would bring under a real-money system. Now, the question — which is of great concern to him, and, if to him, to all producers of all commodities — is, whether he gains or loses by this transaction.

Take a single bushel. He gets ninety cents for it. With that, he purchases six pounds of sugar at fifteen cents. This, he observes, is five cents more than he used to pay for sugar, when his wheat was but sixty cents.* He perceives, that, having paid five cents per pound extra on the sugar, he has just lost all the additional price of thirty cents on the bushel of wheat.

On further reflection, he discovers that he is not so well off as when he sold his wheat at the money price of sixty cents, because it cost him more to raise the wheat. He had to pay more for the labor employed in its production, — equal, say, to five cents per bushel, which, on one thousand

* We here suppose, for simplicity of illustration, that the price of wheat may be enhanced, by mixed-currency expansion, to the extent of fifty per cent; but we shall hereafter show how far agricultural products, in general, are permanently influenced by such a currency.

bushels, amounts to fifty dollars; and that sum he will actually lose, although selling his wheat at fifty per cent advance in price.

This transaction of selling one bushel of wheat for six pounds of sugar fairly represents the result of selling the whole crop, and investing the proceeds in other kinds of property; because all commodities have alike risen in price.

But it may be asked, Suppose the farmer paid a debt of nine hundred dollars with the money he obtained for his wheat, has he not gained by the rise in price? If he contracted the debt before the rise, he certainly has made a large gain in the payment of the debt; for, as things were when the debt was contracted, it would have taken fifteen hundred bushels of wheat at sixty cents to pay nine hundred dollars. Here he has gained three hundred dollars, or saved five hundred bushels of wheat, less, be it recollected, the extra expense of fifty dollars in the raising of the crop. His net gain is two hundred and fifty dollars.

But how is it with his creditor? He finds, on re-investing the money in cattle, horses, sheep, ploughs, wagons, and the like, that the nine hundred dollars will purchase but two-thirds as much as when he loaned the money. He has lost three hundred dollars. The farmer promised to pay "dollars;" but he did not, he only paid the promise of dollars; and these promises were so easily made, became so plenty, proved so cheap, that they were really worth but two-thirds of what they professed to be. This he found when he came to use them in buying articles for his family.

But, to carry the inquiry entirely through, we must ask who gained the fifty dollars the farmer, in the case supposed, lost by the extra cost of labor? The laborer? He was certainly paid an extra price; but he gained no value by it, because all the commodities he purchased with the proceeds of his labor were raised more than his wages, so that he lost more than he gained. The rise in price has, in fact, benefited nobody but the debtor, and him only at the expense of the creditor, who was virtually swindled out of a part of his property. This is the final result, when carefully analyzed, of an expansion of prices through the expansion of the currency.

Every advance in price, occasioned by the depreciation of the currency, is sure to be followed ultimately by a return to the specie standard. Suppose that, during an expansion, a farmer, encouraged by the high price of wheat, purchases land to the amount of nine hundred dollars, in the expectation that he can pay for it with one thousand bushels of wheat, at ninety cents per bushel. A contraction takes place, the price of wheat goes down to sixty cents, and, to pay his note of nine hundred dollars, he must sell fifteen hundred bushels of wheat. He has lost five hundred bushels, just what the debtor, in the other case supposed, gained, less fifty dollars which he will now save in the labor cost of his wheat.

We here see that the effect of raising prices without increasing values is to vitiate all existing contracts to pay money. If the farmer, in the case supposed, had promised to pay so many bushels of wheat, all would have been well; but he promised to pay dollars; and, when the price of wheat was measured by dollars under a contraction, it made the difference stated.

Much misapprehension arises from confounding special and general prices, or the price of an individual article, as distinguished from that of the great mass of commodities. We are told that a variety of considerations enter into and affect prices; viz., demand and supply, cost of production, &c., &c. All this is perfectly true of an individual article, whose price may and does vary from time to time, as compared with other commodities, under the operation of these causes. One article may be very high, while all others are low, or the reverse; but this does not tend to disprove the principle, that general prices are determined by the quantity of the currency. We can take into view all the circumstances which act upon a particular commodity, and by which it is made, for the time being, an exception to the general rule, without disturbing the principle laid down, or casting any doubt upon its operation.

CHAPTER X.

EFFECTS OF A MIXED CURRENCY.

WE stated two principal questions in regard to mixed currency: —

1st, Does it perform satisfactorily the functions of money?

2d, What, and how great, are its effects on public interests, beyond the proper effects of value currency?

In the four chapters immediately preceding, we have discussed the first question, with a result unfavorable to such a currency. We now approach the second of these questions, — What are the effects of mixed currency?

I. A mixed currency endangers domestic tranquillity. This is a proposition which we shall consider solely with reference to society in the United States.

That mixed-currency banks can never, in fact, fulfil their agreements, if called on to do so, we have already shown; and, since they are ever liable to such calls, there is constant danger from this source. At any moment, there may reasonably arise, through this cause, such general dissatisfaction among the lower classes as shall tend to extensive disturbances of the public peace.

This danger is greatly enhanced by the fact, that, within the last forty years, there has been created a vast system of savings institutions, which receive the money individuals are disposed to deposit with them, and promise to return it on demand, or at short notice; generally on demand.

Nº 6.

Bank Liabilities in Massachusetts 1860 and basis of Specie.

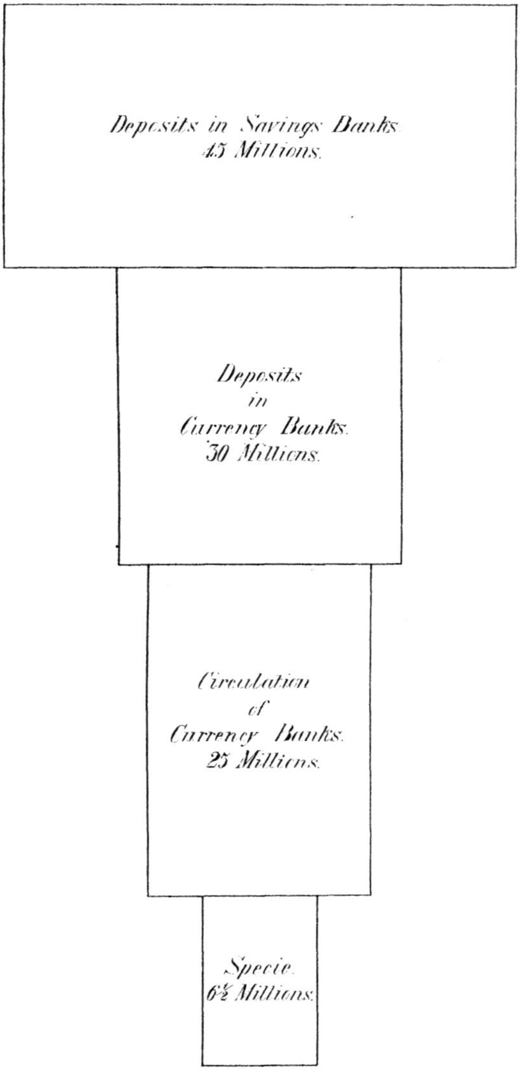

Liabilities 100 Millions. *Specie 6½ Millions.*

Now, should any cause operate by which confidence in the solvency of the general banking system of the country is shaken, it will naturally, nay, inevitably happen that a run will be made on the savings institutions. These can only meet their engagements by drawing on the banks. But, if these have all their resources strained to meet the ordinary wants of the business community, how can the drafts of the saving banks be met? How can currency be supplied for this extraordinary demand? This question can only be intelligently answered by reference to the condition of both these kinds of institutions.

We will, for this purpose, take the currency of Massachusetts as it stood in 1860:—

The savings banks had on deposit		$45,000,000
The currency banks had	deposits	30,000,000
	circulation	25,000,000
Total		$100,000,000
The currency banks had specie		6,500,000
Difference		$93,500,000

This is exhibited in Currency Diagram No. 6.

Here, then, are legal immediate demands, upon the currency banks, of fifty-five millions; and, upon the savings banks, of forty-five millions. Suppose there should arise some dissatisfaction, or public uneasiness, which should prompt to a run on both these kinds of banks. It certainly is possible, not to say probable. Suppose that the institutions for savings are called on for only one-fourth of their deposits. They must look to the banks for eleven millions of currency at once. The banks begin to pay out their bills; but the specie is at once demanded, and of that they have but six and one-half millions against their own immediate liabilities of fifty-five millions. They could not stand a run of two days, because their own deposits would be drawn in specie just as soon as the real state of affairs was discovered. The banks must, therefore, suspend at once. What would naturally follow in a time of great public excitement, when the interests of some party or faction required a general breaking-up of society?

It is not enough to evade this, by saying that such an event has never happened, though the banks have several times suspended. That is quite true; yet it does not follow that it never will. Previous suspensions have originated in commercial causes. Suppose, on the other hand, a run were made on account of political or social disturbances; that the laboring class — factory operatives, railroad gangs, the servants in our families — were incited to demand their deposits in the savings institutions. Could they not prostrate the entire currency in twenty-four hours, by merely demanding their just dues?

Whether such a probability is remote or uncertain, it does not seem wise to maintain a system which can, by any possibility, produce results so disastrous; especially, if there are no advantages whatever in such a state of things.

Premonitory symptoms have not been wanting of such a catastrophe as, under aggravating circumstances, might overthrow all the moneyed institutions of the country, and even endanger the government itself.

We are not the homogeneous people we were. We have elements of weakness and discord that did not exist in earlier times. We have, especially, a large foreign population, as much interested as any other in the funds of our savings institutions, which might, at any moment, if provoked to do so, throw our whole banking system into suspension.

It cannot be wise to ignore these palpable facts, or the consequences that, in the natural course of things, are likely to come out of them. The danger can only be removed by a change of system.

II. A mixed currency has a demoralizing influence upon a community, industrially and socially.

If what has been said in regard to this kind of currency is correct, such an influence cannot for a moment be questioned. If it excites to wild and extravagant speculation at one time, and plunges its victims into bankruptcy and ruin without fault at another; if it excites hopes and expectations which must necessarily come to disappointment and distress; if it increases to an enormous extent the natural risks of trade, and exposes all business operations to an incalculable hazard, — then the mercantile character and the general tone of morals cannot but be unfavorably affected.

The influences that hold men to strict probity, steady industry, and a strong sense of honor, are feeble enough, and have enemies enough, without the discouragements and embarrassments arising from such causes as we have described.

Society should place its premium on virtue, and not on vice.

Those who have witnessed the terrible convulsions occurring in the United States within forty years, know but too well how sad has been the effect on individual and national character.

It is unnecessary to dwell upon a point so evident, and so generally admitted by all who understand the matter; yet its recognition could not properly be omitted in the examination of the mixed-currency system.

III. A mixed currency endangers the national safety in war.

With the existing ideas and institutions of society, and while no preparations are made in time of peace to prevent the recurrence of war, but every effort to meet it, and thus, of course, to strengthen and perpetuate the war system, it becomes a matter of great interest to inquire as to the effects of a mixed currency on the safety of a nation in the event of war.

We have already shown that a mixed currency is greatly affected by a demand for specie to send abroad. Hence, as war must always call for an extraordinary importation of foreign merchandise and materials, and as such extraordinary importation must require the shipment of specie, a contraction and panic, or speedy suspension, must be the certain consequence.

Again, since so great a part of a mixed currency usually consists of credit, and since credit rests wholly on confidence, any thing which impairs the latter compels a contraction or withdrawal of the currency.

Now, war generally, we may say uniformly, does this: for how long it may last, how great may be the demand for money, how large the destruction of capital, and what the final issue, must be a matter of doubt; and therefore its occurrence always impairs public confidence to a greater or less extent.

These two causes, then, are at once brought to bear upon a mixed currency with fatal effect. The result has always been, and always must be, that, under such circumstances, the mixed-currency banks suspend; because their circulation cannot be withdrawn at the time without producing universal bankruptcy, annihilating their own capital, and stopping the wheels of government.

It was so in England during the war with Napoleon; in the United States during the war of 1812, and in the time of the great Rebellion.

What comes in consequence of all this? The nation is obliged to carry on its vast pecuniary operations with a broken-down currency. This, of course, involves the finances in great embarrassment, vastly increases the public expenditures and the national indebtedness. The whole financial system of the country is crippled, and becomes as weak as its currency.

No better illustration of the truth of this statement was perhaps ever afforded than that found in the experience of the United States during its great struggle.

The country was suddenly involved in a stupendous war,

— technically, only a civil war, but, practically, a great international struggle, so vast were its dimensions, so strictly was it sectional; a conflict between two different civilizations, on different though contiguous portions of the American continent.

At the commencement of the struggle, the currency, as we have before said, amounted, circulation and deposits, to four hundred and sixty millions against eighty-three millions of specie. Upon the mere threat of secession, so greatly did it impair public confidence that the banks at the South began to suspend; and their example was followed until most of the Western, and many of the Eastern, were in a state of suspension. After the first shock had passed by, most of the banks in the loyal States resumed specie payments; but the large demands of the government, in the course of about a twelvemonth, compelled a universal suspension by both the national treasury and the banks, and the whole country was thrown upon an irredeemable paper currency.

All this happened, not because the currency was so redundant, but because it was so unsound. Had it been based in full on specie, this disastrous result would have been avoided.

Now, if it ever could be supposed politic or safe to send away the real money of a country and live on credit, if this could ever be regarded as good economy or statesmanship, when should it be done? When the nation is in prosperity, and does not need this little gain, or when it is strained to agony in the struggles of war? If this is really a resource, should it be spent in time of peace for extra imports of wine and silks, or reserved to the great trial of life for the people, when it may bring back the munitions of war?

If we were to dispense with three hundred millions of gold that form our material currency, was it wise to send it off in years of quiet and prosperity, instead of reserving it to the decisive hour of our nationality?

In time of war, a mixed currency always becomes an unmixed paper currency. Being at all times really inconvertible, any disturbance in public affairs which destroys, or even essentially impairs public confidence, will cause a general suspension of the mixed-currency banks, and, of course, of the government, and the substitution of a credit for a value currency.

If this is true, — and all the facts of history go to prove it, — then every nation, which, in time of peace, relies upon a mixed currency, must, in time of war, suffer all the disasters incident to an irredeemable paper currency; must pay a great deal more in all its purchases, require larger loans, and accumulate greater debt, — greater in proportion as the currency is deficient in the element of value.

"A nation may almost as well go to war with paper guns as a paper currency." — J. Y. Smith.

The truth of this was certainly very strongly exhibited in the experience of the government of the United States during the Rebellion. The failure of the currency compelled the national legislature to adopt the arbitrary measure of making its own irredeemable notes legal tender.

This was a palpable violation of the most sacred rights of the people, and involved the treasury in a labyrinth of embarrassment and wasteful expenditure. Necessity, which knows no law, dèmanded all this; and there may be little or no blame on the immediate agents. The law of value had already been violated by the introduction, in peace, of the element of credit into that currency, which the government was obliged to make use of in time of war. It was not easy to change its character at such a crisis, and it was allowed to go on to its proper consequences.

If these are the natural and inevitable results of a mixed currency in such an event, is it not true that a people imposing on themselves a mixed currency can *never be* financially "prepared for war"?

IV. A mixed currency discourages domestic manufactures, disturbs the proper relation of exports and imports, and puts the balance of trade against the people employing the greater proportion of credit.

These effects will be recognized as injurious by all classes of persons; but those who are so solicitous for the positive encouragement of domestic manufactures, and for the restraint of imports, as to favor the enactment of prohibitory or protective laws imposing duties on the foreign article, will, of course, most fully appreciate and deeply feel this tendency of a mixed currency.

The course of this will be best observed in an illustration from the manufacture of a specific article: —

"Suppose that a certain kind of broadcloth can be afforded by the foreign manufacturer, delivered at New York, for two dollars per yard; the same article might be made in this country, but would *cost* two dollars a yard, without any profit whatever. Of course, then, we cannot afford to make the article. The government, in order to encourage its production here, lays a duty upon the imported article of fifty cents per yard; but, at the same time, establishes banks which manufacture a mixed currency, and double the natural amount of money. The American manufacturer now proceeds to erect his mills; but wages and materials have so advanced in price, by the expansion of the currency, that it costs him twenty-five to fifty per cent more than it otherwise would have done. He builds machinery; but this also costs him proportionably high. He proceeds to purchase raw materials, and employ labor in manufacturing; but all are advanced in price for the same reason. His own expenses for living are also greater; and, should he be obliged to hire money, that will generally be found to have advanced in price, or rate of interest. Under these circumstances, he cannot make the cloth so as to afford a profit; and it will not be surprising if he should clamor for more protection. But it may be said, that the same causes that have advanced the expenses of living, and, consequently, of labor, will equally have advanced the price of broadcloth. Not so. The price of the broadcloth will be determined by the rate at which it can be afforded by the foreign manufacturer; and if he can pay the duty of fifty cents per yard, and yet obtain a fair profit, he will send all the market demands.

"There is another view of the matter. Suppose we would export our plain cottons, for example, to India. We there meet the English article, made under a currency more valuable than our own, which can consequently be afforded for less; since, with the *same* amount of the money of India (*i.e.*, value money), the English manufacturer can pay for much more labor in England than the American manufacturer can in America. It is true that the *rate of wages* is lower in England than in this country; but, *in addition to this*, England has the very great advantage of a currency nearer the currency of international exchange, which is always strictly *value money*. In such a state of things, not all the tariffs that ever were or ever will be imposed can adequately protect our manufactures. So far as they have arisen or flourished, it has been in spite of these disadvantages." *

During the continuance of the compromise tariff, established in 1832, and which terminated in 1842, the currency varied from $11.82 to $17.61 per capita, equal to an expansion of more than fifty per cent; while, during the same period, prices (as shown by table V., page 177) fluctuated to a greater extent. The variation in prices was larger even than the percentage of protective duties.

So the tariff of 1842, which began to take effect in 1843, when the currency was $6.18 per capita, was more than counterbalanced by the expansion of the currency to $9.94 in 1846. But the manufacturer suffered as much from the periodical contractions as from the expansions that preceded them; for while, by the latter, the duties were rendered nugatory, all business men met great losses from the failures and the general derangement and stagnation which the former produced. No tariff of reasonable extent, such as the people of the whole nation would endure, can ever place the domestic manufacturer in a position of security and of reliable profit, while competing with such an immense advance in prices as must certainly accompany an expansion of the currency. Nor can it fail to be true, that the normal industrial development of any country, in which such a

* Walker on Money and Mixed Currency, p. 39.

No. 7.

Showing the different Tariffs of the United States with the corresponding consumption of Foreign Merchandise.

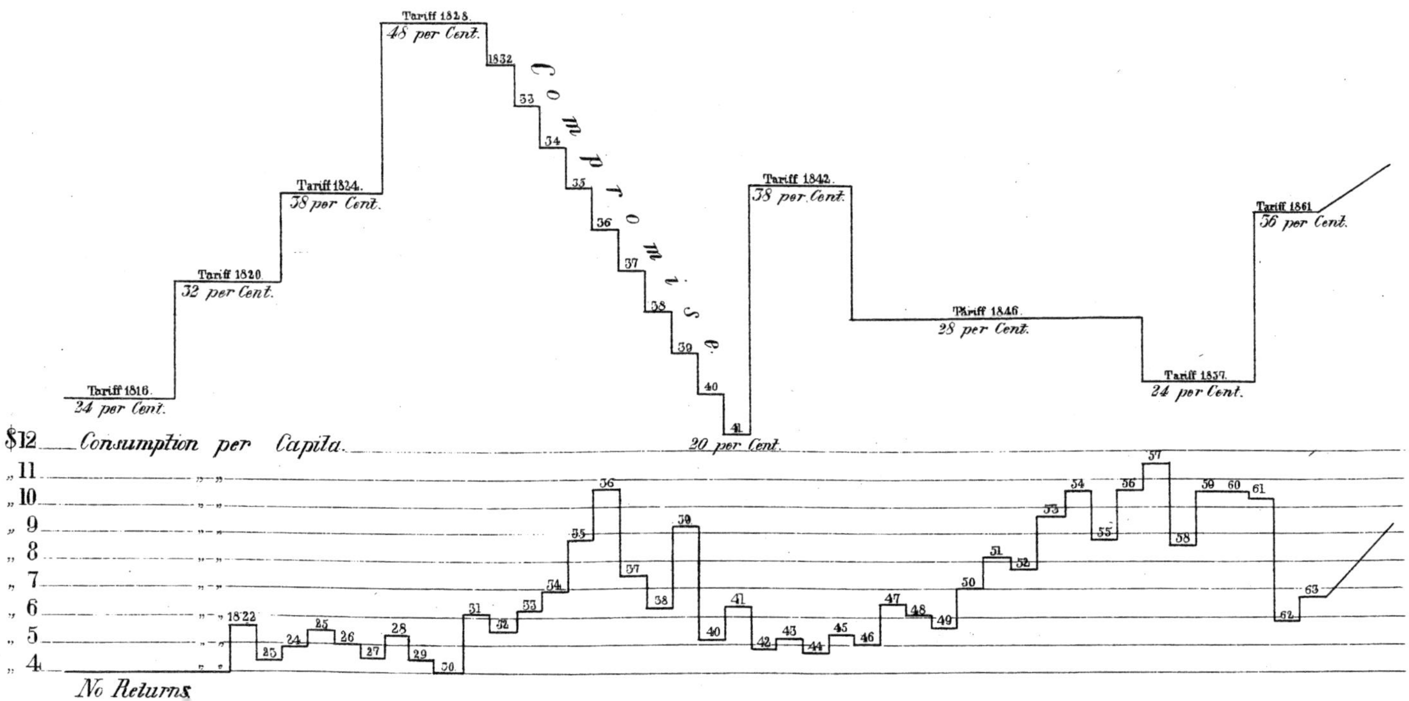

currency exists, must, to a very great degree, be interrupted or distorted. All ordinary business calculations are overturned. An element of hazard is introduced, fatal to the shrewdest schemes.

The terrific struggles through which American manufacturers have passed, ever since the establishment of the first tariff in 1816, have been caused, not by foreign competition, solely or mostly, but by a false and delusive domestic currency. Fully as we are opposed to the policy of protective duties, we are still more opposed to that system of currency which neutralizes them, and renders the legitimate success of home manufactures impossible, even after so great sacrifices to introduce them.

There is a still more striking view of the connection between protection and currency.

It is generally believed that high tariff duties restrict the importation and consumption of foreign merchandise. It is a popular cry, that "government ought to lay heavy duties, so as to prevent an adverse balance of trade, and the consequent shipment of specie abroad."

It is true, as a principle, that, the greater the price, the less the consumption; and that, as the imposition of taxes on the foreign article increases price, so it must, other things equal, decrease consumption. But other things are not equal. They have not been so in this country during this century. The facts in the case do not show that heavy duties necessarily reduce the consumption of foreign articles. On the contrary, it is found that the largest importation has often taken place during the existence of the highest tariffs. Diagram No. 7 will exhibit the relations of the tariffs to the amount of imports, from 1816 to 1861.

Of this diagram, showing the tariffs and the consumption of foreign commodities under each, it must be remarked, that the line indicating the different tariffs does not express with precision the actual percentage of tax imposed by each, because that is not practicable: it is only given as an approximation. Each of the tariffs imposed different rates per centum on different items; and some of the tariffs have a large proportion of specific duties, or so much per yard, gallon, or pound; so that the exact per centum cannot be ascertained, nor is this necessary to our purpose. We are able to determine, with sufficient accuracy, the general percentage of each tariff, to enable us to judge whether the consumption rises and falls in correspondence.

The tariff of 1816 was the first ever laid for protection, and is estimated at twenty-four per cent. Four years afterwards, viz. in 1820, the tariff was increased. Eight years afterwards (1828), a very great advance was made, which is placed in our estimate at forty-eight per cent; but it may have been much higher than that, as many articles were charged with high specific duties, amounting to from one hundred to two hundred per cent. It was almost prohibitory, and gave such umbrage to South Carolina and other cotton-growing States, that the celebrated compromise tariff of 1832 was enacted, which reduced the duties at the rate of ten per centum, on all over twenty per cent, for ten years; so that, at the end of that time, there would only remain the twenty-per-cent duty.

This tariff came down to its minimum in 1842, a time of great depression of prices and trade, growing out of the monetary revulsion through which the country had just passed. A strong and successful appeal was made for an increase of duties; and the tariff known as that of 1842 was established, giving high protection. This occasioned so much dissatisfaction, that, after four years, the rates were again reduced by the tariff of 1846. This remained in operation for the unprecedented period of eleven years, when another reduction was effected by the tariff of 1857. This lasted for four years, when the necessities of the treasury, in consequence of war, required the imposition of higher duties in 1861; since which they have been still further advanced.

№ 8

Showing the Volume of the Currency and the Imports for Consumption for 26 years.

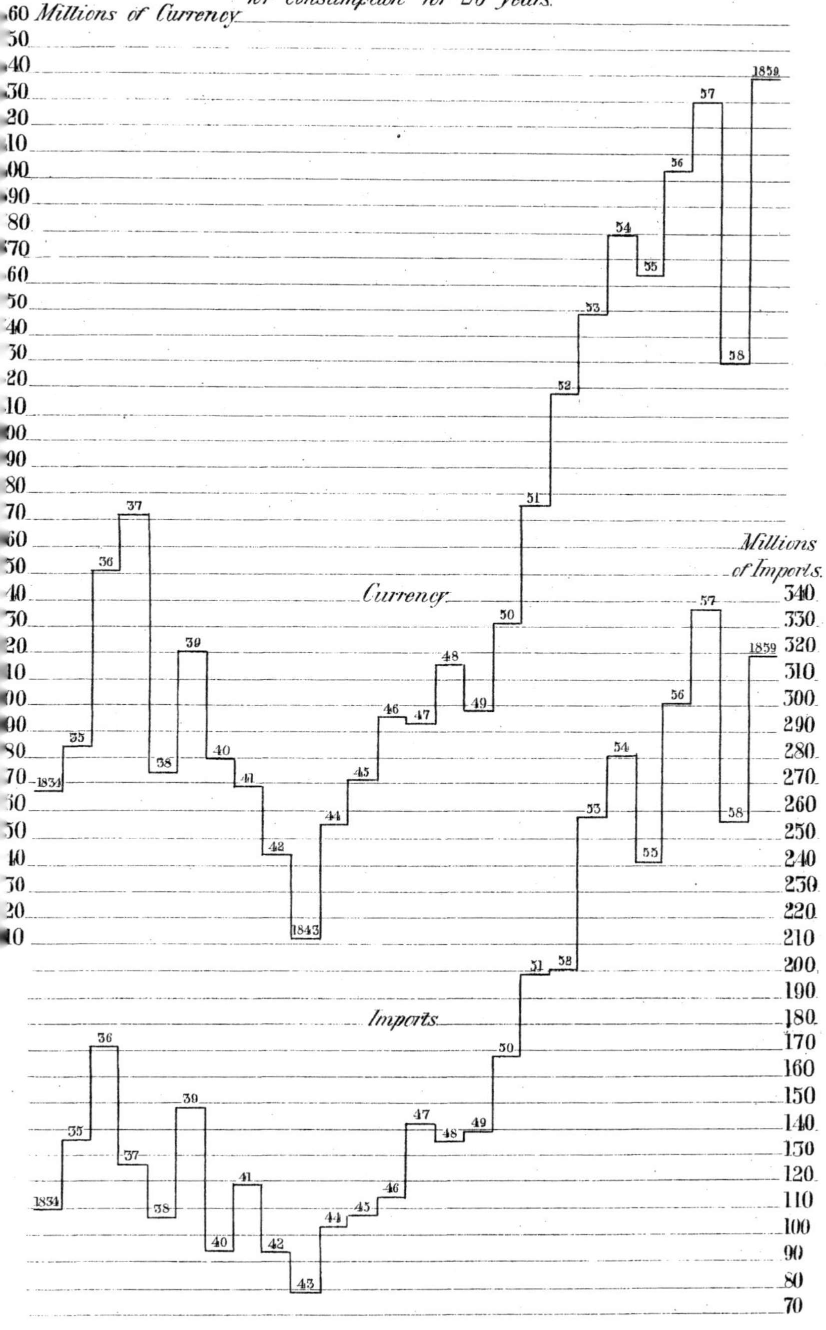

With these explanations of the diagram, we are prepared to inquire into its teachings.

Is there any such correspondence between the two lines as to indicate that one is governed by the other? Does it appear, that, as the tariff rises, importations fall off; that, as it is lowered, importations increase? Certainly not. We can perceive no such striking correspondence between the two lines as to lead us to believe that importations are governed greatly by the tariff.

There seems to be a disturbing influence which deranges the natural movement of the line of consumption.

The two lines clearly do not show such a correspondence as to prove that importations are uniformly governed by the tariff.

A reference to Diagram No. 8 will, we think, show the disturbing cause, or rather by what law importations are controlled.

Here we find a correspondence so uniform and persistent as to decide the question, beyond cavil, that the demand for foreign merchandise depends upon the quantity of currency in the country; and, as that increases or diminishes, so does the consumption of imported articles.

The immense expansion of 1836 carried the consumption up to $10.93 per capita, under a medium tariff; while, under a still lower one, in 1840, the consumption was but $5.21. Whereas, if consumption is governed by the tariff, it should have been higher than in 1836.

According to the natural effects of the tariff (the enhanced price of foreign commodities), consumption should be highest when the tariff is lowest, and *vice versa*. We have seen that such correspondence does not take place. We then conclude that some other force or influence operates to neutralize the power of protective duties, and even reverse the natural effect. The last diagram proves the existence of such a cause, and shows its effects on imports.

Hence we may lay it down as a principle, that a sound currency is more important, as affording protection against foreign competition, than a high tariff.

We close our remarks on this subject, by quoting the following forcible and just statement, found in the "Bankers' Magazine" (New York) for 1859–60, page 2: —

"So far as the currency of a country is alloyed, so far as any thing inferior to bullion is allowed to ride as a dead weight on bullion's back, it is of little consequence whether such dead weight be composed of lead or copper, paper or leather; nor, so far as the country's home trade is concerned, does it matter whether the substitute for bullion circulates in distinct pieces, or is incorporated into the gold and silver coin at the mint. It is of great importance to the profits of our foreign trade, however, that every fraction of gold and silver in our currency should have its own proper share of alloy, or paper inseparably attached to it; so that foreign producers, after they have taken *paper-money prices* of us for their goods, shall not wind up their business (as they have done hitherto) by palming their share of paper money upon us at par for actual gold. As things now are managed, American trade and industry are made to *buy* paper at the banks at the price of gold, and sell gold to foreigners at the price of paper."

CHAPTER XI.

EFFECTS OF A MIXED CURRENCY (*concluded*).

V. A MIXED currency causes unnatural and extreme fluctuations in the rate of interest.

If a mixed currency is in its nature constantly fluctuating, at one time very redundant, at another very scarce, it would seem to follow, as a necessary consequence, that the rate of interest, which is merely the sum paid for the use of money, or currency, would be equally so. Practically, we find that such is the fact. While the currency is *in the process* of expansion, and is enlarged by new issues from day to day, money must be plenty, and the rate of interest low.

When the currency has become largely increased, and speculation has been engendered by the rise of prices, the demand for money will increase faster than the supply, and the rate of interest will begin to advance.

When the banks have arrived at that point at which they must of necessity contract, and they begin to take in their currency, and, of course, to create a scarcity of *the means of paying debts*, then the rate of interest will rise to a very high point, not unfrequently to four or six times its natural rate.

The indebtedness which the expansion has encouraged must now be met, at all events and at any sacrifice. Sales of property cannot be made for cash, because all cash resources are needed to meet existing indebtedness, rapidly maturing; and, consequently, a great pressure is made upon the money market. The severity of this is indicated by the rate of interest.

Such being the facts in the case, we need not be surprised to find that the highest rates of interest are paid at times when there is far more than the average amount of currency.

On the other hand, when indebtedness has been discharged, both by the banks and individuals, and the currency reduced to very moderate dimensions, we find the rate of interest very low.

Take the years 1837 and 1857. Interest was up to thirty-six per cent; yet there was a greater amount of currency, per capita, then in use, than ever before or since. Take the years 1842–43, for an opposite example, when there was less currency than ever before. Money was very plenty and very cheap.

This law has governed the rate of interest at all times under our currency, and is strikingly exhibited in our Diagram No. 9, inserted herewith.

By this diagram, we see,—

First, The frequent and extreme fluctuations in the rate of interest.

Second, That the highest rates of interest occur when there is the greatest expansion of the currency, as witness 1836, 1839, 1854, and 1857.

Third, That the lowest rates of interest are found where there is the smallest amount of currency, as in 1843–45.

Fourth, We observe some remarkable exceptions to these general facts.

In 1834, we find the interest up to twenty-four per cent, while, in the following year, it was down to five. This is easily explained by those cognizant of the facts. The United-States Bank then in existence was extremely desirous of recharter; and, to secure this, it was thought necessary to produce a tremendous pressure in the money market, or, in the expressive language of the day, "put on the screws." This result was a high rate of interest.

The following year, 1835, the bank took the opposite course, and interest fell below the natural rate.

In 1836, there was a great expansion of the currency, as shown in the lower line of the diagram. Speculation was rife, the banks could not meet the demand for money, and interest went up to thirty per cent. In 1837, the banks suspended, then issued freely, and interest went down to a low point. In 1838, the work of contraction began; a multitude of banks in the West and South failed, and the pressure upon the solvent banks became great; interest went up to eighteen per cent. The year 1839 witnessed still greater distress for money. Resumption of specie payments by the banks began to take place, and consequently a great contraction of the currency. There was also a very large exportation of specie that year; and, by these combined causes, the rate of interest ran up to thirty-six per cent. In 1840, on the other hand, more specie was imported than exported. The indebtedness of the country had been, in

№ 9

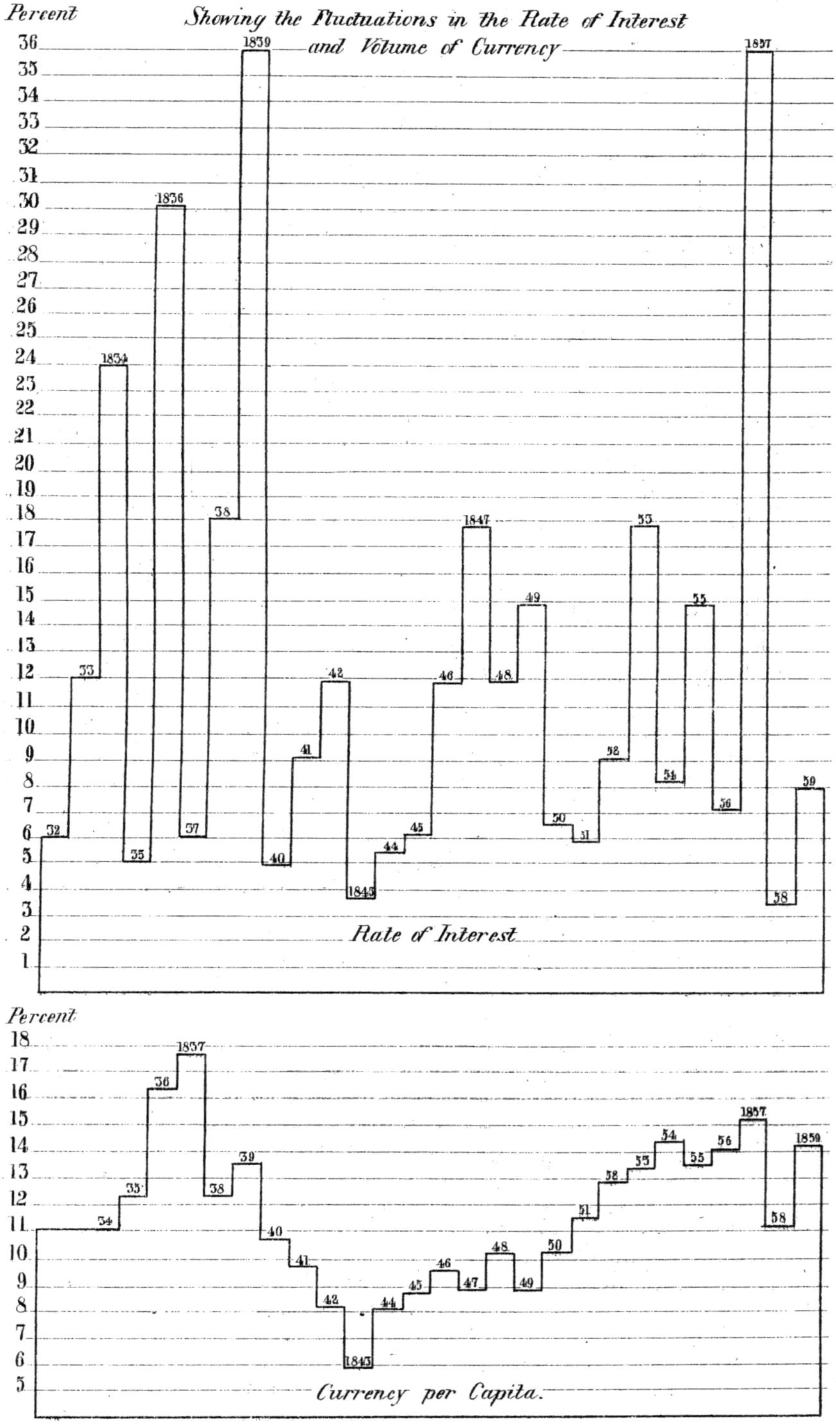
Showing the Fluctuations in the Rate of Interest and Volume of Currency
Percent
36
35
34
33
32
31
30
29
28
27
26
25
24
23
22
21
20
19
18
17
16
15
14
13
12
11
10
9
8
7
6
5
4
3
2
1
32
33
1834
35
1836
37
38
1839
40
41
42
1843
44
45
46
1847
48
49
50
51
52
53
54
55
56
1857
58
59
Rate of Interest
Percent
18
17
16
15
14
13
12
11
10
9
8
7
6
5
34
35
36
1837
38
39
40
41
42
1843
44
45
46
47
48
49
50
51
52
53
54
55
56
1857
58
1859
Currency per Capita.

great measure, discharged, and money was plenty. Interest was down to five or six per cent. In 1841, there was again an export of specie, and also in 1842; and the rate of interest went up to nine and twelve per cent. But, in 1843, the lowest point was reached, more than twenty millions of gold were imported, and money was a drug. Interest was, for a while, almost nominal. Large amounts were negotiated as low as three and a half per cent.

From this time forward, we have only the *natural* results of a mixed currency in its fluctuations. In 1847, the rate of interest was high, — eighteen per cent, — though the currency was not redundant. This was the year of the Irish famine; and we imported twenty-two millions of gold above the exports. From 1849 to 1857, the currency was constantly increasing. Severe fluctuations in the money market took place, but no grand revulsion until 1857, when so great was the inflation of the currency, and consequently the general credit of the country, that an explosion took place; interest going up to thirty-six per cent. All these facts are significant, and form an essential part of the history of mixed-currency banking.

The comparative fluctuations in the United States and England is shown by the following table of rates of interest from 1844, when Sir Robert Peel's act was passed, up to 1858, inclusive, — fifteen years. The rates of the Bank of England are from official sources: those in the United States are furnished by one* who has kept himself acquainted with the street rates in the city of Boston. The banks being prohibited by legislation from taking more than a fixed per cent, the actual value of interest, or the use of money, can only be ascertained from quotations of transactions outside. These are *essentially* correct, as applied, not only to the particular market in which they were taken, but to the other large money markets of the country.

* Joseph G. Martin, Esq., Boston, author of many valuable statistical tables, &c.

TABLE VI., *showing the Fluctuations in the Rates of Interest in England and the United States from* 1844 *to* 1858, *inclusive.*

YEAR.	Rate, Bank of England.	Remarks.	Rate, United States.
1844.	4 — 2½	Passage of English Bank Act.	4 — 5½
1845.	2½— 3½	. . . .	5 — 6
1846.	3½— 3	. . . .	4 —12
1847.	3 — 8	Irish famine	7 —18
1848.	5 — 3	. . . .	12 —18
1849.	3 — 2½	. . . .	7 —15
1850.	2½— 3	. . . .	6½—10½
1851.	3	. . . .	6 —16
1852.	3 — 2	. . . .	5½— 9
1853.	2 — 5	. . . .	6 —18
1854.	5 — 5½	Crimean war	8 —18
1855.	5 — 6	. . . .	6½—15
1856.	6 — 4½	. . . .	7 —11
1857.	5½—10	The great revulsion	9 —36
1858.	9 — 2½	. . . .	3½— 9

The average rate of interest in the Bank of England, from 1844 to 1858, as computed from tables in the "Merchants' Magazine," vol. li. page 465, was . . . . 3.82 per cent.
Approximate average for the same time in the United States. . . . . 10.5 „

We say *approximate average;* for the data are too imperfect in this country to give any exact results. The average of 10.5 may be somewhat too high; and yet, as computed upon transactions made in Boston, New York, Philadelphia, Baltimore, Cincinnati, Chicago, and St. Louis, it is doubtful whether it is much in excess of the true average rate.

The dividends which the banks of this country make, after paying heavy taxes and general expenses, show, that the rate of interest they obtain, notwithstanding the legal restriction, must be high with them; and it is notorious that interest "outside" at all times, when money is in demand, is greater than that charged by the banks. The interest paid upon mortgages and other permanent investments is most commonly six per cent. It is mainly on business paper that the high rates are obtained.

TABLE VII., *showing the Fluctuations in the Rate of Interest at the Bank of England for 160 Years, divided into different Periods.*

DATE.	Term.	No. of Changes.	Average Term.	Rate of Interest.	
	Years.		Y'rs m. d'ys		
1704 to 1814, inc.	111	5	20 5 20	4 to 5	Bank in suspension last 17 years.
1815 to 1835, "	21	3	7 0 0	4 to 5	Bank in suspension first 6 years.
1836 to 1843, "	8	8	1 0 0	4 to 6	
1844 to 1858, "	15	49	3 2	2 to 10	Bank Act of 1844 suspended 1847.
1859 to 1863, "	5	44	2 8	2 to 8	Bank Act suspended 1857.

The foregoing table presents a striking view of the mixed currency of England.

1st, The great contrast between the stability of the rate of interest for the first one hundred and forty years and the last twenty years; only sixteen changes in the rate during the former, and ninety-three changes during the latter period.

2d, The great and violent fluctuations within the last twenty years, ranging from two to ten per cent, corresponding to the variations in the United States from four to thirty-six.

3d, We observe the several suspensions of the Bank of England, and of the Bank Act of 1844.

4th, We observe the same succession of panics as have been witnessed in the United States. Sir Robert Peel, in his speech on the suspension of the Bank-charter Act in 1847, specifies the following: "the panics of 1784, 1793, 1810, 1819, 1826, and 1837." The panics of 1847 and 1857 have since been added.

Between the years 1784 and 1857, inclusive, — a period of seventy-three years, — there have been eight panics, or, on an average, one in nine years, if we reckon that of 1784.

They correspond very nearly with those panics which have occurred in the United States. And here it may not be improper to present some additional facts in regard to the British currency, showing in how far it corresponds to our own in its character and effects.

THE CURRENCIES OF GREAT BRITAIN AND THE UNITED STATES COMPARED.

From 1844 to 1859, inclusive (sixteen years), the average circulation of all the banks — English, Irish, and Scotch — was thirty-seven millions sterling; average specie, eighteen millions.

We have not at hand any account of the deposits in any of these banks, except the Bank of England. In that, the average of deposits, public and private, was about sixteen millions, while the circulation was nearly twenty-one. It is well known that the deposits of the United Kingdom are made chiefly in those joint-stock banks which do not issue currency, but are confined to the operations of legitimate banking. In addition to this, we have the consideration that the Bank of England receives very largely of public deposits, which go to make up the sum already stated. We shall therefore be safe in estimating that the deposits of all the currency banks of the United Kingdom are less in proportion to their circulation than are those of the Bank of England. If, then, we assume the deposits to be on the average, in all the remaining banks, fifty per cent of the circulation, we shall have the following result for the currency of Great Britain: —

Bank of England's circulation	21,000,000
„ „ deposits	16,000,000
Other Banks' circulation	16,000,000
„ „ deposits (estimated)	8,000,000
	61,000,000
Total specie, as before	18,000,000

This would be equal to nearly thirty per cent against eighteen per cent in the currency of the United States, showing a considerable superiority in quality.

But this is only a partial view of the matter. The Bank of England issues no notes of less denomination than five pounds. The banks of Ireland and Scotland issue none less than one pound (or five dollars); while, in the United States generally, bank-notes are issued as low as one dollar (or four shillings sterling). This makes a vast difference in the amount of specie in the hands of the people.

All small transactions are made in gold. A traveller may pass months in England, and expend thousands of dollars, without ever seeing a bank-note in the hands of anybody.

Probably it would not be extravagant to suppose, that there was, on an average, a sum equal to two pounds to each inhabitant. It has, indeed, been estimated much higher; but allowing only two pounds each, equal to ten dollars, we should have, on a population of twenty-six millions, fifty-two millions sterling, equal to, say, two hundred and fifty million dollars.

From the foregoing statements, it will be seen how much greater is the stability of the currency of Great Britain than that of the United States.

The currency of Scotland approaches more nearly to that of this country than any other section of Great Britain. One-pound notes are issued to the extent of two-thirds of its whole circulation; and the proportion of specie held by the banks is smaller.

The consequence is, that monetary affairs are more fluctuating, and the number of bankruptcies greater, than in the other part of Great Britain.

There are no reliable statistics by which to determine the relative proportion of failures in each of the different mixed-currency countries of the world; but, had we the data, it would undoubtedly appear that the proportion of failures in each country was governed strictly by the character of its currency.

In the United States, where the currency for the last thirty-five years has been weaker than any other in the world, the proportion of failures are well known to be greater than anywhere else. The common estimate has been ninety in one hundred. There is nothing mysterious in this result. It is the natural consequence of a fluctuating and unreliable currency. Notwithstanding this greater stability of the English currency, as compared with that of the United States, it is still so essentially defective, so alloyed or adulterated with the element of credit, that it produces in degree, though not in extent, the same evils suffered in the United States. The commerce of the vast empire of Great Britain is kept in a state of continual perturbation. The "reserve" of the Bank of England is watched with the greatest solicitude: as it rises or falls, so every business man in the nation is affected. This has become more strikingly apparent within the last twenty years. The fluctuations in the bank rate of interest have been more frequent and violent than previously, and seem to be growing worse from year to year.

We annex a Table VIII., showing the bank reserve for each year from 1844 to 1858, and the corresponding rates of interest charged by the Bank of England, together with a diagram, No 10, representing the same.

TABLE VIII., *showing the Rates of Interest each Year in the Bank of England, with the Amount of the Bank Reserve at the corresponding Date, from* 1844 *to* 1858, *inclusive, and the Suspensions of the Bank Act.*

YEAR.	Bank Reserve.		Bank Rate of Interest.
1844	8½ millions	. . . .	2½ per cent.
1845	6 "	. . . .	3½ " "
1846	10 "	. . . .	3 " "
1847	1½ "	Suspension of Bank Act	8 " "
1848	11 "	. . . .	3 " "
1849	12½ "	. . . .	2½ " "
1850	13 "	. . . .	2½ " "
1851	7 "	. . . .	3 " "
1852	14 "	. . . .	2 " "
1853	6 "	. . . .	5 " "
1854	4 "	. . . .	5½ " "
1855	12 "	. . . .	3½ " "
1856	8 "	. . . .	4½ " "
1857	1½ "	Suspension of Bank Act	10 " "
1858	13½ "	. . . .	2½ " "

Nº 10.

BANK OF ENGLAND

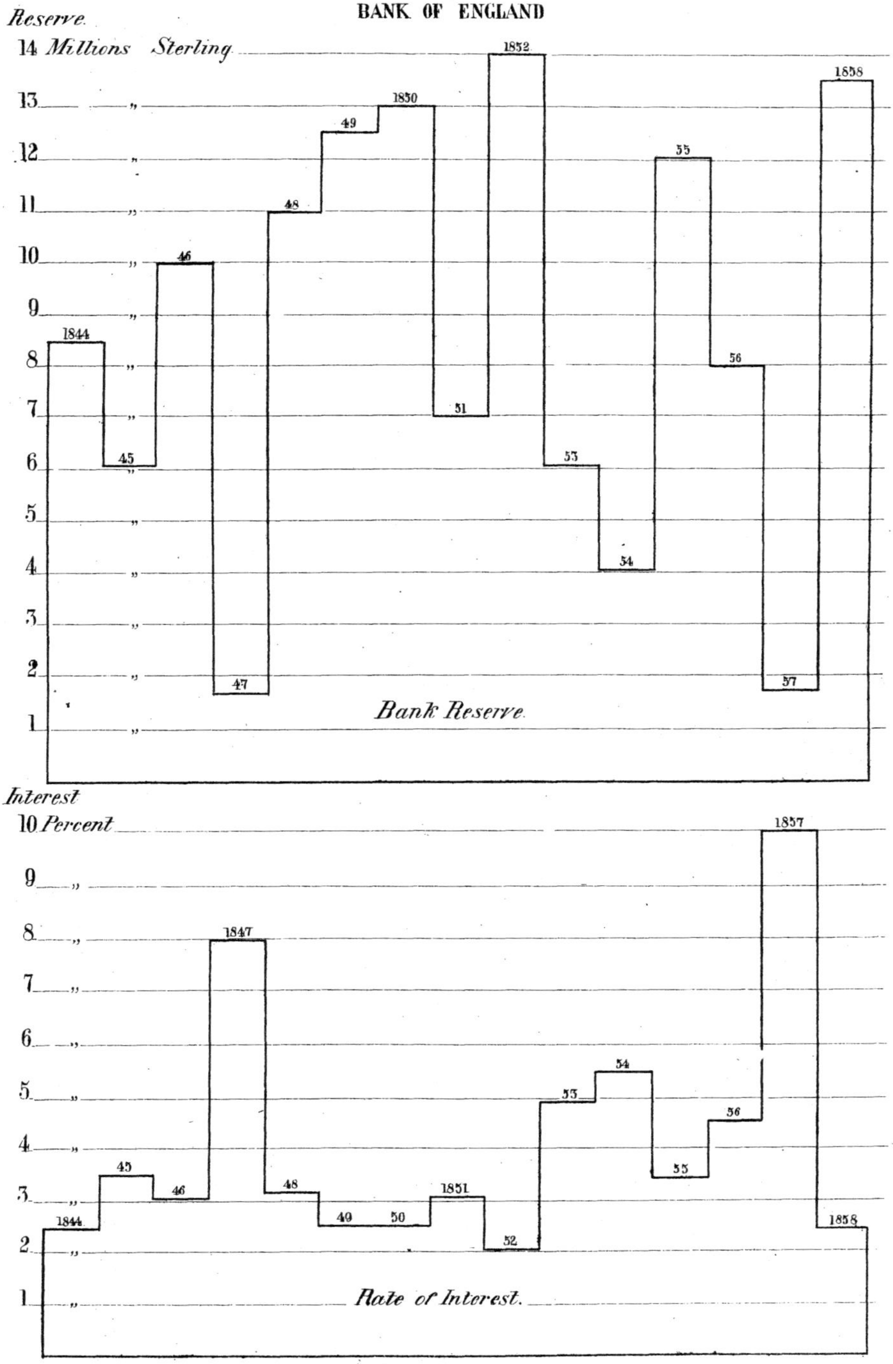

Observe the correspondence between Diagrams No. 9 and 10. The rate of interest in both countries is evidently affected by the same disturbing force, though in different degrees.

EFFECTS OF MIXED CURRENCY UPON AMERICAN AGRICULTURE.

Unfavorable as the influence of mixed currency is upon all branches of industry, the agriculture of the United States is especially injured by it, because, as a people, we have a large surplus of agricultural products, that must find sale in foreign markets. Whatever such surplus is worth for export, determines the price of the whole crop; and the value or price is determined by the value or price of gold. Such products are virtually sold for gold. It is always a matter of choice with the merchant whether to send wheat,* for example, or gold, as a remittance. The produce of the farmer, then, must be sold at a gold standard; but all he purchases for himself and family is bought at currency prices. How much difference this may make is seen at the present time, when commodities in general are one hundred and twenty per cent above par, while gold is but forty.

The currency is now (1865) a credit, or inconvertible one; but we are to inquire whether the principle does not hold good at all times, under a mixed or partially convertible currency. We therefore refer to the statistical tables of the Financial Report of 1863, as heretofore, for prices, and construct a table which exhibits the price of flour and the price of cotton for fourteen years prior to 1860. We also give the *general prices* of certain commodities, as shown in our Table V., previously given (see page 178,) and also the volume of the currency, *per capita*, at corresponding dates: —

* Wheat may be taken as an exponent of all agricultural products exported.

TABLE IX., *showing the Price of Flour and Cotton from* 1846 *to* 1859, *inclusive* (14 *Years*), *with the Currency per Capita, and General Prices at corresponding Dates.*

YEARS.	Price of Flour.	Price of Cotton.	Currency, per Capita.	General Prices.	YEARS.	Price of Flour.	Price of Cotton.	Currency, per Capita.	General Prices.
1846 . .	$5.06	7½	$9.94	$16.69	1853 . .	$5.77	10½	$13.65	$22.47
1847 . .	6.67	8	9.38	20.82	1854 . .	8.94	9	14.95	20.84
1848 . .	5.96	8½	10.67	16.53	1855 . .	8.76	9¼	13.93	22.78
1849 . .	5.50	8	9.18	16.45	1856 . .	6.42	10½	14.64	25.02
1850 . .	5.55	12	10.39	16.20	1857 . .	5.78	14	15.50	25.13
1851 . .	4.52	10	11.86	19.42	1858 . .	4.30	13	11.55	21.92
1852 . .	5.00	9	13.31	21.42	1859 . .	5.10	11½	14.90	22.11

The foregoing table shows conclusively, that, while general prices conform remarkably to the existing quantity of currency, flour and cotton do not rise and fall with its fluctuations. Flour, for example, in 1846, with a currency of 9.94, was at $5.06; while in 1851, when the currency had risen to 11.86, an advance of twenty per cent, flour was at $4.50, a *decline* of ten per cent. Cotton was at 12 cents, under a currency of 10.39, in 1850, and but 9 cents, under a currency of 14.95, in 1854. But we need not point to these facts; they are quite apparent throughout the whole table, and show beyond cavil that the prices of agricultural products in the United States are not governed by its mixed currency, as other products are which the agriculturist must purchase for consumption. Hence he is always a sufferer, as compared with the manufacturer and all other classes whose productions are not exported; for the commodities of the latter, while they are advanced in cost by currency inflation, are also, unless they come especially into competition with foreign products, correspondingly enhanced in price in the home market.

Ordinarily, this operation of a mixed currency is not apparent to superficial observers; but the effects are, nevertheless, always as certain as at the present time, when they are seen by every one.

At the time we are writing, the people of the West are suffering prodigiously from the influence of a redundant currency. All they consume of purchased commodities they pay one hundred and twenty per cent advance upon; while their products, wheat, corn, &c., can only be advanced about forty per cent,—the premium on gold. They feel distressed, and clamor against the tariff, as they have much reason to do; but they suffer a loss of ten dollars from the currency, to one from the tariff. Whenever they see this, the evil will be remedied; for the agriculturists of the nation hold the political power of the country in their hands, and all this class of producers, East or West, North or South, in Maine or Texas, Florida or Minnesota, are alike interested in this matter.

Again, agriculture is more disturbed by speculative operations than other branches of industry. Its products are great staples, the necessaries of life. They are not subject to quick decay; hence can be monopolized and held for a rise of prices. The sudden and excessive expansions of a mixed currency afford great opportunities for operations of this sort; and no products, probably, are so much speculated upon as those of the farmer and planter. The profit of all this goes to those who can command the resources of the banks. The producers are far more injured than benefited by these unnatural disturbances of the market.

CHAPTER XII.

FALLACIES REGARDING A MIXED CURRENCY.

Fallacy 1*st.* That, by means of mixed-currency banks, the capital of a country is greatly increased.

Capital is the portion of wealth employed in reproduction. Money is one form of capital. To the banker or money-lender, it may be his entire capital; but, to the merchant, manufacturer, or agriculturist, it is capital only as the instrument by which he obtains those commodities which constitute his main capital, upon which he does his work, and from which he makes his profits.

Of the great mass of the world's capital, money is but a small fraction. Credit is no part at all. Capital, we have said, is that portion of wealth employed in reproduction. Money is that portion of capital which is employed in reproduction, for the special purpose of effecting easily that exchange of values which itself confers value, because done by labor.

To the greater part of mankind, money is only the means by which capital is obtained from those who have it.

Now, were it not for mixed-currency banks, all the capital loaned in the form of money would be reliable. Mixed currency, for the time being, takes the place of actual money, and becomes an instrument by which capital is transferred. But its nature is, as we have seen, to issue in greater volume than necessary for the wants of commerce, and, by this, to disturb the business of the country, cause an unnatural rise of prices, an increase of imports, a decrease of exports, and finally a call for real money, which will cause the withdrawal of all the extra currency at the very moment when, owing to the increased indebtedness it has caused, it is more needed than at any other period. It will then be discovered that this excess was not capital, or actual value, but credit, in the guise of capital, which the mixed-currency banks had issued, and which they were compelled to withdraw when most wanted.

Fallacy 2d. That mixed currency is cheaper than a value currency, more economical, and therefore more desirable.

Specie costs much labor. Paper costs but little in comparison: therefore, as it answers the same purpose, and is more conveniently handled, it confers a benefit. This is a popular idea.

Money, we have said, is an instrument, nothing else; we do not eat, drink, or wear it. All tools, instruments, or appliances should be as cheap as possible, *provided, always*, they are safe and efficient. It would be cheaper to have ploughs made wholly of wood. They would be lighter, and quite as handsome, as when made partly of iron. But would they be as useful, and, in the end, as profitable?

A paper cap is cheaper than one of leather or cloth; but would it be as durable and comfortable? If not, although in the first instance it costs less, it would not be desirable for use. The same principle applies to money.

If what we have already said of a mixed currency is true, it is wanting in those qualities which would make it cheaper than a value currency. It does not discharge fully or perfectly a single function of money. It deranges trade, because it does not obey the laws of trade. It increases credit enormously, by its expansions, because it is itself credit; and impairs it by its contractions when its own credit is blown upon.

But the gain by this substitution of credit for value in the currency is insignificant, when compared with the great interests of trade.

The average of paper *circulation* in the United States from 1850 to 1859, inclusive, ten years, was not more than $6.25 per capita. If from this we deduct the average specie per capita for the same time held by the banks, viz. $2.25, we shall have left $4.00, as the amount for each individual of credit circulation. On that amount, the saving, if any, is to be made. If we compute the interest at six per cent, we have twenty-four cents as the annual saving to each individual by the use of credit currency; a saving worth the attention of the statesman, if it could be properly and safely made, but paltry in comparison with the losses and disturbances incident to a mixed currency.

In this connection, it seems proper to introduce a distinct

calculation of the damage occasioned to the people generally from this cause.

On the 7th of January, 1841, Congress requested of the Secretary of the Treasury, *first*, a return of the losses sustained by the government from using banks as depositaries, and by its connection generally with them; and, *secondly*, the amount the people had lost on account of the banks and their issues. The replies were in substance as follows: * —

Losses sustained by government to the year 1837 . .	$15,492,000
„ sustained by the public	108,885,721
„ by bank suspensions and by depreciated notes .	95,000,000
„ by destruction of bank-notes	7,121,332
„ by counterfeits beyond losses by coin	4,444,444
„ by fluctuations, revulsions, sacrifices	150,000,000
Aggregate	$380,943,497

Such were the estimates of the losses to the people and the government resulting from the use of a mixed currency up to 1841. There can be no doubt, in the minds of men who were in business during the period covered by these figures, that they are so far correct that they fail only by reason of being set too low, particularly those of the last item; viz., "losses by fluctuations, revulsions, and sacrifices."

Twenty-four years have elapsed now (1865) since the foregoing table was prepared; and, during that time, the currency has been doubled, the country has passed through several contractions and one or two explosions, and has suffered as much probably as in the preceding period. If so, the total loss would amount to seven hundred and sixty million dollars. But suppose it to be only five hundred million dollars: that amount would furnish gold and silver currency sufficient, not only to supply our wants at present, but for generations to come.

Some have supposed that a great saving is made by the use of paper money instead of coin. But it is not necessary

* See "Merchants' Magazine," vol. l. p. 9.

to have a *mixed* currency in order to avoid abrasion of the coin. A mercantile currency, based wholly on specie, would equally avoid loss from this cause, and yet secure all the advantages of a value currency.

But, in fact, the abrasion of paper currency is far greater than that of gold; that is, it costs more to keep out one hundred dollars of currency than it does to keep out one hundred dollars in coin. Gold and silver circulate themselves; but it requires a formidable machinery to circulate paper promises,—a machinery far more costly than the slow wear of the precious metals. No banker would venture to say that a paper currency can be maintained for one-twentieth of one per cent per annum.

It may be said that the banks gain a considerable sum by the accidental destruction of their notes. Doubtless; but what they gain somebody loses. The amount estimated to have disappeared in this manner up to 1841, as we have seen in the table just cited, was put at seven millions of dollars. A very large proportion of this fell on the poorer classes, as also do the losses by counterfeiting.

But, if we would comprehend the question of economy, we must appreciate the expense of maintaining all the officers, managers, and subordinates of fifteen hundred banks, with all the incidental charges of their operations. At a moderate calculation, this would not average less than four thousand dollars to each bank, or a total sum of six million dollars per annum.

This argument of economy in the use of credit money was presented by Dr. Adam Smith eighty years ago. Even then the danger was apparent, though the system had not been developed to its proper character and consequences. Had the writer witnessed the great convulsions from 1797 to 1857, he would have dismissed, as wholly an idle fancy, the scheme of substituting the "Dædalian wings" (say, rather, the Icarian wings) of credit for the "solid ground" of value. He says:—

"The gold and silver money which circulates in any country may very properly be compared to a highway; which, while it circulates, and carries to market all the grass and corn of the country, produces itself not a single pile of either. The judicious operations of banking, by providing, if I may be allowed so violent a metaphor, a sort of wagon-way through the air, enable the country to convert, as it were, a great part of its highways into good pastures and cornfields, and thereby to increase very considerably the annual produce of its land and labor. The commerce and industry of the country, however, it must be acknowledged, though they may be somewhat augmented, cannot be altogether so secure, when they are thus, as it were, suspended upon the Dædalian wings of paper money, as when they travel about upon the solid ground of gold and silver. Over and above the accidents to which they are exposed from the unskilfulness of the conductors of this paper money, they are liable to several others, from which no prudence or skill of those conductors can guard them."

This comparison is full and just in every particular. Nations have been trying to make a small saving by dispensing with the vital condition of all their wealth. These political farmers have always ached to be ploughing up and seeding down the very highways of their industry; far more intent on this than to improve the land already at their disposal. "A wagon-way through the air" is no violent, but rather a modest, metaphor for the schemes by which they propose to make nothing do the work of something. A man might as reasonably try to make a saving by selling his own blood as a nation gain aught by robbing its commerce of money. It is an attempt to cheat the house of its foundation, the animal of its food.

Nor is it even economy, at the first and on the face. Experience has shown that this extensive system of aërial railways is rather more costly in its outlay than the more natural one that rests upon the ground. Industrial ballooning has always been difficult and dangerous.

Fallacy 3d. That the use of mixed currency has been the cause of the great prosperity of the United States.

This is, doubtless, a very idle assumption, unworthy of discussion. Yet thousands are influenced by it.

A *coincidence* is taken, by force, for a *cause*.

The United States have prospered greatly, and at the same time there has been a large consumption of intoxicating drinks. Surely this does not prove that the prosperity of the country was caused by the use of liquor.

Has the country flourished by reason of, or in despite of, such use? Intoxicating liquors stimulate men to greater effort; therefore they increase production. Mixed currency stimulates exchanges, increases prices, promotes speculations; therefore it is favorable to production.

Such is the reasoning, and it is equally good in each case. In both, the misdirection of effort and the certain depression of energy are kept out of sight. Mixed currency never gave strength or wisdom or skill or economy to any human being, and therefore never can have increased the products of the country, or enlarged its wealth, in any manner whatever. Its unnatural excitements are followed by unnatural prostration. Men do not work more, but they trade more, speculate more, and squander more, during the flood-time of an expansion. More is expended for foreign luxuries; there is more extravagance and waste, which superficial observers take to be indications of prosperity. In the time of reckoning, trade is as much depressed as it was falsely stimulated.

Fallacy 4th. That there is not gold and silver enough in existence to form a currency adequate to the rapidly extending operations of commerce; and therefore resort must be had to paper substitutes.

Twenty years ago, this was regarded as an unanswerable argument in favor of credit currency. The recent discoveries of apparently inexhaustible mines, and the immense production already realized, have to a great extent silenced the senseless clamor once raised on this point. Yet the assertion is as true now as ever. Only about one-half of the whole amount of precious metals in possession of man, from the fifteenth to the middle of the nineteenth centuries, was required for coin; the balance remaining in plate and ornaments, mostly in Europe and the East.

The reason of such general error on this point is found in the totally inadequate ideas prevailing as to the amount of currency needed for trade. People are informed, that the annual products of the United States, for example, are, say, four thousand millions; and they fancy that four thousand millions of currency, or something near that sum, is necessary to transfer this immense production: whereas it is true that a very small fraction of the amount is required.

Mr. Colwell, in his "Ways and Means of Payment," estimates that all the securities issued in the United States, including "promissory notes, bank-notes, bank credits, and other currency, — in short, all which intervene between buyer and seller," — amount to one thousand million dollars every three months, or four thousand million dollars per year. Yet we know that all this is wiped off with, at the most, not more than four hundred million dollars of currency, or about one-tenth of the aggregate indebtedness.

Now, that the people of the United States could not command sufficient gold to furnish a currency equal to their wants is preposterous, since the yearly production of California, for at least twelve years, has amounted to fifty millions, — in all, say, six hundred millions of gold; a sum about double our requirements for a *sound* currency.

Instead of using this, we find that the amount of specie in all the banks in 1848, the time of the discovery of the gold mines, was forty-six millions, and that on the first of January, 1860, the amount was eighty-three millions; showing, that, of all the gold obtained from California, only thirty-seven millions, or about one-sixteenth, had found its way into the bank currency of the country. In the mean time, the total exports of the nation had increased from one hundred and fifty-four to three hundred and sixty millions, or more than double. Again, the amount of specie *per capita* in bank for ten years prior to the discoveries, say from 1839 to 1848 inclusive, was $2.07; while for the succeeding ten years, 1849 to 1858 inclusive, it was but $2.10,—showing an actual gain of but *three cents to each individual*, notwithstanding the accessions of gold to the amount of six hundred millions, or *twenty dollars per capita.*

What had become of this gold? It had been exported. Why? Because the credit currency of the country expelled that part, which, but for itself, would have formed a reliable and sufficient currency for the nation. The actual percentage of specie to currency from 1840 to 1849, ten years, was twenty per cent; from 1850 to 1859, ten years, only seventeen per cent,—showing that the quality of the currency was actually poorer after than before the gold discoveries.

But, while it is thus seen to be practically untrue that there is not enough of the precious metals to furnish all the currency needed in the most extended commerce, it is plainly false in theory. We have already shown, that, as the currency is increased, prices advance; so that money becomes no more plenty by augmenting its quantity.

John Stuart Mill says: "The uses of money are in no respect promoted by increasing the quantity which exists and circulates in a country, the service it performs being as well rendered by a small as by a large aggregate amount. Two million quarters of corn will not feed so many persons as four millions; but two million pounds sterling will carry on as much traffic, will buy and sell as many commodities as four millions, though at lower prices."

Sufficient has been said in refutation of a fallacy, which, though popular, is really not entitled to much consideration.

Fallacy 5th. That mixed-currency banks are particularly favorable to those who have little capital, and must, of necessity, depend upon credit, since they increase the facilities for obtaining capital.

Whatever impairs credit and increases the risk of loaning must be unfavorable to those who most need to borrow. Other things being equal, it must be easier to get credit in a community where only one in twenty fails than where one in five fails; the less the risk, the less the hesitation in giving credit. Now, does the credit money of a mixed currency diminish the risk of general credits? Far from it. Common-sense teaches, and statistics prove, that the hazards of credit must be just in proportion to the *credit money* of any country. Instead, therefore, of being favorable, it is adverse to all persons wanting the use of capital. The hazards of credit in the United States are at least four times as great as they would be under a value money currency.

The more credits are extended, the more difficult it is for persons of limited means to do any thing on their own account. Unless an interest can be secured in some large banking institution, business on a large scale is impossible, because the manufacturer or dealer will give long credit, if he can get credit at the banks. If it be true, as we have seen, that introducing credit into the currency extends all the indebtedness of the country, this must operate to the disadvantage of all men of limited capital.

That all this is quite unnecessary, is proved by the condition of things in the years 1863 to 1865, when no credits were given, all transactions being essentially on immediate payment. The war effected this, by destroying all confidence; but the fact that the business of the country was carried on without extensive credits shows that such were always unnecessary.

A mixed currency, far from being advantageous to persons needing credit, has an entirely opposite influence, and is constantly tending to reduce the number of those who can obtain sufficient to participate in the profits of business.

Fallacy 6th. That, without a mixed currency, banks could not exist, and all the advantages now derived from them would be lost.

Such is the general impression among the masses of the people. Propose to them the expulsion of the credit element; that is, to forbid the issue of notes beyond the specie in hand: the reply comes at once that there would be no object in banking, and we should have no banks.

This view of the matter arises from the fact that we have never had in the United States any banks that did not manufacture currency out of their credit. We have therefore come to regard the two things as inseparable. But this is an entirely erroneous view. Banking and currency-making are two perfectly distinct functions, though here uniformly united.

Banking may be carried on to any degree, and in the most profitable manner, without the issue of a single banknote. This is done in Great Britain, to a wonderful extent, by joint-stock and private banks. Only a very small proportion of all the banks in the United Kingdom issue their own notes; yet they make dividends so large as to astonish us.

As an illustration of this species of banking, we mention the fact, that, while the Bank of England, with a capital of fourteen millions, has deposits, public and private, of but twenty millions on an average, the three principal banks of London, with an aggregate paid-up capital of only £2,320,000, have on deposit £46,158,105; and that, while the Bank of England declares a dividend of about six or seven per cent, these banks make an average profit of about thirty per cent, and furnish the commercial and manufacturing interest a much larger amount of capital than the Bank of England itself. And yet they manufacture not a dollar of currency. We present the following statement of their condition: —

	Paid-up capital.	Deposits.	Net profits for 6 mos.	Percentage per ann.
London and Westminster	£1,000,000	£15,629,095	£147,816	29.56
Union	720,000	16,472,279	114,324	38.11
London Joint Stock . .	600,000	14,056,731	80,573	26.86
	£2,320,000	£46,158,005	£342,713	

Of all kinds of banks, with their branches, there are, in the United Kingdom, about five thousand, a small portion only of them being banks of issue. Yet, as a general rule, all make large dividends. Such as are regarded as "successful," divide from fifteen to twenty-five per cent. It is a curious and instructive fact, that, while the average rate of interest is there only half as great as in the United States, the bank dividends are much greater. The largest dividends are made by those banks which issue no notes whatever.

This fact gives sufficient proof, if any were needed, that, in order to make large dividends, it is not necessary for a well-established, well-managed bank to manufacture currency.

Banks belong to civilization. A bank is an institution intrusted by one class of persons with money to loan another class. The existence of such institutions implies the existence of capital and confidence; and these indicate culture and social elevation. Banks are labor-saving machines, of vast power and utility. Their legitimate purpose is simply to facilitate the use of money, to make it more effective in exchange, to give it greater activity in circulation. This they accomplish. A large amount of capital is collected in one building, fitted especially for the purpose. This gives greater security and convenience than if the same were scattered abroad in many hands, and accidental places of keeping. The lender knows where to go to dispose of his surplus funds; the borrower, where such funds can be obtained. The bank introduces these parties, who otherwise would probably remain unknown to each other.

No well-informed man can be opposed to banking institutions conducted in a proper manner. It would be as reasonable to object to railroads.

Banks, until a comparatively recent period, were as harmless as they were useful. They did no injury to any interest, but benefited all. When confined to the loaning of actual values, to the negotiation and collection of notes and bills of exchange, and to the reception and transfer of money, they performed an immense service to the world.

But when they undertook, not only to loan money, but to make it, to issue credit in the form of notes promising value, their character was changed.

The Bank of Hamburg, which has existed since 1619, never promised a dollar which it did not hold in its vaults. It never expanded the currency, and therefore never had occasion to contract it. It has never suspended specie payments for an hour,* and, while so conducted, never will. It has created no panic, and has in no way disturbed the business of the city. It has conferred incalculable benefits on European commerce, while contributing steadily to the growth and prosperity of Hamburg.

Confining itself to the loan of its capital and of money actually left on deposit, to the transfer of surplus funds, and to the negotiation of commercial paper, a bank can, if honestly and ably conducted, make good dividends, and perform valuable services for the community, and furnish the public with all the notes their convenience and that of the banks require.

Fallacy 7th. That a mixed currency can be effectually regulated by law.

Many of the mischiefs arising from a mixed currency are so obvious that all persons desire their removal, and naturally resort to legal enactments for that purpose. The statute-books of every State in the American Union contain laws for the regulation of mixed-currency banks. Commissioners have been appointed in many States, and a Bureau of Currency established. Ingenuity has been burdened to devise regulations by which these evils may be removed or modified, — with what success?

There is but one defect in a mixed currency; and that is, it wants the element of value. There is no sufficient rem-

* Various reports in 1857 to the contrary notwithstanding.

edy, but to supply this, by providing that banks shall issue no promises of their own for which they have not in possession the actual values they promise. But this would be to change the whole system, to make the currency mercantile, and to cut off all the profits arising from the issue of bank debt as currency. The only complete remedy, then, is restoration; that is, a return to the original design and purpose of banking.

Fallacy 8th. That it is for the interest of the public, that the banks, in times of panic or stringency, should be enabled to "stave off" suspension.

On the contrary, this can be obviated only to the misfortune of the business community. A severe pressure for money, as in the United States in 1847, 1851, and 1854, is experienced, and yet the banks do not suspend. But how do they avoid it? By throwing the strain upon the mercantile and business community. This they can always do to a limited extent, and thus maintain their own credit; but it is done at an enormous amount of embarrassment and loss to all engaged in business affairs.

The banks may not only escape damage, but may even profit very much by a pressure, if it does not come to be a panic; for it greatly enhances the rate of interest. The rate of interest in the Bank of England, from 1848 to 1856, did not average three and a half per cent. In 1857, when there was a severe pressure, the bank was able to obtain ten per cent. It had a harvest of profit.

The banks of the United States had a similar opportunity in 1847, when the price of money "in the street" (for we have no means of knowing what it was on an average in bank) was up to eighteen per cent; in 1851, when it went up to sixteen; and in 1854, when it rose to eighteen. In all these cases, the banks profited by the distress they had themselves created; but, in 1857, the pressure became overwhelming, and, after having run the street rate up to three per cent per month, they suspended payment.

If it were necessary, we might multiply instances from the history of the mixed currency of the United States and England of the same kind. A semi-revulsion is sure to take place, under such a currency, every three or four years, and a general break-down once in about nine or ten.

The greater strength of the British banks, together with the temporary suspension of the Bank Act of 1844, enables the Bank of England to throw the sacrifices incident to a great pressure more entirely upon the public than can be done in this country. Indeed, since the law of 1844 just referred to, the bank has increased its average rate of interest, as we have seen, very much.

Practically, mixed-currency banks expand as often and as much as possible; and, when the re-action comes, hold on to specie payments and a high rate of interest, until the bankruptcy of their debtors begins to be so alarming as to endanger their own securities.

They then suspend, allow their debtors to pay up in the notes they cannot redeem in specie, and thus settle the indebtedness of themselves and the public. There is no plan or design to do this; but such is the natural result, and, on the whole, a highly satisfactory one *to the banking interest.*

Fallacy 9th. That, whatever the effect upon other classes, bank stockholders at least are made richer by an expansion of the currency.

That this is not universally true will appear on examination.

An expansion of the currency raises prices: that we take to be indisputable. If so, the stockholder may be made richer or poorer by the cause that increases his bank dividends.

For example: suppose he has an income from various sources of	$5,000
And from bank stock	1,000
Total income	$6,000

In consequence of an increase of circulation by the banks, he gets an increase of $500, equal to fifty per cent on his bank dividends, making his whole income $6,500. But prices and commodities have advanced twenty-five per cent in consequence of the inflation. What he would have bought before for $6,000, now costs him $7,500. The result, then, is, that the bank stockholder has gained $500 in his dividends, and lost $1,500 in his purchases; so that he is actually $1,000 poorer, reckoning the real satisfactions or commodities, &c., which he obtains from his income.

There is nothing fictitious in this statement. The natural and certain operation of an inflation of currency affects in just this way all who hold bank stocks, but have the main part of their income from other sources. But we can suppose a case in which the stockholder would gain by expansion.

For example: he has an income from bank stock of . .	$4,000
From salary	1,000
Total income	$5,000

Now, by expansion, his dividends are increased fifty per cent, as before; and his income stands: —

From bank stock	$6,000
From salary	1,000
	$7,000

Prices have advanced, as before, twenty-five per cent, so that what he could have bought for $5,000, now costs him $6,250; but, since his income has increased to $7,000, he is a gainer by $750.

These two cases present, it is believed, a fair illustration of the effects of an increase of dividends upon bank stocks occasioned by an inflation of the currency. It is seen, that, if a man's income is derived mainly from such sources, he may gain by an increase of his dividends, notwithstanding the rise in price. But few persons are so situated. Nearly all capitalists have a variety of investments, bank stock being only one of them; so that, to the great mass of stockholders even, the gain by increased dividends is more than counterbalanced by the loss from enhanced prices.

Who gains by fictitious currency?

But it may be asked, if stockholders do not gain by bank expansions, who does? There is an increase of dividends: who gets the advantage?

This inquiry brings us face to face with one of the prime mysteries of currency, and, indeed, of political economy. "*Who* gains by fictitious currency?" Before answering this, we will ask, WHAT is gained by a currency not consisting of actual value? We answer, *nothing but price.* Prices are changed by it. Values are not created: they remain the same. By the change in the standard or measure from a value to a mixed currency, prices no longer accurately determine values. Prices are increased. Those who hold commodities while prices are advancing, gain by such an advance. Debtors may discharge their obligations with less value. Speculators may make favorable operations. The value of every commodity has been interfered with; the integrity of every contract to pay value has been impaired. Some are constantly gaining; others, losing: both parties, it may be, unconscious of the cause of such prosperity or adversity. "Times" are said to be good or bad, as men *gain* without earning, or *lose* without a fault. Here we have the answers of the questions,— *What* is gained by a mixed currency? Who gains by it?

Such is the "consummation" of mixed currency. "It is a grand system of insidious swindling." So said "Hardcastle" (who was no other than Mr. Page of the Bank of England) forty years ago; and what that shrewd observer then discovered is apparent now to all who enter into a full examination of the subject.*

* Richard Cobden repeated this remark of Mr. Page to the author at Manchester, more than twenty years since, with his emphatic approval.

CHAPTER XIII.

IV. MERCANTILE CURRENCY.

We have thus far examined three different kinds of currency. 1st, Money, consisting of the precious metals: this we have found to be admirably adapted to the wants of trade, except that, for large exchanges, it is too cumbersome, requiring much labor and time in use. 2d, Inconvertible paper, or credit currency, which, we have seen, never has been, and in the nature of things never can be kept at par with coin, and is therefore highly injurious when introduced into commerce. 3d, A mixed currency, or partly convertible paper, which, as it is constantly varying in quality and quantity, cannot be relied on as a medium of exchange or a standard of value.

We now come to the consideration of *a mercantile, or substitute* currency.

It is quite apparent that a currency is needed which shall combine all the advantages of the two kinds first mentioned, without the disadvantages which we have seen to be inseparable from the third. We want the reliability of coin and the convenience of paper. With these perfectly united, there is nothing more to desire. We have no occasion to increase the currency beyond its natural volume, because that would impair the standard of value. We wish only to have so much currency, and of such a kind, as the laws of trade demand, and, if undisturbed, will always secure.

Is such a currency practicable?

In answering this question, we remark that it would not be an entire *novelty*, since experiments of this character have been made most successfully upon a large scale, and extending over several centuries.

THE FIRST SUBSTITUTE CURRENCY ESTABLISHED.

In the early part of the fourteenth century, the Bank of Genoa, or House of St. George, was established, especially for the management of the public debt. But, in addition, the bank performed all such services as were required by the existing wants of trade, at a period when Genoa was commercially the centre of Europe. Of course, its operations were on a gigantic scale. Its affairs were conducted with the greatest skill and fidelity, and were continued from its foundation up to the time Genoa was united to the French Empire, "when the bank was abolished, and the rentes, 3,400,000 Genoese lire, which they owed their creditors, were transferred to the account-books of France."

This bank, like the Bank of England, had its stock invested in the public debt; but it received deposits of gold and silver, for which it gave credit to the depositor. These deposits, being easily transferable, were employed largely in commercial transactions.

The bank also issued bills extensively; but "*these bills and deposits represented coins of full weight and value, and were payable on demand in such coins.*" The common currency of Genoa, for retail business and *minor transactions*, was coin.

Thus the Genoese were furnished with a currency perfectly adapted to their wants. It had all the reliability of specie, with the convenience of a paper circulation, and conferred immense advantages upon the trade of the city for more than five hundred years.*

The Bank of Amsterdam was established in 1609 as a bank of deposit, receiving gold and silver coins of all denominations and all nationalities, ascertaining their exact value, and passing the amount to the credit of the depositor, or

* For an interesting account of this bank, see "The Ways and Means of Payment" (p. 311 *et seq.*), by STEPHEN COLWELL, of Philadelphia.

giving him a receipt (*recipisse*) for the same. These receipts passed from hand to hand, and formed a circulating medium for large monetary transactions.

The Bank of Hamburg was established in 1619. Like that of Amsterdam, it is a bank of deposit; and all payments are made by checks in the transfer of receipts. It exists at the present day. It never promises more coin than it has in its vaults. It is under the guardianship and guaranty of the city. It has never deranged trade by contraction or expansion. It has always been found reliable. It has contributed greatly to the prosperity of the city, and the convenience of all connected with Hamburg in trade. At the same time, it has paid a considerable and constant revenue to the city, a small *agio* or premium being charged on all deposits.

We have referred to these individual banks, not to give a history of their operations, but to show that the essential principle of a substitute currency has been long recognized, and thoroughly tried in practice. The Bank of Genoa seems to have developed this most fully. Yet none of them would afford a perfect model for the present age.

To keep gold and silver coin in bank, while they are performing all their functions outside, with the perfect accuracy and vastly augmented force, — this is what a mercantile currency seeks to realize. It is beyond doubt that this can be more effectually done in the present, than in any preceding age, since confidence and intelligence are more general and controlling.

England affords the best illustration of the necessity for such a currency at the present day, when the commerce of the world is perhaps one hundred times greater than when Genoa was its chief mart. The monetary condition of England is peculiarly appropriate in this connection, because its present currency is probably the best in quality of all the mixed currencies, and one with which the public generally are well acquainted. Yet, notwithstanding this superiority, we find the currency, on which depend the trade and commerce of the British Empire, in a state of continual fluctuation, a matter of unceasing solicitude: the bank reserve, by which its discounts must be governed, varying from ten millions in 1846, to one and a half millions in 1847; twelve and a half millions in 1849, to four millions in 1854; one and a half millions in 1857, to thirteen and a half millions in 1858; with corresponding variations in the rates of interest, as seen in our Diagram No. 10.

Why all this fluctuation and anxiety? Why this constant watching of the amount of bullion in bank? Why this nervous solicitude about the reserve?

There is only one reason; and that is, that the Bank of England has issued from ten to fourteen millions sterling of notes, for which it holds no specie! That is all the difficulty. It has disturbed the laws of value, by issuing that as money which had only the promise of value; and, consequently, has expelled the actual value from the country in which it was needed.

And what does the Bank of England gain by all this? Why, the interest upon all the excess of its notes over the bullion in bank; that is, if its notes are twenty millions, and it holds eight millions of specie, then on twelve millions it obtains interest, which, at say four per cent, as an average, is equal to four hundred and eighty thousand pounds per annum. So, then, it is for this paltry consideration that the currency of Great Britain is kept in constant fluctuation, and the business community in continual anxiety. This gain is equivalent to about fourpence per head for the population of the nation. Yet for this the public must, on an average, suffer to the amount of many millions per annum.

The people of the United States, having a much larger proportion of the credit element in their currency, suffer still more.

The remedy for all these evils is a very simple one, and perfectly feasible whenever government sees fit to make the needful enactments. Not only so, but, from the nature of the case, there need be no violent change. The experiment may be made as cautiously as the most conservative can desire.

If it be assumed that the banks of the United States have usually twenty per cent of specie, then, if Congress should require an annual addition, to this proportion, of ten per cent, it would require a period of eight years to bring the amount up to the proposed limit. That it would secure one of the grandest results to all the great industrial and commercial interests of society ever known, there cannot be the slightest doubt.

If the principles we have previously laid down, and the practical results which follow, are such as we have stated, then no one nation need to hesitate in making this experiment for fear that other nations may not follow their example; for the community which has the soundest currency will, other things equal, have the most profitable industry and the most advantageous commerce.

With such a currency, as there will be no inducement to issue notes further than convenience demands, none of a less denomination than ten dollars will probably be issued.

The Bank of England issues, we must bear in mind, no notes less than five pounds (twenty-five dollars). In Scotland and Ireland, notes are circulated as low as one pound; and it is found that two-thirds of their circulation consists of these notes. Yet there is no more occasion for one-pound notes in Scotland and Ireland than England. The only result is, that the bankers make profits on their credit issued in those notes, which the people pay for, but for which they receive no benefit whatever; while all their industrial and trading interests are rendered more unstable and fluctuating by the more sensitive currency.

In Massachusetts, where notes are issued as low as one dollar, it has been found from statistical returns that more than twenty per cent of the whole circulation was of notes under five dollars. The exclusion of these notes alone would reduce the credit element one-fifth. If all under ten were excluded, the paper circulation would be reduced at least as much more. If such a result would follow, then, taking the whole currency of the United States as it was in 1857, when the circulation was largest, and amounted to two hundred and fourteen millions, if we deduct from that amount forty per cent, equal to eighty-five million and six hundred thousand dollars, we shall have near one hundred and twenty-eight millions as the paper currency of the country, and that would represent an equal amount of gold in the banks; while all the rest of the currency of the nation would be in specie, in the hands of the people. But there need be no legal restriction whatever upon the issue of such a currency, and it matters not how voluminous it may be; since it will be composed in fact of value money, will obey the laws of value, and, of course, will regulate itself. There would then be no expansions or contractions, except from the legitimate operations of trade; and the currency of the nation would be perfectly sound. Notes may be safely issued, of any denominations, and to any amount; still it would be desirable that no small notes should be put out, because it is better that the people should have the coin, so far as practicable and convenient, in their own possession, rather than that it should be needlessly accumulated in banks, where it would be more exposed to danger in case of a popular outbreak, or a financial *coup d'état*.

That legitimate banking may be made sufficiently profitable under such a system, we have seen in the case of the joint-stock banks of England. All banks, like them, should be authorized to receive deposits, and allow such an interest upon them as they might choose to pay. If there were no issue of promises as currency, which in the nature of the case it was impossible for them to make good, there would be no danger in allowing them to borrow and loan money on any terms they pleased. To attempt to control the operations of such banks would be as useless and absurd as to attempt to regulate the trade in flour or cotton.

There would be no occasion to enact that such a currency should be received in payment of dues. It would take care of its own reputation. It would be good as gold, and easier in use; and it therefore would circulate itself. Of such a currency it might be said, in the language of Mr. Burke, "It is of value in commerce, because in law it is of none."

The transition from an unreliable currency, like that of the United States and England, to a sound mercantile currency, can be made so gradually as not for a moment to retard or interrupt the course of business. It would only be necessary to require that the proportion of specie to circulation shall be gradually increased from time to time, until the final exclusion of credit, as an element of the currency, shall be effected.

If, in carrying such a measure into practical operation, it should appear that there were banks which could not make good dividends, such institutions would be discontinued of their own choice, as not actually required by the wants of the business community. Their capital would be paid back without any essential loss to the stockholders. Those who were concerned in their management would of course be obliged to seek other employments, more beneficial to the country, and perhaps equally so to themselves. The amount of disturbance so produced would not exceed that occasioned, many times, by the invention of a new description of machinery.

Much has been said, at different times, of the desirableness of *free banking*. Of the propriety and rightfulness of allowing any person who chooses to carry on banking, as freely as farming or any other branch of business, there can be no doubt. But it is not, and can never be, expedient or right to authorize by law the universal manufacture of currency. While banking, as at present, means the issuing of inconvertible paper, the more it is guarded and restricted the better. But when such issues are entirely forbidden, and only notes equivalent to certificates of so much coin are issued, banking may be as free as brokerage. The only thing to be secured would be that no issues should be made except upon specie in hand.

With this restriction, however, it is plain that no banker would issue paper for the profits of the circulation, but solely for the convenience of his business.

It may be objected to this programme of a mercantile currency, that no provision is made for the convertibility of deposits, which are as truly currency as the circulation itself. To this we reply, that, if the circulation be represented by its full amount in specie, we think that little danger or difficulty would be likely to arise from deposits; because under such a system, suppose that twenty millions of specie were wanted for exportation, the circulation could only be reduced by that precise sum; consequently there would be much less strain upon the money market. The banks of Louisiana, under the State-bank system, held, on an average, thirty-three per cent of specie to their immediate liabilities. This, it was found, made them very stable, as compared with the banks of other States, and enabled them to withstand panics which drove their cotemporaries into suspension. If the banks were required to hold one hundred per cent of specie upon their circulation, can there be any doubt of their being able to meet all their liabilities without embarrassment? The specie would be held, by the terms of their charter, *for the conversion of their notes.* If specie were wanted, it must be demanded for the notes. Banks standing in that position would be very cautious in making discounts, and passing the same to the credit of their customers *as deposits*, unless they were in a condition to pay the same in their own notes, and ready to cash the latter on demand, if required. They would not lend money unless they had it to lend. Who can question that such a currency would be a stable one?—and stability is the great desideratum.

Panics in the currency would be unknown. Banking companies, public or private, might, and very likely would, often extend their credits so extravagantly as to involve themselves in embarrassment or ruin. That cannot be helped. That is no concern of the government, whose only duty is to forbid a false standard of value, and an unreliable medium of exchange. All notes used as money should be virtual certificates of deposits for coin absolutely held for their conversion. Such a currency can be easily secured, either through present banks, upon the principle here indicated, or through the national sub-treasuries, which might be authorized to issue certificates of any denomination (say from ten to one thousand dollars) for all specie left with them on deposit. In either case, the specie being held for their redemption, all notes in circulation would be actual money, which could neither be arbitrarily expanded or contracted; and that is just what is wanted, — nothing more, nothing less. If it be urged that this latter measure would give the government the power to control the currency, we reply, Not at all: government would be merely *a trustee*, with no power to make currency or loan it to anybody. It could exert no influence whatever on the money market.

We close with the following table: —

TABLE X. — *Characteristics of the Different Currencies.*

KIND.	COMPOSITION.	CIRCULATION.	STABILITY.	CONVENIENCY IN USE.	CONVERTIBILITY.	AS A STANDARD OF VALUE.
Specie	Precious metals	Universal	Perfectly reliable	Cumbersome in large amounts	Needs no conversion	Correct and invariable
Credit	Paper based on credit	Local and arbitrary	Liable to be continually augmented	Convenient	Inconvertible	False
Mixed	Paper based on coin and credit	Local and conventional	Constantly Fluctuating	Convenient	Only partially convertible	Defective and variable
Mercantile	Paper based wholly on coin	Local and conventional	Perfectly reliable	Convenient	Fully convertible	Correct and invariable

CHAPTER XIV.

THE NATIONAL CURRENCY OF THE UNITED STATES.

HAVING given an extended analysis of mixed currency as it has heretofore existed in the United States, it seems proper that we should notice the important changes in that currency soon to be consummated.

In the month of February, 1863, Congress enacted a law establishing a national and uniform system of currency. This has since been put into operation to such an extent as nearly to supersede the State-bank system. We propose now to inquire in what respect it differs from, and in what respect it is like, the latter.

DIFFERENCES.

It *differs* from the old system, in that,—

(1) Being created by national instead of State authority, it is entirely within the control of Congress, which, according to the last section of the National Bank Act, may at any time "alter, amend, or repeal it."

(2) It differs, in that all the notes issued are guaranteed as to their *ultimate redemption* by the government of the United States. This provision we presume to be unique, and without any precedent; for the government is not simply a trustee, holding security for these notes, as in New York and some other States, on the safety-fund principle, where stocks are deposited to secure the circulation, but it absolutely guarantees the final payment of all these notes in full.

Every banking association, on its organization, must deliver to the Treasurer of the United States the bonds of the United States bearing interest, and is then entitled to receive from the Comptroller of the Currency circulating notes of different denominations, in blank, equal in amount to ninety per cent of the current market value of the bonds so transferred, but not exceeding the par value of such bonds. In case the notes issued by the banks are not paid by them according to promise, the Comptroller may sell the bonds left as security, and redeem the notes, making up to the holders of the same any deficiency there may be in the securities. This, it will be seen, does not secure the immediate convertibility, but the *ultimate* redemption, of the circulation.

(3) It differs, again, in that these notes are legal tender in payment of "taxes, excises, public lands, and all other dues to the United States, except for duties," and also are legal tender by the United States in payment of all salaries and other demands owing by the United States, except interest upon the public debt; but they are not a legal tender as between other parties.

(4) Unlike the State-bank notes, those of the national banks, owing to the provision just mentioned, will doubtless have a nearly uniform value in all parts of the United States, and will therefore be generally acceptable as currency.

(5) They differ also in this, that the national banks are compelled by law to keep on hand a certain proportion of "lawful money" to their circulation and deposits. In specified cities,* this proportion is fixed at twenty-five per cent; in all other places, at fifteen.

Under the State systems, there was no legal obligation on the banks to keep any specie whatever, except in a few cases, as in Louisiana and (recently) in Massachusetts, and one or two other States. But this provision in regard to the national banks is practically, to a great extent, only a nominal matter, because the law provides that "bank balances and clearing-house certificates shall be deemed to be

* These cities are St. Louis, Louisville, Chicago, Detroit, Milwaukie, New Orleans, Cincinnati, Cleveland, Pittsburgh, Baltimore, Philadelphia, Boston, New York, Albany, Leavenworth, San Francisco, and Washington City.

lawful money;" and therefore, as these balances may be created fictitiously for the very purpose, the clause obliging the banks to keep a certain proportion of "lawful money" with which to redeem their notes is nearly a nullity. However real these bank balances may be, they are not specie, but, as we have before shown, constitute the most dangerous and explosive element of a mixed currency.

This is one of the great defects of the law, and, until it is removed by the repeal of this provision, would alone make the system a dangerous and unreliable one. Let us look for a moment at the manner in which it may operate.

The Merchants' Bank, Baltimore, has a balance against the Chemical Bank, New York, for twenty thousand dollars. The latter bank has a balance against the Globe Bank, Boston, for twenty thousand dollars. The Globe has a balance against the Merchants' Bank, Baltimore, for twenty thousand dollars. Here is sixty thousand dollars in this circle, which is to be reckoned as equal to so much specie, or lawful money. But is it so? So far from giving any strength to the *currency*, it has the opposite effect. The object of requiring any specie, or lawful money, is, that the currency may be made more reliable; but, if so, does not this provision, to a large extent, frustrate that object? So far from giving strength, every banker knows that these balances are a cause of weakness and peril in time of panic.

It can easily be seen that a very large proportion of the nominal amount of specie or lawful money required may be held in these "balances."

Lastly, the national differ from the old State banks in this, that the latter had almost their entire capital to loan to the business community, while the new banks will have little or none at all, having loaned their capital at the outset to the government, by the purchase of its bonds. They can, therefore, only loan their credit, in the shape of circulation endorsed by the government, together with their deposits.

RESEMBLANCES.

The new currency resembles that of the old State banks, in that it is *a mixed currency*, and in all essential respects as to its nature and effects, of the same character.

(*a*) It will expand and contract from the same causes, and, so far as can be seen, with the same violence and to an equal extent, and consequently will be as fluctuating as the currency it is designed to supersede, except in so far as a larger proportion of specie shall be held for its redemption.

(*b*) It will be an equally delusive and false standard of value, having in itself but a small proportion of value.

(*c*) It will raise prices and cause speculation when in the process of expansion, and depress prices and produce bankruptcies when contracting.

(*d*) It will create an unnatural extension of credits at one time, and a corresponding contraction at another, producing great vibrations in the rate of interest.

(*e*) It will derange the natural current of trade from time to time, causing an increase of imports and a decrease of exports, and thus forcing an export of specie to meet an unnatural balance.

(*f*) It will counteract the influence of both natural and artificial protection, and retard the normal growth of home manufactures.

Lastly, it will create panics, and cause frequent *suspensions* of all the banks in the country.

It may be thought that the fact that the government guarantees the national-bank notes will prevent a run upon the banks; but that will be found an entire mistake. Panics are created because money is wanted to pay notes and discharge immediate obligations, not because the people fear that the banks are insolvent; and, whenever it is out of the power of the banks to supply the currency immediately wanted, the panic must take place, with all its sad consequences.

Such are essentially the points of difference and agreement between the two systems. The national government may change the character of the new currency, and make it approximate a value currency. It will have the power to do this; and, as it is certain that the effects of this currency will inevitably be disastrous, and give rise to grave periodical disturbances in the monetary affairs of the country (notwithstanding its superiority in certain respects over the State-bank system), it seems highly probable that this will eventually be done; the more so, because a large and growing section of the Union is already averse to any other than a value currency. California and all the gold-bearing States are now, and, if they understand their true interests, always will be, hostile to any system which depreciates the value of their great staple.

OPERATIONS OF THE NEW SYSTEM.

The national-bank system being in its infancy, but little can be said of its actual operations.

We have, however, the first Report of the present Comptroller of the Currency (Freeman Clarke, Esq.), from which we can learn its condition on the 1st October, 1865: —

Loans	$485,314,029
Bonds deposited for circulation	272,634,200
Other bonds held	155,097,100
Total securities	$913,045,329

On this last sum the banks were drawing interest at the rate of from 6 per cent in gold to 7.30 in currency. The average rate of interest cannot be less than 7.30; for on the gold interest bonds they get (at 40 per cent premium) 8.40, and they have few securities that pay less than 7.30, to say nothing of the exchange charged in making discounts. We call the rate, however, 7.30 on the whole amount.

$913,045,329 at 7.30	$66,652,309.01

This amount of income is equivalent to a little over twenty per cent per annum on the entire capital invested. It will thus be seen that the system is at least a "paying one" to the stockholders. It is estimated that the net earnings of the banks for 1866 will be twenty-five per cent.

How it affects the quality of the currency (if it can be said to have any *quality* when wholly inconvertible) may be seen in the following statement.

Immediate liabilities of the national banks: —

For circulation	$131,452,158
Individual deposits	393,634,833
Public deposits	58,032,720
Total immediate liabilities	$583,119,711
Total specie	14,966,144
Excess Oct. 1, 1865	$568,153,567

Specie to credit equal to $2\frac{1}{2}$ cents on the dollar. The banks hold $193,094,364 in "lawful money" (greenbacks, compound-interest notes, &c.). The excess of immediate liabilities *over specie and lawful money* is three hundred and seventy-five millions. This excess is some forty millions larger than ever known under the State-bank system.

These statistics only show the condition of the national banks at the date mentioned (Oct. 1, 1865). Since that time, they have been rapidly increasing in number,* capital, circulation, and deposits; yet the general character of the currency they furnish will not essentially differ from what it now is until the government withdraws its own note circulation. Then specie must be had to sustain the circulation and deposits in the same manner, and at least to an equal

* There were over one thousand six hundred, April 1, 1866; and it is expected the number will be increased to two thousand one hundred.

extent, as under the old system. When that is done, the character of the new system will be developed, and its operations and effects made manifest. What they will be, no one who knows the nature of a mixed currency can have any doubt.

As a further illustration, we give the operations of an individual bank in Massachusetts, as shown in the Comptroller's first Report.

The capital of this bank is $300,000. As it is a *converted* one, it has, of its old capital, a "surplus" of $106,000. It has also $33,000 of "profits" on hand; total, $409,000. This is the amount of capital it actually had to loan. Let us see how much it has loaned: —

Loans (on private securities)	$155,000
Loans on public securities, "United-States bonds" . .	334,000
Loans on "other United-States bonds and securities" .	266,000
Total amount on which the bank draws interest . .	$755,000

The immediate liabilities and immediate resources of the bank are, —

Circulation . . .	$275,000	Specie	755
Private deposits .	105,000	Lawful money . .	52,000
Public deposits . .	212,000	Total means in hand	$52,755
Old circulation . .	33,000		
	$625,000		

This is equal to about one mill of specie and ten cents of lawful money to each dollar of immediate liabilities; but it has about $233,000 of bank balances, and, if these balances are sound, they furnish so much of additional immediate resources to this bank, though they do not change the character of the whole currency, because what one bank has due to it another must owe, leaving the result as if neither existed, except that, as both are liable to be instantly called for, they greatly endanger the whole system.

Statistics might be multiplied indefinitely; but enough has been given to indicate the nature of the new currency, and the manner in which the new system is likely to be carried on. Being wholly in the power of Congress, it can be made whatever the people will.

The process, as we have already indicated, is very simple, by which the national currency can be made a convertible or mercantile one; viz., by enacting, from time to time, that the banks shall keep a larger and larger proportion of specie, until the end is finally attained, and the currency made safe and reliable. This is the more feasible, because the government, by making its deposits in these banks, will enable them, with their other privileges, to make good dividends without issuing any notes for which they do not hold an equal amount of specie.

The new system, then, is in so far to be regarded with complacency, as that it is more susceptible of reform, and of being made what a currency should be,—an unalloyed blessing to the public.

CHAPTER XV.

EVIDENCES OF DEBT.

We have already spoken of two different modes of effecting exchanges; viz., (1) barter, and (2) a universal equivalent, money or currency. We now notice a third mode of doing this; viz., by EVIDENCES OF DEBT.

These are mainly of three kinds:—

I. Book accounts. A sells B one hundred barrels flour, and charges him five hundred dollars in account, to be paid, by verbal agreement, in four months.

This is a very extensive mode of effecting exchanges. Very large transactions are made in this manner. Retail trade, especially, is almost wholly carried on in this way. These accounts are often, particularly in country trade, paid in commodities. The farmer makes his purchases of the merchant, from time to time, and sells him his produce when ready for market. Both are entered in account, and the final balance is ascertained and adjusted by money or other equivalent.

(*a*) Book accounts are, in some respects, an undesirable form of transfer, because they are *ex parte*, and may be disputed. The purchaser may deny that he bought such a quantity, or at such a price. An account, if disputed, is always a matter to be proved; and, although the oath of the seller is generally deemed conclusive evidence, there is always opportunity for litigation.

(*b*) Another objection to book accounts is, that they are not negotiable. C cannot readily purchase B's account against A; but, if B had A's note, *that* could be easily negotiated, or transferred. Accounts cannot, of course, be made available at banks, like notes, or left as security for money borrowed. The capital is locked up for the time being.

II. The next mode of credit is that of notes. These are made payable for a given sum, and at a given date. They are generally payable to the order of the payee, and, when negotiated, are indorsed by the latter. This transfers the ownership to a third person; but the indorser is held to pay the note, if the promisor fails to do so.

III. A third form is by bills of exchange, or orders from A to B to pay C a given sum at a fixed time. These differ from notes, in that they involve three parties, — the drawer, the acceptor, and the payee. They have a form usually somewhat like the following: —

$1000. NEW YORK, Jan. 1, 1866.

Four months from date, pay to the order of J. Brentwood & Co. one thousand dollars, value received, and place to account.

(Signed) HENDERSON, WILLIAMS, & Co.

To Messrs. BENNET BROTHERS & Co., Boston.

Here are three parties,—the drawer, the acceptor, and the indorser or payee.

This is first called a *draft*. When presented to the person on whom it is drawn, and by him accepted (which is done by writing the word "accepted" on the face, and signing the name), it is an *acceptance*. When indorsed by the person in whose favor it is drawn, it becomes a complete bill of exchange.

This species of transaction will arise mainly between persons residing in different places, and in this manner: A, in Boston, orders of B, in New Orleans, one thousand bales of cotton, which B sends, with a bill of the same, and then draws on A for the amount.

The commerce of the world is carried on principally by this agency. The transportation of money is thus dispensed with, except to settle the final balance of trade.

BILLS OF EXCHANGE.

Bills of exchange may be divided into two kinds,—domestic and foreign.

Domestic bills are those drawn and payable within the same country, as between different cities and different States. The manner in which these bills save the use of money, in domestic trade, is illustrated as follows:—

A, in Boston, sells to B, in New York, goods to amount of one thousand dollars.

C, in New York, sells to D, in Boston, leather to amount of one thousand dollars.

Instead of sending the money, B, in New York, goes to C, in New York, and gets his draft on D, and remits it to A, in Boston, who receives the money of D; and the transactions are all closed without a dollar in money having been transferred from one city to another.

This is the course of all direct trade between any two places. Not, it must be understood, that, in the case supposed, B actually goes to C; but the merchants in Boston are owing millions to merchants in New York, while persons of the latter place are owing, it may be, an equal amount in Boston.

Bills are drawn on Boston for all due to New York, and on New York for all due to Boston. These bills are, when completed, if not before, generally passed into the banks, who pay out the money for them, deducting the interest (and exchange, if there is any). Then, if a merchant in either city wishes to remit, he goes directly to the bank, which will draw on some bank in New York or Boston, as the case may be, for such sum as he may want. The banks negotiate or collect the whole, and sell or dispose of their own checks or drafts for the amount.

This is a labor-saving arrangement of immense importance, greatly reducing the otherwise inevitable demand for a large amount of money to be kept *in transitu* between the different marts of trade.

INDIRECT EXCHANGE.

But all exchange is not direct between two places.

A, for example, in St. Louis, ships one hundred thousand dollars' worth of lead to New York. He wishes to pay sundry persons in Boston, Providence, Lowell, and Lynn. He draws on his correspondent in New York for all these, in favor of the persons to whom he is indebted; and the drafts are negotiated by the receivers, through bank in the several cities, and finally all sent to New York for collection. All domestic trade thus becomes a great web of exchanges, which adjust themselves by means of these bills; and thus, to their entire aggregate amount, obviate the necessity of transmitting money.

FOREIGN EXCHANGE.

This consists of orders; that is, bills of exchange, drawn upon each other by the merchants and bankers of different countries. They differ little in form from domestic bills, but are usually drawn in sets of three; called, respectively, the first, second, and third of exchange, in something like the following form: —

£1000. BOSTON, June 28, 1859.

At sixty days' sight of this first of exchange (second and third unpaid), pay to the order of A. Brown & Co. one thousand pounds sterling, value received, which place to account.

BRYDONE BROTHERS & CO.

GEORGE PEABODY & CO.,
London.

The party to whom the bill is payable takes these, and forwards the first to London, where it is accepted and paid. But an accident might occur by which the bill would be destroyed or lost while on its way to London; and, in that case, the owner would forward the *second*, which would be paid. The *third* bill is also held, for the same precautionary reasons.

These bills arise in a great variety of ways. Persons wishing to purchase merchandise or other articles abroad go directly to bankers in New York, Boston, &c., and buy a bill of the required amount. So with persons wishing to travel abroad. But the principal amount, of course, is drawn in payment for importations of foreign merchandise. In general, the trade between England and this country is carried on by bills drawn on this side the water, upon cotton and other produce shipped abroad, mostly to Liverpool.

To illustrate the ramifications of this kind of intercourse, we will suppose that A, in Boston, buys merchandise of B, in Liverpool; C, in Boston, sells goods to D, in New Orleans; E, in Boston, buys cotton of F, in New Orleans, and ships the same to G, in Liverpool. Each transaction, we will suppose, amounts to five thousand dollars.

How are all these settled without the transfer of money? A gets the draft of E upon G, and sends it to B, in Liverpool; E gets the draft of C upon D, and remits it to F, at New Orleans, who receives the amount of D.*

Thus four debts of five thousand dollars, in all twenty thousand dollars, have been paid, and no money has been transferred from one place to another.

Observe, now, the saving of time and interest: —

To have transported $5000 from Boston to Liverpool would have ordinarily required	14 days.
The same amount from Liverpool to Boston	14 days.
The transport from Boston to New Orleans	6 days.
The same from New Orleans to Boston	6 days.
Total	40 days.

Saving of interest on $5000 for forty days, at six per cent, is $33.33. From this view of the matter, we see what an immense saving is made in the use of money, the expenses of transporting it, and the interest on the same, upon the thousands of millions of dollars required in the trade of the world.

In 1857, the United States imported	$362,000,000
And exported cotton, breadstuffs, &c., $293,000,000; gold, $69,000,000	360,000,000
Leaving a nominal balance of . . .	$2,000,000

Another thing in regard to exchange may be noticed; viz., England received that year of us (the United States) fifty-four millions *more* than we bought of her. The same year we bought of

Brazil more than sold to her	$16,000,000
China	4,000,000
Spain, Cuba, &c.	29,000,000
France	8,000,000
	$57,000,000

* These transactions go through banking houses, as in the case of domestic exchanges.

These balances were mainly adjusted by drafts on England, by which our balances against England were discharged.

From facts like these, we can readily believe that at least nine-tenths of all the trade of the world is carried on by bills of exchange. Such is the estimate made in England and this country, and there is reason to believe that it is approximately correct.

THE NATURAL RATE OF EXCHANGE.

By the rate of exchange is meant merely the price or cost of transporting money from one point to another; say, from Cincinnati to New York. If the time, freight, insurance, and other charges are equal to one per cent, then that is the natural rate of exchange. We have shown that only a small amount of coin, in the course of trade, is likely to be transported from one place to another. As there is a mutual trade, as Cincinnati buys of New York and New York of Cincinnati, it is only necessary to buy bills of exchange between these places. But on these bills there will be a premium or discount, as the case may be. If New York has purchased more largely in the mutual trade, there will be an excess of demand in that city for bills on Cincinnati. Reverse the supposition, and there will be an excess of demand in Cincinnati for bills on New York. The consequence, in either case, will be a rate of exchange equal to the transportation of specie, as above indicated. The rate of exchange will fluctuate from time to time (other things equal) precisely according to the transactions between the two cities. It becomes, then, in point of fact, the *barometer* of trade; indicating, with perfect accuracy, the state of trade between any two points, at home or abroad. With a sound currency, the rate of exchange may always be relied upon, and is always watched with great interest by every intelligent merchant and banker.

If this be so, we see that perfect freedom of exchange is of great importance, and that no extraneous influence should be brought to disturb this barometer, to which all ought to look with entire confidence.

If, for example, there existed a national bank, having the right to inflate the currency at pleasure, and with branches so distributed over the country that it could bring its whole power to bear upon any given point whenever it chose, it is easy to see that such an institution might control the exchanges, and thus do a great injury to the community; not only by charging excessive premiums, but by disturbing the normal indications of the exchange market. This, it has been charged, the United-States Bank, whose charter expired in 1836, actually did; at any rate, it certainly had the power and the motive to do it.

The Bank of England has never been permitted to deal in exchange.

THE RATE OF BRITISH EXCHANGE.

It is well known, that the ordinary rate of exchange between this country and England is from nine to ten and a half per cent against the United States; but the explanation of this is not generally understood. The transportation of specie between the two countries, all charges and time included, costs only about one and one-quarter per cent. Why, then, this difference?

When the American government was first formed, the old Spanish milled dollar was in use; and $4.44 were equal to the British gold coin called a sovereign, or pound sterling. And Congress enacted that $4.44 should be the rate at which the pound sterling must be computed at our custom-houses.

Since that time, important changes have taken place; the relative value of gold and silver have changed. The latter has advanced, or the former declined. The American dollar, too, has been altered, so that it has a less quantity of silver; and our gold coins, also, proportionately. It therefore now takes $4.86.6, in American coin, to be equal to a pound sterling. Thus the —

Actual value of the pound sterling is	$4.86,6
Legal valuation	4.44,4
Difference	.42,2

which, it will be seen, is equal to very nearly nine and one-half per cent; so that, when exchange is quoted at nine and one-half per cent, it is really at actual par.

Now, if this is the actual par value of the two currencies, it will happen, that, whenever the market rate of exchange rises so far above nine and one-half per cent as to be sufficient to pay the expenses of sending specie and a trifle *more*, then the specie will go forward.

What these expenses are will be seen by a statement of an actual transaction between Boston and London, February, 1865.

Gold purchased		$50,000
Insurance, one-half per cent	$250.00	
Freight to Liverpool, three-eighths per cent .	187.50	
Carriage, Liverpool to London	5.00	
Selling, commission, one-eighth per cent .	62.50	
Fourteen days' time lost, at six per cent . .	83.33	
	$588.33	

These expenses are equal to about one and one-sixth per cent.

There is always some risk that the specie sent forward may not hold out full weight; that is, that, owing to abrasion in use, it might fall short a trifle: so that, probably, instead of one and one-sixth, the exporter of gold might as well have bought a bill of exchange, at one and one-quarter per cent.

Then, if the difference in the par value of the two currencies is equal to	9.5
And the expenses of remitting gold equal to	1.25
Real par value of exchange, total	10.75

it will follow that gold will not ordinarily be exported until the market rate of exchange is about ten and one-half to ten and three-quarters per cent.

The same general principle applies to French exchange, which usually stands at about five per cent against this country. It is only the difference between the value of the coins of the respective countries, as computed here.

The late Secretary of the United-States Treasury, Mr. Chase, tried to induce Congress to rectify the great difference between the nominal and the real value of our coins, as compared with foreign coins; but the proposal was not sustained by legislative action. This measure would have added some ten per cent to the valuation of British imports, and, of course, the same per cent to the revenue derived from them; while it would have removed an absurd and cumbersome mode of computation at our custom-houses.

A change so desirable and expedient cannot be long delayed.

ARE BILLS OF EXCHANGE CURRENCY?

It has often been maintained that bills of exchange are currency, as truly as bank-notes. Let us inquire.

1st, The popular definition of currency is, that which passes current from hand to hand in all transactions between buyer and seller, in large or small amounts; and, also, in payment of all obligations. It is evident that this is not true of bills of exchange, which may be taken as the example of all negotiable paper. It is, indeed, said, that in some countries, as in Great Britain, they are so used, in a limited degree; but even such use does not bring them within the definition.

2d, The wider definition which we gave of currency, viz. that instrumentality by which a general exchange of values is effected and payments are made, does not embrace bills of exchange, which have themselves to be discharged with currency. The fact, that, when found in equal amount on opposite sides, they may be used to cancel each other, makes them no more currency than is the credit side of a book-account, which balances the debit. Bills of exchange dispense with the necessity of transporting currency in a certain number of commercial transactions: they are not, therefore, themselves currency. They allow debts between different States or nations to be discharged in the *local* currencies; but each bill is itself discharged in full by the use of currency, no less.

3d, Currency, if it be equal to money, can be at once exchanged for specie, at the place where issued; but cash cannot be obtained on demand for bills of exchange, as they are generally on time. Here, then, is another wide difference between currency and individual promises. They are, in fact, bought and sold for money, like the merchandise on which they are drawn.

4th, Currency is that in which all persons promise to pay their cash obligations. Is that true of bills of exchange? Quite the reverse.

5th, If a bill of exchange be dishonored, that is, not paid according to promise, the currency of the country is not thereby diminished. Is it so with currency? On the contrary, if a bank fails, so much currency as it has in circulation is at once abstracted from the community.

But how is it with bills of exchange and notes?

Suppose the indebtedness of a country were one hundred millions, and its currency ten millions.

Then, if fifty millions of the bills of exchange and notes of hand fail to be paid, there still remains the ten millions of currency with which to pay the balance; and currency is twice as plentiful, relatively to indebtedness, as before.

Suppose, on the other hand, that one-half the currency fails, while the whole amount of bills of exchange, &c., remain to be paid; or, to go further, suppose the entire currency to fail: then how can the private bills be paid at all?

So far from being currency, then, they are the very opposite in their nature, and can be discharged only by the use of currency.

The more bills of exchange, the less, relatively, is the currency: the fewer bills of exchange, the more plenty, relatively, is money.

How, then, can bills of exchange and promissory notes be synonymous with currency?

6th, Do bills of exchange affect the standard of value, and consequently prices? If plenty, are commodities higher? if scarce, are they lower?

If bills of exchange were passed from hand to hand in exchange for merchandise (which we are sure is not the case to any considerable extent in the United States, if anywhere), it would seem that, so far as thus used, they would affect prices; but this could only be *temporarily*, because, in a short time, the state of the money market would restore the equilibrium. If they do raise the prices, they will in so far prevent exports, and increase imports and consumption; and thus a demand must arise for specie for export, to settle the balance of trade; and this will cause a contraction and a fall of prices.

7th, A scarcity of bills of exchange, however great, can never, under a sound currency, be the occasion of pressure for money, or a panic; but a scarcity of currency may do this, and often does.

Do we not see, then, that there is a wide distinction between currency and all forms of credit? — that to confound them is to destroy necessary distinctions?

BOOK IV.

DISTRIBUTION.

CHAPTER I.

DIVISIONS OF THE SUBJECT.

THE distribution of wealth, like its exchange, arises out of the division of labor.

We have seen, that production might, in strict theory, proceed without co-operation; with feeble and painful steps, it is true: but its laws would still be perfect, should all men refuse to associate in their efforts, and singly seek the satisfaction of their desires. In such a case, there would be neither exchange nor distribution.

We have seen by whom all wealth is produced, have examined the instrumentalities employed in its transfer from one individual or people to another, and have contemplated the nature and extent of that great system of trade by which the products of the world are made to minister to its wants.

We have observed that capital and labor are united in production,—one as the labor of the past, the other as the labor of the present; and that the joint product is divided between them. We now come to consider the laws by which an equal and just distribution of the wealth produced shall be secured among the parties. In doing this, we are obliged to discriminate between the different kinds of labor employed and the various forms in which capital enters into production.

Labor, in the distribution of wealth, falls into three general classes: —

1st, Physical or muscular effort.

2d, Mental effort or enterprise, applied to the union of capital and labor.

3d, Subsidiary labor, or professional services, auxiliary to direct efforts in production.

The reward of the first is called wages; that of the second, profits; of the third, salaries, fees, &c., — but another name for wages.

In these three general forms, labor receives its reward. It is, however, to be observed, that, though the distinction is clear between the wages of direct labor and the compensation paid for subsidiary labor, — like professional services, — yet the laws which govern are so similar as to render separate examination unnecessary. Both are controlled by the proportion of supply and demand.

Capital is *loaned* in two general forms: —

1st, When invested with a permanent character and having a fixed place, — as houses, fields, &c., — its compensation is called "rent."

2d, When in a shape, however solid and tangible, which is not intended to be retained, but may be altered to suit the business, or removed for convenience of location, — *i.e.*, where not the identical product, but only an equivalent, is to be returned, — its compensation is called "interest."

Such, then, are the forms in which capital does its part in production; and such the forms in which it receives its share in distribution. They are, in their nature, the same, and in scientific treatment might properly be discussed under one title; but the common names are so deeply fixed in the mind, so intimately associated with political economy, and so interwoven with daily experience, that only confusion could result from speaking of them as one.

Production, thus far, has been charged with wages (and under this term we include all the rewards of auxiliary labor, salaries, fees, &c.), profits, interest, and rent. Between these parties the product is to be divided. This division is made by natural laws, which, if not interfered with by legal enactments or social customs, will secure to each its rightful share.

But, while this is true, another party enters the field, and makes a peremptory claim to a portion of the wealth which the joint efforts of these has produced. That party is *government*, demanding a revenue for its maintenance, to which all must and should contribute. This is done in the general form of taxation.

Distribution is now complete,—wages, profits, interest, rent, and taxation. These we shall examine in their order.

CHAPTER II.

WAGES.

SINCE labor and capital join together in production, each may rightfully claim, and in the nature of things must receive, a share of whatever is produced.

The share which labor receives is called "wages;" and by this general term is meant that compensation which the employer pays to the employed for his personal services. The law of value is the law of wages. Wages confer value, and are measured by it. They depend essentially on the conditions of cost, supply, and demand. Competition comes in to influence their rate, as it does the price of other commodities.

Wages vary greatly in different countries, and in different parts of the same country; they vary, too, in all the employments and occupations of society. These differences, however, are neither accidental nor arbitrary, but depend on certain laws which it is our purpose to point out.*

* A part of this chapter appeared in the "Merchant's Magazine" in 1857.

The joint instrumentality of labor and capital being necessary to the production of wealth, it follows that the interests of the two parties are closely connected; that capital is as dependent on labor as labor is upon capital.

If this is so, the probabilities of an equitable division will depend on the freedom with which both parties are able to act, and the equality on which they stand when the contract or copartnership is formed.

Whatever, in social arrangements or civil institutions, destroys the natural freedom and equality of the parties, gives one an advantage over the other; and the party having the advantage will profit by it.

Wherever, by class legislation, capital is allowed to tyrannize over its copartner, or concentrate itself in vast aggregations, and thus increase its natural power over labor, which cannot be thus brought into powerful and permanent combination, the latter will be compelled, in one form or another, to take up with less than its just reward.

But, however unjust or arbitrary laws or institutions may be, it is evident there are certain limits beyond which the wages of labor cannot be reduced.

The cost of labor is identical with the cost of maintaining the laborer in such circumstances that he can not only support himself, but rear a family of children sufficiently numerous at least to keep the supply of laborers good.

Hence he must receive what has been properly denominated *necessary wages;* that is, to use in part the definition of Adam Smith, "such wages as will enable him, not only to obtain the commodities absolutely necessary to the support of life, but whatever else the customs of society render it indecent for persons in his rank in life to be without."

There being, then, no uniform and established standard of wages, they vary according to the expenses of subsistence in different countries, and the condition in which the laboring classes are willing to live.

The cost of labor, or the current rate of wages that can

permanently exist, depends on the necessary expenses of living; and these expenses, in turn, depend upon the condition of the laboring classes. Hence, other things equal, the more educated and morally and intellectually elevated any community of laborers may be, the higher will be their standard of wages.

Wages are not high in proportion to the wealth of a community, but rather to the disposition that exists amongst those possessing wealth to pay it out for labor; and this disposition will depend much upon the security and profitableness with which capital can be employed in production, and the enterprise and aspirations of the people.

We make the following divisions of our subject: —

NOMINAL AND REAL WAGES.

There is often a considerable difference between the nominal and real wages, or between the wages of the employé when received in money or when realized in such commodities as his wants require. As this is a question of fact, we refer to pages 177, 178, of this work, as shown in Table V. In that table we find the prices of ten commodities, which the laborer would be likely to use in his ordinary consumption, such as sugar, coffee, molasses, pork, cheese, rice, salt, &c.

By taking the wages of the laborers at certain periods, and the prices at corresponding periods, we ascertain the desired results. We have added the year 1864 from the best unofficial sources at hand: —

	1836.	1840.	1843.	1864.
Wages*	$1.25	$1.00	$1.00	$1.50
Commodities . . .	29.46	20.73	14.82	46.96
Labor required . .	$23\frac{1}{2}$ days	$20\frac{3}{4}$ days	$14\frac{4}{5}$ days	$34\frac{6}{10}$ days

* It is to be regretted that we have no carefully prepared tables of wages in the United States. Such are greatly needed. We have taken the rates mentioned according to our own observation, and believe them essentially correct.

Nominal wages fell from 1836 to 1840 by one-fifth, or twenty per cent; yet the real wages (as shown by the less number of days required to procure the same commodities) were higher in 1840 than 1836 by more than thirteen per cent. In 1843, when the nominal wages were but one dollar, real wages were about sixty per cent better than in 1836, when the nominal wages were twenty-five per cent higher. In 1864, when nominal wages were at one dollar and fifty cents, real wages were but little more than half what they were in 1843 at one dollar.

In this connection, it seems appropriate to mention the great difference to the laboring classes between a value and a credit currency. If the latter, as we have endeavored to show, raises prices and causes speculation, and if the price of labor does not rise in proportion to the rise of prices, then it must follow that wages were really less at all times of inflation than when the currency is in a natural condition. How great these fluctuations are we have seen in Table V., pages 177, 178, from which, as an illustration in point, we give the following triennial synopsis: —

Years . . .	1834.	1837.	1840.	1843.	1847.	1850.	1853.	1856.	1859.
Prices . . .	$19.13	$28.40	$20.73	$14.82	$20.82	$16.20	$22.47	$25.02	$22.11

Every one acquainted with the rate of wages will realize at once that they have not corresponded to their fluctuations in prices, and that the laboring and salaried classes must have suffered great injustice in consequence.

CHAPTER III.

PROPORTIONATE RISE AND FALL OF WAGES.

ALTHOUGH wages rise and fall with the general rise and fall of commodities, they do not in equal proportion. The fact is one of common observation; but the reason of this dif-

17

ference we do not recollect to have seen stated by any writer. For nearly all products there is both an actual and speculative, or a present and prospective, demand: for labor there is only an actual, present demand. When business begins to be particularly prosperous, there is a general demand for all kinds of merchandise, and prices gradually begin to improve. This at once occasions a speculative demand; for to buy will be to realize an advance: the larger the purchases, the greater the amount of profits. Every operation pays. The rise continues until every article bought and sold as merchandise goes up to the highest point.

But no one speculates in wages. No one can, if he would, buy a hundred thousand dollars' worth of labor, and hold it for an advance, as he can of flour, sugar, or tea. Of course, labor has no advantage from this kind of demand, but must rely entirely on that which is immediate and actual. Therefore it is that a general rise of prices, so far as occasioned by speculation, must always operate against the laborer, or the person employed on salary or wages.

But wages not only never rise so much as commodities, but do not rise so soon. The reason is, that the rise of commodities is greatly accelerated by speculation; while labor, as before stated, is not affected by that kind of demand. Hence it does not begin to rise until speculation has engendered a spirit of extravagance and increased consumption; then wages make an advance about half as great, on an average, as that of merchandise in general.

And, again, wages fall *sooner* than merchandise, because the latter may be held for high prices, if need be. The fall of merchandise is broken by the disposition and ability of the owner to hold on, and, as far as possible, prevent loss; but the laborer cannot do this,—he must sell his commodity at once for the most it will bring.

It is for those obvious reasons that wages, in times of depression, must fall, not only sooner, but lower, than property in general.

A real rise or fall in wages is a matter difficult to ascertain with certainty. Fluctuations, since the introduction of mixed currency, have been frequent and violent, not in the rate of wages only, but of those commodities upon which the laborer subsists, and in which his real wages must be estimated. To determine whether actual value wages have advanced or not since the commencement of the present century, for example, we must have the nominal rates, say, in 1810, also in 1860. We must then take the prices of commodities at the two periods; and, by comparison, we may arrive at a general conclusion. We should undoubtedly be satisfied that there has been a decided increase in the average value of wages. In our investigation, we should find that some articles were higher and some lower in price in 1860 than fifty years before. For example, while one dollar per day for labor was probably as high wages in 1810 as one dollar and a half in 1860, corn was worth the same at each end of the half-century; but cotton cloth, which was worth forty cents a yard in 1810, could be bought in 1860 for ten cents. In all manufactured articles, the difference is against the earlier labor; so that it is true the laborer of to-day enjoys many comforts to which his predecessors could not aspire. The *wants* of the laborer have immensely increased. It would be impossible to give an inventory of them; but, could we compare the consumption of those classes in 1810 with their consumption in 1860, we should find the advance surprising. The amount expended for pleasure-travel, for example, by this class is immense, while fifty years ago it was hardly appreciable. So of the luxury of newspapers, magazines, &c. Some part of the expenditures of the poorer classes are for articles (like photographs) which were absolutely unknown a generation since.

Workmen may be less satisfied with their compensation now than fifty years ago; but it is really far greater. We do not say they have no cause for complaint, yet they are vastly better off than those who went before them. Wages, when realized in commodities, have increased. The general product has been enlarged by the introduction of labor-saving machinery, and therefore their absolute share is greater. Whether their relative share, as compared with that of the capitalist or employer, is greater, we shall find place elsewhere to discuss.*

The laborer suffers nothing, but gains much, in the progress of civilization, if he is not despoiled by an unsound currency. That is his greatest oppressor, because his real wages — what he obtains in commodities for his labor — is determined to a considerable extent by the character of the circulating medium of the country. If the value of that, or its purchasing power, is less than it professes to be, he cannot fail to be injured by it.

DIFFERENCE OF WAGES FROM DIFFERENCE OF EMPLOYMENTS.

Occupations which manifestly involve a great amount of personal danger command higher wages than those regarded as perfectly safe. The risk of life must be taken into account. The man who works at powder-making gets a higher price than the man who works upon a farm; the man employed in blasting rocks, than the man who shovels gravel. So it ought to be, and so to some extent it is, in regard to mining and other dangerous employments; though, from the smallness of the difference, it is often quite manifest that human life is placed at a low valuation.

Any occupation which public opinion brands as odious and revolting will usually be found to pay a large compensation, for the reason that honorable or conscientious men will not engage in it.

* The very low rate of "corn wages" received by the English laborer in times past may be seen from the statement of Mr. Matthews (Pol. Econ., p. 228, Lond. ed. 1836), that wages had advanced, and wheat fallen, so much "that, from 1720 to 1750, a whole peck of wheat could be had for a day's labor."

UNHEALTHY TRADES.

Those occupations which, although not immediately dangerous, are nevertheless unhealthy and abridge human life, ought to command more than ordinary wages.

If a man is liable to be made sick, and consequently exposed to loss of time and expense for medical attendance, he should be compensated for that liability. If he shortens life in a particular employment, that should be a matter of consideration in determining the rate of wages.

It is not for us to inquire here whether a man may rightfully engage in that which he knows will abridge life; but that multitudes do so is beyond a doubt.

Regarded in a merely economical point of view, it is obvious, that, on this account, some laborers should receive much higher compensation than they do at present. To determine what that increased pay ought to be, we should be obliged to ascertain the value or expectation of life in the different occupations.

The expectation of life should be a matter of consideration with every one choosing his business, and should have importance in determining the rate of wages. That this is not adequately the case now is quite evident, because wages paid for labor in unwholesome employments do not correspond with the consequent abridgment of human life; so that the laborer not only loses a good part of his life, but also a share of the wages he ought to receive while he does live.

Agriculture is evidently the normal employment of man, that in which he lives longest and enjoys the greatest health. Every other calling is unwholesome to the exact extent in which it departs in its condition from the agricultural; and the rate of wages should be adjusted to a scale constructed on this principle.

THE EDUCATION OF THE LABORER.

Other things equal, the man who has received merely a common-school education will obtain higher wages in any employment than one who is entirely illiterate. He has some mental discipline, will therefore be more intelligent and capable, will better understand and recollect the directions of his employers, better comprehend the nature of his duties. If need be, he can keep an account of what he does. He has in some measure learned to think; he will have a higher sense of self-respect, and be more reliable.

The difference in favor of a workman who is so far furnished with intelligence that he can do his own share of thinking, instead of relying entirely upon his employer for every exercise of judgment and forecast, is very great to the employer. If the latter is compelled to supply all the head-work, he must be in constant attendance, and exercise the utmost vigilance. Five stolid workmen will cost him as much time as ten intelligent ones, and a great deal more care, vexation, and loss. Hence intelligent labor is worth more, and will bring more.

THE FRUGALITY OF THE LABORER.

Another important consideration in connection with this part of our subject is, that the educated laborer will be more likely to appreciate his true interests, and *save* a part of his earnings. Every dollar he saves and accumulates in the shape of property, of whatever kind, will render him more independent; and the more independent he is, the more likely he will be to get fair wages. He becomes, to a certain extent, a capitalist, and can measure strength with capital on better terms.

The man who has nothing upon which to subsist to-day must work to-day, at whatever price, or starve; while he who can get on for a fortnight without employment may choose whether he will work for less than a fair price to-day or not.

This is a matter of great importance to the laborer; for the *natural* advantage the capitalist has over him is, that the latter can wait a little, while the former must work NOW. The laborer or employé of whatever kind (for all are subject to the same law) should strive earnestly to make himself as independent in his position as possible. Hence, self-denial and economy, when exercised by those who live on wages or salaries, are amply repaid by better terms of service. There is a homely adage, "that a man is poorer for being poor," which laborers, of all others, should bear in mind.

DISTINCTION OF SEX.

Women receive less wages than men. This is doubtless true in all the so-called civilized countries. The difference may be stated at about fifty per cent to their disadvantage; that is, where the man receives one dollar, the woman receives fifty cents.* And this, too, not only where the services of the two sexes differ, but where they are identical, as in school-teaching, type-setting, &c. Why this disparity?

Political economists, so far as we know, have not troubled themselves much about it. Philanthropists have taken cognizance of the fact, and have sought to apply a remedy, but generally, we may say uniformly, with little success. We shall not go at length into the subject, only endeavor to state the causes from which we suppose the difference arises. These may suggest the remedy.

The first consideration to be noticed is the fact that the

* The average monthly wages of male teachers in the public schools of Massachusetts, 1857–8, was $49.87
The average monthly wages of female teachers in the public schools of Massachusetts, 1857–8 . . . . $19.63

two sexes exist in remarkably equal numbers throughout the world. There are as many women as men.

The second, that, while almost all occupations and employments are accessible to the male sex, but comparatively few are, by the opinions and customs of society, regarded as proper for women. One, therefore, has the whole field of life in which to act; the other is limited to a part.

On the principle, then, of supply and demand, the number of females being as great as that of males, while their employments are so much fewer, they must of necessity work for less reward. The supply is greater than the effective demand.

A third fact is, that the part of labor assigned to women is of a more dispensable character. A great part of the labor of women is connected with the comforts, conveniences, and luxuries of life: hence it can and will be dispensed with, unless it can be had cheap. The staple productions — corn, cattle, iron, cotton, and the like — must be had, at whatever price or cost of labor; but not so with the thousand-and-one little articles of beauty, taste, and fashion which female industry creates in every household. For example: suppose a farmer employs two men to carry on his agricultural labors, and usually the same number of females in the work of the house. Now, if he should be so pushed for means as to be obliged to dispense with one of his employés, which would it naturally be, one of his hired men or hired maids? Doubtless one of the latter; because, by doing so, he would only lose some of the conveniences and comforts of life, without, perhaps, much sacrifice of property; while, in the other case, he would lose part of his crop.

There seems to be a prevalent feeling at the present day that the wages of woman ought to be increased; that her position ought to be less dependent. But those who are satisfied with the existing customs and opinions of society, by which the sphere of woman is restricted to its present limits, ought to be equally well satisfied with the compensation allotted her; for it is just such as must follow.

No attempt to enhance her wages by appeals to human sympathies or benevolent organizations need be attempted; for there is a law that overrides all these,—the law of supply and demand; a law founded in nature, inexorable and immutable. An increase of her wages can only result from an increase of her employments,—of employments, too, of an equally indispensable character as those of the other sex.

That a change of this sort is fortunately in progress in most civilized countries, and especially in the United States, is apparent. The introduction of machinery is doing much to equalize the wages of the two sexes. Water and steam are now made to accomplish that which could once only be done by human strength, leaving the residue of labor, which is, to a great extent, the exercise of intelligence, care, and attention, to be performed by persons of either sex. Hence, there is now a great demand for the labor of females where there was once none at all. There is less demand for muscle, and more for mind: this brings woman nearer an equality with man.

In the department of education, too, the sphere of women's labor is vastly extended within the last forty years; and, from existing indications, the present century will not close before a considerable part of the business of the medical profession will be in their hands. Women are also employed extensively in public offices and trading establishments.

All this is the natural result of our civilization, and especially of a free common-school education. In a great part of the United States, the same advantages are furnished to both sexes. The consequences are, that as the females are more docile, have a quicker apprehension, and are more studious generally, they acquire a better education in our lower schools and seminaries than the other sex.

ANOTHER CLASSIFICATION OF WAGES.

There have now been presented most of the considerations we have room to offer in regard to the subject before us, and in somewhat the usual manner of arrangement. We propose, in conclusion, to give what may be a new, but is, as we think, a more natural and scientific classification of wages.

Properly considered, wages are paid for three different kinds of *power;* viz.,—

1st, PHYSICAL POWER, or mere muscular effort with the spade, shovel, hoe, and the like; the kind of labor least elevated above that of the horse or ox. This power is most plenty, comes by nature, costs the least, and is therefore cheapest. It would be so regarded theoretically: it is so practically. This has ever been, and will be, the lowest priced.

2d, MENTAL POWER. Those faculties of mind that give ability to manage complicated affairs, the general operations of agriculture, manufactures, commerce,—all services, in fact, that require the exercise of judgment, discretion, reflection, calculation. Such power is more rare than physical force. It will therefore command a higher price, especially in a progressive state of society. To this class may be referred all persons of natural ingenuity, inventors, authors, and men of genius. Such often receive great rewards. In this class may be placed the greater proportion of those professional services which are subsidiary to production, and indispensable to its fullest development.

To prepare men for the exercise of their intellectual powers, a considerable amount of education and training is necessary. Hence such powers are not only more rare, but more expensive, than brute force, and therefore rightfully command higher compensation.

3d, MORAL POWER. As man advances in civilization; as

wealth, its great concomitant, increases; and social combinations are multiplied, — it becomes more and more necessary that important trusts should devolve on individuals occupying particular stations. With all the checks and securities that can be devised, the greatest reliance must ever be placed on the character of the person to whom the trust is committed. Oftentimes the honor and interests of vast bodies of men must be committed to a single hand.

Hence arises a necessity for something more and higher than physical and mental faculties or qualities combined, — something that shall furnish a guaranty, irrespective of all contrivances, that these high trusts shall be faithfully discharged. That guaranty is found in the moral power of the individual, — the power which gives such a control over appetites, passions, and propensities as affords assurance that under no circumstances of trial or temptation will he ever depart from the strictest line of duty. This confidence can be inspired only by the conviction that the individual to be trusted has firm, abiding principle ; that he will be honorable and true, not merely because it is for his immediate interest to do so, but because such are his sentiments and convictions that he cannot be otherwise ; that no change of circumstances will ever induce him to deviate from the path of rectitude.

When men are found possessing this high moral power over themselves and the accidents of their position, they will, of course, be called to places of responsibility and trust.

Now, as such men are more rare than those having only physical power, or physical and mental power combined, they will command higher rewards, — the highest paid for any class of services.

The merchant must often intrust all his fortune to a single confidential clerk. He must put himself in the power of that clerk to injure, it may be to ruin, if he will. Hence, should he find a man to whom of all others he is willing to commit this power, he will be disposed — he can afford — to give him large wages. The incorporated company, with its capital of millions, must put into the hands of its officers, sometimes of a single man, its whole wealth. And, after all the bonds and guaranties that can be devised, reliance must be mainly placed upon the moral character of the man.

In affairs of state, in the highest public trusts, how much must always depend on personal honor and integrity! What other assurance can the people have, that their servant may not, under great temptation, prove recreant to duty, and injure and disgrace himself and his country? Looking at all rewards in the light of political economy, it is here that we find the highest plane of human effort.

It may be objected to this new classification of labor, that we confound economic with moral science, and depart from our appropriate sphere. We reply, that men, if truly moral, are so not because it is profitable, not because it will enlarge the value of their services, but because it is right, because they love integrity for its own sake. This must be their motive, or their morality has no reliable foundation. Yet from this cause it occurs that their services are more desirable, and they will receive greater remuneration, — will be paid for honesty as truly as for intelligence, activity, and strength. So a man must preserve his health, if he would receive wages for even the lowest form of labor; but that will not be his motive. The love of life and the pleasures of health will form the grand consideration in his mind why he should abstain from all that will impair his physical energies; yet, as a consequence, he secures the ability to command wages, and is paid for his abstinence and discretion.

We cannot, therefore, acknowledge the validity of the objection to that which seems to us the most natural and scientific classification of wages.

CHAPTER IV.

LABOR COMBINATIONS.

In connection with the subject of wages, it seems necessary to inquire somewhat in regard to the rights of the laborer, since upon these his compensation must to some extent depend.

Under a government acknowledging the rights of all men, the laborer must, of course, have the same rights as his fellow-citizens, neither more nor less. He asks no favor, and grants none. He demands the same justice, the same freedom, accorded to others. He should be able, so far as law is concerned, to work when and for whom he chooses, and for such consideration as he can get in the great competition of industry. The law cannot say how much he shall accept for wages, how many hours shall constitute a day's work, nor how much the employer shall give him. Each is left perfectly free, and the competition is simply between labor and capital.

But the laborer is not under obligation to act as an insulated individual, any more than the capitalist. If the latter is permitted, and even authorized and encouraged, to combine with his fellows in order to enhance the power and profits of capital, it is equally the right of the laborer to do the same, and equally the duty of the legislator to give him any facilities for doing this he may justly demand.

If capital is incorporated, labor should have the same privilege. If favors in any case are awarded to one party, they should certainly be furnished to the other.

Laborers, then, may combine, if they deem it best to act in concert in regard to their interests.

As a matter of fact, they do form associations for mutual benefit. In England, these "friendly societies," as they are called, are numerous, and often exert a very happy influence. They are formed for a great variety of specified objects. One class, for example, provide,—

1st, For assisting members when they are obliged to travel in search of employment.

2d, For granting temporary relief to members in distressed circumstances.

3d, For the relief and maintenance of members in case of blindness, lameness, or bodily hurt through accident.

4th, For the purchase of necessaries to be supplied to the members.

5th, For the purpose of assuring the members against loss by disease or death of cattle employed in trade or agriculture.

6th, For the purpose of accumulating at interest, for the use of the member, the surplus fund remaining after providing for his assurance.

Some societies provide for a variety of other contingencies,—sickness, old age, and death. These associations are so numerous and important in Great Britain that the government has appointed a registrar (John Tidd Pratt, Esq.) for their general supervision, and his reports are annually made to Parliament. All associations like these, if properly managed, have a tendency, not only to relieve the misfortunes of the laboring classes, but to enhance their wages by making them more independent.

Societies are also formed for the diffusion of intelligence amongst these classes, and for their moral and social elevation,—like temperance associations, lyceums, mechanics' institutes, &c. These, too, have the effect to influence favorably the rate of wages, since they tend to bring laborers more upon a level with the more favored classes, to increase their intelligence, and especially to divert them from low and degrading occupations and amusements.

Associations of this kind will, in the progress of events, undoubtedly contribute more and more towards an equal distribution of the wealth which labor produces in conjunction with capital, provided they are formed for proper purposes, and conducted in an orderly manner.

TRADES' UNIONS.

One of the forms in which these associations make their appearance is that of trades' unions. The principal object of these, generally, is the increase of wages. The different trades often combine for this purpose, and endeavor to fix the rate at which they will work. This, it would seem, they have an undoubted right to do: whether it be good policy is another question.

Men may mutually agree, for example, that they will work only ten hours per day, and will have two dollars per day as wages. All who voluntarily join such an agreement are in honor bound to keep it; and, if the association binds itself to support those who are turned out of employment, they have also the undoubted right so to do.

But, while all this is conceded, it does not follow, that, if a member violates the rules of the society, his associates may inflict any punishment upon him for doing so, except such as the law of the land authorizes. A trade's union is not an *imperium in imperio*. It has all the rights which each individual member has, and no more. Hence any attempt to inflict punishment upon such delinquent is as much an infringement of his rights, and of the laws of the country, as if it were done by an individual.

Again: nor has a trade's union any right whatever, moral or legal, to interfere in any manner with those of their craft who do not choose to enter into their association. If such persons prefer to work at a less rate of wages than that established in the tariff of the union rather than not work at all, they have the most unquestionable right to do so; and any attempt to prevent them by brute force is an infringement of personal rights which government is bound to resist to the utmost. Such an act is merely the act of a mob, and has no justification. Nay, more: under a free government, where these very men who have thus combined are citizens, with the right of suffrage, and, in common with others, elect those who enact the laws under which they live, any outrage of this kind is an overt act of moral treason against republican institutions. It is a virtual declaration that these institutions *have* failed, and *must* fail, to give adequate protection, and therefore these aggrieved parties are obliged to resort to violence; in other words, to override the government, the Constitution, and the laws.

STRIKES.

The foregoing argument covers the whole ground of right or wrong in regard to strikes.

Members of a trade's union, believing that their wages are inadequate or less than their employers can well afford, by mutual agreement *strike* for higher wages. If not granted, they *turn out.* To produce effect, and aid in obtaining what they demand, they parade the streets with banners and music. Very well, so far; for other associations do the same, whenever they see fit. If these demonstrations do not interfere with the general avocations and pursuits of the public, there can be no reasonable complaint. The economy and utility of such demonstrations is another matter; but the right to make them need not be disputed.

But when, in addition to this, a procession, instead of peaceably passing through the streets, proceeds to compel by force every person engaged in a particular trade to quit his employment, the case is entirely altered. The procession has become a lawless mob, and is to be dealt with like any other body of men disturbing the public peace.

All demonstrations of violence, of this kind, are in utter antagonism, not only to the institutions of society in general, but to the real and permanent interests of the party which makes them. They do harm, and only harm, in the long-run, both economically and morally, and degrade, instead of elevating, the laboring classes, who really have much to hope from their associations of various kinds, if they be peacefully and properly conducted. There is no one thing by which the interests of the laborer can be more effectually promoted than by associations for good and useful purposes, managed in a sensible and becoming manner; and, on economical as well as moral and social considerations, they would then be worthy the approbation and patronage of the capitalist, whose interests would be promoted thereby: but it should ever be remembered that individuality is to be interfered with as little as possible, since the more there is of individual responsibility, socially and politically, the better; the less men are called upon to resign their freedom of action and personal reliance and choice in the various duties and emergencies of life, the more advantageous to their welfare and happiness.

But strikes cannot permanently raise the rate of wages. Combinations of workmen, taking advantage of the peculiar state of trade when commodities are in great demand, may, for the moment, extort, from the necessities of their employers, an addition to their compensation; but they gain no substantial advantage. When trade becomes dull, they are certain to be placed again in the power of the employer. Especially is it injurious to the interests of the workmen, where by strikes they have forced out of employment large numbers, whom they are obliged to support out of previous accumulations. In such cases, they consume their own little savings, injure the interests of those who have employed them, and render them less able to pay wages in the future.

Freedom, protection, and justice are what labor needs, and must have, or its condition will be depressed, and its productiveness diminished. With freedom, the laborer can work for whom he will: with the ballot, he can insure to himself and his interests protection and justice.

CO-OPERATIVE ASSOCIATIONS.

There is yet another mode in which those who depend upon wages may secure very great advantages to themselves; viz., by co-operative associations, formed for trading or industrial purposes. These are already somewhat extensively introduced into the United States; and, so far as are known, have been attended with a good degree of success. Mr. Fawcett (now M.P.), in his "Manual of Political Economy," has given a very full and interesting account of the operation of certain co-operative societies in Europe, from which we extract the following: —

"The co-operative movement in England was first commenced at Rochdale.* About 1844, a few working-men in that town suspected, and no doubt justly so, that they were paying a high price for tea, sugar, and other such articles, when they, at the same time, believed they were not free from adulteration. They therefore said, 'Why should we not club together sufficient amongst ourselves to purchase a chest of tea and a hogshead of sugar from some wholesale shop in Manchester?' This they did; and each one of their number was supplied with tea and sugar from this common stock, paying ready money for it, and giving the same price for it they had been charged at the shops. When all the tea and sugar had thus been sold, they agreed to divide the money thus realized amongst themselves, in proportion to the capital each had subscribed. They found, to their surprise, that a large profit had been realized. The great advantage of the plan became self-evident; for not only were they provided with a lucrative investment for their savings, but they obtained unadulterated tea and sugar at the same prices they had been previously obliged to pay for the same articles when their quality was deteriorated by all kinds of adulteration. A fresh stock of tea and sugar was, of course, purchased. Other laborers were quickly attracted to join the plan, and subscribe their savings; soon the society was sufficiently extended to justify them in taking a room, which they used as a store, and the success of the plan fully kept pace with its enlargement.

* The residence of John Bright, M.P., and where his family carry on a large manufacturing business. A. W.

"In 1856, this society, now famous as the Rochdale Pioneers, possessed a capital of about £12,800. The business was not long restricted to articles of grocery: bread, meat, and clothing were all sold on the same plan. Their capital so rapidly increased, that they were soon enabled to erect expensive flour-mills; and a supply of pure bread, as well as unadulterated tea, was thus insured. During the last few years, this Pioneers' society has attracted frequent public attention; for it has gradually grown into a vast commercial institution, embracing a great variety of trades. At the present time (1863), its capital is £32,000, the amount of business done is £170,000, and the profits realized twenty per cent. The general management of this society, and the mode in which the profits are distributed, are both excellently arranged. A ready-money system is so scrupulously adhered to, that even a large shareholder cannot make the smallest purchase on credit. The managers of the business are chosen by the general body of shareholders; and, in almost every case, an excellent selection has been made. The accounts are made up quarterly, and placed before the general meeting. London accountants have audited these accounts; and they express a unanimous opinion that no business in the country is better conducted. With regard to distribution of the profits, a sufficient sum is at first allotted to pay a dividend of five per cent on the capital; the remaining profits are divided on the following plan: Every person, when he purchases goods, receives one or more tin tickets, on which is recorded the amount of his purchases. At the end of every quarter, each person brings these tin tickets, which form the record of his aggregate purchases; and the remaining profits are distributed in proportion to the aggregate amount which each individual has expended at the store. Thirteen pence in the pound (equal to about five and a half per cent on the amount purchased) is the average amount which, in this manner, is received as a drawback."

Professor Fawcett then proceeds to give the causes of this remarkable financial success: —

"The ready-money system, invariably adopted by these societies, has probably promoted their prosperity more than any other circumstance. All bad debts are thus avoided; and, where credit is not given, a certain amount of business can be transacted with much less capital than would be required if large sums were locked up in book-debts. Under a ready-money system, the same capital may be turned over perhaps twenty times a year; and, if one per cent only is realized upon such transaction, the capital will sum an aggregate profit of twenty per cent in the course of the year. When goods are sold for ready money, they can be bought for ready money from wholesale dealers. This is always a guaranty that the purchases will be made on the most favorable terms. Again: the shareholders of the society form a nucleus of customers; and therefore, directly business is commenced, a certain amount of trade is insured. If an individual commences business, he must attract customers either by advertising or costly shop-fronts; he is compelled to conduct his business in crowded thoroughfares, where rents are extremely high: but a co-operative society is saved all these expenses. Its shareholders are its customers; it therefore need not advertise; it does not require a showy building; for its position is rather in the centre of the homes of the laboring population. These and other advantages sufficiently account for the large profits which have been realized, not only by the Rochdale co-operative store, but by a great number of similar societies, situated in almost every other part of the country."

The author here enumerates a long list of different places in which these stores are established, as Manchester, Huddersfield, Dover, Blackburn, &c. He then proceeds to state some of the advantages of these institutions: —

"The advantages which the working classes derive from a co-operative store are apparent. In the first place, it provides them with a most eligible investment for their savings. This is important, because the absence of good opportunities for investing small savings operates powerfully to increase the improvidence of the poor."

Again, he says: —

"The co-operative principle, when applied to trade and manufactures, enables the laborer to support his industry with his own capital, and, in this manner, to rise from the mere status of a hired laborer. . . . There can be no doubt that these societies promote a most healthy social intercourse between workmen; for, at frequent meetings, the shareholders consult each other upon matters of business. They have to show their discrimination in selecting the proper persons to be managers; and, in fact, the experience of the Rochdale store proves that a co-operative society can succeed in carrying out many a social improvement, which would not otherwise be introduced. Thus, two and a half per cent of the profits realized at Rochdale support an excellent reading-room and library, which the shareholders, as well as their wives and families, are permitted to use gratuitously; the society organizes excursions, and often performs some united work of charity: not long since, its members presented a magnificent drinking-fountain to their fellow-townsmen. A co-operative store may, moreover, become a particularly powerful agent in benefiting the working classes, because it can be conducted on the smallest possible scale. The experiment can be made without involving any expense: any half-dozen working-men may try the plan, as it was tried in 1844 at Rochdale, by clubbing together sufficient to purchase a chest of tea from a wholesale grocer. If their first effort is successful, they may gradually develop their plan, until, at length, it becomes a great and important trading establishment."

The same writer gives the following account of an industrial co-operative association: —

"A small society of co-operative masons was established in 1848, in Paris. This society was reproached for holding certain political opinions, and the government attempted to discourage it by refusing to loan any capital. This intended hostility secured its future success; for the societies which were assisted by the government, in almost every instance, proved to be failures. The co-operative masons endured many vicissitudes; and, in the year 1852, they determined to re-organize their society. It then consisted of only seventeen members, and borrowed no capital. They resolved to create a capital, by depositing in a common chest one-tenth of their daily earnings. At the end of the first year, a capital of fourteen pounds and ten shillings was in this manner created. At the end of 1854, the capital had increased to six hundred and eighty pounds; and, in 1860, consisted of one hundred and seven members, and the capital possessed by them was fourteen thousand and five hundred pounds. The Hôtel Fould, the Hôtel Rouher, the Hôtel Frescati, &c., &c., were erected by this industrial association. At the present time, these co-operative masons are building an hotel for M. Girardin, on the Boulevard of the King of Rome, and an hotel at Montrouge, for M. Pacotte. No laborers, except the shareholders, are employed by the society. The laborers are paid the ordinary wages, current in the trade, and the net profits realized are proportioned in the following manner: two-fifths of these profits form a fund, from which the annual dividend is paid; and the remaining three-fifths are appropriated to provide an extra bonus on labor. The bonus each laborer thus receives is proportioned to the amount of labor he has performed throughout the year. No arrangements that could be devised would more powerfully promote the efficiency of labor. This is the secret of the remarkable success achieved by this society."

The advantages of these associations is further stated, as follows: —

"In the first place, it may be observed that the laborers receive the whole profits which result from their industry; for they supply the capital which is required. Another most important effect seems likely to result from these associations; for they appear to hold out a fair prospect of correcting a very disadvantageous tendency, which is associated with the present rapid accumulation of wealth. For we have previously remarked that each year the production of wealth is conducted on a greater scale: manufactories are enlarged, farms are extended in area, and in every branch of industry there are those that seem, from the very vastness of their capital, to monopolize the additional profit, and thus compel the smaller producer to succumb. Hence, each year it becomes more difficult for the laborer to engage in any industry on his own account. . . . Hence, the industry of the country must be conducted by two distinct classes; namely, employers who supply the capital, and workmen who provide labor; unless those who labor agree to form themselves into associations, and subscribe amongst themselves sufficient capital to carry on production upon a large scale. It must be quite evident, that co-operative trading establishments, when successful, as it were intensify many advantages which laborers derive from co-operative stores. But we have separately described these two classes of institutions, because we think that the success of the former may be imperilled by many circumstances which do not affect the latter. In fact, we have already stated, that, in the case of a co-operative store, success may almost be guaranteed. . . . But the case is very different with regard to a co-operative society carrying on some branch of industry for profit."

This the writer shows to be more hazardous. He gives, in connection with this, a statement of a very successful agricultural co-operative enterprise, commenced some thirty years since, in which the results were in the highest degree satisfactory.

The description here given, by Professor Fawcett, of co-operative societies abroad, furnishes satisfactory evidence of their feasibility, and the great advantages the laboring classes may derive from them. If true to their interests, they will direct their attention to the formation of such associations in this country. By so doing, they will violate no legal enactment, in no way disturb the public peace, or interfere with the laws of trade. They will simply avail themselves of their just rights, for the use of the power which legitimately belongs to them.

CHAPTER V.

PROFITS.

By the term "profits," we mean that share of wealth which, in the general distribution, falls to those who effect an advantageous union between labor and capital.

All wealth, being the product of labor and capital, would be divided between them, were it not necessary that still another agent should take part in production; viz., an employer, manager, undertaker* (*entrepreneur*), projector, contractor, business man, merchant, manufacturer, farmer, or whatever else he may be called, whose services are indispensable.

Capital cannot move itself; labor cannot command capi-

* "It is to be regretted," says J. Stuart Mill, "that this word, in this sense, is not familiar to the English ear. French political economists enjoy a great advantage in being able to speak of *les profits de l'entrepreneur*."

tal, and therefore has little power: hence the necessity for an employer, or *business man*, to effect a union, and put both in successful operation. Capital without labor is an infant; labor without capital, a cripple.

The parties, then, to production are, (1) the laborer; (2) the capitalist; (3) the employer, or manager. Each has a distinct province, and a separate interest; and each must receive his reward, or share of the general product.

This is, undoubtedly, the natural division of the subject. To confound the capitalist with the employer, as often is done, throws the whole matter into confusion. There is no occasion whatever for this. The man who owns the capital, and receives his compensation for its use in the shape of rent, or interest; the laborer, who applies muscular or mental power to the production of value; and the man who, as employer or manager, relieves the first from the anxiety and risks of trade, and furnishes the second with the means by which alone he can work to advantage, — are separate persons, with distinct interests.

The capitalist, as such, has no share in the profits of business. He does nothing but loan his wealth, which, by the value of its services, brings him an income, in the shape of rent for real, or interest for personal estate.* If he is careful in regard to the securities he takes or the credit he gives, it is of no immediate consequence to him whether trade is dull or brisk, whether profits are high or low; but, of course, it is true that the capitalist has a general interest in the profits of business, to this extent, — that unless profits, in the long-run and on the average, are such that the business man can afford to pay the usual rate of interest, the compensation of the capitalist, or his share in the general distribution, must be reduced. He must rent or loan his capital on such terms as those who employ it can afford,

* The term "personal estate," in distinction from real estate (land, buildings, and the like), is generally used in the United States to describe every kind of movable property, and all evidences of debt.

over and above all the charges and hazard of business, besides making a satisfactory profit. On the other hand, to the employer, in whatever department of business, the question of profits is vital. His success depends upon the amount he can secure, after meeting all his necessary expenditures for labor, rent, interest, taxes, insurance, bad debts, &c.

It often happens that the employer (manufacturer, merchant, &c.) is the owner, in whole or in part, of the capital used. This in no wise alters the case; for then he receives income both for his capital and his labor, or efforts. He saves all the interest he would otherwise pay to the capitalist; he pays interest to himself. He may own the buildings he occupies; and in so far he is a capitalist, paying rent to himself.

It is, then, by this triple alliance of enterprise, capital, and labor that all production is effected; and between them, in the final result, it should be shared. The economical question is, How shall an equitable division be attained?

We have previously said, in relation to capital and labor, that there must be a just proportion of each to the most efficient production,—sufficient labor for the capital, and capital for the labor: so there must be sufficient enterprise, business talent, and tact to use both; and the several parties must be left to act voluntarily, under the instincts of human nature and the laws of value. Indeed, the great difference in the wealth of nations is made by the business class: mind is more effective than muscle. Each party, too, must be protected in his just rights, and be insured against the encroachments of the other. No advantage should be given by legal enactments to either. The capitalist should be free to loan his money to whom he will, and at whatever rate he can get; the employé, to work for whom he pleases, and at such compensation as he can obtain by the competition of employers. If the laws allow capitalists, by concentrating their wealth, to increase its power, laborers should have an equal right to combine their efforts; and employers should be free to secure the services of either, on the best terms they can.

With this perfect equality, each will certainly obtain the share that belongs to him. Laws in regard to this, as all other property relations, are not needed to direct human industry, but to control human passion; to prevent one party from trespassing upon the rights of the other.

All these parties are equally necessary. In one respect, labor has the advantage, since it can accomplish a little without capital, while capital can produce nothing without labor. On the other hand, capital can rest, without extinction; while labor, if not employed, will soon perish by starvation.

It has been common to speak of the profits of capital, instead of the profits of business. This is a mistake which confounds necessary distinctions. The profits of trade, or business, are to be reckoned *upon the amount transacted*, not upon the capital employed. The difference between the two modes is often very great.

We give the following table as an illustration of what we mean: —

An Illustration of the Difference of Profits as computed on the Capital employed or the Business transacted.

CAPITAL EMPLOYED.	Sales.	Rate of Profits on Sales.	Gross Profits.	Expenses, including Interest.	Net Profits.	Net Profits, if reckoned on Capital.	Net Profits, if reckoned on Business done.
$100,000	$500,000	15 per cent	$75,000	$25,000	$50,000	50 per cent	10 per cent
20,000	150,000	10 " "	15,000	7,500	7,500	37½ " "	5 " "
10,000	30,000	30 " "	9,000	2,000	7,000	70 " "	26⅔ " "
50,000	350,000	5 " "	17,500	7,500	10,000	20 " "	2⅞ " "

The actual transactions of business present an endless variety, of which the above may be taken as samples.

The object aimed at by the business man is to get as large a net profit to himself as possible, irrespective of the per centum of profit on the capital employed. On his capital, if borrowed, he pays the interest; if he owns it, he computes the interest as a part of his expenses, reckoning the latter as the income on his capital.

RATE OF PROFITS.

There is a constant tendency, in the progress of society, to a decline in the rate of profits; *i.e.*, as has just been said, of profits upon business done.

1st, From the acceleration of exchanges, or the rapidity with which capital is used; in consequence of which, the same absolute remuneration can be obtained with less charge on each transaction.

2d, From the increasing number of those who, by education and training, are qualified for independent business.

3d, From increasing facilities for intercourse by steam, on land and sea, and the consequent diffusion of intelligence in regard to prices and markets.

The rate of profit can never be arbitrarily fixed where there is free competition, any more than the wages of labor; yet in a given country, or mart of trade, there may be an actual average rate which all individuals strive to attain; say, for example, ten per cent. As a matter of fact, such individual obtains all he can. He does this, especially in places of large trade, by charging as much advance on every article as he finds it will bear. If his rate is too high, he will find his custom fall off; or, if he has customers, they will be of a hazardous class, by whose delinquencies he will lose more than he can gain by their patronage. Then, again, it is practically true, that scarce any two commodities pay the same profit; some, it may be, only two, some ten, some twenty per cent. And, further, while in the same street one man sells his goods at ten per cent, another is selling at seven and a half per cent, and is making a larger *amount* of net profits at that. Why is this?

First, The latter buys more shrewdly. *Secondly*, he carries on his business more by his own efforts, and with less expense; and, *lastly*, sells, as he will be likely to do, to reliable men, who most certainly discover where they can purchase to the greatest advantage.

RAPIDITY OF EXCHANGE.

The *necessary* rate of profit depends greatly on the rapidity of sales, as compared with the capital employed and the expense of conducting business.

This may be shown in the following illustration: —

A, with a capital of $10,000, which he turns every six months, charges twenty per cent profit.

B, with same amount, turns his capital once in three months, at fifteen per cent.

C, with same amount, turns his capital every thirty days, at seven and one-half per cent.

Result: —	A sells $20,000 at 20 per cent		$4,000
	Interest on capital	$600	
	Rent	600	
	Labor and other expenses	800	2,000
	A's net profit		$2,000
	B sells $40,000 at 15 per cent		$6,000
	Interest on capital	$600	
	Rent	600	
	Labor, &c.	1,200	2,400
	B's net profit		$3,600
	C sells $120,000 at 7½ per cent		$9,000
	Interest on capital	$600	
	Rent	600	
	Labor, &c.	2,500	3,700
	C's net profit		$5,300

Large sales, with small profits, or a rapid turning of capital, is the natural tendency of trade, as population and wealth increase, and especially as credits are diminished.

Those who sell for cash have immensely the advantage of those who give long credits, particularly under a mixed currency, which so largely increases the hazards of trade.

In those communities in which the people are generally poor, and their wants great and pressing, as in newly settled countries, credits are naturally much extended, and, of course, the rate of profits proportionally increased. This is known to be the case over a large part of our Western States. The people can afford to pay large profits, if by so doing they can get the use of capital, because capital produces so large a return; as, for example, one thousand dollars invested in the spring in ploughing the prairie, and getting in a crop of wheat, will, not unlikely, give a net profit, within six months, of one hundred per cent. But when such communities accumulate capital, and are able to pay as they purchase, they come to buy at greatly reduced rates, and profits fall to the minimum. This is the general law in all countries, though most clearly seen in new settlements. The average rate of profits in a country is determined by the same law as wages. Profits are merely *wages received by the employer*. This idea should be kept constantly in mind. The wages of the laborer depend upon supply and demand: why not the wages of those who employ him? The employer is as truly a laborer as the man who toils with the spade, only on a higher plane.

If there are more laborers than are wanted, wages fall; if fewer, they advance: just so with employers, or business undertakers. If there are too many competing for profits, the rate will fall until the excess is driven back into the ranks of labor. As there are, however, comparatively few, in proportion to the whole number of persons capable of labor, who have the requisite capacity and training required for transacting business successfully, and fewer still who can command the necessary means or capital, it will follow that the rewards of the employer will be larger than those of the persons employed. But we must not forget that this difference is less than at first appears, because our observation shows us, that, of all who undertake to trade or manufacture, a large majority become bankrupts; and, consequently, the average difference between the employer and the employed is greatly reduced.

There is, undoubtedly, a constant tendency to an equalization and reduction of profits from continual improvements in the means of locomotion, and the increasing intelligence of the people. The opening of railroads has wrought a great revolution in this particular. These not only greatly reduce the cost of transportation, but the average rate of profits. For example, a given town is one hundred miles from the mart of trade, by which it is supplied. There are only common roads, and those of bad construction. Eight or ten days are required to pass teams to and from the city. Under such circumstances, the people generally will be likely to know but little of the market value of commodities. As they must very rarely visit the places where merchandise is obtained, and, consequently, are ignorant of the worth of the articles they are obliged to purchase, and quite unable to supply themselves directly, they are charged large profits on what they buy. Let a railroad be put in operation, so that the time distance is reduced from eight or ten days to four or five hours, the price of all commodities in market will be known, and those who supply them must do so at a small advance; while yet, it may be, the dealers will make as large aggregate profits from increased sales.

EFFECTS ON PROFITS OF A TEMPORARY RISE OF WAGES.

The effect of a temporary rise of wages upon profits may be illustrated as follows: —

A manufacturer of kerseymeres is able to produce an article for one dollar per yard, for which he can get one dollar and twenty cents in the usual state of trade. A sudden rise of wages advances the cost to one dollar and ten cents. The result, under ordinary circumstances, will be that the manufacturer will not be able to obtain at once an advance equal to the enhanced cost. He will be fortunate if he can get one dollar and twenty-five cents for his goods, leaving him but fifteen cents profit. But, if the rise in wages holds on until the market has been cleared of the stock of goods on hand, the price will then be easily brought up to one dollar and thirty or one dollar and thirty-five cents.

But a rise of wages, especially if occasioned by an expansion of the currency, is sure to be followed by a corresponding decline when contraction takes place. The manufacturer will then gain the advantage he lost by the rise of wages. His goods will not fall at once as much as the fall in wages. This is the practical experience of business men; and they can safely calculate to gain as much on the one hand as they lost on the other. Wages, we have previously shown on page 258, fall faster than commodities. It is from the operation of this law that the *entrepreneur* gains in the fall as much, ordinarily, as he lost in the rise of wages.

DIVIDENDS.

A large share of the income received by owners of capital, at the present day, comes in the form of dividends on stock, held in corporations and joint-stock companies, formed for almost every conceivable purpose. The introduction of railroads has caused immense investments, the income from which is received in dividends. How are these to be classed? They cannot be regarded as synonymous with interest, or rent: they must be considered as profits. They are received for the profits of business done by proxy. The capitalist may not have the slightest agency in the affairs of the company from which he gets an income; still he is a partner, though a limited and silent one, and receives his share of the profits or loss.

It may be objected, that bank dividends must surely be classed with interest, since they are made up wholly of interest received for the loan of capital. This is not strictly correct. No inconsiderable share of profit to the banks of the United States is derived from the premiums charged for exchange. American banks are exchange-brokers. Besides, nearly one-half of all the income of mixed-currency banks is derived from the manufacture of currency, not the loaning of money or capital. Although the dividends of banks, of this kind, approach nearer to interest than those of ordinary business corporations, still they are most properly classed with profits.

Through associations, capital is largely connected with the industrial operations of the country, and shares directly in their prosperity or adversity. This result is in so far a favorable one, as it unites the interest of capital with the industry of the country.

CHAPTER VI.

INTEREST.

WHAT is paid for the use of money, or any other form of loanable capital, is called "interest." Hence the term "usury." It is all the reward that capital receives, not embraced in the term "rent." It ordinarily insures the return made for the employment of money, because loans are commonly made in that form; but the idea of interest is general to all articles having value, but not bringing rent.

Interest has its justification in the right of property. If a man can claim the ownership of any kind of wealth, he is the owner of all it fairly produces. Past labor has all the sacredness of present labor, and as justly claims its reward. An associate in production, it is entitled to a share in the product. Whoever by labor produces wealth, and by self-denial preserves it, should be allowed all the benefit that wealth can render in future production. This is the only condition upon which the largest accumulation of wealth can be secured; it presents the only motive that can withstand the impulse to immediate gratification. The desire to gain and the desire to spend are both in human nature, and are conflicting passions. What one takes, the other must relinquish. If, therefore, the desire to spend is unchecked, all wealth and physical well-being disappear in riot and wastefulness. There is the further consideration, that, since to loan capital is to incur risk, that risk should be compensated. It has been a favorite idea with many visionary writers, that interest can be entirely done away with. Proudhon and others have speculated and theorized much on this subject; but nothing can be more idle. We can no more get rid of interest than value: both are in the laws of nature. Yet this has been, in the view of many, the philosopher's stone, that was to transmute all baser metals into gold. It is akin to the idea that credit can be made to take the place of value, and is sustained by the same sort of reasoning as that "property is a crime; a monopoly that must be destroyed."

We will notice briefly a few of the main principles that govern the rate of interest the world over.

1st, Interest, in its general rate, will be determined by the productiveness of labor in the community where it is employed. It is evident the reward of capital cannot be larger than the total profits of business, because it would no longer be used; nor can it be equal to these profits, for no one would be disposed to employ it and pay out his whole profits for its use. Interest must, therefore, be less than the aggregate amount of the returns of production; and finding, as it does, a competitor in the power of present labor, capital will be obliged to submit to an equitable division.

If, then, the productiveness of labor is very great, if the industry of the community yields easily and richly, capital will naturally obtain a large reward; while, if Nature be niggardly in her gifts, each of the parties must be content with a pittance.

2d, Interest will be governed by the law of supply and demand. This is so evident as not to require argument or proof, hardly illustration. Old countries abound in accumulations of capital. Interest is there found cheap. In all new countries, there is a youthfulness of capital; there has not been time to develop the powers of production; and hence interest is high. The United States of America afford a most striking example in point. There is a vast amount of uncultivated but fertile land, while the amount of capital with which to cultivate it is comparatively small. So of its manufacturing capacities. Hence there is a high general rate of interest. This is governed by the supply and demand, *i.e.* by the laws of value alone, and should never be interfered with by legal enactments.

This is a lesson mankind have been slow to learn; yet the most commercial nation in the world (Great Britain) has abolished all usury laws. The experiment was at first made with great caution, limiting the exemption to a particular kind of paper, and the time in which it should operate to a few months; but it was found so perfectly satisfactory to the community, that, after a fair trial, the abolition of the usury laws was made final and complete.

But, upon a question so much in dispute, it may be desirable to give the principal reasons why the matter of interest should not be interfered with by law.

(*a*) When it is made a penal offence to take over a certain per cent interest (say six), if money is worth more, as it often will be, it must be obtained by some indirect process. Most persons do not like to directly violate a law, however foolish or unjust they may deem it to be; consequently, they will attempt to evade it. There is no difficulty in this. A note may be sold to a broker for what it will bring; and the broker buys it with funds furnished by the capitalist, who stands behind the curtain while the borrower pays the broker for getting the money he might otherwise have obtained directly of the capitalist himself. The law has not prevented the usury, only increased the rate. The broker feels no responsibility; for he is only an agent between the parties. The capitalist has no scruples; for he is not known in the transaction. Instead of this, the borrower and lender should be brought face to face, in an open market, where each could be protected by law in the transaction; and then a fair, unrestricted competition would assure the lowest rate of interest, obtained in the most economical manner.

But for usury laws, the current rate of interest would be as well known as the price of stocks or corn or wool, and would, like them, be determined by the laws of trade; and men would act as intelligently and as freely as in the purchase of merchandise. Freedom is as essential in the disposal of money as in the intercourse of nations. To hamper it with laws regulating the rate at which it shall be loaned, is as absurd, and as repugnant to the laws of wealth, as to fix the price of wheat or cotton.

(*b*) Usury laws create an injurious distinction between different kinds of mercantile paper, and thus occasion embarrassment and loss to borrowers.

For example, the law says in Massachusetts that only six per cent interest shall be taken by the banks. But money may be worth twelve per cent; and there are ten applications for it, at that rate, to one that can be supplied. What is the result? Why, the bank will make no loans except upon such paper as it can charge for exchange. Exchange is legal, whether it is real or fictitious. A and B apply for discount at a bank in Boston. A offers notes of the most undoubted character, payable in Boston; B offers notes or drafts payable in New York, and he gets accommodated. His drafts have sixty days to run; he is charged one per cent exchange, and thus pays twelve per cent interest. A, having only notes on which no such exchange can be legally charged, must "go into the street," and employ a broker to sell the notes for him at the best rates he can.

This state of things occasions great annoyance and loss to borrowers; yet it must continue so long as usury laws exist.

(*c*) Usury laws are the principal cause of compulsory deposits, or deposits made to secure large discounts. These are, as we have shown, exceedingly burdensome to the business community, and most dangerous to the currency. If the rate of interest, as at the Bank of England, was left entirely to the state of the money market, these deposits, now peculiar to American banking, would disappear. If every man could borrow money at what it was worth, there would be no motive to bribe moneyed institutions indirectly.

3d, Interest will be influenced largely by the safety or hazard of capital. This will depend,—

(*a*) Upon the moral character of the people, whether essentially honest or dishonest, whether honorable or dishonorable, whether industrious, frugal, and temperate, or otherwise.

(*b*) Upon the general thrift of the community; for however well disposed to pay, if decay and decline are general, the hazards of capital must be greatly increased. It must share in the general losses of business.

(*c*) Upon the justice and efficiency of the laws by which the rights of property are secured, and the obligation of contracts enforced. This, as can readily be seen, is one of the most important considerations in regard to the safety of loans; and, of course, the rate of compensation in the shape of interest.

4th, Again, the uniformity of the rate of interest, and its general average, will depend mainly upon the soundness of the currency. If it consists wholly of value,—that is, if the credit element constitutes no part of the circulating medium or standard of value,—the rate of interest will be as uniform and as low as the laws of trade admit. The rate can never be absolutely fixed at one point; yet, where no credit is used as *currency*, the credits of the country will be so based upon values that the vacillations will be very moderate. They were very slight in Europe until within the last thirty years.

We have already shown, when speaking of a mixed currency,* how frequent and excessive are the fluctuations in the rate of interest in the United States. In no other civilized country have they been so great, for the sufficient reason that no other country has a *mixed currency* so deficient in the element of value.

We have shown, at the place referred to, that these variations have been from three and one-half to thirty-six per cent. Now, no commodity, in time of peace, has varied to an equal extent. The reason is, that commodities are not wanted to pay notes; but, to meet pecuniary engagements, money is, and must be had.

Under a currency in which credit is the principal element, the fluctuations in interest are in proportion to the extent of that element; because, as we have shown, a mixed currency, whenever there is any panic or distress for money, withdraws from circulation with a rapidity proportionate to its weakness, or want of value. Hence the frightful revulsions we have witnessed. And we may doubtless expect that these will increase in force and frequency in the future, since the mixed-currency system, once almost exclusively confined to England, France, and the United States, is being extended throughout the commercial world. The risks of credit will therefore be greater, and the average rate of interest will, so far as risk is concerned, be enhanced.

But, in regard to a legal rate of interest, it may be asked, whether a limit should not be established by law, in all cases where the parties have not themselves agreed upon one. Certainly, it would seem desirable and proper, that, in the absence of all agreement or contract, the law should say

* See Diagram No. 9, p. 197.

that a given rate should be awarded. This would not be regulating the rate of interest, but establishing justice between the different parties in those cases where, from any cause, no fixed rate of interest had been agreed upon. This legal rate would properly be the general average rate obtained for the use of money.

CHAPTER VII.

RENT.

RENT is paid for the use of land and its appendages, which together are called "real estate." The question of the rent of land is of much less practical importance in the United States than in Europe, since it is here generally held in fee simple by those who cultivate it. Yet, as an economic question, it deserves consideration. And there is an especial inducement, since we certainly have in this country the best opportunity to investigate, in their simple primitive form, all the phenomena connected with it. Constantly entering upon new lands, we have exhibited for our observation the working-out of problems which long puzzled the philosophers of the old world.

1st, Rent implies ownership, since no one would pay for the use of that to which all had an equal title. This may be called the first condition.

2d, It implies society, so that more than one person shall desire the use of the same land or appendages. If exchange, as M. Bastiat says, "is civilization," rent is society. This is the second condition.

From our definition, it will appear that rent is paid (*a*) for land, (*b*) for whatever is added to its value or desirableness. We cannot separate the two considerations, nor would it be of practical utility if we could; as, from what we have already endeavored to show, value is not derived from the gifts of nature, but the labor of man: "land, water, steam, electricity, and the like, confer no value."

Land may be said to be the foundation of rent; and, since the rightfulness of appropriating it has been disputed, it may be proper to remark that we deem it a sufficient answer, that appropriation is indispensable to the production and accumulation of wealth, to the progress of civilization, and the welfare of the human race: therefore it is right.

Man, in his original or savage state, is a *hunter*. He needs no appropriation of land; for he roams at large through the forest. He accumulates little or nothing; and it is of small importance where he builds his temporary cabin. His means of living are precarious; he is often exposed to starvation, has nothing permanent, pays no rent, and population but slowly increases.

Nor in the second or nomadic condition, when man becomes a *shepherd*, does rent make its appearance. His business is no longer mere destruction, but preservation and use. This elevates his condition; the employment has a far more ennobling effect upon character; higher faculties and better feelings are developed. But still he lives in a tent, and removes from place to place to find pasturage for his flocks. In the natural progress of events, he becomes an *agriculturist*. His chief business now is to till the ground. How can he do this without preparation of the soil from which he is to draw his sustenance? And why should he do this, if another may at will dispossess him of his labors? The land *must* be divided, appropriated, and held by some tenure that can be relied upon; and, when this takes place, rent makes its appearance, and increases in intensity as man becomes more and more advanced in social condition; for with agriculture come the mechanic arts, manufactures, commerce, villages, towns, cities, — civilization.

We now come to the elements which enter into the rental of land.

THE FIRST ELEMENT OF RENT.

Location. — This grows out of the social condition of man, to which we have alluded. If men lived as isolate beings, and there were land enough for all, and the whole equally fertile, there would be no rent; but, once gathered into villages and communities, rent would make its appearance, *although there were as much land as all desired, and each part equally productive.*

This point we shall endeavor to make plain by an illustration.* A colony of thirteen families settles along the shore, where all the land is unclaimed, and immigrants have only to choose where and how much they will occupy. We will suppose the land all equally fertile, agreeable, and accessible. In point of fact, there shall be no natural difference between one lot of one hundred and sixty acres (what each family desires) and another; absolutely no choice arising from any thing appertaining to the land. They accordingly lay out thirteen lots half a mile square. This allotment and location upon the shore we represent as follows: —

1	2	3	4	5	6	7*	8	9	10	11	12	13

In this arrangement, it will be seen, the lots commencing on the left are numbered 1 to 13. No. 7 is, of course, the middle lot.

Now, all being equally eligible, the land equally accessible and good, and there being as many lots as settlers, and each as large as any one desires, will there be any value to them? Yes: because all will prefer No. 7, for they perceive that it is most desirable, inasmuch as it is central; and, if public buildings are erected for the accommodation of all (schoolhouse, church, &c.), they must be

* This illustration was given by the author in the "Merchant's Magazine," in 1860, vol. xlii. p. 306.

placed on that lot. If a landing-place is made, or a warehouse put up, for the commerce of the settlement, it must be on No. 7; for the obvious reason that it is the point at which the whole population can most readily assemble, and it thus forms the natural centre of business.

All this is so apparent, that each man prefers No. 7; but only one can have it. What follows? It must be sold to the man who will give the most for it. Some one will give one hundred bushels of wheat, or its equivalent, — six bushels rent per annum. All this does actually happen in every case of new settlement; not, indeed, in a manner always so distinct and striking as in the case we have supposed, but in principle as certain and absolute.

If this is so, we have established the fact, that, though all land were equally fertile, and there were enough for all, and all equally desirable in every other particular, yet that rent would arise from the social wants of man, which make mere *location* a circumstance affecting its value, and create a rental independent of all other considerations.

THE SECOND ELEMENT OF RENT.

Difference of Fertility. — We will suppose four different tiers of land, of unequal fertility. The first will yield forty bushels of corn; the second, with the same labor, thirty; the third, twenty; the fourth, ten.

Now, while there was enough land of the first to produce all the corn wanted, nobody would give any rent for the first tier on account of its fertility; but when, by the increase of population, it became necessary to cultivate No. 2, which would only yield thirty, No. 1 would command a rental of ten bushels, because a man might as well give ten bushels rent for No. 1 as to cultivate No. 2 without rent.

When, again, necessity compelled the cultivation of No. 3, No. 2 would pay a rent of ten bushels, and No. 1 of twenty bushels. And further, when tier No. 4 must be brought under culture to produce the quantity of corn needed for consumption, then, as it would with equal labor produce but ten bushels, No. 1 would yield a rent of thirty, No. 2 of twenty, and No. 3 of ten; while the last, or No. 4, would afford no rent.*

THE THIRD ELEMENT OF RENT.

We will further suppose, that, from the increase of population, more corn is wanted than can be raised; and, consequently, importations are made at an increased price, — equal, say, to fifty per cent. Now if, for the sake of convenience, we take the price of corn to have been originally one dollar a bushel, and to have advanced to one dollar and fifty cents, it will come to pass that tier or quality No. 1 will have a rent of $45; No. 2, of $30; No. 3, of $20; and No. 4, which now for the first time produces rent, of $5.

This represents the condition of Great Britain, which, besides raising all the wheat her highly cultivated fields can profitably produce, imports some eighty millions of bushels annually. This causes a large increase of prices; consequently, of money rent.

FOURTH ELEMENT OF RENT.

Application of Capital to Land. — This is done in various ways, — by the use of fertilizing materials, drainage, deep ploughing, &c. For every such appliance, wisely made, a rent is received, supposed to be equivalent to the expenditure incurred.

And here it may be found that the same expenditure, applied to the different qualities of land, produces unequal results. Five dollars, expended per annum on No. 1, may return but a profit or additional rent of eight dollars; while

* Mr. Ricardo, we believe, first brought out this principle clearly in his "Political Economy," London, 1819.

the same amount, applied to No. 2, will give seven dollars; or to No. 3, will give six dollars, &c.

This will cause a variation in the relative rentals of the different qualities or tiers of land we have supposed.

Improvements, more or less permanent, are investments of capital in real estate, changing the income from the form of interest to that of rent. They are made to an immense extent in the older countries of Europe. Their profitableness depends, like that of all other investments, upon the wisdom with which they are made: but men are more disposed to invest capital in real estate, other things equal, than in any thing else, for the reasons that it has the greatest security; that it gives a certain degree of social importance to the holders in all countries, and, in some, confers political rights and privileges.

LAND APPENDAGES.

We have, thus far, noticed only the rent of land, without reference to what may be placed upon it for other purposes than direct production.

We now come to speak of real estate, consisting of dwellings, stores, warehouses, and the like.

When buildings are placed upon farms, they form a part of the preparations which are indispensable to agriculture; and, if erected with suitable reference to economy, will add to the value of land as much as shall be equal to their fair annual rent. Farming cannot be carried on without buildings; therefore, so far as buildings are absolutely necessary, they will command a rent as certainly as the land itself. This must be true; and yet all know that "improvements," as they are called, in the shape of buildings, seldom increase the value of farms in proportion to their cost. For example, if the land alone is worth three thousand dollars, and buildings are put up costing two thousand dollars, the whole will not, ordinarily, sell for five thousand dollars. Facts of this sort are observed everywhere. Farms may, as a general rule, be bought, especially in all the older States, at much less than their cost, after making all due allowances for depreciation of buildings, &c. We observe, first, that buildings are not generally put upon farms for the purpose of selling or letting them. They are almost invariably erected by the owners of the land, in order to create for themselves a home. To make that home pleasant and desirable, a dwelling is erected according to the tastes of the owner and his family, rather than the direct profit of the farm. There is a natural and becoming competition among agriculturists to have pleasant, and, as far as may be, elegant residences. Hence, they build upon a more expensive scale than the business of agriculture will fully justify; and though they may be able to keep on, and even thrive, with their establishments, these are, nevertheless, a heavy charge upon their industry. Whenever, therefore, such farming properties must be sold, the purchaser will rarely, if ever, give more than a fraction of the original cost of the buildings. If, as is generally the case, he must make the money off his land to pay for the estate, he cannot afford the cost of buildings erected to gratify the taste of somebody else. He gets the extra improvements gratis, really paying only for the useful and necessary.

And, in the competition of cultivation in a community like the United States, it is to be remembered that its agriculture is a unit; that the products of the accessible and fertile prairies of the West are brought into the same markets as those of the hard and sterile hills of New England. And it is also to be taken into account, that a farm in Illinois, for example, with a productive power of five thousand bushels of corn, will probably not have upon it buildings worth more than one thousand dollars; while on many Eastern farms, of a productive power of but two thousand bushels, the buildings may have cost three thousand dollars. Now, as these farms are, in fact, competing in the same general markets, it is clear that the extra expenditures upon Eastern farms can pay but little, if any, rental, though they may be very pleasant to the occupant.

It is on the same principle that the amount expended in clearings, building walls around farms, and the like, do not, in the aggregate, return much rent or income, compared with their cost. They become, in the progress of years, to a considerable extent, like the gifts of nature, gratuitous. This is true of all countries, at all times.

In cities, where the value of real estate consists principally of buildings, and improvements made upon the land, we find that the land itself feels the operation of the first cause of rent or value, viz. location, far more intensely than anywhere else. An acre of land, once of the value of fifty dollars for agriculture, becomes worth five hundred thousand dollars for city purposes. Such, and even more extraordinary, instances may be found, showing to what extent the principle of location may be carried. The estimated wealth of cities consists, to a considerable extent, of the appreciation in the value of land which the increasing density of population and the concentration of business enterprise has occasioned.

Investments in commercial cities depend, of course, for success, upon commercial prosperity. Changes likewise take place in the business centres of every great city. There is much of mere whim and fashion in this; but, whether the commerce and trade of the city moves "up town" or "down town," rents move with it.

City property, in all thrifty communities, is sure, on the whole, to advance in value with the lapse of time; and hence it is always a favorite investment. Yet so great is the competition, so large the amount of capital in cities, that the net average rental is probably not greater than the ordinary rate of interest. Rents are based on permanent property that requires much care; interest, upon securities that may prove worthless, but which demand but little attention.

The absence of all restrictions upon the ownership and transfer of landed property and real estate, of all entails and mortmain holdings, makes the question of rent one of small practical importance. Where owning is the rule, and hiring the exception, as is the case with us, rents regulate themselves; or, in other words, are governed entirely by the operation of the laws of value. They advance or recede with trade and population.

CHAPTER VIII.

WAGES, RENT, INTEREST, AND PROFITS, AS RELATIVELY AFFECTED BY CURRENCY INFLATION.

It is an important fact, not to be overlooked in our examination of incomes derived from wages, rent, interest, and profits, that all of these are not only greatly affected by the condition and character of the existing currency, but also in very unequal degrees. We have already spoken of the influence of an inflated currency upon wages and interest; but we are now to show its *unequal* operation upon all these different kinds of revenue.

The enormous inflation of currency during the rebellion has given a most favorable, because a most striking, illustration of the degree in which different interests may be affected by any inflation.

Take, for example, the years 1864 and 1865. Wages were, on an average, fifty per cent above their usual rate. Where a skilful workman had previously obtained two dollars a day, he now got three: where the common laborer got one dollar, he now got one dollar and a half. From extensive inquiry and personal observation, we are satisfied that the rise of wages, take the country through, was equal to fifty per cent: such we have found the uniform testimony of employers.

Rents, during the civil war, except in some large cities, advanced but little, on an average, throughout the country: it is much to be doubted if they advanced more than ten, certainly not more than twenty, per cent.

The rate of interest advanced generally from 6 per cent to 7.30; but this was mainly from the action of the government, which negotiated large loans at that rate, and consequently fixed that as a general standard. Yet, of the immense amount loaned on mortgage, it is doubtful if a tenth part of it has been raised beyond what it was previous to the war. But we may safely assume that the rise of interest has been from 6 to 7.30 per cent, or about twenty per cent.

Profits may be safely estimated, during 1865, at a hundred per cent higher than ordinary; that is, where they were ten per cent on the business transacted, they were increased to twenty per cent. This we suppose a very low estimate. To recapitulate: —

Interest and rent, the remuneration of the capitalist, advanced	20 per cent.
Wages, the remuneration of the laborer, advanced .	50 per cent.
Profits, the remuneration of the business man, advanced	100 per cent.

What is the result of this? Who wins, in consequence of this rise of wages, interest, rents, and profits, occasioned by the inflation of the currency? Prices rise, as we have seen, to an unprecedented height; say, one hundred and twenty per cent. Then we will suppose that —

A, the capitalist, has an income from interest and rent .	$4,000
Gains twenty per cent by rise of rate	800
Whole income in currency	$4,800

If he expends this amount in general commodities, at the advanced prices we have stated (one hundred and twenty per cent), he can only purchase with his $4,800 the same commodities he could have obtained before the general rise for $2,181.81.

From original income	$4,000.00
Deduct	2,181.81
Loss by change of prices	$1,818.19

equal to a loss of 45.4 per cent, notwithstanding the nominal rise of twenty per cent in his income.

And now as to the laborer. His wages were three hundred dollars: they are now four hundred and fifty dollars. This last sum is laid out in commodities, and brings him $204.54 worth, as reckoned at the prices before the rise. So, from $300 deduct $204.54, and his loss (in commodities) is found to be $95.46, or nearly one-third (31.82 per cent) of his sound-currency wages, or what they were before the expansion.

But how with regard to the third party, *l'entrepreneur*,— the merchant, manufacturer, &c. His income, at first, was $10,000: it is now $20,000. If laid out in commodities, the $20,000 would purchase, at the advanced prices, but $9,090.90 worth; which sum deducted from $10,000, his original profits, will give a loss of $919.10.

It is not to be presumed, however, that the whole of the income of the business man is expended in commodities, but a large share added to the capital. Suppose, before the rise of profits and prices, his expenses were five thousand dollars, and he purchases the *same commodities* now. He will then expend eleven thousand dollars, leaving him nine thousand dollars to add to his capital; while, before the general rise, he added only five thousand dollars. So that he is making a net gain of eighty per cent upon his income.

Recapitulation, on the foregoing suppositions:—

The capitalist makes a loss of	45.4 per cent.
The laborer makes a loss of	31.8 per cent.
The business man makes a gain of	80 per cent.

Or, to state the result in another form: —

The capitalist gets but 54.4 on the dollar of his just due.
The laborer gets but 68.2 on the dollar of his wages.
The business man gets 180 cents where before he got $1.00.

This statement, which we think will be found correct in principle, and approximately so in the application we have given it, shows the position of each party in reference to the change in the standard of value occasioned by the war expansion of the currency. The two first classes lose, — the capitalist most heavily, but the laborer, perhaps, most distressingly; because, as a general fact, the latter must expend all his income, and, under such circumstances, can get only about two-thirds of the commodities to eat, drink, and wear which he could obtain with his wages under a sound currency. But one of the classes mentioned is getting rich; viz., that engaged in trade, manufactures, and general business. Nor will this class, perhaps, in the end, be so greatly benefited as might be at first supposed; for it must sustain the entire loss which will take place upon all the merchandise of the country, as the currency comes down to a specie standard. One class we have omitted; viz., speculators. To them, an expansion like that we have experienced affords a *golden* and most plentiful harvest; and they are not slow to enter the field of labor and fruition. To them an expansion is always a good; for it necessarily causes a rise of prices, and of course an opportunity for speculative operations. Expansion warms them into life and activity: contraction, to a sound standard of value, suspends their animation.

Upon certain facts, in regard to this matter, all will doubtless be agreed: —

(*a*) That those who live on fixed incomes from rent, interest, or salary, were never so straitened as during the war inflation.

(*b*) That laborers got less commodities for their services than before the expansion.

(*c*) That merchants, manufacturers, and business men generally, made extraordinary profits.

(*d*) That speculators flourished beyond all precedent.

But the importance of all these facts and considerations consists in this,—that all we find to be true, theoretically and practically, during the great expansion occasioned by the war, has always been true, *in degree*, during every expansion of the currency, though never before so palpable, because never before so excessive. There is nothing new in these phenomena: they are only more strikingly exhibited. The same effects have attended all previous expansions: the same process has always been going on, always must go on, under a currency capable of unnatural inflation.

CHAPTER IX.

TAXATION.—PRINCIPLES OF TAXATION.

SINCE government, or social organization, is among the wants of man, as truly as food or clothing, we must recognize it in the science of political economy, and provide for it. Government implies functionaries and expenditures. How shall these be maintained? Evidently by the contributions of all, for all are interested in its existence.

It may, therefore, rightfully claim a share of all that labor and capital have created.

The aggregate of all sums collected by government is called its REVENUE; the system by which it is collected is called TAXATION.

Although the single object of taxation is to obtain a given amount of wealth (generally in the form of money), yet the modes by which that object may be secured are various.

In ancient times, taxation was often imposed by the arbitrary fiat of the ruler, with little or no reference to equity, or its effect on the prosperity and happiness of the people; but, in modern civilization, it has come to be regarded as altogether the most difficult and delicate task government is called upon to perform.

The question of taxation, in its various bearings, is now made the subject of examination and discussion in all legislative bodies; and taxes are imposed, in all constitutional governments, not at the caprice of the ruler, but by the representatives of the people.

Until within a few years, the people of the United States have been so fortunately exempt from heavy taxation, that it has been felt to be a matter of small consequence what the expenditures of the government amounted to, and still less whether they were wise and necessary. That day has gone by, probably not soon to return.

If, then, the property of the citizen must be taken to meet the exigencies of government, it becomes highly important that those from whom it is taken should feel that it is equitably done. Nothing in relation to all the acts of government is more to be desired than that its mode of raising a revenue should be so wisely and economically arranged, so manifestly just and equal, and so well understood by all, that no opposition to its demands shall arise from a sense of oppression.

Desirable as this would be under any form of government, it is manifestly quite indispensable in a country where there is no force superior to the public will, and where it is certain no taxes can be collected but such as are believed to be both necessary and just.

In the distribution of wealth, as has been before stated, government makes a peremptory claim to so much as its necessities, real or supposed, may require.

This claim is not only peremptory, but prior to every other claim. The laborer must contribute a part of his wages; the business man, of his profits; and the capitalist, of his interest, or rent.

Every man knows, or should know, that when he creates any kind of wealth, a share of it belongs to government. He, in fact, creates a fund out of which government is to be supported. For example, should a man pre-empt a section of land on the western prairies, and by his labor make it of the value of ten thousand dollars, government has a lien upon it equal to all the taxation it may choose to impose. The value of the farm is just so much less than it would otherwise be, by the burdens which it is known the government will lay upon it. For example, if the owner could sell it, free of all taxation, instead of ten thousand dollars, he could get, say, eleven thousand dollars for it. If we suppose that the annual tax imposed on the farm will be equal to the income on one thousand dollars, then the farm is worth one thousand dollars less on this account.

If the seller buys another farm, or any other property, with his ten thousand dollars, he gets it at just the same reduction as he sold his own farm; and, for the same reason, all property, whether personal or real, whether land or merchandise, is exchanged under these conditions; and therefore all parties creating wealth are placed on a level.

The paramount question, in regard to taxation, is, On what principles shall it be founded? Adam Smith, in his "Wealth of Nations," written almost a century ago, laid down four maxims, or principles, which have been so generally concurred in from that day to this, that, as J. Stuart Mill says, "they have become classic."

I. "The subjects of every state ought to contribute to the support of the government, as nearly as possible, in proportion to their respective abilities; that is, in proportion to the revenue they enjoy under the protection of the state. In the observation or neglect of this maxim consists what is called the equality or inequality of taxation."

In examining this proposition, our first inquiry is, What is meant by "subjects"? We answer, Every inhabitant, old or young, male or female. Women? Certainly: if they have a revenue or income, they are as justly bound to contribute to the government as men, and in the same proportion. Many women have large wealth: why should it go untaxed? Children? There are some such who are millionaires: why should they be exempt?

Idiots, lunatics, cripples? Yes, if they have "revenues." Many such persons have large estates, which should contribute to the public treasury.

It is not the ability to hear or see or walk that is taxed, but the income, or "revenue."

We next notice the condition mentioned, "as nearly as possible."

This implies that it may not be practicable to secure perfect equality; indeed, we know it is not, but such should be the aim of government.

II. "The tax which each individual is bound to pay ought to be certain, and not arbitrary. The time of payment, the manner of payment, the quantity to be paid, ought to be *clear and plain* to the contributor, and every other person."

(*a*) "Certain, and not arbitrary." By this, Dr. Smith evidently meant that the taxes should be assessed by competent authority, and upon fixed and well-known principles. In many countries, taxes have been, and in some are still, farmed out in gross to a publican, or tax-gatherer, who, under the authority of government, imposes such sums as he pleases to exact.

(*b*) The time of payment should be "clear and plain." The citizen should know *when* he pays; be conscious of the fact that he *is* paying the government a certain sum at the time he actually does it. Otherwise, he will be liable to great impositions, in one form or another.

(*c*) "The manner and the quantity plain." This for

the same reasons as just stated. He certainly ought to know *how* he pays, and *how much*.

(*d*) Should be known "to the contributor, and everybody else." In the method of taxation, the people are joint partners: what one does not pay, another must. If A pays less than he should, B and C must pay more; hence the right of every man to know, not only what he pays, but what his neighbor does. Otherwise, how can he judge whether he is overtaxed or not?

It is on this account that the publication of tax-lists is a duty on the part of the taxing power. Then, if any property is omitted by accident or design, it will probably be found out; for, being a copartner, each man is interested in the taxes of every other, and has a right to know what they are, and will or ought to give notice of any omission or incorrect valuation.

III. "Every tax should be levied at the time, or in the manner, which is most likely to be convenient to the contributor to pay it."

As, for example, when the harvest has been secured, and is ready for market; when the fisherman returns with his "fare," &c. This, though not a very important consideraeration, will readily be admitted as proper.

IV. "Every tax ought to be so contrived as to take out and keep out of the pockets of the people as little as possible, over and above what it brings into the treasury of the state."

Although the soundness of this principle would seem indisputable, and will doubtless be theoretically admitted by all, yet Dr. Smith proceeds to enumerate several modes in which the opposite result may be brought about.

First, By levying the tax in such a manner that a great many officers will be required for its collection, who will consume a great part of the produce of the tax. This will depend in great measure on the machinery employed in collecting the public imposts.

Second, By diverting a portion of the labor of a community from a more to a less profitable employment. For example, so heavy a tax might be laid on carriages as to reduce their use or consumption to such an extent that the manufacturer might be compelled to go into some other business less productive. This has often been done by unwise legislation.

Third, By attaching such heavy duties as to occasion smuggling, and thus create a multitude of officers to guard the revenue.

This result has often been brought about in European countries, and is now beginning to be seriously felt in the United States, under the heavy duties at present imposed.

Fourth, By subjecting the people to frequent and inquisitorial visits, and interruptions in the pursuit of business and in their domestic affairs, thus causing annoyance and dissatisfaction.

We now add still another principle, which, though not among those laid down by Dr. Smith, has been adopted in every country having any considerable taxation: —

V. The heaviest taxes should be imposed on those commodities, the consumption of which is especially prejudicial to the interests of the people.

Having stated the maxims or principles which should govern the imposition of taxes, we now come to consider the different forms of taxation which have been adopted, and, to a great extent, are still in use, by the different governments of the world, in order to ascertain in how far they conform to principles universally admitted as correct.

FORMS OF AMERICAN TAXATION.

Preliminary to an examination of the different modes of taxation, it may be proper to say, that there are, in the United States, two general systems; viz., by national and by State authority. The national government imposes taxes in every form, direct and indirect, except upon the poll. The State governments generally rely upon direct taxation; and the poll-tax is one of the forms adopted.

Under State authority, counties, cities, towns, and school-districts impose taxes; so, also, parishes and religious corporations: but the latter, generally, only on voluntary membership.

Taxes may first be divided into two kinds, — *direct* and *indirect*. A direct tax is demanded of the person who it is intended shall pay it. Indirect taxes are demanded from one person, in the expectation that he will indemnify himself at the expense of others. Such are customs and excise.

In our further examination of the subject, we shall refer to the national taxation of the United States, and the State taxation of Massachusetts; selecting the latter State only for being the most convenient, and as representing that of the individual States generally with considerable exactness.

CHAPTER X.

NATIONAL TAXATION. — I. CUSTOMS.

THESE are taxes upon importations, and collected through the custom-houses. Government establishes a tariff; that is, a list of duties upon such articles as it deems best: these are paid by the importer before he can gain possession of his goods.

Duties are generally of two kinds, — specific and *ad-valorem*. *Specific duties* are imposed by the pound, yard, gallon, &c. *Ad-valorem duties*, as the term imports, are charged upon the value of the goods, as twenty per cent upon an invoice of silks, hardware, sugar, &c.

In some of the American tariffs, the specific principle has predominated; in others, the *ad-valorem*. There has always been a struggle when the tariff was to be changed; those favoring specific duties, for protection, being in favor of *specific*, those of the opposite views contending for *ad-valorem* duties.

There are difficulties attending both. If specific duties are laid, they operate with great inequality. For example, suppose a duty of twenty-five cents per pound upon tea. This would be equal to a taxation of one hundred per cent on that which cost, originally, twenty-five cents, which the poor man must pay; while the rich, who would purchase tea that cost seventy-five cents, would pay but thirty-three per cent, or one-third as much per cent as the former.

This was the character, to a large extent, of British taxation. The tax on tea was, for a long time, two shillings and sixpence per pound (over sixty cents), paid alike by the hand-loom weaver and the wealthy nobleman.

When laid upon cloth, for example, a specific duty frequently operates in a most oppressive manner. By the American tariff of 1828, a duty of so many cents was laid upon the square yard of coarse woollens. In applying the principle, it was found that negro cloths, as they were called, paid more than two hundred and fifty per cent. This gave rise to great dissatisfaction, and was the ostensible cause of the nullification movement.

In regard to *ad-valorem* duties, the practical difficulty has been, when the rates were very high, to prevent fraudulent invoices. For example, the importer must present his original invoice at the custom-house, and make oath to its correctness. If dishonest, he may, by connivance with the shipper, furnish false papers, showing the cost to be much less than it really was.

Precautionary measures have been adopted. Appraisers have been appointed to determine the actual value; but, with all possible care on the part of the government, there is danger of deception, and consequent loss to the revenue, as well as injustice to the honest importer.

Of all modes of raising a revenue, that by customs is confessedly the most effective, and the most readily accomplished; and its great importance, as one of the chief sources of national revenue, demands that we give it a careful consideration.

The first principle we laid down was "that all should contribute, as nearly as possible, in proportion to their respective abilities."

As all duties are laid upon articles of general consumption, it will at once be seen that such taxation cannot have an equal bearing, because men are thus taxed in proportion to what they consume, not in proportion to their wealth. The poor man, with a large family, may pay more than a millionnaire. A case is personally known to us of one of the latter class, who actually paid less on dutiable articles than a printer, with a family, who received but fifteen dollars a week. Men are taxed in this way according to the mouths they have to feed, and the bodies they have to clothe.

In the second place, we inquire, Is "the time and manner plain to the person who pays" this indirect tax? The farmer who purchases a carriage, — is he aware that he is paying a government tax by so doing? If so, does he know how much he is paying? Does he understand that all the materials, except the wood, have paid duties to government; that the linings, trimmings, and ornaments, the paints and varnish, and the tools with which it was made, have all been taxed; and that he is to pay the sum total of the whole? Even if so, can he or any one else easily compute the amount of taxation which enters into the carriage? So of all commodities which have passed through the custom-house: people seldom realize when or how much they are taxed. Then the second principle we have laid down is violated.

But we shall not have a full view of the operation of duties on foreign merchandise, unless we take into consideration the fact that they raise the price of the home product, if there is one, to an equal degree with the foreign article, and, in that way, largely increase the burdens of the people, without adding to the public revenue. We will take the article of sugar as an illustration: —

In 1858, there was imported into the United States to the amount of		$23,000,000
There was raised in the United States, same year .		25,000,000
Total original cost of sugar consumed . . .		$48,000,000

On all the imported sugar a duty was charged of twenty-four per cent; and, of course, the home product was raised to an equal extent; say, together: —

$48,000,000, at twenty-four per cent		$11,520,000
Now, as all this sugar must pass through the hands of wholesale and retail dealers, if we allow them, altogether, only twenty-five per cent, we have .		2,880,000
		$14,400,000
Of this last sum, the treasury gets the amount paid as duties	$5,520,000	
Less expense of collection, ten per cent	552,000	
		4,968,000
Loss to the consumers		$9,432,000

Hence it appears, that the government gets in the present case but about thirty-five per cent of what the people have paid. We have estimated that the merchant charges a profit upon what he pays as duties, just as much as upon any other part of the cost of his commodities. We have put the profits of the merchants at twenty-five per cent. This, we are aware, is a low estimate; but we are governed by the consideration, that there would be no *importer's* profit on the amount produced at home, and also that sugar is a "leading article," in the language of trade, upon which less aggregate profits are made.

It is apparent, from this illustration, that the real taxation of a people will depend very much upon the proportion of duties which, designedly or not, are positively protective.

If, in the case presented, instead of a duty upon sugar, the same impost had been laid upon tea and coffee, which articles were *free* in 1858, and of which together we imported in 1858 about the same amount as of sugar, while we produced no tea and coffee ourselves, the case would stand as follows: —

Tea and coffee imported		$23,000,000
Duties, twenty-four per cent		$5,520,000
Importers' profits, twenty-five per cent		828,000
		$6,348,000
Jobbers' profits, ten per cent		634,800
		$6,982,800
Retailers' profits, twenty per cent		1,396,500
Total, paid by the people		$8,379,300
Of this amount, the government received	$5,520,000	
Merchants' profits, paid by the people .	2,859,300	
		$8,379,300

The saving to the people in this case would stand thus: —

Paid by the sugar taxation, as shown before . . .	$14,400,000
Paid by tax on tea and sugar	8,379,360
Saved to the people, in one year	$6,020,640

Such is the wide difference between duties imposed for revenue and those laid for the advantage of home productions. Some cases of protection would exceed this; others would come far short: but the principle is shown by this illustration.

CUSTOMS AN EXPENSIVE MODE OF TAXATION.

But, setting aside all consideration of the additional burden of taxation occasioned by *protection*, as just illustrated, we find this system is entirely at variance with our fourth maxim, which was "*that no more should be taken or kept out of the pockets of the people than absolutely necessary.*" This will be seen by the following illustration: —

Supposing the custom-house duties collected to amount, as in 1864, in round numbers, to . .	$100,000,000
Expenses of collecting, in all	10,000,000
Total amount received by the treasury . .	$90,000,000

We estimate the expense of collecting at ten per cent; but including all salaries and charges, and interest upon investments made by government, the expense is, doubtless, somewhat greater; but, to prevent dispute, we assume that the net amount is ninety million dollars. To get this sum, how much is paid by the people?

We will suppose that the importer's profit is fifteen per cent, the jobber's ten, and the retailer's twenty per cent. The matter then will stand thus: —

Original duties paid	$100,000,000
Importers' profits, fifteen per cent	15,000,000
	$115,000,000
Jobbers' profits, ten per cent	11,500,000
	$126,500,000
Retailers' profits, twenty per cent	25,300,000
Total, paid by the people	$151,800,000
Deduct gross amount paid into the treasury . . .	100,000,000
Taken out of the pockets of the people, and not paid in the public treasury	$51,800,000

or more than fifty per cent extra taxation.

In regard to the general correctness of these estimates, no well-informed person can have any doubt. Hon. George Opdyke, a distinguished merchant, late Mayor of New York, in a small but excellent work on "Political Economy," published in 1851 (page 200), computes the importers' profits at fifteen, the jobbers' at ten, and the retailers' at twenty-five. He had the best of means for knowing the amount of the importers' profits. The retailers' were a matter of estimate with him. We have supposed that they might be somewhat too high, and have therefore placed them at twenty per cent. This, considering that it is to be applied to all retail sales, not only in cities and towns, but in the most remote districts of the country, is undoubtedly within actual limits. As long ago as 1849, we made such investigations as satisfied us of the correctness of the estimates we now give, and published tables at that time, illustrating the principle laid down.

In regard to customs duties, then, we cannot but conclude, that, while they are a convenient and prolific source of revenue, they are very unequal and expensive, and little in accordance with the principles of justice and equality.

BOUNTIES.

At this point, it may be most proper to speak of the *effect of bounties*. If a home product is to be encouraged by government, it is desirable that it should be done as economically as possible; or in such a manner as to impose the least taxation and loss upon the public, while it shall be as effective as possible in securing the object.

Let us take the sugar crop of 1858, just referred to, as an illustration. It amounted to $25,000,000. To protect this to the amount of twenty-four per cent, the people paid, as we have shown, $14,300,000, of which the government realized but $4,968,000. Here was a clear loss to the consumers of $9,332,000.

Suppose, now, that instead of this protective duty of twenty-four per cent, a bounty of equal amount (twenty-four per cent) had been paid by the government. The matter would then stand thus: twenty-four per cent on $25,000,000 is $6,000,000, which the people would pay to the sugar growers, instead of $9,332,000 they were obliged to pay through protection; a saving of $3,333,000, equal to thirty-three per cent of the amount paid under the protective system.

This principle applies, in all cases, where an article is actually protected, and shows that bounties are by far the most economical form of governmental assistance. Bounties, as a means of protection, have been but little resorted to by governments. The reason is obvious. The evident injustice of giving to one class of men a premium upon their productions, in order that they may be encouraged in a branch of industry that cannot live without contributions from the public treasury, is so apparent, and evidently unreasonable and unwise, that the people of no country would long tolerate it. It is, therefore, vastly more feasible to give protection by duties on the foreign article, although much more wasteful and onerous.

EXCISE.

Excise are the opposite of custom-house duties, being laid wholly upon articles of domestic production, and paid first by the producer; and, after the articles have passed through the hands of the merchants, with their profits added, the sum total is paid by the consumers.

This mode of taxation is obnoxious to the same objections that may be made to customs. Excise is unequal, because it falls on rich and poor alike; not in proportion to their wealth, but what they consume. The merchants' profits are not quite so large on these as on custom duties, because home products do not ordinarily pass through as many hands as foreign merchandise. The expense of collection, though only perhaps about one-fourth part as great, is still a heavy charge upon the revenue; but the most popular objection to excise is the espionage which it necessarily requires. It is, notwithstanding, a very productive source of revenue, and must be resorted to by governments heavily indebted. Domestic manufacturers are not injured by excise duties, unless they so increase the cost of their commodities as to expose them to foreign competition. Profits upon such duties are charged upon commodities as a part of the general expense of their production.

TAXES ON DISADVANTAGEOUS CONSUMPTION.

The principle has everywhere been acted upon by governments, that heavy taxes are to be laid on commodities "the consumption of which is especially prejudicial to the interests of the people." This is in accordance with our fifth maxim.

There are two strong and sensible arguments in favor of this kind of taxation. One is, that, if it should cause a falling-off in the consumption of the articles so taxed, no detriment would come to individuals or the public; but, on the other hand, their moral and social condition would be promoted, and the power of production increased.

The other consideration is, that all those who choose to abstain, as they can do without injury, from the specially taxed articles, will avoid the payment of the tax altogether: such taxes are voluntarily assumed by those who pay them.

This kind of taxation is found to be far more productive, in proportion, than any other; and consumption is less affected by heavy imposts. According to Professor Levi, the *working classes* of Great Britain pay over ten millions sterling annually, in taxes upon tobacco and intoxicating drinks. The whole amount raised upon these two articles in 1858 was as follows: —

British and foreign spirits and wine	£18,500,000
Tobacco	5,500,000
	£24,000,000

or about one hundred and twenty millions of dollars, equal to four dollars to each inhabitant; or, allowing five persons to a family, twenty dollars to each family. More than a third part of the whole British revenue is raised by the taxes upon these articles alone; a remarkable fact, especially worthy the attention of the American government at the present time.

STAMPS.

There is still another mode of supplying the treasury; viz., by the sale of stamps. This is an important branch of the public revenue in all highly taxed communities. Stamps are required upon all letters, newspapers, and other matter carried through the mails; upon all bills of merchandise and bills of lading; upon legal instruments of every name and nature; upon patent medicines, &c.

This is cheap and efficient, and as desirable as any form of indirect taxation. Of course it bears unequally upon different classes, and is more or less vexatious, particularly when first introduced; but habit will, after a while, reconcile the people to it, and it is as little likely to be resisted or evaded as any other form of exaction. It is also collected with very little expense, as no functionaries are necessary. It should therefore be carried out, as far as practicable. The British government raises a large sum in this way: eight millions sterling are received for stamps. The United-States treasury received, for the year ending June 30, 1865, the sum of $11,162,392.

LICENSES.

These are granted by both national and State authority, for a great variety of purposes. It is a more economical and convenient mode of raising a revenue than by excise on manufactures, &c., requiring only annual renewal. There is also less opportunity for fraud and evasion. It is therefore a very desirable form of taxation; and the United-States government has already availed itself of this mode of raising revenue, to the extent of $12,613,478 for the financial year 1865; and this sum may doubtless be greatly increased in the future.

CHAPTER XI.

NATIONAL TAXATION (*continued*). — INCOME TAX.

It is unnecessary to say that this tax is in perfect accordance with the first maxim laid down by Adam Smith, that "every man should be taxed according to the revenue he derives under the state," and also consistent with every other principle we have stated. It is "clear and plain" to the contributor, and every other person. The income-tax payer knows when and how much he pays; and it can be collected as conveniently and economically as any other.

This kind of tax was established in England in 1798, during the wars with Napoleon, but was abolished soon after the close of that struggle. About 1842, however, the government, finding its revenues fall short of the expenditures, restored the tax; and it has been continued to the present time.

This tax was unknown, we believe, in the United States, until the civil war, when it was laid by Congress, and has been continued thus far. Total amount collected for the year ending June 30, 1865, was $20,740,451.33; while the whole internal revenue, for the same time, was $211,129,-529.17; so that the income tax produced nearly ten per cent of the amount.

Of all modes of taxation, this is the most just and equitable. Every man *can afford* to pay according to his income, and ought to do so. There is no other *perfect standard* of taxation; none other which does not inflict more or less hardship and injustice.

The tax comes upon the annual private revenue of each year, out of which the government should receive its share for the annual revenue of the state. If the private revenue is increased, so should be the contribution to the public revenue: if the former is diminished, the latter should be also. This is fair and just. Were it to supersede all other forms of taxation, perfect equality would be established; property and labor would bear each its just share of the public burdens. To do this, it would be necessary to ascertain the income of every man; of every laborer, whether his wages amounted to one hundred or one thousand dollars a year; of every professional man; of every operative, male or female; every capitalist, banker, merchant, and mechanic. Upon the gross income, thus ascertained, the general tax should be levied, *pro rata*. In this way, it is clear, equality, as far as that is practicable, would be established; and each member of the community would be made to bear his just proportion, and, of course, would be obliged to *save*, in his expenditures, to that amount.

The objection to this form of taxation is the difficulty of ascertaining what a person's income actually is. In the *first* place, it is said that many do not know their affairs so as to be able to state their true income. There is doubtless much of truth in this; but the very fact that such a tax is certain to be enforced every year will, in a short time, remove this difficulty to a considerable extent, because men will be compelled so to keep their accounts as to know what they gain or lose. The operation of the law in this respect, therefore, is favorable to private interest; since the more intelligent every man is in regard to his affairs, the better for him. Such, we believe, has been the operation of the income tax in England.

Secondly, It is said that some men will be dishonest in their disclosures and statements, and therefore a correct result cannot be reached.

That many men are dishonest there can be no doubt; but, when the law taxing incomes is regularly enforced from year to year, the difficulty of concealment, on the part of the tax-payer, is constantly increasing. His neighbors and competitors in business have an eye upon him, if they believe he is making false statements; and he cannot long escape detection. Besides, as a man *may* be put under oath (and, by the way, *ought always to be*), the crime of perjury must be committed with every misrepresentation of his affairs. The immense difference between the reported incomes of the United States in 1864 and those of 1863, even after allowing for the general rise of prices, serves to give an idea of the advance that will naturally be made in the application of the income tax.

The *third* objection made is, that men do not always like to have their incomes known. But why should they not? We have already said, that, in the matter of taxation, all are copartners, having a *pro-rata* interest. What one does not pay, others must. All, therefore, may rightfully demand such information as shall furnish the means of assessing a correct tax.

Besides this, an income tax well enforced will be the means of diffusing a large amount of information most important in regard to the credits which business men are required to give. The position and ability of every man will be better understood. This is not an unimportant consideration. It is difficult to see any reason for objecting to a disclosure of income for taxation, which does not equally apply to the disclosure of property for the same purpose.

Estimated Income. — But it may be said that the income-tax principle would not work well in some communities, because a considerable share of its wealth produces no income, and therefore would go untaxed; that this is especially so in the new States, where vast quantities of land are held which yield no rent or income whatever.

But this is a mistaken view of the matter. If these lands are appreciating from year to year, — and, as a general fact, owing to the increase of population, they are, — the income from them is as real as any other; but it is a *deferred income*, which is sure to come in the end. All such property, whether in city lots or farms, should, if an income tax only were levied, be estimated yearly, according to its increasing value, and be assessed upon that principle.

We do not advocate the adoption of the income tax as a substitute for all other modes of taxation: our purpose is to show, that, so far as practicable, it is the most just and economical mode of raising a revenue.

TAXATION UPON EXPORTS.

Whenever a people produce more of any commodity than is required for their own consumption, the surplus must find a foreign market, or the production will not be extended beyond the home demand. Any thing, therefore, which has a tendency to prevent the sale of domestic products in a foreign market must discourage home industry. Such being the case, what must be, in general, the effect of duties laid upon exports? Evidently to reduce the amount exported, and benefit the *foreign producer* of the articles thus taxed. Take the article wheat as an illustration. It can be produced in almost every country, and is an article of export from many. Such are the facilities afforded by commerce, that the wheat of one country must enter into competition with the wheat of every other country; and it may therefore be taken as a fair exponent of commodities in general.

If the price of wheat in New York is one dollar and fifty cents under a currency at par with specie, it is because it can be shipped to Liverpool or some other foreign port, and, after paying freight and charges, make a remittance equal to one dollar and fifty cents in specie. Under these circumstances, we will suppose an export duty of twenty-five cents per bushel is laid on wheat.

Would the New-York dealer now pay one dollar and fifty cents per bushel for the wheat? Certainly not, since he could not export it without paying, in addition, a duty of twenty-five cents per bushel; and, unless the article should rise abroad, he would lose to the amount of the duty paid. Of course, he now offers but one dollar and twenty-five cents instead of one dollar and fifty cents, and the difference is the loss of the producers, who, in consequence of the export duty, are at a disadvantage of twenty-five cents per bushel, as compared with the wheat-growers of every other country. They have nothing left but to accept a reduction of twenty-five cents per bushel, or limit their production in the future to the amount required for home consumption. When they have done this, the price of wheat will correspond with the prices of all the other agricultural products of the country, whatever that price may be: for all such products will be affected by an export duty laid on the great staple of agriculture; every kind of grain and meat, as truly as the wheat on which the duty was laid, though not, perhaps, in the same degree. But, since the foreign market has been to a large extent dependent for its full supply upon American wheat, will not the price advance to such a point as to bring up the price of the American article? If the American wheat *must be had*, such a price must be offered as will bring it. But, as soon as wheat begins to rise abroad from this cause, a larger supply will be attracted from other wheat-growing countries, in which production will be stimulated to the extent it is depressed in the United States. The price having risen, a limited amount will go from our ports; but wheat will not rise permanently to such a point abroad as to make it twenty-five cents higher in the United States. The American producer must, in any event, take a part of the loss, and the foreign consumer the balance; while foreign producers, having an unnaturally high price, will extend their cultivation as far as possible.

The unquestionable effect of export duties is to lessen production at home, and give encouragement to foreign labor. This is a general principle, applicable to every commodity of home growth or production, *except such as one nation may have a virtual monopoly of;* that is, may be able to produce in so much greater perfection, or at so much lower rate of cost, or both, that no other nation can compete with it. In that case, the exporting nation might impose a duty, which, while it should create a revenue, would not lessen production materially, if at all.

TAXATION OF COTTON.

Many persons are of the opinion, that an export duty, or its equivalent in the form of excise, might be laid upon cotton without any detriment to the general interest of the trade of the country, while it would produce a considerable revenue at the expense of the foreign consumers.

It is, then, an important economical and financial question to the people of the United States, whether the peculiar advantages they have over all other cotton-growing countries give them such a monopoly as to enable them to lay an export duty upon it, without any immediate or remote injury to themselves.

There are several considerations which go to prove that such is the case, some of which we shall notice.

I. UNIVERSAL DEMAND FOR COTTON.*

"There are only four articles of any considerable importance used in the manufacture of clothing. These are wool, silk, flax, and cotton; two animal and two vegetable productions. The first of these, though quite indispensable in the high latitudes, is only partially available in the lower, and can be used but little in the tropics. Silk, while an article from which beautiful and elegant fabrics can be made, is not adapted to general use, and being, like wool, an animal product, cannot be furnished in sufficient quantity, or at so low a rate as to be made available for the greater part of mankind. Flax being a vegetable production, and its culture adapted to a great variety of soils and climates, might doubtless be produced in any desired quantity; but, like silk, it would but partially meet the wants of that large portion of the population of the globe where snows and frost prevail a considerable part of the year

* Extract from the author's speech in Congress, Feb. 18, 1863.

"After looking at these several commodities, then, we find that an article is needed which shall, as nearly as possible, combine the peculiar properties and advantages of all of them; one that can be cheaply and bountifully produced, and that may most readily be converted into clothing, having, at pleasure, the warmth of wool, or the elegance or lightness of silk or linen. Cotton we find to be just that article, combining in a most wonderful degree the advantages of wool, silk, and flax. The earth has one thousand million inhabitants, and each and every one of these need cotton. There is no exception. Not, indeed, that human beings cannot possibly exist without it, but their welfare and happiness are promoted by its use."

II. RESTRICTED CULTURE.

"While cotton is one of the greatest necessities of mankind, we find its successful culture confined to a very limited portion of the earth's surface. I say successful culture; for although it may be raised in India, Egypt, and other countries in similar latitudes, yet the quality is so inferior, the quantity to the acre so limited, and the labor so ineffective, that the countries in question do little more than supply their own wants.

"It is reserved to the States of the American Union lying in immediate proximity to the Gulf of Mexico to furnish the world with the article in such quantities, and of such quality, as to meet the general demand. The culture of the article began prior to the Revolution; but it did not become an article of foreign export till 1784, when eight bales were shipped to Liverpool. These were seized by the custom-house officers, on the ground that they could not be of American production."

III. INCREASE OF PRODUCTION AND ADVANCE OF PRICE.

"No very great extension of the cultivation of cotton was realized until 1792, when Eli Whitney invented the cotton-gin; but, from that moment, it increased with wonderful rapidity. The value of the export of cotton was, —

In 1821	$20,900,000
In 1830	29,000,000
In 1840	63,000,000
In 1850	71,000,000
In 1860	191,000,000

"This amount, it will be observed, is over and above the amount consumed in the United States. The whole product in 1850 was 2,096,706 bales; in 1860, 4,669,770 bales. Mark especially the great increase from 1850 to 1860, of one hundred and thirty per cent!

"But the more striking and noticeable fact is, that, while the production had increased at this enormous rate, the prices also had advanced twenty-five per cent. According to the financial report of 1861, the average price of cotton from 1840 to 1850 was but 8.2 cents per pound; while, from 1850 to 1860, the average price was 10.5 cents per pound, — a difference, it will be seen, of a little over twenty-five per cent.

"The difference between the value of the entire crop of cotton, including all consumed at home and exported, is still more remarkable. In 1850 it amounted to but $117,619,947; while, in 1860, it was $308,865,280, — showing an increase of value of nearly two hundred per cent, owing, of course, to the increase of quantity and the advance of price.

"Here, then, is the singular fact, unparalleled, perhaps, in the commercial history of the world, that, while the production was increasing at a rate so prodigious, the price was constantly advancing. This is contrary to all the ordinary laws of trade. As production increases, prices fall; but in this case, instead of a decline, we find a great advance of price."

Do not these facts and considerations show conclusively, that the United States have such advantages over all others in raising cotton that they may to a certain extent dictate the terms of sale? In just so far as this is true, might an export duty be laid which would fall entirely on the foreign consumer, without any injury to the American cotton-grower.

Suppose an export duty of five cents per pound. The superiority and desirableness of the American article are so great that it cannot be supposed the demand would be lessened in any appreciable degree. From what we have seen during the Rebellion, need we fear that the demand would be perceptibly curtailed? If not, then no damage would come to the grower; while a large revenue would be secured by the government at the expense of the foreign consumer.

The whole cotton crop of 1860 was 4,669,770 bales, which, at 500 pounds to a bale, give a total of 2,334,500,000 pounds, which at five cents duty, or excise, would yield $116,725,000. To determine what rate of duty or excise should be laid must be a matter of experiment. If the rate were found too high, — that is, so high as to reduce consumption, — it should be lowered; or, if too low, it could be raised.

The immense extent to which the cultivation of cotton in the United States may and doubtless will be carried is shown by Edward Atkinson, Esq., of Boston, a most reliable statistician, in his map of the cotton kingdom; from which it appears that while the whole area within the United States adapted to profitable cotton culture is 666,196 square miles, only 10,888 are in actual use for that purpose, or but 1.634 per cent; that is, less than two per cent. He remarks, that, "with free labor, the capacity of the South to raise cotton cannot be less than one hundred million bales" against about four and a half millions in 1860; so that less than one-twentieth of the capacity of the country has yet been developed.

The principal point to be considered in regard to cotton, or any other domestic product, is whether an export or excise duty will essentially restrict the consumption of the article, either at home or abroad.

CHAPTER XII.

STATE TAXATION.

A GENERAL valuation of all real and personal property is made by the authority of the State, according to which all State taxes are apportioned to each county, city, or town. The municipal authorities then assess the amount allotted them upon the property and polls of their constituents, together with the amount required for city or town expenditures.

Thus all taxes, whether for State, city, town, or school-district, are direct, and laid wholly on property, except the small amount of poll-taxes. There may be some slight variation in different States from the course we have stated; but it is quite unessential, and does not materially change the grand result.

The law makes it the duty of each person to furnish the assessors annually a true invoice of his estate, and to its correctness he may be required to make oath; and, if any person neglects or refuses to make such inventory, the assessors make one for him, according to their own judgment.

The rate of tax varies from year to year, and is widely different in different towns and cities. Before the Rebellion, the rate in Massachusetts was seldom less than sixty cents, or more than one hundred on a hundred dollars; but such have been the expenditures caused by the war, that few now have a rate less than one hundred, and some have been as high as three hundred and fifty, cents on the hundred dollars.

This tax, if the valuation be fairly made, approximates to justice and equality. It is assumed that every man's ability to pay is in proportion to the property he holds; that his revenue corresponds with his wealth. This may, or may not, be true; and, as we shall have occasion to show, there are circumstances which disturb, to some extent, the equal operation of this tax.

And here we may notice some of the objections to this compound system of poll and property taxation. Poll-tax payers vote directly upon the public appropriations; yet they have no personal interest whatever in the amount of expenditures. No matter whether a proposal to expend money is wise and necessary, or frivolous and wasteful, the poll-tax payer can vote for it with entire impunity. It is nothing to him whether the sum be one thousand or ten thousand dollars. Indeed, the influence of poll-tax payers is often in favor of the most lavish expenditures. A new road, for example, is proposed in town meeting. It may be quite unnecessary, and ought not to be made; but the poll-tax payers, a large share of whom are laborers, will be immediately benefited by the demand that will be made for labor, and will be very likely to go in favor of it. It needs no argument to show the bad effects of such a state of things, regarded only in an economical point of view. If men may vote away money in the payment of which they have no interest, is it likely to be done to the advantage of the public interests? Is it not certain that there will be unwise and reckless expenditures?

This false position of the poll-tax payer has attracted the attention of those who are narrowly watching the effects of equality of suffrage without equality of taxation. The result of popular votes during the civil war, by which immense, and often quite unnecessary, burdens were imposed upon towns, has caused no small anxiety amongst those who have noticed the natural consequences of giving to a class numerous and powerful, at the ballot-box, the power to impose taxes upon the public, from which they are themselves exempt.

On the other hand, the poll-tax payer, while he contributes heavily towards the national expenditures through customs and excise, has no direct vote in regard to them. He can vote where his own interest would lead him to vote wrong, but has no power to vote directly where his interest would lead him to vote right.

The *income-tax* principle, if universally adopted, while it would doubtless relieve poll-tax payers of their present taxation, would, at the same time, bring their interests into harmony with those of property-tax payers, and thus promote the general welfare of the public.

The property and poll tax being the two modes * by which all revenues are raised by the individual States, we will look for a moment at their operation as between the different classes upon which they are imposed. To do this, we refer to a valuation and tax list before us, and find the following examples.

The *poll-tax* is one of the oldest and most general of all taxes imposed by State authority. In Massachusetts, "every male inhabitant over twenty years of age is included, except persons who, by reason of infirmity and poverty, are, in the judgment of the assessors, unable to contribute fully to the public charges."

It hardly need be said, that this form of taxation is not in accordance with the maxims laid down by Adam Smith; those who pay it not having equal ability, or enjoying "an equal revenue." It is a tax founded on no sound principle whatever; and, if it were, the *only* tax imposed would be as unjust as a tax could well be. It forms, however, only a part of a system which must be looked at in all its bearings, in order to form a correct judgment of the operation of the particular tax, which by law is a limited one, deter-

* States have, in some cases, derived a revenue from a tax upon banks. In Massachusetts, it was for many years the greatest source of income; so great, indeed, as to render any direct State tax unnecessary. Licenses have also been granted, by State authority, in some instances; but the amount received in any other mode, except by direct taxation, is too small to affect essentially the public burdens. The establishment of the national-bank system has cut off bank taxation from the States as a source of revenue.

mined by State legislation. In Massachusetts, the maximum poll-tax is now fixed at "not over two dollars," but may be, as it has been, changed from time to time. It has never, we believe, been higher than at present.

B. H. —	Buildings and 45 acres of land	$1,000			
	Stock, &c.	345	$1,345.	Taxes,	$15.47
				Poll,	2.00
					$17.47
T. G. —	Buildings and 43 acres of land	$1,500			
	Stock	238	$1,738.	Taxes,	$19.99
				Poll,	2.00
					$21.99
L. G. S. —	Buildings and 56 acres of land	$1,200			
	Stock	300	$1,500.	Taxes,	$17.25
				Poll,	2.00
					$19.25

Average property, $1,661. Average tax, $19.57.

We here find that these small farmers pay $19.57 each, equal to nine and a half times as much as the poll-tax contributors. Does any one suppose that the incomes of the former are *nine and a half times* as great as the latter? Let us test the question.

Suppose each of these farmers derives a *net* income of ten per cent on his capital, over all outlays and repairs; and that his labor is worth to him four hundred dollars per annum. This is a large allowance: —

Land and stock, as above, at ten per cent	$166.10
His own labor equal to	500.00
Total income	$666.10

Now we will assume that the exclusive poll-tax payers have an average income of four hundred dollars. We include in this list not only all common laborers, but all skilled workmen, mechanics, and others, whose labor is worth, under a sound currency, $1.50 to $2 per day; and also all clerks, and other employees, whose salaries are six hundred dollars and under. Then if all these classes average four hundred dollars per year, as no one will dispute, it will appear that the income of the poll-tax payers is charged $2, while these small property-holders are charged $19.57.

Here is a great disparity, but there is no exaggeration in the statement. From the same valuation and tax list, we take three farmers, having about one hundred and twenty-five acres each, with buildings and stock, and find their farms and stock average $3,757; and their average taxes, poll inclusive, amount to $47.03.

On the same calculation as before, —

Farm and stock, $3,757, at ten per cent	$375.00
Value of farmer's own labor	625.00
Farmer's total income	$1,000.00

Then, if the poll tax-payer is charged $2, with an income of $400, what ought the farmer to pay with an income of $1,000? Answer, $5.

Instead, then, of $5, the true proportionate amount, the farmers, as before shown, pay $47.03, or more than nine times as much.* There is no escape from these conclusions; and we appeal with confidence to those best qualified to judge, whether the estimate placed upon the incomes of farmers of the description we refer to is not essentially correct. In whatever way we look at the matter, we cannot fail to see great inequality. But the poll-tax is not only unequal as between those upon whom it is assessed, and whose incomes range from $150 to $600, and also unequal as between this class generally, and all property holders, but it is also very disproportionate to the advantages it confers. Let us see what these are.

1. Entire protection to persons and property.
2. Right of suffrage, and eligibility to office.
3. The most ample means of education in common and

* And the hardship, in this case, is often increased by the fact that the farmer is indebted for a large part of his capital, and paying interest upon it.

high schools, without charge, and a chance for a scholarship, provided by the State, in one of the colleges.

4. Complete maintenance, and the highest scientific treatment, for life, if need be, if himself or any member of his family should be deaf and dumb, or afflicted with blindness, idiocy, insanity, or, last of all, helpless poverty. What individual or corporation could be found to insure a laborer's family against all accidents and deprivations, physical and mental, from every source, through life, for one-half of one per cent on the income of the family head, or for twenty times that sum?

For all this, and much more that might be added, the recipient of a revenue from any occupation, trade, or profession, of any sum not exceeding six hundred dollars, if he has no visible property, pays an annual tax of not over two dollars, or four cents per week! As we have already said, considered in itself, disconnected from other forms of taxation, this is very unequal, and consequently unjust, as between the different classes. The obvious result is to transfer an undue share of the burdens of *State*, *county*, *and town* expenditure from the mechanical and laboring classes to the agricultural; thus promoting the interest of the former at the expense of the latter.

But all this applies, it must be remembered, to taxes imposed under State or municipal authority *only*, from all which the poll-tax payer escapes entirely by paying two dollars.

Effect of the Two Systems.—We are now able to compare the results of the two different systems; viz., national and State taxation. In the national, we find that the greater part of all taxes are indirect: the State and municipal taxes are, with slight exceptions, direct. The former fall almost wholly on consumption; the latter, upon property. The first is unjust to labor, or the non-property-holding classes: the other is unjust to capital, or those who hold taxable estate. One operates as an offset to the other.

Neither is just in itself, nor does the action of the two systems conjointly establish perfect justice; but it approximates as nearly to it, perhaps, as any other system of taxation ever adopted, or likely at present to be adopted.

Before leaving the subject of State taxation, we will briefly notice the inquiry often made, why the United-States government does not assign to each State its share of the public burdens according to its general valuation, and allow the State authorities to collect the amount at the same time, and in the same way, as all the direct taxes of the State are levied and collected. In reply to this, it may be said, that, if the national government could rely implicitly upon the fidelity and promptness of every State, it would be by far the most economical and efficient mode of collecting the revenue. The expense of collection would be almost nominal, probably not exceeding one-tenth of the sum now required; and an army of office-holders might be left free to engage in productive employments. But such *has been* the state of society in some of the States in times past, that reliance could not be placed upon their promptly assessing and collecting a national tax; nor can it be expected that the time will soon come when such a measure would be practicable.

TAXATION OF CREDITS.

It has sometimes been maintained that credits ought not to be taxed, but all assessments be made upon values, or property, personal and real. Taxes, it has been argued, ought not to be laid upon persons, but upon that out of which they can alone be paid; viz., property.

But credits are taxed as well as values. A holds a farm worth $10,000, mortgaged to B for $5,000. A pays taxes upon the whole valuation, and B upon $5,000, as money at interest. A, it is said, is doubly taxed. This is a practical question, that has puzzled legislators in every age and country. Let us therefore carefully examine it.

Suppose A and B aforesaid form an entire community, and that the whole tax of $150 is imposed on property. The whole valuation will then be $10,000 (A's farm), and the rate one and a half per cent, which A pays, and B goes untaxed. We will now change the principle, and have both property and credits taxed. The valuation will then be, A's farm, $10,000, and B's money at interest, $5,000; total, $15,000; and, with the same amount to be assessed ($150), the rate will be one per cent, of which A pays one hundred, and B fifty, dollars. So, then, we discover that A is not doubly taxed, as assumed, but at the worst pays only twenty-five dollars, or one-third, more than his share. Such must, in principle, be the result of this kind of taxation, taking a whole community together. All the amount taxed upon credit is so much relief to taxation upon property. This seems to be clear; and the justice of the thing is established by the fact that A bought his farm knowing that it would be subject to a full taxation, and bought it cheaper, as we have shown in another place, on that account. B, on the other hand, accepted his mortgage on the same ground, knowing it would be subject to tax on the common valuation. Is either party, then, wronged?

But perhaps another reason may be given why A should pay taxes upon the whole value of his farm; viz., that, having the usufruct of the whole, he is entitled to all the profits on the farm. "But he don't own the whole of the farm." True, that is his misfortune: if he did, he would obtain a larger amount of net profits; but his obligation to pay tax on the whole is not impaired, because he has the use of a part of B's capital. As the owner of the farm, A has a chance for all the profits that can be made from the whole; while, by the taxation of B on the mortgage, the former saves a part of what he would otherwise pay in taxes. One pays taxes for the profits of business; the other, for the income on his capital.

In this case we find another very clear illustration of the

correctness of the *income-tax* policy. If there were no other tax than upon income, the matter would stand thus: —

A's income from his farm, say	$900
He deducts the interest he pays B	300
A pays tax on his net income of	$600
B's income is taxed upon	300
Total income to be taxed	900

Amount to be raised, one hundred and fifty dollars: of this, A will pay one hundred dollars, and B fifty; and there would be no question as to the justice of the system by which both were thus taxed. If A's income should be more or less than nine hundred dollars, he would pay more or less, and B must pay less or more accordingly.

In the absence of the income-tax principle, what can be more equitable and just than the practice of taxing both mortgagor and mortgagee? If the former were allowed to deduct from his inventory the amount he owed the latter, it would often happen, that, the mortgagee not living in the same town or State, so much property would escape taxation altogether. This in some communities, especially our Western States, would be a great evil. That much hardship may often result from taxing credits as well as property is undoubtedly true; but that only affords additional evidence that the income-tax principle is the only correct one. Next to this would be the levying of all taxes upon property exclusively; and if adopted at the very commencement of a social organization, as at the landing at Plymouth in 1620, it would secure a just taxation, because all property would be created, held, and transferred under that well-known condition.

TAXATION OF GOVERNMENT BONDS.

The question of taxing credits assumes great practical importance, when regarded in relation to the national debt of the United States. We will assume that debt to be three billion dollars ($3,000,000,000). This forms a lien or mortgage upon the national wealth, which the Secretary of the Treasury, in his report, December, 1865, estimates at a little over fourteen billions: for convenience, we will call it fifteen billions. In that case, the national debt will be equal to one-fifth of the national wealth. On this debt of three billions, the interest, at six per cent, will be one hundred and eighty millions. If we suppose that all other demands on the Treasury amount to one hundred and twenty millions annually, we have an aggregate of three hundred millions as the amount of taxation. The national debt, if included in the national valuation, would increase it twenty per cent, or from fifteen to eighteen billions. This would reduce the rate of taxation by one-sixth, or $16\frac{2}{3}$ per cent; that is, if only property was taxed, the rate would be two per cent; if property and national stocks, the rate would be 1.66.

Should the national debt be exempted from taxation, there will be one hundred and eighty millions of *income* that will go untaxed; and that, as can be readily seen, is a large share of the *net income* of the whole nation, or what the people save annually after supplying their necessary consumption. The subject, therefore, is one of surpassing interest to the country. Quite fortunately, however, the matter is wholly within the control of Congress, which can, as fast as the present bonds and other securities become due (and they may all be redeemed* within seven, and most of them within three years from 1865), convert them into bonds not exempted from general taxation.

Public faith should be kept inviolate, but public justice should also be secured as soon as possible. Better far to pay a high rate of interest, if need be, than have so large a share of individual income, and, consequently, of ability to pay taxes, escape its proper responsibilities. This is desira-

* Except the twenty-year bonds, which mature in 1881.

ble, not only as a matter of policy in removing a prominent cause of popular dissatisfaction which may sooner or later endanger the security of the debt itself, but as an economical advantage to the country.

The effect of exempting the public debt from taxation may be illustrated as follows: A has an income of one thousand five hundred dollars, derived from a salary; B has an equal income, derived from coupons on the national stocks. A must pay taxes, and, of course, must economize accordingly: B pays no taxes, and consequently has no occasion to save on that score. Now, as all national capital comes from the savings of the people, it can be seen at once, that, if one-sixth part* (in amount) of the tax-payers are exempted from taxation, they are, to an equal extent, exempted from all necessity of saving.

We are aware that the holders of public stocks pay indirect taxes (customs, excise, &c.), but so also does the man who has no interest in the funds. What we intend to say is, that so far as a man's wealth is invested in untaxed securities, in so far he has no motive to save arising from a taxation to which all others are liable. Looking, then, at its economical bearings merely, ought not all public securities to be included in the general schedule of taxation, both by the national government, and the States, cities, and towns in which the holders reside?

CONSOLIDATION OF THE NATIONAL DEBT.

While this work is passing through the press, a proposition is made in Congress to consolidate the debt of the United States into a uniform five per cent stock, having thirty years to run, payable, interest and principal, in gold.

It is, doubtless, desirable to effect such a consolidation,

* It is, doubtless, far more than one-sixth part of the net national income, probably at least one-fourth, or 25 per cent. A large share of the estimated fifteen billions of aggregate wealth is of a character to escape taxation.

provided it can be done in an economical and proper manner; but the proposal to exempt the consols from taxation is quite another matter. We have already spoken of the invidious, as well as unjust, operation of a system which exempts from taxation one-sixth part of the national resources; but, since the proposal has been made, it becomes desirable, we think, to give the subject some further consideration.

We shall not dwell upon the political bearings of a measure sure to create abiding dissatisfaction; sure to be a most dangerous weapon in the hands of political aspirants, and certain to endanger eventually the security of the debt itself. We shall speak only of its economic bearings.

1st, The exemption of three billion dollars from taxation for all national, State, county, town, school-district, and parish purposes, will create a very considerable and influential *class of persons*, who, while they will have the legal right to vote appropriations for all public objects, will be under no obligation to pay a farthing of the amount raised; who, while interested in having large public improvements made, will have no responsibility for the expense of them: a class to whom it will be a matter of entire indifference how large the assessments may be, or how unwisely or wastefully the public finances may be conducted. Can any reasonable man think it expedient and proper to create such a class? Does any one doubt that its influence would be unfavorable to the public welfare? We already exempt labor, to a great extent, from the burdens of State and municipal taxation, by limiting the poll-tax to a fixed and very trifling amount, so that the poll-tax payer can vote any sum he pleases with entire impunity. By exempting three billions of the national credit from taxation, it is now proposed to place capitalists, so far as they are owners of the public stocks, in the same favored position. The interest of these two parties will then be identical in regard to all public expenditures paid for by a direct tax on property, as State and municipal charges generally are. Both can vote away money, and leave the unfortunate property-holders to settle the bills. By the exemption proposed, government creates a great antagonism in the body politic. It grants a special and most important favor to one class, at the expense of others. It may be urged, that the favor has been paid for by the creditors of the government, in that they took the stock at a less rate of interest than they would have done had it been subject to taxation. But can government, with any propriety, make any such condition? Can it rightfully grant, for any consideration whatever, a dispensation to one class of citizens from all pecuniary obligation to State, city, and town authority throughout the nation? Surely not, consistently with justice and equality, because in one community the favor granted may be worth one per cent, in another two. In one locality, it may advance the general valuation one-half; in another, only one-tenth: in one municipality, it may increase the general rate of taxation five mills on the dollar; in another, twenty.

Can that be just and equal? And yet all taxation, under a free government, must be seen to be clearly impartial and just, or the people will not submit to it.

2d, Such an exemption will create a powerful influence against the payment of any thing but the interest of the debt. This can be readily seen, and hence we perceive another unfavorable effect from the proposed policy. The debt should be paid off as soon as practicable. It should not all be placed out of reach for thirty years, and exempted for all that time from contributing to its own discharge, unless we are prepared to resign ourselves to never-ending taxation for the payment of interest.

In a *sectional point of view*, the exemption principle will be very unequal in its bearings. In the new States, where capital is comparatively scarce, and local taxation necessarily heavy, its operation will be especially oppressive and odious. Every available dollar will be put into government bonds, unless it will command an excessive rate of interest on individual security. Will not this enhance the rate of interest, where capital is most scarce? If so, will it not be most burdensome to those who can least afford to bear severe taxation and high rates of interest?

3d, A consideration is, that the contemplated exemption has a direct and powerful tendency to cripple the industry of the country by absorbing a large proportion of its wealth into the debt of the government. If the national bonds should be relieved of taxation for thirty years, no more will go abroad for sale, and those now in Europe *will be returned upon us.* Of that there can be no doubt. The difference occasioned by the exemption here, which does not attach to bonds held abroad, will be so great as to insure their return to the American market. That this will make the working capital of the country scarce and high, and thus greatly injure all the industry of the nation, especially that engaged in manufactures, is beyond a question.

The last consideration we shall name is, that the proposed measure is *entirely unnecessary.* Such a policy should never have been entered upon. It was bad financiering, even in the darkest hour of our national struggle, and is wholly inexcusable now.

But it may be replied, "The government cannot negotiate its loans at five per cent, unless the exemption is made." Very well; then promise six. The rate of interest is far less essential than equality in the taxation by which that interest is paid. If one-sixth more interest is to be provided for, there will be one-sixth more property on which to assess the tax that is to meet it; the burden upon the people is not increased, only equalized.

The British government pursued a wise financial policy during its great contest with Napoleon. It consolidated its national debt, issued only three-per-cents, and negotiated these on an average discount of about forty-one per cent. Her exigency was great, but the United States is under no such extreme necessity. If a policy is adopted which commends itself to the capitalists of the world, American consols, at a low rate of interest, will, like the British, command money on the most favorable terms. But there must be no tricks, no subterfuges, no unjust exemptions, which sensible men well know are certain to breed public discontent, and imperil the national securities. All must be fair, honest, and just; the resources of the United States are ample, and rapidly increasing; we only need a wise and faithful administration of them.

We have said there was no necessity for the proposed measure; but it would be well to decide fully and finally upon the policy of consolidation into *one stock, at one rate of interest;* yet it is in no wise necessary to bind the government to issue the whole amount, as proposed, in thirty years. The debt is not all due at this time: if a part, say one thousand millions, were now authorized for thirty years, when that was taken up the expediency of issuing more on so long a time could be more judiciously decided upon than at present; besides, if only a part were now offered, it would be taken with more avidity than if the whole were put at once on the market. Policy, therefore, as well as economy, requires a limitation of the issue of thirty years' bonds.

The proposal to save thirty millions per annum, by issuing bonds at five per cent, untaxed, instead of six per cent, in order to form a sinking fund, we regard as idle and delusive. The project never will be carried through. National sinking funds have always failed of success, and, in the nature of things, always will; besides, if such a fund were to be provided for, it could be done more advantageously without exemptions from taxation.

CHAPTER XIII.

FOREIGN INDEBTEDNESS. — I. ECONOMY OF FOREIGN INDEBTEDNESS.

PECUNIARY obligations, between different nations, may be of four different kinds: —

1st, *Individual Indebtedness.* — This can only be of limited and temporary duration, since it must soon be paid, or wiped out by insolvency.

2d, *Corporate Indebtedness.* — This is of two kinds: (*a*) the bonds or other obligations of incorporated companies formed for industrial purposes, the building of railroads, &c.; and (*b*) the bonds of municipal corporations, cities, towns, and counties. These have been issued to an enormous extent in the United States, and a large amount have been disposed of abroad. These two kinds of indebtedness are alike in this, that they may be enforced by law upon the promisors. Property may be attached and sold, if it can be found; and as, in the case of municipal corporations, there is rarely any deficiency in that respect, the latter are quite sure of ultimate, if not prompt payment.

3d, *State Indebtedness.* — Nearly all the States of the American Union have contracted debts, and issued coupon bonds, which, to a considerable extent, have been sold abroad. These rest upon a different footing from the preceding, since they cannot be enforced by any legal process. They are secured only by the honor of the promisor. The Constitution of the Union gives no authority to the general government to compel a delinquent State to regard its obligations; and no foreign power, if disposed, would be allowed to enter the national territory. So there is no remedy. State indebtedness abroad must amount, at the present time, to many millions.

4th, *National Indebtedness.* — Great Britain has a debt, as heretofore stated, of eight hundred millions sterling; but it is almost entirely held at home. The rate of interest on her consols is only three per cent, and there is little inducement for capitalists in America to invest in them; but it is quite otherwise with the United States. Interest here is at least six per cent on the best securities.

We may safely assume, that the civil war has caused, or will cause, the issue of United-States stocks to the amount of three hundred thousand million dollars. According to the comptroller's statement, seven hundred millions of these have already gone abroad; and it is certain, if the credit of the government is preserved, a large part of the balance will take the same direction. Is this desirable, or otherwise, economically considered?

II. THE EXPORTATION OF PUBLIC STOCKS.

Whether the sale of such stocks abroad is desirable or not, will depend entirely upon the character of the commodities sent in return for them, whether these be for advantageous or disadvantageous consumption; and this again will depend upon the financial and commercial condition of the country from which they are sent. Suppose one hundred millions sent to England, and returned in railroad iron, which, put into use, pays a net income of ten per cent, besides facilitating the transport of cotton and wheat, and thus adding to the national wealth. As these stocks pay the American holders but six per cent, and by selling them and investing the amount in railroads they get ten, there is a clear gain *in income* of $66\frac{2}{3}$ per cent. The foreigner, on the other hand, who could only get four per cent for his money in home investments, now gets six, an improvement upon his income of fifty per cent. Both parties are benefited. On the other hand, if the amount sold were returned in fancy goods, jewelry, &c., which increased the consumption of luxuries, but in no way contributed to reproduction, the country would in a short time be poorer to the whole amount. The foreigner would hold his bond, and get his interest; but the American would have nothing to show for it. Or stocks may be exported in payment for an actual balance of trade. If, with all our export of commodities and specie, there still remains an adverse balance, American stocks of one kind or another may be sent and sold to adjust it. By this last operation, the debt is merely "extended," or postponed; and as the interest upon this must be annually paid, a larger export of commodities, specie, or stocks must be made in the future.

If the foregoing illustrations of the manner in which a foreign debt may be contracted are correct, as we think will not be disputed, the remaining question is, what policy on the part of the United-States government could have secured in the past, or can secure in the future, a desirable return for its bonds sent abroad.

If all bonds were sold for cash, and the specie sent in return, the operation would be simple, and its effects apparent; but bonds, when sent abroad, in reality enter into the exports of the country, are negotiated through bankers, and their proceeds become "exchange." If a railroad sends its bonds abroad, the returns will probably be in the iron used for its construction; but, if a city or State, the funds are to be expended at home, and the currency of the country is all that is desired by the sellers. The bonds go into the hands of a banker or agent, who negotiates them abroad, and holds the amount as foreign exchange, which he sells to the merchant, who wishes to remit for purchases abroad. As these operations increase the quantity of exchange for sale, they naturally promote importations, not of money, but of merchandise. And here we must ask pardon for again referring to the hackneyed theme of an inflated currency. If, at the time when bonds are thus being sent abroad, the currency of the country is expanded, prices generally advancing, profits enlarging, and there is great inducement to extend trade, the importer, consciously or unconsciously, is affected by this state of things, and sends forward large orders. The consumption of foreign goods is encouraged, since they are easily paid for (in promises), at home and abroad. It will not be surprising if the consumption of the country is thus increased to the full amount of the bonds sold; at all events, there can be no doubt that it will be increased to a very considerable extent.

The fact that the sale of these bonds has brought into market a large amount of foreign bills of exchange gives the banks an inducement to *increase their discounts*, because there will be no call for specie to be sent abroad, the only thing they ever seriously fear. Thus, on every hand, facilities for expansion and additional consumption are multiplied. At present (1865), American stocks are exported under circumstances absolutely appalling. With gold at forty per cent premium, foreigners can obtain them at 71½ per cent; that is, at a discount of 28½ per cent. With the amount so disposed of, merchandise is purchased and returned to the United States, where it is sold at the extravagantly inflated prices of a redundant credit currency. What the consumer of the imported commodities is thus taxed, and what the country actually loses, it is neither easy nor agreeable to calculate. But such is the condition of our financial affairs at present; and it is quite likely to continue, as no effectual measures are being taken at the present time to contract the currency.

There are those who advise, as a remedy for the evils of over-importation under such circumstances, the imposition of a very high tariff, so that this influx of foreign goods may be prevented. But, however disinterested such counsel may be, the remedy proposed will not meet the case. We have already proved, if we have proved any thing in this work, that the quantity of currency is *more influential* in determining the amount of foreign importations than *the rate of tariff duties.* While there is a great excess of currency, twice or thrice the legitimate amount required by the exchanges of the country, as at present, nothing short of absolute prohibition of all trade will prevent importations, however high the tariff, which, although it does have a tendency to reduce the consumption of foreign goods, may be more than counterbalanced by a superabundant currency. The remedy lies in another direction; viz., in the restoration of the currency to a specie standard. This, although it should be a gradual process, would, as soon as it began, check importations and increase exports; the premium on gold would be reduced; and our stocks, when sold abroad, would bring us in return the full amount of their value. The process of saving amongst all classes would at once commence. Debts, principal or interest, can only be paid by savings; and economy will begin when contraction is inaugurated.

With the present inflated currency, with high prices, large speculative operations, and extraordinary profits, the idea of *economy* is simply absurd. Hence the great necessity of a change of policy. No country was ever being more rapidly depleted than the United States at the present moment (1865), though the fact will only be realized when the consummation of the present disastrous policy has been reached.

FALLACIES RESPECTING FOREIGN INDEBTEDNESS.

No sentiment or opinion is more common, perhaps, among the people, than that it is very undesirable, or dangerous even, to have the national debt held abroad. Is this opinion well founded?

1st, A debtor cannot always choose who his creditor shall be. If deeply involved, those will hold his securities who are most able to hold them. They will, like commodities, go where they are most wanted, where they will bring the highest price.

2d, It makes little difference to the debtor, if he can meet his obligations when due, who may hold them. There is no friendship in trade. Native or foreigner will alike demand his pay, when he has a right to do so.

If these propositions are true, we see that it is quite impossible to prevent foreigners from purchasing our national securities, and of little importance if we could. It is a great misfortune, that we are deeply in debt as a nation. If that indebtedness were wholly to our own people, it would be quite favorable; for then, *as a people*, we should owe nothing at all, since what was to the debit of one citizen would be to the credit of another: but if this cannot be, and if capital is worth more to us than it is to others, then is it not fortunate if others are ready to loan us theirs, that is, are ready to take our public indebtedness? As an admitted fact, the use of capital is about twice as valuable in the United States as in England: why, then, should we not allow Englishmen to hold our public debt?

We are aware that there is a deep prejudice in the public mind against this. That prejudice has influenced the financial action of the government. When the war of the Rebellion broke out, and vast demands were made upon the national treasury, instead of looking abroad for capital, and offering our loans in foreign markets, on favorable conditions, such a course was officially denounced as derogatory to the American people. Foreign capitalists were actually *snubbed*, if we may use so unscientific a term. The Confederates on the other hand, took the wise precaution, from the outset, to establish their credit abroad, and negotiated loans as extensively as possible. This fact gave strength to their cause, since they soon built up in Europe a large pecuniary interest in their success. A foreign loan to the United-States government of one hundred millions in the latter part of 1861 would have saved the country several hundred millions, inasmuch as the suspension of specie payments might thus have been postponed for a twelvemonth, and perhaps even been avoided through the war. By this means, the prices of all the government had to purchase would have been kept down to the natural standard. This measure, if accompanied with the expulsion of all bank currency from circulation and with the issue of government notes to take their place so far as desirable, would, in the end, have saved a great part of the present national indebtedness.

But, whatever may be true in regard to the past, it is unquestionably an object of much importance to secure foreign loans in the future at a low rate of interest. It is not a question whether we shall owe a foreign debt, for that is certain; but whether we shall negotiate it abroad at par at five per cent in gold, or at home at six per cent in a depreciated currency. If bonds were made payable, principal and interest, at London, Paris, Hamburg, and Frankfort, in the currency of those places, and suitable efforts were made to inform foreign capitalists in regard to the resources of the United States, there is not the slightest doubt that most advantageous operations might be made.

But this, we are aware, cannot be done so advantageously now as if we had a sound currency. At present, we could only negotiate at a discount proportionate to the discount upon our currency; say, about thirty or forty per cent: but even that rate would be more favorable than negotiations at home. No financial operations can be made to the best advantage anywhere, until the currency is restored to a specie basis. Then the credit of the nation will be fully established, and its loans at five per cent may be sold at *real par;* that is, for a currency equal to gold.

What the objections to foreign loans are, we have never heard stated; those who have opposed such loans having, so far as we have seen, contented themselves with denunciation: but the argument which seems to be floating in the public mind is, that such a debt will give foreigners an advantage over us, since they may, at any time, combine to send back our bonds, sell them for what they will bring, carry off the specie, and throw our banks into suspension. A frightful result, indeed. But is there any foundation for such a supposition? Do not men act according to their interests? When hundreds of millions of our stocks are held abroad, is it likely that the holders will "combine" to send all, or any large amount, of them back, and force a sale, when they cannot do so except at a great loss to themselves?

What object would be gained by it? What damage would they do us? If they sacrificed their stocks, we should buy them in at great advantage.

But it may be said, that they might drive our banks into suspension. Possibly they might; but what of that? The banks are accustomed to it: it would be nothing new or uncommon. Besides, if the stocks were held *at home*, and money became scarce, or the credit of the government was suspected, the public stocks would be thrown upon the market at once, and with the same result. British consols are thus thrown upon the market: why not American stocks?

From whatever point of view we may look at the subject, we find there can be no well-founded objection to the sale of American stocks in Europe. On the other hand, such a sale of them must be advantageous, *when made under a sound currency*.

FALLACIES RESPECTING A NATIONAL DEBT.

1st, *That a national debt is public wealth.*

"The funded debt of the United States is, in effect, the addition of three thousand millions to the realized wealth of the nation. . . . It is three thousand millions added to its available capital." *

* See pamphlet *issued* by "Jay Cooke, General Subscription Agent for the Sale of Government Bonds," entitled, "How our National Debt may be a National Blessing." Philadelphia, 1865.

If this is so, it is fortunate, so far as the financial condition of the country is concerned, that the Rebellion took place; that it continued so long, and cost so much. Had it lasted long enough to have made the debt tenfold greater than it now is, the "available capital" of the nation would have been correspondingly enlarged; and, of course, its power of production so much increased. It must be a misfortune, economically considered, that the war closed so early. But let us examine into the truth of the assertion that "a national debt is public wealth."

How was it created, and for what?

It was contracted for war expenditures. The operation was simply this: A certain part of the people, having the ability to do so, furnished the nation with the means to carry on the war. These persons became the creditors of the government, and they now hold the public stocks. All the rest of the people are debtors, and jointly owe the amount of the debt. It is a lien upon estates, personal and real, and must remain so until liquidated. Are those who are the debtors to the bond-holders any richer in consequence of the existence of the public debt? Certainly not: they are just so much poorer. They must subtract from their incomes, each year, so much as they have to pay for interest on the national debt. Are the bond-holders any richer in consequence of the creation of this debt? If they actually loaned money, that is, coin, as some did in 1861, for which they are receiving only the usual rate of interest, they are neither richer nor poorer for the operation. They have got public, instead of private, securities for their funds. If they subsequently loaned mere credit currency, or capital at prices advanced in consequence of the depreciation of the currency, then, in so far, they gained what the government lost; or, rather, what that part of the people lost who must pay the debt and interest. There was no increase of wealth in consequence of the increase of prices, but merely a transfer of commodities from one party to another, without an equivalent.

But "the national debt is public wealth." Then it follows, that, if the national debt were repudiated, the nation would be three thousand million dollars poorer. Is that so? Surely not. The holders of the stocks would be poorer, doubtless, by the amount of their bonds, which entitle them to interest semi-annually, and final payment in gold; but just what they lost their debtors would gain, and the general wealth of the nation would not be affected to the amount of a dollar, except, that, in so far as the debt is due to persons abroad, the repudiation of it would save that amount to the nation. Other than this, neither the security nor the insecurity of the national debt has the least effect in determining the national wealth.

2d, But, again, it is said that "*the debt is active, available capital;*" and, in illustration, it is said "that a man having, say, twenty thousand dollars of the bonds, can engage in any kind of business at once, just the same as if he had so much cash capital."

Now, what is the fact? The bonds being good securities, the holder can exchange them for cash, and with this can obtain any description of capital he may need. The bonds, then, are not capital, but only the security upon which capital may be had. If the holder had notes against individuals of unquestionable credit, he could do the same. Are private notes, then, capital? Surely not. The man who, having invested his money or capital in public securities, wishes to exchange them again for capital, can do so readily, because the nation is pledged to repayment, with interest. Bonds, while the credit of the government is sustained, are only a very convenient form of credit. They have no element of capital about them. A thousand billions of them would not add a farthing to the capital or wealth of a nation, or increase the productiveness of any department of industry.

So far from aiding production, a national debt has an effect directly opposite. It depresses industry by the taxation it imposes, and reduces its power to compete with other countries. If a laborer pays fifty dollars per annum more for the commodities he consumes, in consequence of taxation occasioned by the interest upon the public debt, then he must have fifty dollars more wages, or reduce his style of living to such an extent as to save that sum. If the former, his higher wages will enhance the cost of products, and he will be less able to compete with the foreign manufacturer or producer.

3d, The third fallacy is, *that a public debt gives stability to government.*

Upon what should the security of a government depend? Evidently upon the convictions of the people that it is a good government; that it secures to them life, liberty, and the pursuit of happiness. Any people who know they have such a government, will need nothing to assure their loyalty and attachment. Where government rests upon universal suffrage, the power is wholly in the hands of the people, and no law or constitution can have any permanancy, that does not receive their approbation. Any thing that is regarded as oppressive and unjust will certainly be abolished.

France has a large national debt; yet her government has been revolutionized time and again, without any reference to that fact, and without at all disturbing the security of the rentes. National debts will be paid, if the people please to pay them; and governments will be sustained, if the people choose to sustain them.

But it is said, that, since every person who owns a part of the public debt will be interested in the permanency of the government, all such will certainly be loyal; and, as these will be in great numbers scattered over the whole country, and belonging to the most influential classes, their social and political co-operation will afford security to our political institutions. Such reasoning assumes, that every man who owns a certificate of stock, will, on that account, be loyal to the government. Let us examine the matter. How numerous are those bond-holders who are expected to sustain the government and its debt?

(1) There are those who directly hold the bonds.

(2) Those who have stock in State and national banks whose capital is invested in government securities.

(3) Those who have deposits in savings institutions, the funds of which are largely invested in public stocks and in banks, whose capital, as just stated, is in the same kind of investment.

These are the classes on whom reliance is placed to give stability to government, in consequence of the *interest* they are supposed to have in the public tranquillity, as security for the national debt.

What the aggregate number of persons in all these classes may be, we have no means to determine; but it is, doubtless, much less than most people imagine. For—

(*a*) Some seven hundred millions of the bonds are held abroad.

(*b*) Many millions are held by aliens in this country.

(*c*) A large amount is held by females.

(*d*) Vast sums are held by trustees and guardians.

(*e*) Of the savings-banks depositors, who are interested to a limited extent, a majority, probably, have no vote.

(*f*) It is well known, that the capital stock of the currency banks is held largely by widows and orphans.

(*g*) A large part of the debt is absorbed by great capitalists, holding $50,000 to $500,000 each.

How many votes, then, can all these parties give? The whole number of *voters* in the United States is some five millions. What portion of the whole belong to the above classes? Certainly a very small share indeed.

But this is not a full view of the case. Of those who do own stocks, and can vote, very few—*not one in ten*, probably—have a sufficient ownership to counterbalance the amount of taxation they encounter in consequence of the debt. The average amount to the credit of each person in the savings banks of New York and Massachusetts is about $225; and we may safely assume that to be the general average throughout the country. Then it is quite certain that an immense majority have an interest in the savings banks of not over $200. What is the interest of all these small holders, in reference to repudiation?

For example, a laboring man, having $200 in bonds or in a savings deposit, expends $400 per annum, derived from his wages, for articles required in the support of his family. What amount of taxation will he incur annually, in consequence of the national debt? Is it not a very moderate estimate, that ten per cent of all his expenditures will be occasioned by the higher duties, taxes, excise, &c. Ten per cent on $400 is $40, which this man must pay annually; while his whole income from the $200 in bonds, or savings-bank deposit, is only $12. Is it for his pecuniary interest that the public faith be kept inviolate? If he must pay $40 annually, while he gets but $12, how long will it take to use up the $200 he has in government bonds? In less than eight years, he would have lost a sum equal to the amount of his stock, and then be for ever after liable to the same amount of taxation. Very clearly, the sooner the public debt is repudiated, the better for this laborer, though holding $200 in the public funds.

We make the same comparison in regard to a man who holds $1,000 in stock. His income we will suppose $2,000, which he expends. On the scale before given, he will pay, in increased prices, $200, while his coupons are but $60 per annum; a balance against him of $140. How long will his interest require that the coupons be paid? Clearly, the sooner they are worthless, and the taxation they impose removed, the better. Another view may be given, of the relations of the debt to the population of the country. It may be assumed, that the debt will be equal to about $100 to each person, if the population is thirty millions. Then a family of five persons owe $500 of the public debt, and, on an average, must pay the annual interest upon the same; say, from $30 to $40. A little reflection will satisfy any one, that the number of families that hold $500 of the national bonds, compared with the whole number, must be very small; and, therefore, that a vast majority can have no pecuniary interest in securing the payment of the national indebtedness.

In these illustrations, we see the folly of the assumption that a public debt gives security to government. Of all who are directly or indirectly owners of the public obligations, not one in twenty has so large an interest that he would not be greatly benefited by its repudiation. Of those who *vote*, probably not one in fifty has an interest in the public debt sufficient to counterbalance the taxation he must endure in consequence of its existence. How idle, then, to talk of the stability a national debt gives to a republican government, under which the will of the people is the supreme law!

On the other hand, who does not see plainly that such a debt, from the necessary taxation it imposes, must be a constant source of irritation and dissatisfaction; that a party will inevitably be formed for its overthrow, and that in such a party will be found sectionalism and all the bad and dangerous elements of society? The future peace and prosperity of the nation is more endangered by the national debt than by all other causes. In a country where the people have little or no power at the ballot-box, a public debt may, doubtless, be made an effective engine of tyranny, and contribute to the enslavement of the masses; but it is quite otherwise where suffrage is universal.

4th, A fourth fallacy is, that a national debt ensures protection to home industry, since the heavy taxation it causes will, if laid on foreign goods, secure that object. Having already discussed the question of protection, we need not now enter upon it; but remark, that a large national debt does not make it certain that there will be a high protective tariff. Great Britain has the largest debt of any nation in the world; yet she has abandoned her protective system. She has become satisfied that such a luxury is too great a hinderance to her commercial prosperity, too heavy a burden upon her home industry; and that she can only compete with other nations, in her manufactures, by maintaining freedom of trade. No nation has had a larger experience of the operation of a severe protective system than Great Britain, and in none is it more heartily repudiated.

5th, But, again, it is said that a national debt is desirable, as a basis for a national currency. That this is an idle assumption, we have already endeavored to show. No such foundation is needed for any currency which the good of a nation demands. It is a false and pernicious system which requires any connection with national indebtedness. Debt is no sound basis for banking. Banks should be created to loan capital that exists, not *debt* for capital that has disappeared.

We will briefly notice one other fallacy in regard to a national debt; viz., that the generation which contracts it is under no obligation to pay it; since, having been contracted for the good of the country, posterity ought to share, at least, the burden of it. What is the principle involved in this statement? Clearly, that one generation has the right to create a debt for such purposes, and to such an extent, as it deems best, and impose on another the payment of the whole, or of such part as it does not choose to discharge out of its own resources. Can this be true? Does it not follow from this, that one generation has the right to enslave another, since, if it can impose a tax, it can enslave? for, to the extent of the tax, it is slavery, or labor taken without compensation. Suppose the tax carried to such an extent as to consume all the products of the laborer over that which is absolutely necessary to existence. If the present generation may lay a tax of ten dollars on each producer for all time to come, it may lay one of a hundred dollars, or a thousand. If it may take away a fourth of a man's income, it may take a half, or why not the whole? The right to tax posterity at pleasure is the right to establish a most terrific despotism; and yet this is one of the popular sophisms of the present day.

A slave is one who does not enjoy the fruits of his labor, further than to preserve his efficiency, and to keep good the number of laborers. It is little matter in what way this is brought about, whether by lawless violence or legal exactions. The result is the same. The British laborer feels it, has always felt it, and, so far as we can judge from the present, always will. He cannot be bought and sold. That is chattelism; that would convert him into capital: but his earnings can be taken from him to pay interest upon debts contracted long before he was born, and for purposes that all now admit were useless.

If such is the effect of the principle which establishes the right to entail upon posterity unlimited indebtedness, can it be safe, economically considered? Surely no man can give an affirmative answer. "But nations must sometimes create debts." To this we reply, —

1st, That the occasions when nations are really so compelled, or can rightfully do so, rarely occur. The great struggle through which the United States has just passed, is one of the strongest cases that has ever been presented; and yet, had the currency been sound at the commencement, and had a sufficiently effective system of taxation been adopted, there is little doubt that the war expenditures might have been met as incurred. It is certain that almost all the service and material was furnished by the country; and therefore, had the taxation been so laid as to apportion the amount judiciously and fairly, the whole cost might have been provided for, and we to-day be essentially free from debt. Without entering, however, upon this question, we can safely assume that the whole should be paid off within the present century, which will also be within the present generation, as a generation is reckoned. We are told by the Secretary of the Treasury (Report, 1865), that two hundred millions paid annually, for principal and interest, will extinguish the debt within the period named. Does any one doubt the ability of the people to do this, if they will? Is it not their duty, if they can?

Unless it is the settled policy of the nation to have a permanent debt, it should *at once* commence the payment, and continue to discharge it in a regular, systematic manner; for, unless the work is commenced promptly, it will never be done. Like England, and other European countries, we shall submit to never-ending taxation for mere interest.

We need not pursue the examination of these fallacies further: indeed, an apology is demanded for noticing them at all. And that apology must be found in the respectable and semi-official source in which they originated. The pamphlet referred to would be of little consequence, however, were it not for a prevalent popular delusion, that, somehow or other, a national debt is real wealth. It is that fallacy which we have attempted to expose.

In conclusion, we will only observe that any people capable of maintaining self-government, and worthy of free institutions, will need no other bond of union than their common loyalty; no other sentiment than that of honor and honesty, to induce them to sustain a national debt, contracted in good faith for the preservation of national existence.

CHAPTER XIV.

RISE AND GROWTH OF THE MODERN FINANCIAL SYSTEM.

No large national debt has ever been paid, or in any way discharged, except by repudiation. The debt of the old French monarchy was wiped out with the "assignats."

The debt incurred in the American Revolution vanished in worthless "continental money." The present debts of England, France, Austria, and other European countries, are so large, the constantly increasing demand for more extensive and costly armaments so pressing, so absolutely overwhelming, that the hope of any payment of the principal cannot be reasonably indulged. A national debt may be regarded, under the existing war policy of the world, as a fixed institution, an inevitable appendage of government.

The United States, which, up to the time of the great Rebellion, formed the only exception among the principal nations of the earth, has entered upon the same course. That general system of finance, of which national indebtedness forms so important a fact in its influence upon the industrial interests of mankind, deserves a careful consideration.

When William of Orange succeeded to the throne of England, Louis XIV., then at the zenith of his power, refused to acknowledge him as a legitimate monarch, and espoused the cause of the exiled Stuart. War, of course, followed. But fighting, in consequence of the invention of gunpowder, and the changes it gradually introduced into warfare, had become an expensive luxury; a game which kings, with their limited and uncertain revenues, could ill afford to play at, particularly for a great length of time. War with one so powerful as the *Grand Monarque* could not be safely commenced or successfully prosecuted, while every penny must be extorted from a reluctant and now independent Commons, and the taxes immediately assessed on the large land or other property holders of the realm.

Such was the difficulty which King William encountered; but, fortunately for his fame, he was a shrewd financier, as well as an able soldier. Up to this time, England had never had a permanent organized national debt, a national bank, or any regular and reliable system of revenue. Grants and subsidies had been voted, from time to time; duties and special taxes had been imposed; but these were not to be depended upon.*

The monarch might and did borrow money from time to time, in great emergencies, but on the most disadvantageous terms. The credit of the government was always low, because there was no regularity or system in the public finances. Men had no confidence in the responsibility or punctuality of the government. William changed all this. He borrowed for a specified period, and promised the punctual payment of the interest semi-annually, and the principal when due; and pledged "the public funds" for the fulfilment of his promises. Hence the public securities were called "the funds."

He negotiated loans and issued stocks. He granted annuities, upon the payment of specific sums. Interest and principal were secured by a pledge of the public funds, or revenues derived from various sources.

This put a new face upon the financial affairs of England: but something further was desirable; viz., an agency by which the national debt would be readily managed, and its semi-annual interest promptly paid.

This was accomplished by the incorporation of a national bank, consisting of the holders of the public stocks, to the amount of £1,200,000.

One thing more was wanting; viz., a permanent and sufficient income, to meet not only the interest on the accumulated debt, but the current expenses of the government, already large, and constantly increasing. To effect this, a land-tax was established; small, indeed, in amount, and upon a *fixed* valuation, so that it could not be increased with the increasing value of the land.

* That this has been disputed, on the authority of Mr. Macaulay, we are well aware; but we do not find any thing in his statements that contradicts our views of the subject. Partial efforts, more or less successful, for the establishment of a thorough financial system, had already been made in England, Italy, and some other countries of Europe; but the great work was at length successfully inaugurated during the reign of William and Mary.

A system of duties on all imports was also enacted, and an excise laid upon all home manufactures and products. In short, a system of *indirect taxation* was adopted, far more general and effective than any which had before existed.

Thus was completed the grand triad of the system of finance, inaugurated by the English Revolution; viz., —

FUNDING, BANKING, AND INDIRECT TAXATION.

The immediate, as well as ultimate, results of the new system are alike remarkable and worthy our attention.

1st, The credit of the government was now firmly established.

It could borrow more money, and at a lower rate of interest, than ever before. Men of small means could now loan money to the government, and with entire confidence. The whole community could be laid under contribution.

2d, Government was enabled to carry on war by borrowing, instead of imposing taxes. War could be waged with credit, instead of cash. Parliament had only to vote a loan. No expenditure need be stopped for want of funds, while the national credit was unimpaired. This was a great change. Many a war had been abruptly closed for want of funds. There was to be no such necessity hereafter.

3d, This course removed the fear of immediate and pressing taxation from the rich, because the greater part was now to fall upon the masses of the people, who pay taxes, not in proportion to property, but to consumption. This was an agreeable consideration to the wealthy classes; and the more so, because, as the public stocks were multiplied, better opportunities were afforded for investments.

4th, Especially was the new policy acceptable to the aristocracy, who, at that time, even more perhaps than now, monopolized the public offices, and whose revenues and patronage were increased by governmental expenditures.

We have said that William became involved in a war with France. In eight years, besides expending all he could raise in taxes, he increased the national debt from £1,200,000 to £21,500,000. A peace of five years followed Anne's accession (1701), during which five millions of the debt were paid off. Then came the war of the Spanish succession. The ostensible object was "to humble the Bourbons, and deprive Philip V. of his crown." This lasted eleven years, and added £37,500,000 to the debt, besides consuming £6,500,000 raised in taxes; so that, at the peace of Utrecht, the national debt was £54,000,000.

In 1727, the House of Hanover succeeded to the throne, in the person of George I., and then came a peace of twenty-six years; but, in all this time, the public debt was reduced to the extent of only £7,500,000. Why? Because it was no object with the ruling class to pay off the debt, since the national stocks had become the most eligible investments; so the resources of the nation were squandered upon the court. In 1739, therefore, the debt was £46,500,000, when the war of the Austrian succession took place. Its specific object was to secure the throne of Austria to Maria Theresa; and the debt was carried up to £78,000,000. Then came eight years of peace; but the debt was reduced only three millions.

In 1756 commenced what was known in this country as "the old French War," or "the Seven Years' War." It was caused by a dispute about colonial boundaries, or, as the wags of those days said, "about a few acres of snow in Nova Scotia;" but it eventually involved a great part of Europe, and the American colonies of both France and England.

Then followed a peace of twelve years; but only £10,500,000 were paid off. The war of the American Revolution lasted seven years, and carried the debt up to £239,000,000. In the ten years of peace and prosperity which followed that great contest, the public debt was reduced but £5,000,000,

No 11.

Rise and Growth of the British National Debt.

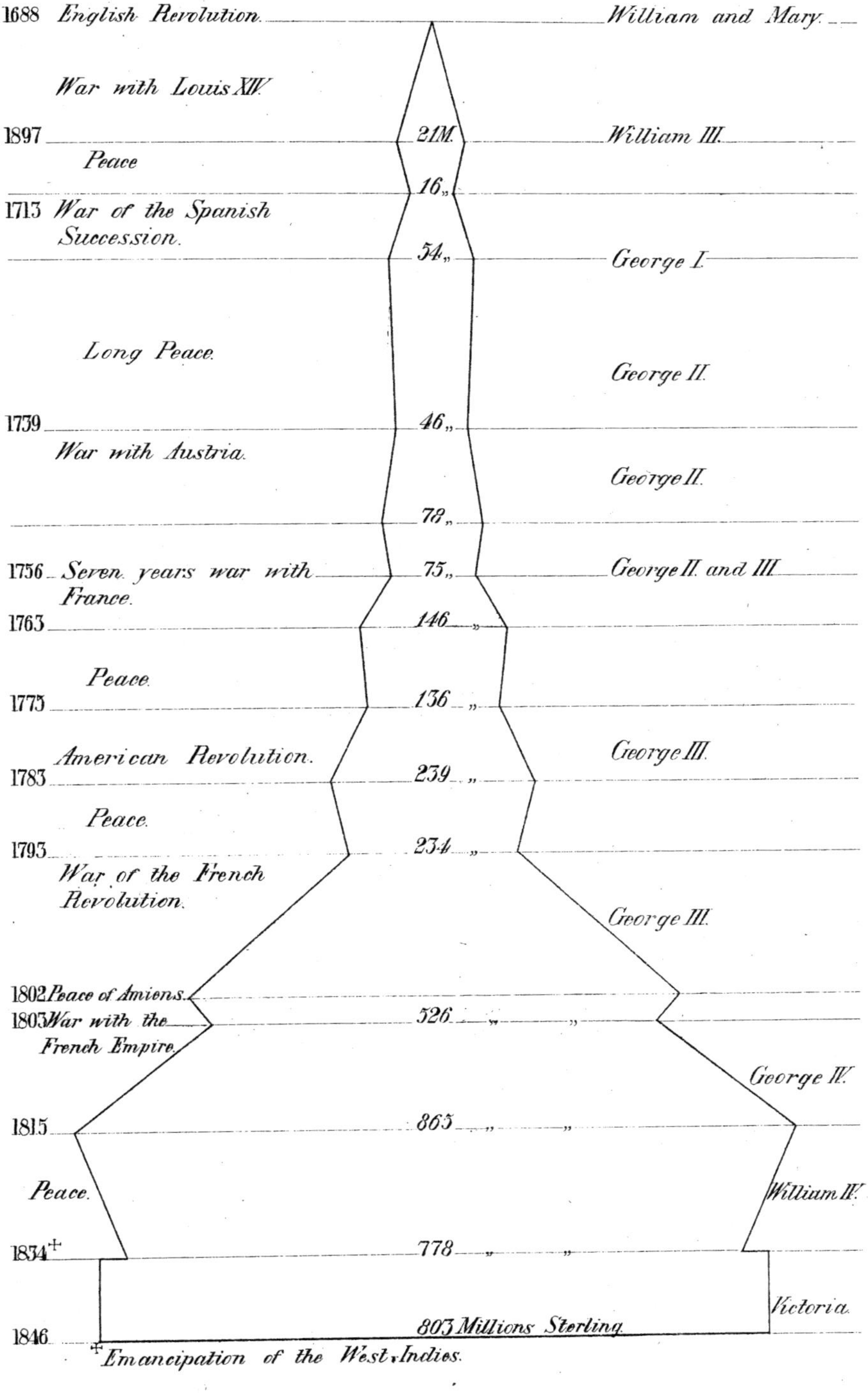

notwithstanding that the resources of England were largely increased, and her ability to reduce the national indebtedness was ample, if the disposition to do it had existed.

In 1793 began the war that grew immediately out of the French Revolution. This lasted for nine years, and increased the debt to £526,000. Then, in consequence of the Treaty of Amiens, a period of one year's peace intervened; but it was only an armed truce: military preparations were continued, and the public debt was increased £3,000,000.

In 1803 commenced the final struggle with Napoleon, which terminated in 1815, leaving the British debt at £865,000,000 sterling. During the twenty years following, £87,000,000 were paid off. This was from necessity, rather than choice; a measure of policy adopted to secure the credit of the government. In 1835, the debt was but £778,000,000; but the emancipation of eight hundred thousand slaves in the West Indies added to the debt £20,000,000. It has stood at £800,000,000, very nearly, ever since. We give in Diagram No. 11, inserted here, an illustration of the facts as we have stated them.

We have given this history of the rise and p ogress of the debt of Great Britain, as exhibiting the natural effects of such a system as she inaugurated during the reign of William and Mary. But we have shown only a part of the system. The history of the national bank is interwoven with that of the national debt. It was incorporated in 1697, with a capital, as we have said, of £1,200,000. As the public debt was enlarged, the capital of the bank was increased; that is, more and mo e of the debt was incorporated into the bank organization, until it amounts, at the present time, to £14,475,000. This bank, as before stated, has never had a shilling of capital to lend to the people; it has simply held a certain amount of the national stocks, and, upon the credit of these, has issued its own promises to pay; and these promises, having been made a legal tender by Parliament, have circulated as money.

The government has no interest whatever in the bank, so far as its profits are concerned; but it has always stood by it, sustained it by its influence and legislation, besides allowing a large annual sum for its services, in paying the dividends on the public debt. When the bank was obliged to suspend payment, in 1797, the government came to its rescue, by legalizing the act; and the bank went on issuing its notes during the twenty-three years that followed, and sometimes to an amount so excessive, that gold was carried up to a premium of twenty-five to forty per cent: generally, however, during this period, the difference was small,—some ten to fifteen per cent. The last feature to be noticed in this connection is that system of INDIRECT TAXATION which became so general and efficient under the new financial policy. Duties, as we have said, were laid upon every description of foreign merchandise, and excise upon all articles of home production. This measure was indispensable to the full development of the system. When the masses of the people can be taxed in such a manner that they are almost unconscious at the moment that they are taxed at all; when the amount taken is in very small sums, so that, if the fact were understood, it would hardly be appreciated; when the aggregate amount for a month or a year cannot be ascertained, except approximately, and then only by long and intricate calculation,—taxation may be carried to its utmost possible limit, so far as to leave to the poorer classes only the bare necessaries of life. Such a people may feel that they are very poor, but they will regard this as the consequence of their low wages; they may feel that they are oppressed, but will naturally attribute it to the want of justice or generosity on the part of their employers. The true cause of their poverty and suffering they do not perceive. The gross taxes imposed in Great Britain in 1859 amounted to seventy-three millions sterling, equal to $14 per head, through the whole population, or $70 for a family of five persons. Such a taxation, if collected at all, must be taken, as it is taken, imperceptibly, as it were a penny at a time. This grand system of currency and finance, so fully established in Great Britain, has at this time become the policy of all civilized, and to some extent even of uncivilized countries,—funding, indirect taxation, paper-money banking.

RESULTS OF THIS FINANCIAL SYSTEM.

1st, *An immense extension of the war system.* Prior to the introduction of this policy, standing armies and armaments were exceedingly limited. Now all Christendom is armed, by land and sea. France leads the van, with an army of some 700,000; and each nation is struggling to create and support the largest possible military and naval establishment: and all this can be done of credit, if need be; there is no limit to these prepartions, while national credit holds out.

2d, *Universal and constantly increasing indebtedness.* This is true of nearly every country in the world. England, indeed, has not increased her debt for the last thirty years; but almost every other government has been borrowing money from year to year, until many of them are as much burdened by their indebtedness as England, because, in proportion to their wealth and resources, they are as deeply involved. France, we suppose, is really more oppressed by taxation than England. France is a great nation of poor people, compared with England or the United States. She has but a small margin for taxation. The same, indeed, may be said of many other European nationalities.

3d, *Impoverishment of the masses.* This is especially apparent in England. What has become of that YEOMANRY, once the pride of the country? Their little estates have disappeared, have been swallowed up by the terrible system of taxation to which they have been subjected. The pleasant hedges which still surround the small enclosures, once constituting the freeholds of her yeomanry, may yet be seen in all parts of the country. They are the monuments of an industrious, brave, and independent class of men, now extinct. These lands are indeed tilled by the hands of their descendants, no longer yeomanry, but peasants, almost the paupers of the nation. How strikingly true this is, may be seen in the fact that there are but one-third as many "holdings" at the present time as one hundred and fifty years ago, while the wealth and population of England have doubled many times. How this has been accomplished, may be seen from statements made by Professor Levi of the whole taxation of Great Britain for the year 1858.*

Total Taxation.	Paid by the Upper Classes.	Middle Classes.	Working Classes.
£73,000,000	£22,550,000	£30,930,000	£20,320,000

From this analysis, it appears that the amount paid by the middle and working classes is equal to five-sevenths of the entire revenue, while those who monopolized the landed estates of the country, and an enormous proportion of its public stocks and circulating capital, paid but two-sevenths.

We have said that no large national debt has ever been paid or discharged, except by repudiation; nor does it appear that such debts are likely ever to be paid, unless the war policy of the world is changed. All have been created by war, and are perpetuated by constant demand for additional armaments.

The economy of a national debt, under the modern financial system, must always impoverish the productive classes. Its entire influence on them is oppressive. It deprives them of their honest reward, by a false currency, which robs them of a large share of their nominal wages; it imposes upon them, through indirect taxation, an undue proportion of the public burdens, and is, in fact, a stupendous enginery for depressing them, though perhaps not so

* Levi on Taxation, p. 32, London edition.

intended. Hitherto we have known little of its effects in the United States. Until the present time, we have felt little pressure from public indebtedness and consequent taxation; but the case is now altered. We have an immense debt, and a larger amount of annual interest than any other people on the face of the earth. Hence the great importance of understanding the whole subject of modern finance by the people themselves; for without such an understanding of it, however much they may suffer, they cannot hope for relief. They must know the cause of their sufferings, or they cannot apply the remedy.

CHAPTER XV.

ON THE LAWS OF INHERITANCE AND BEQUEST.

MEN die, and the property they have acquired or held during their lives must pass into the possession of others. May the person who is about to leave the world say to whom his wealth shall immediately descend? May he go farther, and say to whom it shall descend for all coming time? May he go farther still, and determine what specific use shall be made of his wealth for ever? Or shall the laws of the State decide the questions, — to whom, for what purposes, and for how long, the wealth of deceased persons shall descend? Does the world and its wealth belong to the living or the dead, or to both in common? If to both, what portion should belong to each? If the dead are allowed to control a part, why not all? Which party, the living or the dead, will most intelligently decide how wealth can be advantageously employed in production, or in any other mode, for the benefit of the living?

These are the points involved in the subject of Inheritance and the testamentary disposal of property, and are important in an economical point of view, irrespective of all other considerations. These questions have been practically decided by the laws and institutions of society in different ages and countries. Governments have always interfered in regard to the estates of deceased persons, to such an extent as to prescribe limitations and conditions. So far as these have been in harmony with instincts of humanity, and the laws of value, they have been beneficent in their operation. But all the wealth, all the institutions, all the interests of society, should ever be regarded as fully under the control of the existing generation of men. This should be a fundamental principle in civil polity; and, if law may interfere in this matter at all, it may do so to any extent the public interest shall demand.

Mr. McCulloch,* in his "Principles of Political Economy" (page 267), says: "Every man should have such a reasonable power over the disposal of his property as may be necessary to excite his industry, and to inspire him with a desire of accumulating. But if, in order to carry this principle to the furthest extent, individuals are allowed to chalk out an endless series of heirs, and to prescribe the conditions under which they shall successively hold the property, it would be taken entirely out of the market; it might be prevented from ever coming into the hands of those who would turn it to the best account; and it could neither be farmed nor managed in any way, however advantageous, that happened to be inconsistent with the will."

Mr. McCulloch here recognizes the correct principle; viz., that the interests of those who are laboring and suffering now, are paramount to the whims and caprices of those who have passed from the stage of action; in other words, that the earth belongs to the living, and not to the dead. To exhibit the enormous abuses and perversions to which these mortmain holdings must lead, we need only refer to the old

* Author of the "Commercial Dictionary," and one of the best writers of his time upon Political Economy.

countries of Europe, England especially, where millions on millions of wealth are held and used, not for the purposes originally intended, but often for the very opposite. Many of the objects for which benefactions are thus made, become obsolete or absurd; yet the property must be held and misused, if really used at all.

It has been said, that nothing is more unwise than to attempt to bind posterity with parchment; and, the more enlightened the public mind becomes, the more apparent will be the utter folly of allowing the past to govern the present.

Yet the author just quoted, advocates, with the most surprising inconsistency, the laws of primogeniture, and makes an argument, though a very weak one, in favor of giving the whole estate to the oldest son! — an illustration of what has too often been found in the writings of English economists, who seem generally to assume, in advance, that the laws and institutions of their own country are right, and therefore the laws of wealth must be made to appear in conformity with them. Mr. McCulloch would probably never have been made a public officer, and held a lucrative position under government, if he had taught the opposite doctrine.

In some countries, the laws have not only provided for the manner in which wealth *may be* disposed of by testamentary provisions, but have often ordained that certain estates *shall be* inalienable. Thus, the landed property of a people, seized by violence, has been made a perpetual inheritance to the favored parties and their descendants for ever. This class of persons has often been invested with the powers of government; and class legislation has strengthened and increased what force or fraud had achieved.

So far as a class, more or less strictly limited, or highly distinguished, reaches a position of property or influence by moral perfections, by high intellectual endowments, or by successful business operations, agreeably to the laws of wealth, and under the test of ordinary competition, it is not taken out of the principles heretofore laid down. But so far as it has been placed arbitrarily in the possession of large properties, and is maintained so by thwarting the action of natural laws, it is by that removed from the primitive rule of distribution, and requires to be separately considered. We shall regard it only from an economical point of view.

The nobilities of the world have, in fact, been formed off-hand, generally out of the personal favorites of the monarch, or distinguished soldiers, by the grant of large privileges and valuable estates. Would this perpetuate a nobility? On the one hand, we have the argument, *a priori*, that the possession of wealth tends to secure its own continuance, both because possession is nine-tenths of all the points, and because the *vis inertiæ* is against a change; that the family which has property to-day has a better chance, other things equal, to have it next year or next century, than those who have it not. But other things are far from equal, which introduces the argument from experience; viz., that estates tend to go out of the hands of any special class. The forces that scatter are stronger than those that hold together. Outside is a hostility to the individual appropriation, that never ceases, arising out of the desires of the entire community for that particular property. There is not a sentient being who has not the instincts that would impel him to seize it if he could. Within, to hold the gates against the assault of the whole world, is the solitary possessor. His strength must some time fail; his vigilance, some time relax.

Such, in a figure, is the tendency of wealth to scatter. By an order of things in which we can seem to see great benevolence, no family or class can secure the integrity of its estate. Otherwise, property would tend to aggregate itself, so as to crush competition, and leave the greater part of the world destitute. As it is, the foolish son dissipates the gatherings of the wise father, and alienates the lands that have been annexed, acre after acre, by prudence and frugality. A single break in the succession of industry and economy will scatter the accumulations of ages. *This liability of the rich is the property of the poor.* Just as surely as the lapse of ages wears down the craggy mountain-tops, to form the soil of the humble valleys, so surely do aggregations of wealth gravitate every hour to the general level.

To contravene this provision of nature, the law of the land often shuts in these estates by arbitrary enactment or judicial interpretation, and so keeps out the busy, unrelenting competition, which otherwise would, sooner or later, bring the proudest structure to the ground. All such legal arrangements may be summed up in —

THE LAWS OF PRIMOGENITURE AND ENTAIL.

1st, Of the rightfulness of such laws.

In the order of nature, no man brings with him into the world a store of wealth for his subsistence and support through life, or finds it waiting especially for him. His means of livelihood are to depend on the inborn faculties of appropriation, on the store of wealth already existing from which these may draw, and on the natural agencies of production which they may employ. But if the latter conditions are removed, and the man is forbidden access to the fields of labor, he is condemned to be destitute, in a greater or less degree, no matter how well endowed, or how fully he obeys all economic laws. With these open to him, he is certain of success. It hinders not at all, that all the wealth of the world is now taken up, that every inch of ground is possessed. Though utterly without legal claim, he is yet, in his faculties of industry and appropriation, sure to become the owner of some part of it, at least sufficient for his wants.

The tiny tree pushes its way through the matted sod. It comes out, one little stem, two little leaves. The squirrel looks disdainfully over it. The ant can gnaw its trunk. Pounds of atmospheric weight are already on its fluttering expanse. Yet it stands. The world and the air are now absolutely full, present not one inch of vacant space. The universe seems to have no room for the little stranger. Yet it grows. Simply confiding that the world had need of it, the seed broke its shell, and crept upward to the light. And in the same unshrinking faith of a mission and of room that shall be provided, it grows, atom by atom, till the biparted leaf has become the giant tree, and takes its place in the crowded universe, with always room to grow, and never an inch to spare.

So, in the state of nature, man enters on life, feeble and destitute, but with powers of absorption and assimilation as evident as those of the tiny tree. These, not human charity or human justice, award the world's wealth, and sustain the lives for wise purposes created. But, if the tree is planted in a pot, its capacity of growth is dwarfed to the dimensions of the place in which it finds itself. It cannot enlarge; not because its vital germ is deficient, but because it is placed in a false position, and deprived of natural aliment. If the confines are too close, the tree starves and dies.

This is precisely the injustice and mischief done by laws of primogeniture and entail. So far as they operate, they shut off the industry of the world (and the wants which that industry must supply) from its proper field. We have said that the liability of wealth to dissipate is the property of the poor. It is so. A man entering the world may have no claim to any share of its previous gains; but he *has* a claim to a *chance at them.* This is the provision nature has made for his maintenance. This is his inheritance. He has a right, at least as complete as the plant, to get his growth and his support out of the soil about him. There is nothing in this view agrarian or communistic. It admits that property should be sacred; but it asserts that it should be alienable. The right of property does not include the right of the wise to get wealth, and of fools to keep it. To shut up any part of the world, for the benefit of one, is to rob all others, not of it, but of their chance to acquire it lawfully. A system of entail dwarfs all existing industry, so far as it operates. It has even proceeded to beggar an entire people. There is, therefore, no economic censure too severe for it.

2d, But, besides the general objections to such a system on the grounds of justice, we meet certain considerations of expediency that deserve notice.

(1) The capital thus kept together by laws forbidding alienation is often so large that it cannot be managed by individuals for the best economic advantage. Of course, a government might provide for the preservation of properties not excessive. But it is not such that have been made perpetual; and there can be no occasion to lock up, in this way, moderate estates. Great accumulations will be made under any free and peaceful government; and it is neither the right of government, nor the interest of society, to interfere to scatter them. The sacredness of property makes a greater demand than the mere productiveness of capital. Besides, this has been collected, and is kept together, by economic virtues, which should ever receive their natural reward. But it is not in the order of things that such mountains of wealth should remain. They will be rent asunder, or worn away, in the lapse of comparatively few years.

Many reasons might be given why wealth, in such aggregations, is never so efficiently managed; but the assertion hardly requires proof. We find, in certain countries, extensive systems of polygamy; but it is notorious that population does not advance as with those people where the Christian law of marriage is observed. Monopoly of wealth no more tends to reproduction than monopoly of wives. All this is true, even if the desire of increase remained the same; but, —

(2) Such aggregations of wealth destroy, in great part, the desires which lie at the root of all activity. The spring of industry is want. Let us take into calculation the sum of one million of dollars. It cannot be doubted, that this, as a reproductive agency, would be quickened by more desires if in the hands of one thousand men, than if in the hands of only one hundred. Without an attempt at mathematical accuracy, it is certainly true that the machinery of reproduction would be set in motion by a deeper and broader stream of human wants. It is evident, that the impulse of the mass, the one thousand, will be greater; but it may be questioned whether the impulse of each one is not greater in the former than in the latter case. Certainly the necessities of each will be more pressing: why not his activities more aroused? How much mightier, then, the current of energy with which the greater body moves on to its object!

On the other hand, if we suppose the sum to be vested in the possession of one person, we shall have the desires greatly weakened. This is not the man who, "from the rising of the lark to the lodging of the lamb," toils with unrelaxed nerve; to whom every gain is needful bread; from whom every saving removes a pain.

Erskine, as his courage sank in dismay on his first pleading, seemed "to feel his children pulling at his gown," and so took heart to go on. Everywhere it is the hands of the little ones, plucking at the sleeve, that elevates labor into heroism.

(3) Such aggregations draw off an undue proportion of wealth into luxuries. This is the necessary consequence of what has just been exhibited; while its own results will appear more specially in the department of "Consumption." When the stern pressure of necessity is removed from human activities, they bound into a thousand sports and caprices.

(4) Such aggregations of wealth often come to men not competent to administer them, either in use or enjoyment. This appears in the very necessity of a law of entail.

Under a free system, capital is sure to go into the hands best fitted to manage it for the highest economic good. It may pass through strange experiences, and take on many doubtful forms; but it never, for a moment, escapes from the grasp of economic laws, and must, at the last, reach and rest upon true economic desert.

BOOK V.

CONSUMPTION.

CHAPTER I.

DIVISIONS OF THE SUBJECT.

THERE is a production, and there is a destruction, of wealth; but the latter is not the subject of scientific inquiry. Its phenomena may, at times, be prodigious, terrific; its effects may be most baneful and grievous; but there is no philosophy of it. It is all either unintelligent or malicious. Science is only of what is good, or may be made good; and of what is amenable to laws, either of human direction or of human comprehension. The flood that drowns a thousand farms, the storm that whelms a fleet, the earthquake that shakes a city to the ground, are not so important to the eye of philosophy as the difference between yesterday's leaf and to-day's.

It is not, therefore, with wealth, as disposed of in destruction, but in consumption, that we have to speak.

Consumption is the use of wealth. It is precisely the converse of production. If production were, on the one hand, the creation of an article, consumption would be its annihilation. But as human labor cannot bring one atom into existence, so neither can it return one to nothingness. Since man's efforts expend themselves in arranging matter into certain desirable forms, so man's satisfactions do, directly or indirectly, soon or late, exhaust those properties or peculiarities of form that have been imposed on matter; and leave it, in the act and for the time, vacant of the elements of value. This result is reached in the consumption of wealth.

There can be no use of wealth, without this change of form; while the merest change of form oftentimes answers all the conditions of consumption. This consumption may be for any purpose,—for luxury, wastefulness, or reproduction; may be within any time,—from the slow wear of the precious metals to a perishing that is almost simultaneous with the making; may be in any degree,—from a total disappearance, as when wood is burned, to a change which the most practised eye can hardly detect.

In the economical sense, iron ore is consumed when it is wrought into chains and bars. These, again, are consumed when they are arranged into a bridge, though each may still retain its single shape. And, when the bridge has been worn out in time, it is said to be consumed, though it still remains as an element in all articles which have received value by carriage over it.

Each one of these changes is an act of consumption; and at each the character of the change determines the new state, and the result, both in individual or national wealth. At each, there is an application to a new purpose, and a new economical direction is imposed.

While the iron remained in bars, it was liable to be wrought into a bridge, as it was; or into ploughs, for the tillage of the earth; or into weapons, for the destruction of man. When it was directed to one of these, a new object was produced: it was consumed; not annihilated, but changed in its form and purpose. It is evident that the effects on society and on industry would be vastly different, as one or the other of these directions should be taken. The bridge itself might be used for facilitating commerce, or for transporting armies; and, in each case, the new application would be a consumption of the article, the new product and the new result in wealth being determined in the choice of uses to which it should be put.

The seed is consumed when it is planted in the ground to bring forth one hundred-fold. The cigar is consumed when it goes off in smoke.

Such consumption of wealth is constantly taking place in industrial society; and in this light we see the great importance of the principles which govern in this department: what momentous decisions are made at each change of the form imposed by labor on matter; how the wealth of the world goes up or down, with the new direction given it. Although such consumption comes far more slowly in some instances than in others, and seems at times to be indefinitely delayed, yet it is true that wealth has its generations, like the race of man; that, in so long a time, all the present accumulations of labor will have expended themselves; and that upon the provision made for reproduction will depend the condition of the future. The world might be stocked full of useful and precious goods, yet become seedy in ten years, and beggarly within the life of man. And not only is the change of form and the new direction of vital importance; but it is made so frequently, in such multitudinous ways, often so silently and unobserved, always with so much of complication and uncertainty, that the principles which should control it have an interest at once, and a difficulty beyond those which belong to any other part of political economy.

It would be impossible to give a catalogue of all the distinct acts of consumption that take place in the narrowest field and in the shortest time. It might be even impossible to decide distinctly when any one of them actually began or ended; so that, if the science depended on determining them accurately, we should be forced to close our inquiries at once, as useless. No eye can detect their processes; no thought can reach down to the real spring of economical life. But we can find in the general results, as they come out in national or individual experience, enough for practical instruction and guidance.

We cannot see the grain grow, or fix its daily increments; yet we know the fact of its growth, and can study the conditions of its best development. So we cannot mark the periods of wealth, or note its phases; yet in its great harvests we can see the kindness or unkindness of the soil, the refreshing of the showers, or the parching of the drouth.

To employ a figure: Exchange and distribution form the trunk of the tree, between the two branching worlds, above and below. Through that narrow compact body passes all that the intricate web of roots has to give, the product of their silent, humble work; all that the interlacing limbs and boughs, more fortunate and conspicuous, have to spend. Below is the world of production, where myriad agencies appropriate and assimilate the properties of the soil. Above is the world of consumption, where is given off, in every variety of foliage and flower and fruit, of use and beauty, what has been long and patiently gathered.

The consumption of wealth may be regarded as of four kinds,—mistaken, luxurious, public, and reproductive. We shall speak of them in that order.

CHAPTER II.

I. MISTAKEN CONSUMPTION.

WHAT shall we do with that large class of industrial actions which bring no reward to those who perform them?

We find labor and capital applied with the purpose of reproduction, but without result. And this not occasionally; but the share of failures can almost be determined with certainty, and is found to bear no inconsiderable proportion to business enterprise the world over. Indeed, in some occupations, entire success forms the exception.

These cases of mistaken industry would present very few questions but for the secondary uses to which we sometimes find them applied. Gibbon describes the towers, citadels, and palaces of Rome as built on the foundations of the ancient temples, theatres, and arches. We can draw a figure thence to our modern industry. The fortunes of one generation often rise from the failures of that which went before. If we trace the history of many of the most flourishing establishments, we shall find them resting at last on some great outlay of capital, or expenditure of labor, that ruined some man or corporation, and finally went to pay taxes or office rent. Such has been the fate of many of the railroads of the United States; so much so, that it has passed into a proverb that such stock must be sunk once to pay at all. A railroad is established, starts with brilliant prospects, and, after a descending course for a few years, arrives at bankruptcy. Even so, when the stock can be had for nothing, it may not pay for running, and lies idle, or half run. But perhaps the industry of the country takes a sudden start, or pushes up gradually, finds the old track there, and demands that its goods be carried to market. The experiment is made; and soon the road is worked to its utmost capacity, enriching holders, who had forgotten the existence of their stock.

The same thing occurs frequently in the course of individual enterprises. Men undertake great matters, launch into immense expenses, and, after sinking the full amount of their capital and credit, stop hopelessly. The works stand idle and melancholy for years, till some new industry or some shrewder manager takes them at half cost or for nothing, and gets a fortune out of them.

When one of the later emperors would build a monument of his achievements, he was forced to use fragments of older architecture; and so, history tells us, the head of Trajan frowned from the arch of Constantine. Many a modern fortune is pieced out of the wreck of earlier industry.

This, of course, presents only the best view of such mistaken investments. There are cases where industry, instead of coming back to re-animate the lifeless body by sudden movements, forsakes even the habitations it has delighted in; and the machinery of to-day becomes old-fashioned and useless under the surprising inventions of to-morrow. Every locality has its "folly," named from some helpless adventurer, who undertook more than he could carry, and which has reached a death from which there is no resurrection. Long lines of railroad stretch across the country, forsaken, apparently for ever, of passengers or freight. Mills and factories stand tenantless till they crumble. These only enumerate the gigantic failures of industry; while the amount of labor and capital misapplied in ordinary ways is beyond computation. The three causes for these industrial misadventures are as follows:—

1st, Capital is fallible in its calculations. Plausible schemes, based on views that are partial or temporary, draw even the ablest financiers into such investments. It would be out of reason that such errors should not be committed, even with the keen scent of personal advantage and trained observation.

2d, Extravagance is, however, the prime cause of business failure. Men, in originating enterprises, sanguine in feeling, and exhilarated by the possession of large capital, almost invariably indulge in a scale of outlay which the return does not justify. They find it unpleasant or undignified to omit any thing from the completeness of preparation out of considerations of economy. The result is, that the expense of starting drags on them through the whole course, and perhaps ruins them. They are kept down all the time by the original outlay, and often have to vacate their magnificent establishments for the entrance of parties who, getting them at half price, can afford to keep and work them.

3d, Another reason is found in those accidents or great

developments which transfer business from one seat to another, just as wells give out with no apparent cause. The axis of commerce shifts its place, and leaves tropical bones and tropical fruit high on the northern hills.

What shall we do in our discussion with such investments of labor and capital? Shall industry carry them on its books, like bad debts, in the hope that something may some time come of them? Political economy here takes a lesson from the legislation by which obligations are outlawed after a certain time, and declares that wealth, unproductively applied, is not capital; that it must be struck out of the account of the world's goods, to be reckoned either as loss or luxury. Whatever, from any cause, fails to recompense its outlay, though it may still have some utility, is to be considered as so much added to the common agencies of society. If any thing comes out of it, this is to be counted as so much received from the gratuitous gifts of nature. Whoever, by shrewdness or chance, has possession of them, is fortunate. A canal or railroad, whose stock has been once sunk, stands in just the same relation to political economy as do rivers and natural causeways, which facilitate travel, and render production easy, but are not capital, in the scientific sense of the term.

CHAPTER III.

II. LUXURIOUS CONSUMPTION.

LUXURY, — what is it, and what are its effects, economically considered? Noah Webster defines it as "a free or extravagant indulgence in the pleasures of the table, as in rich wines and expensive diet, or delicious food and liquors; voluptuousness in the gratification of the appetites, or the free indulgence in costly dress and equipage." We must give a far wider definition for our purposes, in the science of which we treat. A fine house is certainly as much a luxury as fine clothes or costly wines ; so are statuary and paintings ; so are a vast number of articles of common consumption in every condition of life. It is quite clear, too, that what would be esteemed a great extravagance in the royal establishment of Dahomey would be far otherwise in the humblest dwelling of Europe. The wigwam and the cottage exhibit very different phases of luxury. The loathsome poisons of " Gin Lane " are as truly luxuries, perhaps in the sense of Webster more so, than the " rich wines " and " delicious liquors " of the palace. Idleness is a cheap enjoyment in some spheres of life ; but many a seamstress's wealth cannot buy her the time to weep.

> " My tears must stop, for every drop
> Hinders needle and thread."

It is apparent that a *specific* definition of the term " luxury " is impossible ; yet we can give a general formula that will be sufficient for our purpose. Luxury in the community is indulgence in those expenditures which are beyond the reach of the great mass of the people : luxury in the individual is indulgence in those expenditures which are beyond the strict necessities of maintenance, according to the customs of the social or economic class to which he belongs. It is not luxury for the ambassador of a nation to pay thousands of dollars for a great disagreeable state carriage, if the etiquette of court prescribes it : it *is* luxury for a laborer to pay five cents for a ride to his work, if he could as well walk.

Of course, this standard will vary in different countries, the inhabitants of one being able to command many indulgences which are denied to others. The luxuries of Europe are daily fare in Asia, while articles of common decency in an Irish hovel are unknown in the court of Delhi. Nor only this : the scale of luxury changes with every year.

Those articles which in one generation indicate wealth, become common property in the next. This results from the general progress of society and the constant advance of economic powers. As production rises, it covers the monuments of earlier taste or grandeur.

The direction, too, of luxurious consumption varies with the culture and the aspiration of those able to indulge in it. In one circle, it will run to horses and hounds; in another, to paintings and statuary: some will turn for enjoyment to architecture; others, to dress and equipage; more, still, to feasting and dissipation.

The ground of luxurious consumption is, perhaps, best determined by the boundaries of its neighbors. It embraces nothing that is spent in the purpose of a reproduction, more or less immediate and direct. The *necessary* consumption of a people depends chiefly on absolute wants, is not greatly a matter of choice, fancy, or taste; but its luxuries, those things which it may or may not have, depend entirely, for their kind and degree, upon moral and intellectual characteristics. Consequently, they furnish an index of the national civilization.

1st, Do luxuries directly encourage industry?

We shall reach the truth of this by illustrations. When William IV. came to the throne of England, he erected a tower at one of the entrances of the palace where he made his residence. It cost $500,000. There was no pretence of utility whatever in the building. It was pure luxury. It was an elegant structure. It gratified the monarch's taste. It was highly ornamental to the castle and the grounds: What was the economical effect? The erection gave employment to mechanics and laborers; it made a call for materials and architectural skill; it made trade brisk in the neighborhood. Was it therefore beneficial? Suppose it had accorded more with his majesty's views to take the same money, and with it erect two hundred cottages on the crown lands, at an expense of $2,500 each. This would have called for as much labor and materials as the tower; would have given as great an impetus to trade. At the same time, it would have brought into existence comfortable residences for the families of two hundred laborers. If the cottages were rented at a moderate rate, the income would be equal to a fair interest, and the dwellings would stand for generations, a valuable property, conferring happiness and comfort on a thousand people.

But there is more to come. We said, "take the same money." What money? Whose money? Now, in arguments for govermental luxury, it is always assumed that the money is in the treasury. But how came the money into the public coffers? Who furnishes the money? The sober, steady industries of the country. The money to make King William's tower came from Leeds and Sheffield and Manchester. It encouraged one class of artisans. True. Whom did it discourage? A class that is always out of sight in such reckonings, — the class that pays the taxes.

Then, so far, it only amounts to changing the capital of the country from one hand to another; employing one class by turning off another; a change that is never made without distress and loss.

There is still more to be said. If the wealth had remained in the hands of the manufacturer, say, it would have been capital, and supported workmen this year. So has the tower. But, in the latter use, next year it will be no longer reproductive; while, in cotton-spinning or land-draining, it would grow with every day, and furnish unfailing employment for labor. A thousand dollars *spent* in luxury will pay a thousand dollars of wages (less certain little items). A thousand dollars *employed* as capital will, in ten years, pay twenty thousand dollars of wages. Such is the difference in results.

A similar instance is that of a man expending ten thousand dollars on an enlargement of his house for purposes of grandeur or enjoyment, or laying it out in draining and improving fifty acres of land. In either case, he pays a certain amount of wages; but, in the latter, he has added a permanent value to the country; increasing his own annual income, and affording the means of employing a certain amount of labor to the end of time.

Wealth, employed as capital, is an annuity made out in the name of the laborer, and good for life.

There is no possible case in which the employment of wealth, for purposes of luxury, as opposed to reproduction, can be said directly to advantage industry. It is only the fierce blaze of the burning house, at which a few may be for a moment warmed, but which goes out, leaving desolation where was habitation and home.

2d, Do luxuries indirectly encourage industry? Here we must turn sharply on our previous decision, and see a further meaning in luxurious consumption than first appeared. Unquestionably, a wholesome luxury is one of the most important principles of production. What is it that kindles the desire of acquisition; that keeps the hand strong to labor? Is it not the hope to spend? For what else, the wretched miser excepted, do men toil early and late? It is the promise of future enjoyments that calls out half the work of the world. It is this that makes the difference between nations. No man passes by the abode of leisure and refinement without receiving an incitement to effort.

There is one practical limitation of this principle, which is of great social and economical importance. It arises from the relative position of those who do, and those who as yet cannot, indulge in luxurious consumption. If a few are very rich, and the many very poor, the expenditures of the former have very little effect on the condition of the latter. Since these cannot aspire to the enjoyment of their superiors, their ambition, instead of being excited, is depressed. If, on the contrary, the interval between the classes is narrow, and the differences moderate, the luxuries of the rich exert strong and increasing desires in those who are less wealthy. These desires create wealth. It is not the gifts of nature, nor the constraints of law, that heap up the stores of value. It is the force with which man moves to production, wholly determined, as that is, by his economic desires. The luxury of European courts has no elevating influence upon the masses: quite otherwise. Robbed to furnish the means of others, they are hopeless of ever attaining to such fortune themselves. But where the grades of society are fixed only by differences of natural endowment, and so are moderate and regular, rising by easy steps, the entire population becomes inspired with the purpose of reaching a higher position. In such a state, the imagination can hardly run ahead of wealth.

We have, then, attained the principle, that luxurious consumption, while it directly gives no help to industry, but rather spends in one hour's enjoyment the provision of months or years, may yet, by its influence on man's desires, create a productive force which shall make its extravagance seem economy, its waste appear frugality itself.

But this is only true of harmonious, temperate, and well-proportioned luxury. There are indulgences, great courses of indulgence, which, while they excite momentarily to production for the means of gratification, do yet, by their certain and inevitable effect on the physical and mental powers of the individual, by their demoralizing and perverting influence on the community, prostrate industry, and overturn the foundations of the state. Many as are the unfortunate possibilities which attend upon production and distribution, they are all inferior in interest to the momentous decisions of consumption; and here in luxury, as we find the spring of all beneficent activity, we also find the root of all economic evils. So vast and so important are the issues here involved, that many of them are taken away from the political economist by the statesman or the moralist. We do not propose to follow these principles into all their results; content with only indicating their starting-point and direction.

Such is luxurious consumption, in its definition and its general principles. We shall further discuss the degree to which it is, or may be, carried in any community.

CHAPTER IV.

ON THE DEGREE OF LUXURIOUS CONSUMPTION.

We mistake, if we attribute luxuries to the rich alone. It is estimated, on the best authority, that of the taxes paid by the laboring poor of England, out of every twenty-one shillings, eleven shillings and fourpence were paid for what was, in the economic view, not necessary, and, in the sanitary view, not beneficial. If we estimate the amount expended for luxuries by the corresponding class in our own country, we shall find it as much greater as nature is more liberal, labor more free, taxes lighter, and the working-man more ambitious and sanguine; while, if we turn to France, we find the proportion much smaller; yet even here the laborer has his holiday, and his theatre or fair.

Paradoxical as it may sound, it may be said that a certain amount of luxuries forms a part of the necessary wages of the laborer in these countries. Indeed, it is true of all countries; for the human mind and the human body will have rest and recreation in some form. Man is not all laborer. Some indulgence is the demand of that part of his nature which looks out on another field than production and accumulation. And in this light we see the vast importance of such social and moral influences as shall determine the laboring classes to those relaxations and amusements which really refresh both mind and body, and elevate the whole tone of being. If we mistake not, a mighty industrial revolution, that promises effects more searching and permanent than many illustrious victories in arms, is now being accomplished by the divergence in taste and amusements of two nations. Great Britain has, thus far, maintained supremacy in useful and ponderous manufactures; while the artisans of France have been almost alone in the department of elegant and delicate fabrics. But the signs are clear that France is rapidly rising into superiority in the former class of industries, and may yet attain the primacy throughout the world. The French workman is so economical, not only in his personal habits, but, in handling materials and tools, has such generally correct and wholesome tastes, and is so simple in his wants, that his work is cheap as well as efficient. On the contrary, the English laborer seeks more and more the delusive relief of strong and impure liquors, and, by this, adds so much to his expenses, and takes so much from his power in production, as to place him at a real and increasing disadvantage. It hardly admits of question, that, if the present causes operate for twenty years to come, the close of that period will find the most mercurial and sensitive people of the world enjoying the supremacy of its weighty and useful manufactures.

National taste determines, in a great measure, the demands of wages. It is only required, by our present object, that we take a good look at the luxuries of the poor; not by any means grudgingly. Indeed, we may ask why laborers are not everywhere allowed more time and means for enjoyment, outside the dull routine of work and the dry subsistence of life. It is a wise and Christian statesmanship that seeks to enlarge the simple pleasures of the poor. It is a capital charge against despotism in every form, that it breaks down the power of the humbler classes, to claim them. As the intelligence of laborers increases, and their political franchises extend, they will assert a larger share of the products of industry; and very much of this will go into what we call, not invidiously, luxuries.

But it is with regard to the richer classes that the question of luxuries becomes especially important. The amount of wealth directed to these objects can hardly be overestimated.

The excise and customs authorities of Great Britain recently made an attempt to ascertain the shares of certain articles consumed, severally, by three classes into which they divided the population of the kingdom. The result is shown in the following table:*—

Class.	Persons.	Tea consumed.	Sugar consumed.
1st, Upper . .	1,000,000	17½ per cent.	22½ per cent.
2d, Middle .	9,000,000	38 „	38 „
3d, Lower . .	18,000,000	44½ „	39½ „
	28,000,000	100	100

In these simple articles, which are almost included in the strict necessaries of life, we see the great excess of the expenditure of the upper classes. When we rise to take in services of plate and sets of jewelry, galleries of pictures and parks of deer, studs of horses and packs of hounds, we shall be impressed with the immensity of outlay devoted to the luxuries of society.

We are not surprised to hear that at Rome "almost any profession, either liberal or mechanical, might be found in the household of an opulent senator;"† that one thousand barbers, one thousand cooks, and one thousand cup-bearers were employed in the imperial service of Constantinople, while the chief cook had a retinue of twenty menials; that the baggage of a Persian monarch was carried by twenty thousand camels, even in campaign; that Zingis Khan maintained seven thousand huntsmen and seven thousand falconers; that the revenue of two thousand villages supported the temple of Sournat; that four cities were allowed for the personal expenses of the dogs of a royal establishment;‡ that the household of Philip II.

* Levi on Taxation. † Gibbon.

‡ The poodle of the Empress Livia seems to have been neglected. If the authorities may be accepted, it enjoyed the entire services of only one man. — Gibbon, ch. 49, n. 155.

numbered one thousand five hundred, while the queen was attended by four physicians.

Nor was the luxury of those times of barbarous might greater than that of to-day. An easy walk with any people, whether in city or country, will afford contrasts as striking and painful as that between the palaces of Susa and the corners into which the common people crept for sleep; between the mansions on the Quirinal and the holes in which "Rome's rats" hid their wretched lives.

1st, What are the causes that set wealth apart for luxury?

(*a*) The most essential is the existence of a surplus. Other things equal, the degree of luxury will be as the surplus. The latter, however, will depend not so much on the general mass of wealth as on its apportionment among producers.

(*b*) The desire to gain and the desire to spend are antagonistic. They meet in every act of life, and one or the other must have its way. Luxury is the victory of the latter passion. The mere possession of a surplus is not enough. Some men remain eagerly devoted to gain, when their wealth is counted in millions: others retire, satisfied with the most moderate competency. The force of either motive will be greatly influenced, both by the security and the profitableness of investments. Every thing that renders business unsafe, makes withdrawal more desirable. On the other hand, every thing which raises the reward of capital, takes something from the zest of luxury.

2d, To what extent can wealth be devoted to luxury?

Gibbon gives countenance to the theory, that no state can, without soon becoming exhausted, support more than a hundreth part of its population in arms and idleness. This is to be understood as a hundredth part of the population, taken out of the able-bodied males; say, a twentieth part of these. The estimate is interesting, and has a certain share of truth; but its form shows it to be a very rude one.

Does it make no difference whether this portion is simply unproductive or also destructive? Does it make no difference whether these idlers are maintained in the dreamy, half-naked indolence of Asiatics, or in the splendid luxury of courts? no difference whether the general production of the country is large or small; whether the wants of the people and the necessities of government are few and simple, or many and great; whether rice enough for a year can be had by the labor of two weeks, as in India, or a bushel of grain costs the labor of eleven days, as in Lapland? The Athenian was content with his figs and philosophy: the cultivated Roman craved the brains of birds-of-paradise for his food, and was positive he wanted a palace on the Quirinal. Which maintained the larger share of its population in idleness? When Frederick the Great faced all Europe in arms, rye bread and potatoes, powder and lead, were all he served his army, — marshals and drummers alike. By such parsimony, he was enabled to make Prussia what she was, — "all sting." France, with the perfection of her warlike equipment, and the fastidious taste of her citizens, could not maintain a proportionate number of troops, even under the conscriptions of the empire.

It is in this light that we see the impossibility of fixing, for all nations, all climates, all ages, a common proportion of luxury that can be maintained, without bringing down the standard of industrial well-being. At the same time, it is plain that for each nation, at any time, there must be a point beyond which wealth cannot be spent in enjoyment, or time in idleness, without first oppressing the laboring class by hard exactions, and afterwards debasing the entire state.

We have already anticipated the remark, that idleness or leisure is a form of luxury, — a form of luxury that, in either sense, is almost unknown, to some peoples, whirled about, as they are, on the untiring wheels of manufacture and trade; a form of luxury that, as idleness, is the most costly of all indulgences, that corrupts all manners, perverts all the offices of nature, wastes all the powers of labor, and has its complete result in poverty, ignorance, and political servitude; a form of luxury which, as leisure, adorns life, and makes it worth living, compacts the acquirements of study and toil, re-creates and refreshes the whole man, and leads upward to an eternal rest and felicity.

OF LEARNING AND ART.

These, in the economic view, may have value, and so may be produced, exchanged, distributed, and consumed. The reward they receive, the price they bring, is in no sense due to them in their own right, because they are true, beautiful, or good; but arises legitimately out of the desires they gratify, and the labor they cost. It is the appreciation of a service rendered. That reward will vary in form and degree, at every state of society. The wandering Homer was content with the most simple hospitality. The modern man of letters has his rooms, his club, his carriage, his opera, paid for perhaps out of very mild criticisms on the blind bard of Greece. There is not a real scholar of the present day who would not work ten years in the mines, to hear Homer recite the parting of Hector and Andromache. So differently is the same service counted in different ages. Cicero, long before he reached the height of his fame, had received, by will, £170,000, as a tribute to his genius. The younger Pliny was loaded with wealth by his admirers. The laureate of England drinks to the royal bounty in royal wine. Blackstone's legal profits did not permit his marriage till his thirty-eighth year. A popular novel or sketch-book to-day earns a fortune.

Thus it is that learning and art enter into wealth. While their rewards are uncertain, and apparently wayward, they have yet, from the mythic days, had a place with the most substantial industries. Whatever may be true of the quality of such productions, the amount of labor bestowed on them obeys strictly the same laws of supply and demand which govern the growth of cotton or wheat. Economical science has no occasion to take them out of the same category. When one man gives his efforts to any work of this character, and finds one other who has a desire for it, that work begins to have value, comes hereby into the domain of political economy, and must submit to its principles. Milton, chaffering for the price of "Paradise Lost," forms no royal exception to the sovereignty of the empire he has entered.

What is the character and effect of such consumption? This is a question doubly interesting, having an importance to general scholarship, as well as to our immediate science. Of course, learning and art have not necessarily to establish an economic usefulness, in order to justify their pursuit. In their own names, they have sovereignty, and claim homage. But there is an economic relation which we cannot overlook, and which must affect, somewhat, the place which they shall be accorded in the world. In brief, their effect upon industry may be defined as follows: So far as they give dignity to human aspirations, furnish new objects to human desires, enlarge ambition, develop the useful sciences, and suggest the application of new powers, as the telegraph, the locomotive, and the magnet; so far as they unite and harmonize social and political divisions, — they are of inestimable value; and such consumption of wealth as rewards and encourages them is seed thrown into a soil more grateful than any land of fable or story. But so far as learning or art tend to produce that unmanly sentimentalism which shrinks from dirty details, present duty, and simple fact; that mawkish cosmopolitanism, moral or political indifference, which weakens each nationality, without promoting the union of all; that softening of the mental fibre, that dissolution of the will, which makes man the slave of his circumstances, and even of his fellows; and, worst of all, that selfish fastidiousness which shuts itself in from human activities and social alliances, to dwell in dreams and idle imaginations, whether of philosophy or art, — why, in so far, we must call such an employment of time and labor, not merely unprofitable, but mischievous, consumption.

SUMPTUARY LAWS.

No subject stands so peculiarly related to scientific inquiry as this. There is no scheme of governmental action which can present a more clear and convincing argument, drawn from the nature of things, and even from experience, prior to actual legislation; while none has been more effectually exploded by trial. There seems to be a perfect reason for sumptuary laws; yet the general sense of civilization has, after full experiment, settled decisively against them.

It is impossible to look about the smallest community, without being grieved at the manner in which much of its labor and wealth are expended. What enlightened person can pass once through any street of human habitation, without seeing very many instances of folly, extravagance, perversion, and indolence, which are wasting the best gifts of God and the fairest hopes of man? And, when this view is carried out to all the communities of a nation, it is not strange that philosophers and statesmen have come to believe most earnestly, that by salutary curbs on expenditure and spurs to exertion, by reforming dress, diet, equipage, and establishment, they could multiply manifold the comforts of the people, the resources of the state, and the means of social and moral culture. And why not? That there is no reason manifest in the nature of things is proved by the fact, that everywhere, and at all times, the most benevolent, temperate, and sagacious, alike of political rulers and of political writers, have agreed in recommending stringent sumptuary provision and inspection by law.

And yet nothing has more utterly and conclusively failed. It is not that the evil is imaginary; for enough wealth and power are wasted to make every human being comfortable and happy. It is not that the state of things is unsusceptible of reformation; for the matter is one wholly of human choice, and open to the control of the public sanctions. It is not that the aggregate sense of the community, in matters of consumption (not of production), is not, on the whole, more enlightened and less fickle than that of individuals. We say, on the whole; for there have been instances in which laws were even behind the instincts of the community, and proposed to compel the popular energies and tastes to less advantageous forms of consumption. As instances, we may cite the enactment in the reign of Charles II. of England, prescribing, under penalties, the interment of the dead in shrouds made of wool, for the encouragement of that manufacture; the Spanish Cortes, petitioning in the same breath for the prohibition of coaches and encouragement of bull-fights; and all of the recent legislation of this country, in any form, which has taken for its principle the absurdity, that to issue bonds for expenses incurred in the work of destruction adds any thing but weight to the national burdens, and can introduce aught but grievance and faction into our politics. Yet, as we said, the major will of the community would, on the whole, prescribe a more harmonious and healthful consumption of wealth than that which follows individual choices. Why, then, has law, acting to this end, failed of its purpose so universally and so manifestly, that such enactments are hardly ever proposed at the present day, even by the most sanguine of philanthropists?

It is difficult to give a full and satisfactory explanation. One reason is, that such enactments are very easy of evasion. Expenditure is not a matter that submits readily to inspection and proof. The interest of the producer and of the desire of the consumer are against the enforcement of the law. Then, again, luxury can take on so many forms, can slip so readily from the grasp of definitions and specifications, that the law becomes a greater trouble to its officers than to its offenders.

But the grand reason is, that it is against human nature; and with this we may fairly close our objections.

But all these furnish no conclusion against the regulation of public morals and manners in things that affect the happiness and safety of the community. It is no longer legislation to supplement the wisdom of the individual or instruct industry. It becomes the defence of the general good. It is not a breach of personal rights, but the safeguard of public liberty. If there is any habit or practice which brings disease and suffering and disorder, which abridges the power of labor and the span of life, which inflicts misery upon the innocent and unoffending, which entails expense upon the whole community for the charge of pauperism and the punishment of crime, there can be no doubt of the right and duty of the people to protect themselves, through the power of their government, by the most severe and efficient laws that can be devised. To deny this is to deny the validity of government itself.

CHAPTER V.

III. PUBLIC CONSUMPTION.

THERE is an economical reason for government. Without the strong arm of the public force, men could not work unmolested, or retain the results of their labor. Without law, production would be hindered directly, by the confusion of society and the interruption of violence. But far more serious would be the secondary effects on industry. All motives to the accumulation of wealth would be withdrawn, by the insecurity of property. Its possession might even become an object of terror.

We cannot, indeed, trace society back to anarchy; for a state of anarchy is impossible with human nature. Even the savage tribes take on political forms. Like a drop whose cohesion is violently broken, the public body seeks to form itself anew, or at least to aggregate itself about two or three new centres. Absolute isolation is not merely impolitic: it is impracticable. But, as far as we can go back, on the path of social order, we find industry answering to law.

To what share is government entitled in the general production? If, as we have seen, it is the indispensable condition of all wealth, it can rightfully claim a part of all wealth; and that part will be, *at the least*, enough to sustain itself in this economical function. It owns just as much of this wealth it has helped to create as is necessary to continue itself; for, without this, wealth could not be. The absolute necessities of government, then, afford the minimum measure of its share in wealth.

Has government no right to more than what is essential to its support in this economical function? Its industrial work embraces a wider field than appears in the simple statement. In America, education is required as a part of the public police; and our eminent statesmen have estimated the outlay of schools and colleges cheap, in the results on order and security. In Great Britain, the church has been held to be a legitimate agent of the public force, and its maintenance is provided for out of the public purse. Government may employ means of influence, numerous and remote, all in the interest of peace.

But has it no right to property beyond this? Plainly it has. We must not be as stringent in our scientific views as young Gobbo, and complain that "this making of

Christians will raise the price of pork." Political economy recognizes that humanity has other interests than wealth, and respects the claim of government to duties and services for the sake of a moral good. But such reasons should appear clearly. Nothing should be taken arbitrarily, or for contingent use. Man is the direct producer, and the product remains in his hands. If government, as indirectly engaged with him, enters with a claim to share the profits, it must show cause distinctly for whatever it takes. It is the part of the statesman, not of the economist, to judge of occasions like these.

Having defined the right of government economically to participate in wealth, two considerations naturally precede the discussion of methods: —

1st, Government should undertake nothing that can be left to individual enterprise.

If we admit that the difficulties which surround industry are imposed for our good, and form a part of our discipline and culture, political society palpably acts on a false idea when it relieves the citizen of his own proper responsibility, care, or labor, and assumes his natural duties. This, however, is not the only reason against such interference. Government never does the work of individuals as well as it can be done by individuals.

It is related of Herodes Atticus, that, having come upon a great treasure concealed in the ground, he took it to Nerva, and pressed it on his acceptance, saying, "it was too considerable for a subject to use." — "Abuse it, then," replied the emperor. The anecdote has great significance as to the employment of wealth. Its abuse by the citizen is almost preferable to its use by the state. If government were conceived to be always wise, it would still be better, on the whole, that citizens should direct their own industrial matters, wisely or unwisely, as might happen. But, when the liability of government to err is confessed, we have a double argument against taking the fee or use of wealth out of private hands. It cannot be too often or earnestly insisted on, that individual, interested supervision is the grandest economical condition, and should never be departed from till the work becomes too vast for single hands.

2d, Government should do nothing for display.

For ages the science of politics might be summed up in the word "pageantry." To dazzle the vulgar eye, and overawe the common sense of the people, by splendid equipage and stately building, has been the main theory of rulers. The system certainly has not failed for want of trial. There have been governors who earnestly sought to prove, that the power of the law and the peace of the subject did not depend on show. The simplicity and austerity exhibited by Carus of Rome, Julian of Constantinople, Elizabeth of England, the Great Frederick of Prussia, and the Saracen caliphs in all ages, stand in marked contrast with the wicked and ruinous extravagance that has marked the administration of most of the governments of the world.

It is gratifying to believe, that, in some countries, the advance of economic principles has relieved the people of great burdens by limiting the display of government. Imagine the storm in Parliament, had it been proposed to buy the great Sanci diamond * for the British crown. Yet, two centuries ago, the heart of England would have craved it for the royal brow.

3d, The expense of government will vary according to the circumstances and character of the people.

Some peoples have a government as simple, primitive, and cheap as their clothing; while others, no more highly civilized, manifest an inclination to complicated and refined forms of administering law, which bring a heavy burden of taxation on the present, and entail permanent debt on posterity. Some nations are obliged, by their position, to build themselves around with fortifications, and maintain extensive forces, just as some countries can keep out the ocean only

* Disposed of at private sale in 1865.

by artificial dikes and levees; others have a natural strength, or an isolation, that is good to them as strong armies. Some peoples can be governed readily in the plainest manner by rulers who, like the caliphs, sweep their own floors, patch their own shoes, milk their cows, and live on soldier's fare; others are supposed to require an immense amount of pageantry to dazzle the public eye, and occasional wars, wasting thousands of men and millions of money, to divert the common mind from troublesome questions, and keep the peace at home.

Russia spends yearly three dollars a head in governing her people and supporting her armies; Prussia, five dollars; the United States, up to 1860, two and a half dollars, reckoning only the federal establishment; Great Britain runs her expenditure up to ten dollars. Political economy has great charity for claims based on public considerations. It allows that whatever is really necessary for peace and order and property, in full view of the national peculiarities or geographical difficulties, is economically well spent and a good investment of capital.

It is not alone the direct office of preventing immediate crime, and protecting present property, that government performs at so great cost. Civil law is an educator. It gives a prospect and a security for the future; it multiplies the ambitions and the desires of all who live under it; it elevates the self-respect and trains the self-control of all good citizens.

Yet government charges heavily for what it does. The yearly revenue of the European states is, at present, very little, if any, short of fifteen hundred millions of dollars. The expenditure of the United States, even if no attempt is made to liquidate the public debt, will not, probably, be less than three hundred millions; and this, exclusive of all the service of State and municipal government.

On the whole, it may be said of this duty of capital to support government, that it pays, as an investment, whatever it may necessarily cost; but that the expense should be strictly held down to the lowest practicable figure.

DOES PUBLIC CONSUMPTION ENCOURAGE INDUSTRY?

We shall get the principles of such a discussion, in their bare form, by taking the extreme actual cases of this mode of consumption.

There have been instances in which the people of cities, and even generally of States, have claimed work at the hands of government, to support life; and we find that such provision has been at times really made.

We will suppose the claim to be founded on absolute necessity, no work whatever being offered at private hands. The state, in compassion or from fear, employs the mass of its laborers on public works, and pays them from the public purse.

What is the real condition of things? It is one of two: —

1st, If the work so performed is unnecessary, having been arranged solely to meet the popular emergency, this is merely a mode of government charity. So much is taken out of the resources of the state to maintain its indigent citizens. It comes finally as a tax on all *productive* industry. The classes that create values are called on to contribute, it may be largely and painfully, to feed and clothe those which do not.

How does this answer the conditions of a successful charity?

(*a*) Such artificial industries require great expense beyond the simple wages which the laborer receives from the national treasury. If these workmen were employed only in digging trenches to fill them up again, the additional cost would be only for tools to work with and land to work over. But government, in such cases, always maintains a certain semblance of purpose. There is a pretence of usefulness, immediately or remotely. This generally calls for a great amount of material, in one form or another, all of which makes a dead loss to the community, not even the poor getting it as charity. Such is the case where costly public buildings, or vessels of war, are constructed simply to provide labor for the destitute. Often the expense to the state is many times greater than the sum which is divided among the suffering poor. There are, besides, the salaries of officials, in great numbers, to superintend the labor; no inconsiderable item in public industries.

(*b*) We have, on the other hand, an advantage; viz., that this mode of receiving charity saves the self-respect of the workman. If government adjusts the rate of wages intelligently, it is certain that none but those who really need employment will seek it; and in receiving wages for work, even if that work is fictitious, they will not feel degraded. Of course, it is economically very desirable that the instinct of self-support should be kept strong and keen among the laboring class.

(*c*) There is also the consideration that these artificial enterprises entail a burden on the future. The work, when completed, is handed over to the public authorities, to be an object of costly maintenance, till happily destroyed by time or violence. In this way a tax is perpetuated on the community for a relief that was perhaps of the most temporary character.

2d, If the work to be performed is, in whole or in part, necessary or desirable, the pay of the laborer is so far taken out of the denomination of charity. He has rendered a real advantage, — it may be to the full extent of the wages he receives. Neither government nor his fellow can question his right to the remuneration, or taunt him with pauperage. Still, supposing this mode of employment necessary, we have some important considerations presented.

(*a*) Though the laborer renders the full value of his wages, the public often does not receive it. It is a perfectly established principle, that, in most departments of industry, government cannot compete with individuals. The dishonesty and indifference of its agents need not be dwelt on here. It is a recognized maxim of business, that self-interest and personal observation are the conditions of that intelligence and economy which secures success. How entirely evident it is, that the public will seldom, if ever, be fortunate enough to obtain officers who can, if they would, manage its affairs as their own!

(*b*) There are times and cases in which this wholesale employment by government may be useful, even if we allow the superior cheapness of individual work. There are great enterprises which can be undertaken only by the constituted authorities of the nation. There are duties, not only too large for private or corporate power, but too important to be left to the chances of individual management. Such, of course, is the maintenance of civil and military police, which, so far as it is necessary, must be in public hands, and cannot be let or farmed out, consistently with the honor and dignity of government.

(*c*) But these occasions for government to enter the field of industry are few and definite. They cannot be exceeded without loss of wealth and demoralization of labor. Government should not only refrain from undertaking any work not necessary *in its own interest*, but should, as far as possible, let out what *is* necessary to competition and individual enterprise. Wherever the character of the operation is not such that its reliability concerns immediately the existence of the nation or the lives of citizens, it should be left to the general industry.

We have, thus far, discussed the employment of laborers by government, on the strict supposition of a necessity existing at the time. We have seen that such a necessity might overrule economic laws, and justify governments in such a course; but we have also seen those evils, even in this case, which will save us any very extended consideration of the question, whether governments should, without reference to an immediate distress among its people, enter the market of labor; and, in the consumption of wealth, become a competitor with individual industry, even when the objects selected are wholesome and natural.

(*a*) In a free people, and with fair laws of distribution, there will seldom be occasion for such employment by governments, except in its own interest. No able-bodied laborer can render to an official as much service as to an individual employer; the reason being, that the former is not capable of receiving the service so perfectly. And it ought never to be true, that an able-bodied laborer is compelled to seek work at the hands of government. It will not happen, until wicked laws have deprived him of that employment, which, in a natural order of things, he obtains simply in virtue of his ability to achieve the satisfaction of human wants.

(*b*) Such employment by government perpetuates dependence. It has been found strikingly true in the history of great experiments after this fashion. Men once accustomed to feed at the public board, whether as princes or day-laborers, are very loath to return to the primitive fare of private life. Relief from the stringent but necessary laws of competition becomes almost a second nature; and few are found willing to break off from this reliance on government support.

(*c*) Such employment by government demoralizes the general industry of the country. A false scale of prices is established, since government does not buy or sell under exactly the same motives as individuals. An unnatural competition is introduced into labor. The market is improperly controlled by the immense resources of the administration: in consequence, all other branches of production are, to a greater or less extent, disturbed and kept restless.

(*d*) Such employment by government induces political corruption. It is not consistent with our purpose to enlarge upon this subject, but only to show its place. The fact is undeniable; and while government must accept, as a necessity, a certain amount of improper influences attending its operations, this should be a potent argument against any assumption, on its part, of unnecessary work.

A great part of the discussion of this question would more aptly come into the department of "Production;" but it is so bound up with popular theories of government expenditures, as encouraging industry, that it is fairly brought within the present field of inquiry: and it is from the point now reached that we get the best view of that absurd doctrine which proclaims that national extravagance stimulates trade, and promotes the general welfare.

We have seen, that any expenditure by government, even for necessary purposes, is made at a disadvantage to itself, and is attended by many marked inconveniences and mischiefs to society; and that, so far as consistent, individual enterprise should be substituted. In how strong a light, then, do we see the folly of that scheme of national prosperity which looks to lavish outlay by government for any purpose, whether productive or destructive, of luxury or war! The share of some interested portion of the community may be larger, or come more easily; but the sum of wealth is diminished, and the healthful laws of distribution are disturbed.

Yet, in the recent gigantic warlike operations of the United States, it was a daily experience to hear the accepted teachers of political philosophy gravely pronounce the condition of the country to be most gratifying, loudly congratulating the public on the stimulus given to industry by the outlay of government. Trade was brisk, because the nation was running three thousand millions in debt, to be just so much poorer for centuries. We do not question that the occasion justified the expense; but this was none the less an unfortunate necessity, and the liveliness of business was the most melancholy feature of the national condition.

CHAPTER VI.

CHARITY AND POOR-LAWS.

IN its broadest sense, half the world exists on charity; and the amount of wealth so distributed, exceeds calculation.

Man comes into the world a helpless being. If left alone, he dies. He has not the faculties of self-defence and self-support that brute young possess. Years pass before he attains the power of maintaining his own existence.

Even in the best states of society, woman is, to a great degree, rendered, by delicacy of constitution, incapable of self-support. At times, the fierce competitions of trade may be hushed when she comes among them; yet she must always subsist somewhat by the sufferance of the fiercer and stronger sex. In the barbarous state, she is the tool and slave of man.

Besides these large classes, the field of adult manhood is trenched upon by accidents of birth or circumstance, that render thousands incapable, physically or mentally, of earning a livelihood.

All these must live by charity.

But in the sense of economy, in our modern civilized state, the field of this agency is greatly limited. The family relation adopts by far the greater part of all who are helpless to control their own condition. There have been peoples where children were the property of the state, and were reared at the public charge. There have been communities where women were had in common, and their maintenance was included in the budget of the treasurer. But the world has settled down to the family relation, and so we are to consider it.

But there are yet melancholy outcasts from society,—aged folk and cripples and young children,—who have lost their staff and stay by the natural course of life, by the ravages of vice, by appalling accidents, or by the devastations of war. These form a great community, over which the state is called to watch with tender care; a solemn trust, appealing to the holiest feelings of our nature. For these it has to provide, not food and shelter alone, but healing for their diseases, correction for their vices, help for their infirmities of body and mind, instruction and useful arts, as far as they are capable of receiving them.

Such are the natural constituents of this class; but unfortunately, by social obstructions and political oppression, we find, in some communities, thousands of able-bodied and hard-working men dragged down into the mire of beggary, compelled by wicked institutions to shameful want.

There is hardly any social result so distressing as the reduction of the healthy workman to the low ground of charity. This, found in almost any degree in a political system, must be held to offset a great many splendid merits; while freedom from such conditions must be accepted as satisfaction for many conspicuous defects. Legislators should ever consider the independence of the poor man as the visible "fulfilment of the law." It is a crying curse, that ever a stout man, glad to work, should be forced to beg.

In the United States, the question of charities has not that engrossing interest which it commands in the older peoples of the world. Land here is so cheap, labor so much in demand, that no able-bodied man has any excuse for pauperism. And even a large share of those disabled by severe accidents are yet competent to earn something for livelihood, in a country where every hand is wanted for work. It is probable, that the pauperage of the nation is not, in ordinary times, equal to one-half of one per cent of its population; while England and Wales had, in 1859, four and a half per cent; Holland, in 1855, eight and a half;

Belgium, in 1846, sixteen; East and West Flanders rising that year to thirty per cent.

The methods of charity have not, therefore, the same importance with us which they bear elsewhere. It is a matter of profound concern with others, that pauperism should be in every way discouraged, and that what of it is necessary should be as cheaply arranged as possible. Here, the only occasion for anxiety is, lest some unfortunate should be overlooked in the general prosperity of the country. It will not, however, be without interest and instruction to regard carefully the practical principles which should govern the administration of charity.

1st, What classes are entitled to charity?

Manifestly all who are unable to subsist in human decency without it.

But should government provide nothing for those who, having wantonly wasted their means and gifts of labor, find themselves, and those dependent on them, suffering for the necessaries of life? We answer, that the liberty of the subject is not a privilege to become a pauper; that government has the right to protect itself; that it may, by stringent enactments concerning vagrancy and indolence, anticipate the operation of such causes; that it may encourage industry by rewards, or compel it by pains and penalties; that it may apply to vicious pauperism the same severity as to crime. Yet, when all this is granted, and all this done, there will still remain a certain degree of physical want, the result of sinful and slothful habits. Of this the state must have charge. No man may be allowed to starve, however clearly his destitution may be the effect of his own folly or wickedness. "It is better," said the Roman law, "that vagabonds should die of hunger, than that they should be supported in their beggary." In the light of Christianity, we have a wider view of political duties. The sharpest incitement to labor, the sternest punishment of vice, is equally just to society and kind to the subject; but that the vilest outcast should perish of hunger by the actual permission of government, would eclipse the brightest glories of conquest or commerce which a Christian nation can acquire.

Here we have an important practical precept concerning governmental or individual charity; viz., the frequent and careful revision of claims to assistance. There should be no prescription in beggary, nor any thing taken for granted. The inability of self-support should be distinctly proved, or the applicant forced to work.

2d, Who should administer charity?

An argument might be made from the principle of benevolence and the sensibility to another's distress found in the constitution of our nature, that charity was not alone designed for government, but that the relief of the poor is appropriate to private hands. And there is a plain, economical reason, in that such contributions can be made more timely, more judiciously, and more cheaply, by the offices of individuals than by public agencies. There is a further reason, not less economical than moral, that assistance rendered in this form does less hurt to the feelings of the recipient. The interests of production, not less than the law of kindness, object to the unnecessary lowering of the self-respect of any class or person. To accept charity from a neighbor, under the pressure of extraordinary misfortune, could impeach the honor of no one; but to take bread from government carries with it a sort of taint of beggary through life.

But this does not in the least excuse mendicancy, whose principle is directly opposed to that of intelligent, equable charity. It is prohibited, under severe penalties, in almost all communities, though the sympathy of the solicited and the condition of the solicitor take much from the terrors of the law.

Here, then, in individual contributions, we have one of the main instruments by which the relief of the poor should be effected.

There is another class of voluntary agencies, standing between individual charity and that of the state, consisting of mutual-relief societies and trade associations, established for the purpose of assisting their members over the rough places of life. When honestly formed, and held to their legitimate work, they have, economically, all the advantages of division of labor. With this they unite a considerable share of intelligence, as to the special deserts of applicants. There is also, and principally, the consideration, that relief from this source is thought to have nothing degrading, and so preserves the self-respect of those who receive the aid.

This agency is very extensive in all the countries of Europe, and in all the States of America. By the most recent statistics available, the voluntary associated charities of London alone include the efforts of four hundred and eighty-six institutions, with the annual expenditure of £1,222,529, while the mutual-relief societies of France number 4,125, with a membership of 535,233, which, with four persons to a family, would give a sphere of activity embracing more than two millions of people.

Prominent, too, in this view, we see the noble, economical, and Christian scheme by which the great body of Quakers, or Friends, throughout the world, assume the care and support of all the infirm or helpless of their order; so that no one can come upon the colder charities and harsher discipline of public maintenance.

Yet all these methods cannot be relied on, by themselves, for all times and at all places. The state should assume the responsibility and control of the poor everywhere. It is a part of the national concerns that no subject shall suffer from want. After all that individual and associated charity can do, there will be an immense amount of the most repulsive and unromantic want and misery awaiting remedy by government.

3d, By what branches of the government should public charity be administered?

We answer, that, in the mere relief of poverty, local authorities be charged with the dispensation, though the state may, and indeed should, compel them to do it, and perhaps regulate the degree and manner of it. Wherever a pauper has his residence, there he should receive whatever assistance he is to have. More work can be got out of him, his character and claims will be better understood, he will be nearer to returning into the condition of self-support, and each community will have an active interest to diminish its pauperage. All this is additional to the greater expense of monster workhouses, and the corruption they are sure to breed.

We said, "in the mere relief of poverty." But government charity has to do with other classes with which the rule of assistance is directly opposite. Hospitals for the disabled, asylums for the insane, schools for the blind,—these should be aggregated to secure the best scientific treatment and the greatest natural advantages.

4th, To what extent should charity be given?

To the full extent of the necessities of the subject. The destitute, whether maintained in their own homes or in houses devoted to that purpose, should be required to do all the work they are really able. This is just; for the government has the right to diminish its own burden. It is kind; because, by keeping up their habits of industry, it preserves self-respect and bodily vigor, and may in time enable them to return to a condition of self-support. To render any more assistance than is really necessary, is not to relieve pauperism, but to create it.

The English system includes two methods: 1st, The allotment, which is the cheap rental to the poor of certain portions of land, from which, by their own industry, to procure some of the necessaries of life; 2d, The parish allowance, which affords weekly assistance to a certain amount, — say, two shillings, — to eke out wages. These, in some circumstances, may give a real and permanent relief; but it is found in England, that this kind of charity is so general, that employers reduce wages still further, in expectation of it, and the laborer is soon brought to distress again. Such a state of things is a misfortune, arising, not from defects in the system of charity, but jointly from the want of independence and intelligence in the laboring class, and from the operation of vicious institutions, which lock up the natural means of subsistence, or take them away in excessive taxes.

It is in this failure — acknowledged equally by government and by scientific writers — of the English charitable system, under which one million families have been kept in substantial pauperism, while there was found at least another million "just above the paupers, always in peril, lest they should become paupers," * — it is here we reach the true principle of this matter of public charity.

Poor-laws may be effective, to the full extent, in providing for all pauperism that results from natural or accidental disability of body or mind for self-support. Government may relieve every form of such distress with entire satisfaction of the individual need, and with perfect justice to the community. But, as soon as the necessities of a people bring able-bodied workmen within the scope of poor-laws, it is certain that, while temporary relief should be afforded, the remedy must be sought elsewhere. The reason is as follows: Charity to the disabled is simple gratuity, wholly outside the laws of value, and involving a definite expense; but charity to the laboring class is an absurdity, only explained by the wickedness of human institutions. It is an absurdity liable to indefinite repetition. It indicates that the point has been reached below which oppression and greed cannot go. The Creator of this bountiful order has made provision for the support, the comfort, and the

* John Bright, 1865.

gratification of all our kind. Poor-laws, permanently embracing in their charity able-bodied workmen, simply show that the gratification was long since abandoned; that comfort was afterwards denied by oppressive requirements or restrictions; and that now the lowest plane of injustice has been reached, in the inability of the laborer for self-support. There is no further descent; nor have poor-laws any virtue to bring back the right order of things. The great, the sole, regulating principle of economical life, viz. the entire self-sufficiency of labor, has been destroyed; and nothing but laws returning labor to its own full rights, not affording it charity, can restore health and harmony. There is no proper ground for charity but the inability to labor; and, when under the stress of government injustice and social falsehood, it departs from these limits, it begins a wandering that has no end. The pauperism of America is the result of accidents, and expires with its special causes. The pauperism of Europe is the effect of system, and perpetuates itself.

England will retain her million of pauper families; her other million of families, suspended over pauperism by a cotton thread; her three millions more, scantily subsisted and nourished, — until the axe is laid by giant hands at the root of the evil.

The quackery of the Middle Ages applied herbs and balms, not to the bleeding wound, but to the injurious sword. Such are poor-laws for pauper populations. It is not poor-laws, but rich-laws, that are needed. The relations of capital to labor, of government to the people, of the soil to the hand, need to be re-adjusted.

5th, In what form should charity be administered?

In deciding this question, we shall find it convenient to distinguish between two classes of recipients; viz., permanent paupers and those occasionally destitute. Of the former class we need hardly more than refer to the alternatives of in-door or out-door, mechanical or agricultural employment, of home-relief or poor-house maintenance. The habits and circumstances of each community must determine the methods of its charity. This class, being in the main composed of those hopelessly dependent, does not present such perplexing questions as arise, when, by national calamities or natural causes, great bodies of helpful industry are deprived of support. The famine of 1693 reduced twenty-five thousand in Paris alone to a starving condition, and for a while overwhelmed the laws relating to mendicancy. The great number of persons now dependent on government support,* throughout the Southern section of the United States, strikingly illustrate that class of calamities which may reduce a population almost to general beggary. These, when they come, must be promptly and amply provided for: labor must be saved at all expense, humanity out of the question.

(1) Such charity must not be administered in connection with stated pauperism, or in public institutions.

(2) This is the best field for individual benevolence, unless the prostration of business is so universal that nothing but the credit and authority of the government can intervene.

(3) Government may, by foreign loans or other means, remit the pressure of ordinary taxation.

(4) Government may appropriate the necessaries of life for the public good, if the emergency is as great as would justify the same invasion of property in war; not otherwise, not merely to save expense or extinguish speculation.

(5) Government may very properly employ its marine and its finance in furnishing subsistence promptly, at low rates, and on easy terms.

(6) Government may, in exceptional cases, offer employment on works of public concern. This should be done at least to the extent of such enterprises as are in themselves desirable and profitable. The time of general distress is

* Winter of 1865–6.

the only time in which government can largely enter the field of industry without working a considerable share of disturbance and mischief. All works of manifest utility should be undertaken at such a time. This will cost less, and be a mighty kindness to the suffering poor. Governments have often proceeded much further than this, have undertaken works that involved a far greater expense to itself than relief to labor, and entailed a permanent burden on the country. This was done in Ireland during the great famine, and has more than once been done in France. The policy of such employment is very doubtful; for, —

(7) Government should administer its charity to the necessary amount by direct personal assistance, generally of supplies in kind, through its own local agencies. The degradation of accepting relief is, in such cases, removed by the universality of the distress. It is the most appropriate and least costly remedy. For example: it is not a matter of question, that the assistance which the United States furnished during the Irish famine, in its cargoes of provisions and clothing, was more sensible and effective, in proportion to the expense, than the outlay of the British Government on useless roads.

But the occasions for such extraordinary charity are few. The greater the freedom of intercourse, the wider the ramifications of trade, the quicker the sympathies of industry, the less frequent and the less destructive will be all local and temporary calamities. In the present winter, when, by the unusual severity of war, hundreds of thousands of families have been thrown on the public support, government, both State and national, has adopted, without hesitation and without discussion, the most simple, economical, and beneficial method of relief. There has been no loud outcry for grand public works. No useless costly piles will remain as tokens of this hard winter, and burdens to every succeeding year. The hungry mouths have fed off the hand of government, open now in charity, as lately clenched in wrath.

6th, In what spirit should charity be administered?

In that of kindness and respect. No condition of life and character is so abandoned that it needs or deserves that marks of ignominy should be attached. When the murderer, with his bloody hands, is to be executed, the sentiment of the community shrinks from the idea of adding insult to his doom. He is treated among no magnanimous people with contumely or outrage. If his manhood is respected, even in his crime, should not those who are the victims of misfortune, or at the worst of only passive vices, be free from more than the disgrace which is necessary to their condition? It is unchristian, it is cowardly, to insult by word or badge the unfortunates of society. No true man will do it: no brave people will allow it to be done. The followers of Mahomet would not suffer a tattered bit of paper to blow by them or remain on the ground, but would reverently pick it up, lest it should contain some fragment of Alcoran. There is no broken piece of humanity in the mire of poverty and crime on which the proudest of earth can place his foot, and not crush God's image. Tenderly, reverently, should we bear ourselves to all; but to none more kindly, more ourselves rebuked, than to the forlorn and helpless.

Yet there should be no weakness or paltering in charity. While all harshness and contumely are avoided, public maintenance should never be made desirable to the able-bodied workman, nor should even the feeble be allowed to escape just so much of labor as their condition permits. This is justice to the community, and kindness to the unfortunate. Especially should the public sense discourage and banish that shameless and obtrusive mendicancy by which the bold and bad snatch away the portion of the weak, the honest, the retiring poor. The truly helpless and suffering should be sheltered under the wings of charity; the indolent and wasteful, driven out into the storms of the world.

CHAPTER VII.

I. THE FINANCE OF WAR.

THE finance of war is greatly perplexed to the popular mind by one fallacy, which is, that a vastly greater amount of *money* is needed in time of war than of peace. Bewildered by this notion, than which none can be more absurd, the public are easily induced to sanction a whole class of measures that would be generally recognized as injurious in ordinary times, but are imagined to have some virtue to bring out a greater amount of money to meet the supposed emergencies of war. The truth of it is, if we suppose no extra importation of foreign material for consumption (and nineteen-twentieths of the expenditures of all wars are for domestic labor and material), there is no larger production, no more commodities to be exchanged, no more services to be rewarded, and consequently no more occasion for the use of money.

But *government* now becomes the great operator, employs perhaps ten times its usual number of agents, expends ten times its usual resources. It then has need of more money: but as it only takes the place of former employers, of former consumers, so it only needs to take their place in the receipt of money; and that may be effected by prompt, equal, and thorough taxation, — taxation, too, conducted by the established methods, and in accordance with such principles as we have laid down. A state of war, therefore, instead of being, as it is usually made, a reason for departing from the ordinary rules of public economy, is an additional reason for adhering closely to them in every particular.

War is a business as much as agriculture. The same resources are necessary: there must be materials, provision, tools, labor. This is all that is needed in either; nor is there the least difference in the two, considered as modes of production: their principles and methods are the same. It is only when considered as modes of consumption that they have separate relations to the science of wealth. "Raising money" has been generally accepted as the great business of a nation in war; but it is no more so than in ordinary times. What is wanted is labor, tools, provision, and materials: that is what is to be "raised." And at least an equal amount, though of different kinds and for different purposes, is "raised" every year or day of peace. Government, however, is now the great employer; and, as it is to furnish these, it must get them from the community which has them, and has been operating them. This, as we said, requires taxation, but needs no financial jugglery, as is supposed; and involves no departure from ordinary principles.

Indeed, war might be carried on without money; has been, to a great extent. The public force might always, as it often has, fill its armies by conscription; its granaries, by a tax in kind; its arsenals, by compulsory labor. The greatest armies the world has ever seen were raised, supported, and disbanded without a money chest. In the advance of civilization, it has been found more expedient, as it is more just, that government should purchase all it consumes in war, obtaining the means in money by taxation. But, as war does not increase the number of laborers or augment their power in production, it remains true that there can be no greater occasion for the employment of money, whose only office is to exchange the products of labor.

But it may appear, that, if foreign labor (as mercenary soldiers) or foreign material (the products of foreign labor) is introduced, there will be a greater demand for money to make the exchanges of services and values. Of the first, it may be said, that the employment of mercenaries is, in fact, too small to be of any account in the great calculations of warlike expenditures. The latter is of importance, but really forms a small fraction of the actual outlays of war, probably not equal to the reduced wages of domestic labor in arms, as against the same labor in peace; it being true of almost all armies, that their pay is below the average of industrial occupations. But, if we allow all the actual importation of foreign material to be so much added to the necessity for money, the effect will be simply what has been already indicated in the philosophy of currency. Money will be exported up to a certain point to pay for imports: this will lower home prices, diminishing the domestic expenditures of government, and encouraging the export of produce, which will continually tend to restore the balance. Beyond the point at which money cannot be sent off, without domestic distress, government must resort to credit by loans. Such loans, however, cannot increase the money in the country; for, even if they first assume that form abroad, they are turned into *material* before imported.

This discussion, it should be borne in mind, has only regarded the amount of *money* acquired in war.* We have had nothing directly to say as to the amount of capital employed. Of this we express no opinion; while we maintain that it is unquestionably true, that no greater volume of money is needed to effect all the exchanges incident to a state of war.

* For an able discussion of the subject in all its bearings, see "A Critical Examination of our Financial Policy," by Simon Newcomb. D. Appleton & Co., New York. 1865.

CHAPTER VIII.

ECONOMY OF THE WAR SYSTEM.

WAR is the greatest fact that presents itself in this part of our general subject. Its consumption, its expenditures, are wholly for unproductive purposes, and not only unproductive, but absolutely destructive of those by whose labor wealth is produced. War demands by far the largest part of all the revenues of civilized governments throughout the world. It therefore claims consideration as far as our limits will permit.

That war is a political necessity while no preparation is made for preserving peace, cannot for a moment be denied. So also were private combats and the wager of battle in bygone ages. Disputes will ensue between nations as between individuals; and, if no provision is made for umpirage or arbitration, a resort to the sword is inevitable. Hence the great system of war. But for established laws and courts of justice, individuals would, of necessity, be compelled to seek redress for private grievances by an appeal to brute force. This would not, indeed, determine which of the parties were in the right, only which was the stronger or more fortunate in the struggle. So of nations. When differences arise between them, how can they be settled except by a trial of strength? There is no well-defined, well-established code of international law; there is no tribunal of international justice: how then, except in battle, can their disputes be adjusted? It is a well-established principle, that a man should not be a judge in his own case; and therefore, as between individuals, it is decided, that, instead of the wager of battle, the aggrieved party shall submit his case to the arbitrament of his fellow-citizens. But, as between nations, no such arrangement has as yet been made.

Hence we are to contemplate war as a political necessity, until the nations of the earth shall establish a code of international law, and institute a high court of appeal, to which their disputes shall be referred for adjudication.

War, then, in the sense in which we are to look at it, is not an accidental fact, but an established system; and, as an economical question, is to be regarded from three different points of view.

1st, As consisting of a permanent military force, a standing army, with all the paraphernalia of war; and, if the nation be maritime in its position, a naval force, somewhat proportioned to its military establishment.

2d, A system of constantly increasing preparations for war, — arsenals, dockyards, and manufactories.

3d, A heavy indebtedness for wars of the past, with unceasing taxation for the payment of accruing interest and the extension and perpetuation of the system.

These three items may be said to constitute the war system of the civilized world at the present day. Looking at war in its economical bearings only, the great feature that presents itself is the immense and constantly increasing expenditures it requires.

In proof of this, we first refer to the statistics of Great Britain, not because they are peculiar, but that they are full and reliable. Her naval and military expenditures from 1815 to 1865, during which period of fifty years there has been no protracted war, have been £1,084,330,507, equal to $5,000,000,000, or nearly twice as much as the whole present debt of the United States: from 1855 to 1865 inclusive, £769,612,936, of which £301,618,920 were required to pay interest on the national debt; £331,887,258 for current expenses of army and navy; for the cost of collection, £48,733,823 (or about six per cent of the whole revenue); and only £105,472,935 for all the expenses of civil government. So that, in paying interest upon the debt wholly created in war and in meeting present expenses, the war system swallowed up six sevenths of the entire revenue.

The "Annuaire Encyclopédique" has the following statement of the armies of Europe for 1863: —

	Army.	Population.	Cost per Soldier.	One in	Total Cost.
Russia	1,000,285	64,000,000	$105.29	64	$105,848,000
France	513,349	37,500,000	268.18	73	137,729,075
Austria	467,211	35,019,058	144.00	75	67,310,840
Turkey	429,000	39,000,000	76.00	91	30,000,000
Italy	314,285	21,920,269	209.79	70	65,934,225
Great Britain	300,323	29,193,319	446.18	97	135,485,875
Prussia	214,482	18,500,446	147.60	86	31,346,730
Spain	120,000	15,500,000	209.20	129	25,132,370
Sweden	67,867	2,855,883	50.39	56	3,417,320
Holland	59,431	3,569,486	158.18	60	9,381,580
Denmark	50,000	2,605,024	71.37	105	3,507,729
Belgium	40,115	4,671,183	160.29	117	6,450,525
Romania	20,000	4,000,000	118.00	200	2,360,000
Norway	18,157	1,433,764	93.00	79	1,689,540
Greece	10,291	1,096,000	99.60	100	1,084,500
Roman States	8,845	684,306	100.00	77	886,965
Servia	2,500	985,000	71.39	344	178,880
Switzerland	. . .	. . . .	. . .	. .	. . . .
* Total	3,815,217	299,494,195	$168.87	77	$644,283,888*

But this sum of $644,283,880 is but a part of the cost. If we take the loss to production to be equal to $150 for each soldier (a low estimate), we shall find the additional amount to be five hundred and seventy-two millions of dollars per annum.

The following statistics from the muster-roll of the British army show its entire strength and composition: —

Regular troops	218,971	Pensioners	14,768
Local and colonial	18,249	Yeomanry	16,080
Foreign and colonial	218,043	Irish constabulary	12,392
Indian military police . . .	79,284	Volunteers	170,000
Depot establishments . . .	28,141	Total number of men . .	820,928
Militia	45,000		

If from this total amount we deduct about 270,000 for the constabulary, the militia, volunteers, &c., we have 550,000 men, as the non-productive force required by the war establishment of Great Britain.

* The Report of the Secretary of the United-States Treasury for 1863 showed, that there was expended for the army $747,359,828, and for the navy $82,177,510; total, $829,532,338, or about thirty-three per cent more than all the war expenditures of Europe for that year.

The following is a statement of the national debt of each of the nations mentioned: —

Great Britain (1862)	£	800,000,000,	equal to	$4,000,000,000
France (1865)	Francs,	11,902,000,000,	" "	2,380,000,000
Austria (1860)	Florins,	2,360,000,000,	" "	1,120,000,000
Spain (1864)	Reals,	14,531,000,000,	" "	726,000,000
Russia (1861)	Roubles,	418,000,000,	" "	300,000,000
Prussia (1862)	Thalers,	301,000,000,	" "	215,000,000
Portugal (1862)	Milreis,	149,000,000,	" "	168,000,000
Turkey (1864)	£	31,000,000,	" "	155,000,000
Belgium	Francs,	655,000,000,	" "	131,000,000
Denmark	Rix-dollars,	95,000,000,	" "	53,000,000
				$9,248,000,000
If the debts of all other European powers may be estimated at				752,000,000
We have a total of				$10,000,000,000
To this we add the debt of the United States (say)				2,750,000,000
Grand war total				$12,750,000,000

The following table, which we take from the "Financial Reformer" (British), is more impressive than any statements we could make in regard to the expenses of the war system in England, and the *small proportion* required for the civil department of the government: —

From 1834 to 1861 inclusive (nineteen years) the total expenditure was			£1,125,689,474
For army	£226,084,027		
For navy	177,654,537		
Operations	16,164,290		
		£419,902,854	
Interest and charges on the debt		546,400,540	
Total for fighting purposes and debt			966,303,394
Leaving for *all other purposes*			£159,386,080
Hence it appears that there was expended during this period for war, preparations for war, and debt, a consequence of war, an average, every year, of		£50,858,073	
And for civil government		8,388,741	
Difference		£42,469,332 per annum.	

Another important point to be noticed in relation to the war expenditures of European nations is, that they have been constantly increasing, and at a fearful rate.

The increase of taxation in England between 1863 and 1865 was fifteen millions sterling per annum over the previous decade.

The cost of the army, navy, and ordnance combined, in 1835, was less than twelve millions; in 1850, it was fifteen millions; in 1861, it had increased to thirty millions sterling. Mr. Gladstone stated in 1861, that "the total expenditure (imperial and local) had grown nearly twenty million pounds in the space of seven years; and that, taking the annual savings of the country of £50,000,000, the whole interest of eight years' accumulation was absorbed and swallowed up in this expenditure."

Mr. Laing, Ex-Finance-Minister of India, in a late lecture, said that "the national debt of France had, in ten years, increased £150,000,000, while that of Austria and Italy had increased £68,000,000. Spain was at its wits' end to make both ends meet; while Turkey was knocking at the doors of every banker in Europe, ready to accept any thing from any body who was ready to lend them, on any terms. . . . During the last ten years, there had been an extra expenditure of £300,000,000, incurred by two great European wars; £300,000,000 more added by minor wars and an armed peace."

Mr. Gladstone has made the following statement,—"that, between the years 1842 and 1853, the income of the wealth of this country (Great Britain) was at the rate of twelve, and that her expenditures were at the rate of $8\frac{3}{4}$, per cent; while, between 1853 and 1859, the national wealth grew at the rate of $16\frac{1}{2}$, while the national expenditure was at the rate of 58, per cent."

Such, then, is the condition, not only of England, but of all the European powers; and the United States of America are now to be placed on the same level. All have an immense indebtedness, the interest upon which consumes a large part of their current revenue. Each finds its annual budget increasing at a fearful rate; each finds itself obliged, under the present competition in armaments, to expend an increasing sum, from year to year, for warlike preparations by land and sea.

These facts should be kept distinctly in mind, when we look at the economic bearings of the war system of the present day; and it should, moreover, be remembered, that they apply generally to that system as it existed prior to the civil war between the American States. But that conflict greatly changed the war system of the world: it perhaps would not be extravagant to say, that it *revolutionized* naval warfare. In November, 1861, the British Government had, *in process of building*, fifty-four steamships of war, with a tonnage 95,855, with 10,930-horse power, and 1,254 guns. On the 8th of March following, the Confederate ram "Merrimack" appeared in Hampton Roads, and in a few minutes, with its formidable prow, sent to the bottom the "Congress" and the "Cumberland," two of the finest vessels in the navy of the United States, and demonstrated that, in the future, no reliance could be made upon wooden vessels in naval warfare. This great fact disposed of "*wooden walls*." On the next day, the "Monitor," with her turret, entered the Roads, engaged the "Merrimack," and she, in her turn, fell before a new and still more powerful enginery. Iron sides were no sufficient protection against the turret. This was the second important fact; and, together, they turned the whole current of preparation for naval warfare in a new, ay and much more costly, direction.

These considerations have most important economic bearings; but their political significance is still greater. In the first place, they destroyed the vast supremacy which England had held up to that time. Her previous preparations and accumulations of war-ships were almost annihilated at a blow; and the nations were thus left to commence together a new race of competition. In the second place, the immense appropriations hitherto made for naval purposes must, if the competition is to be kept up, be increased tenfold; and since, as we have just shown, all the principal nations of the civilized world are deeply involved in debt, it becomes a very grave and embarrassing question, by what means, and out of what resources, all these new expenditures are to be met. Besides, the question may well be started, whether invention and discovery in regard to military and naval engineering and architecture have arrived at their *ne plus*, so that there is no danger that all these now extraordinary means of destruction will not be superseded by others as much in advance of these as Enfield rifles are in advance of the old flint firelocks. Such, fortunately or unfortunately, is the condition and aspect of the war system to-day. To the political economist, as well as the practical statesman and financier, it must be a matter of serious consideration whether the time has not come when new and improved ideas of international intercourse are not quite as desirable as new engines of human destruction; whether the important events to which we have referred, do not suggest a different policy from that which has prevailed in the past.

To take the United States as an example: The national debt, when consolidated, will not be less than three billions, the interest of which will be at least one hundred and eighty millions. To this must be added the vast *pension list* which a four-years' war has created. To this still is to be added the immense amount which is sure to be awarded for *claims* on the government for spoliations and damages occasioned by the operations of war. And if we are to enter into competition, under the present policy, for iron-clads, monitors, land fortifications, and standing armies, we must have an enormous addition to our current expenses. Of necessity there must be a very heavy and constant taxation to meet all this, and that, too, with no prospect of paying off the debt.

The war debts of modern times are not paid off, and never will be, until the policy of increasing preparations for war is discontinued. But the condition of the United States in this regard, as we have already shown, is the condition of Christendom; and therefore, if a change is to be brought about, all are alike interested, and must unite in effecting it.

We have said, that, under existing circumstances, war may be a political necessity; but is it a *moral* necessity? Is there any thing in the nature of man which makes the destruction of his fellow-men in war unavoidable? Is it not as feasible and as consistent with his nature to dispense with appeals to brute force amongst different communities, as between different individuals in those communities? Would not the same principle, the same common sense, which establishes a court of justice for the settlement of private disputes, establish a similar tribunal for the settlement of international differences?

If it is indispensable to the preservation of peace amongst individuals, that there be a well-defined code of laws, which all may understand, and all must be required to obey, is it not equally indispensable amongst different communities?

At present, as we have said, there is no established code of international law, or any common tribunal for the settlement of international disputes. Is the attainment of these admittedly important objects practicable? In what manner can they be secured? Evidently in the same way in which all social institutions are formed; viz., by the voluntary, harmonious action of those who are directly concerned. And this can only be secured by concerted and concentrated effort. "Concentration," says M. Guizot, "is the highest element of civilization." The parties must come voluntarily together; must consult upon their mutual interests; in short, there must first be a general international convention, or congress. This is a necessary preliminary. Is it feasible? Can the human mind achieve this advanced step to a higher condition?

We answer these questions, without hesitation, in the affirmative, and for the following reasons: —

First, Because the present system is at war with the plainest dictates of common sense, and the highest interests of mankind.

It may be safely assumed, that any system, policy, or practice, which, in the course of events and the lapse of time, has become, not only absolutely useless, but positively pernicious and absurd, cannot long continue; that the advancing tide of intelligence will sweep it away as the rubbish of the past.

FOLLY OF RIVAL ARMAMENTS.

Each nation, as we have seen, has its standing army, its navy, fortifications, dockyards, arsenals, &c., &c.; and, consequently, each is endangered by the military and naval preparations of every other, and they live in constant mutual jealousy. Hence, if it is known or suspected that France is making an addition to her navy, England at once makes as large or larger one to hers. And, having done this, is either any safer than before? Are not both *as relatively defenceless as ever?* But France lays down still other keels, and the dockyards of England are again in motion, until the fleets of both are yet further enlarged; but has the relative condition of either, as to security, been improved? Has not each increased its means of *aggression* as well as *defence?*

That which is true of France and England is true of all the nations of Christendom. Russia does her utmost to create a vast navy. Austria, Prussia, Turkey, Sweden, do all in their power *to prepare for war*, however great the burden and sacrifice. And yet does this general system of mutual armaments make them any more safe, respectively, than if no such preparations were made by either? If this question must be answered in the negative, is not the arrant folly of the system fully demonstrated?

CHANGES IN WAR ARMAMENTS.

Secondly, Because the changes to which we have already referred, that are continually taking place in the machinery of war, are so great and frequent as to forbid *all hope* that nations can ever be fully prepared for war. We need not dwell upon this point; for its importance is obvious to any one who looks for a moment at the subject. What terrible engines of destruction, what unheard-of forces, are yet to be brought into use for the destruction of mankind?

The mind stands aghast at the awful possibilities of the future, if the present senseless and inhuman competition in war preparations is to be continued. The moral sense of the world revolts at the thought of such stupendous folly and crime.

INFLUENCES ADVERSE TO WAR.

A *third* consideration which leads us to expect that the present war system will be superseded by a general confederation for the preservation of peace, is, that all the influences of the age are against its barbarities.

(*a*) Commeree, as well as common sense, makes a strong plea in favor of peace. Extending with almost inconceivable rapidity, its influence is every day advancing, and its interests becoming more identified with the harmony of nations. No stronger illustration of this was ever afforded than that presented by the war of the Rebellion in the United States. Although a civil war, confined, of course, within the territories of our government, it deranged, to a wonderful extent, the commerce of the world. How tremendous its effect upon European industry! How rapidly did it transfer the wealth of Europe to India and other Eastern nations! How severely did it affect the commerce of the United States, driving nearly half of it from the ocean in the short period of three years!

But how circumscribed were the effects of that conflict to what would be felt, should a war arise between Great Britain and the United States! In such an event, how painful and wide-spread would be the devastation to the commerce of the two most commercial nations on the face of the globe! How terrible the results to trade and industry in every part of the earth! Yet no preparation is being made to prevent the occurrence of such a calamity; but every thing is done to make it as destructive and ruinous as possible, should it take place. It does not seem reasonable to suppose that such a state of things can be permanent; that all the great social, moral, and material interests of mankind can, in the present advanced period of intelligence, be allowed much longer to be thus imperilled.

(*b*) The rapidly increasing intercourse by travel between the different peoples is making them more acquainted with each other, and dissipating much of that ignorance and prejudice which, in times past, has been a prolific source of jealousy and distrust.

(*c*) The education of the masses, their gradual progress in knowledge, and their growing influence in public affairs, is another very hopeful indication. The people are being enlightened, and are becoming too "wise" to be made the dupes of a system of which they are the greatest victims.*

(*d*) The neutralization of the Black Sea, by the treaty

* It may perhaps be expected, that we should mention "the onward progress of the gospel" as one of the influences adverse to war: but we are indisposed to enter upon the theological question, whether Christianity condemns war as sinful; and, consequently, as we cannot assume that it does so, can make no argument as to its influence in preventing war. Christianity, certainly, has no direct tendency to abolish any system which it does not positively condemn, still less any practice which it openly sanctions and approves. We have our individual opinion, that war is not in accordance with the teaching and example of the great Founder of Christianity, but shall not moot the question here. We prefer to look only at the economical, political, and social bearings of the subject.

made at Paris, 1856, at the conclusion of the war of the Crimea, is a very significant fact, as connected with disarmament and the permanent peace of the world. By that treaty, the parties agreed that no ships of war should enter the Black Sea, but that its waters should be sacred to peaceful commerce. This was the introduction of a new principle into European diplomacy, although the idea had before been adopted in the Treaty of Ghent, made, in 1815, between Great Britain and the United States, which contained a provision, that the great lakes, lying between the territories of the contracting parties, should be neutralized, and neither party build fortifications or maintain a naval force upon them. This treaty has been observed down to the present time, upwards of fifty years, to the great advantage of both parties.

The argument suggested by these two facts is, that, if the neutralization of the American lakes and the Black Sea is found so feasible and beneficial, the same principle might, with still greater advantage, be extended to all the seas and oceans on the globe.

A CONGRESS OF NATIONS PROBABLE.

But our *fourth* reason for expecting that the great object of disarmament will be accomplished, arises from the consideration that public sentiment has been evidently turned in that direction for the last fifty years, and much has actually been done towards bringing the subject directly before the different nations.

(*a*) Associations have existed for a long time, whose object has been to bring about permanent and universal peace; and one of the prominent measures insisted upon as necessary to this end, has been a congress of nations. To bring this idea distinctly before the public mind, an international Peace Congress was held in London, in 1843; in Brussels, in 1848; in Paris, in 1849; in Frankfort, in

1850; in London, in 1851; besides several other general convocations in regard to the same subject. At all these, the prominent idea has been the establishment of a general congress, organized by the representatives of all the states of Christendom.

The result of these movements has been to awaken an interest in the public mind in relation to this subject.

(*b*) In addition to these voluntary and merely philanthropic efforts, the question was distinctly presented in the British House of Commons by the late Mr. Cobden, who took great interest in the movement, and had perfect faith in its ultimate success.

So far back as June, 1851, this distinguished member of Parliament moved, "That an humble address be presented to Her Majesty, praying that she will direct the Secretary of State for Foreign Affairs to enter into communication with the government of France, and to endeavor in future to prevent that rivalry of warlike preparations in time of peace which has hitherto been the avowed policy of the two nations; and to promote, if possible, a mutual reduction of armaments."

Lord Palmerston expressed his high approval of the motion, and said, "I am glad the honorable member has taken advantage of the meeting of the world (the Great Exhibition), to declare in his place in Parliament those principles of universal peace which do honor to him and the country in which they are proclaimed." Yet his lordship objected to being "bound into negotiations;" and, of course, nothing was ever done.

(*c*) A still more encouraging fact is found in the action of the French emperor in relation to this matter. Placed at the head of the most military nation in Europe, he proposed a congress to devise, amongst other measures, the means of reducing those enormous standing armaments which are the curse and peril of the world.

This proposal England alone, of all the governments of

Europe, declined. The Emperor of Russia, in his reply to the invitation of the French Emperor, said: "A loyal understanding between the sovereigns has always appeared to me desirable. I should be happy if the proposition issued by your majesty should lead to it." The King of Prussia replied, "In such a work I will join with all my heart, and in perfect liberty only to consult my own solicitude for the general interest of Europe." The King of Italy said: "I adhere with pleasure to the proposal of your imperial majesty. My concurrence and that of my people are assured to the realization of this project, which will mark a great progress in the history of mankind."

The King of Norway and Sweden, the King of Denmark, the King of the Netherlands, the King of the Belgians, the Queen of Spain, the King of Bavaria, the King of Hanover, the Pope, the Germanic Confederation, the Kings of Saxony, Wurtemburg, and Greece, all replied to those pacific proposals of the French Emperor in terms of high and cordial approbation.

(*d*) The public press in Europe has also spoken very strongly in favor of disarmament.

The subject is thus referred to in the Paris journal, "La France:" — "Now let us for a moment suppose, that by an understanding with the great powers, a disarming in the proportion of one-half was effected. Immediately, 1,907,924 men of twenty to thirty-five years of age, constituting the flower of the population of that age, are restored to the labors of peace, and at once a saving of three hundred and twenty million dollars is effected in the totality of the annual European budgets; with that sum Europe might add, each year, to the railways at present existing, six thousand two hundred and fifty miles. She might establish in every commune, and even in each section of the communes, a primary school. These great improvements once realized, she might, if she decided in maintaining the same sum in her budget, apply it to the payment of the public debt. The annual interest upon the debts of the different European states being about four hundred and sixty-five millions of dollars, they might be paid off in about thirty-six years. If, on the contrary, the countries interested preferred applying the four hundred and sixty-five millions thus saved, to the reduction of those taxes which weigh most heavily on the production or consumption of articles of necessity, what an alleviation to the people, and what a stimulus it would give to business! The labor of these 1,907,924 men, at only two francs (about forty cents United-States currency) per day, would amount to about $1,500,-000,000 per annum."

The "Journal des Debats," of Dec. 14, 1864, says:— "The immense majority of the intelligent inhabitants of Europe have pronounced a preference for peace rather than war, for economy rather than enormous budgets, for productive rather than unproductive outlays; and yet the attitude of nations would lead one to believe that war is possible and imminent, for on every side the system of great armaments devouring so much capital is persisted in."—"La Presse" says: "Disarming is the order of the day in Italy, is in course of realization in Austria, and, being proposed by the Palmerston ministry, has formed the subject of discussion in the English journals. Spain is thinking of reducing the number of men in her army and navy, thanks to the still-increasing probability of a European congress, the present necessities for which begin to popularize the Utopian character of the scheme. . . . We are pleased with the transformation: it is the outset of a prosperous career; it is the triumph of a truly great policy. It is not the congress itself, but, as a Spanish journal said a few days since, *it is the preface to the congress.*"

In view of the encouraging facts we have presented, does it not seem highly probable that a general congress of nations will not be delayed much longer? The necessity for such an institution, in an economical and commercial point of view, is becoming every day more apparent and pressing. The matter rests entirely with the three principal nations of the world,—Great Britain, France, and the United States of America. They have the power to do as they will. *Acting in concert*, their influence is irresistible, and they can achieve any object that commends itself to the common sense of mankind. There is no adverse interest in the case, and it is only requisite that some one of the great powers should take the initiative. True, the French Emperor's proposal failed; but the condition of the world has greatly changed since it was made. The American Union has been restored, republicanism has been vindicated, the barbarism of slavery abolished, and the civilization of the world has received a powerful impetus.

CHAPTER IX.

ON THE ECONOMY OF PUBLIC EDUCATION.

It is difficult for Americans to sympathize in the least with the objection which is made in England, even by those distinguished for liberal sentiments, that compulsory education is a breach of the liberty of the subject. Our incapacity for understanding or even respecting that sentiment arises from the fact that such education was early made one of the foundations of our social and political organization, and we have grown up to regard it as an accepted principle of good government. Our intolerance of the English theory, however, is not helped by the consideration that their own state makes the support of a particular religion compulsory on all inhabitants.

This is not the place to discuss whether legal provision for the instruction of youth is an invasion of that field which is recognized, in all governments moderately free, as belonging to personal rights; but it may not be inappropriate to remark, in passing, that the period to which compulsion is applied in this matter is that which cannot, for a moment, by any rational philosophy, be contemplated as capable of liberty. It is the period of youth to which restraint always attaches. Nor can it be urged that such compulsory instruction is a breach of the rights of parents; for their rights are not perfect and primary, but depending on the gift of the state, which can resume the functions of control in any degree for the public good.

The economic results of public education are manifestly in two directions.

1st, It is intended to effect the prevention of pauperism and crime. To use a popular American phrase, "It's cheaper to build schoolhouses than jails." In looking at this matter, we need to take a view between that of the optimist who expects the extinguishment of sin and vice by the advance of knowledge, and that of certain grossly material philosophers who compose statistical tables to prove that general enlightenment rather encourages crime. The first notion is refuted all too quickly by sad experience. We may fairly decline to consider the latter till it receives the sanction of one practical statesman. Such is the theory of our government on public education. We will not argue this. We will say that it is an Americanism to rely on general instruction to check the grosser inclinations of society, refine its manners, foster its self-respect, and multiply its restraints.

2d, Public education is intended to bring about, positively, a higher economical condition.

It is mind that gives man power over the brute creation; and it is by enlarging and instructing the mental power that the greatest possible factor is introduced into his effort.

We do not speak now of the education of the laborer in art or science for their own sake, but solely for his advancement as an individual being; nor do we refer now to the indirect influence on social order and national power, enlarging the desires, stimulating the activities, and promoting the frugality of a people. We allude only to the education of all who labor, whether as masters or apprentices, inventors or drudges, governors or soldiers, in order that they may more intelligently and efficiently discharge their parts in production.

It pays to do so. A few years of boyhood spent in practical studies has taken many a man out of the class of day laborers, and placed him among those who superintend the work of hundreds, or by scientific discovery multiply the power of industry manifold. Nor is it alone in these marked cases that a fortunate result has appeared. It is perfectly practicable in any country to raise the whole body of the people one distinct grade in industrial character; to make every hand and every eye more strong and accurate, while giving to each the *repeating power of mind.*

The two modern communities which earliest connected a general education with the agencies of government were Scotland and New England. In each, the advance of local industry, and consequently of wealth and social power, has exhibited most strikingly the economical advantages of such a system. But it was when the inhabitants of these regions went abroad to engage in the industry of foreign countries that the triumph of public education became complete and conspicuous. For more than a century, their intelligent labor has reaped the richest harvests of the world. Not to speak of social and civil honors, the Yankee and the Scot has everywhere risen, by virtue of early and thorough training, general information, and ready resource, to the mastership of all enterprises, all sciences, all arts. He never remains on the lowest plane of labor; for he always finds enough who are condemned to it by ignorance and that want of self-respect and social confidence which results from ignorance. He becomes "boss," overseer, master, employer, contractor, projector, from the force of that character which was impressed by early education, and those accomplishments which it bestows ; nor only this. Although we may remember that for the greatest inventions we are indebted to inborn genius or fortunate accident, we cannot but admit that genius is more likely to be born in men of such a stock, and that accidents are more likely to be fortunate under this mental training and industrial activity ; and accordingly we find, that beneficent discoveries, whether in comprehensive laws or little useful "knacks," have repaid a million-fold all that education ever cost Scotland or New England, let alone morality, honors in scholarship, happy homes, and civil peace. In plain speech and literal truth, no miner, who at the first blow broke into one of nature's sub-treasuries and found gold rolling out upon his feet, ever by miracle of fortune hit upon a richer reward than every people may secure, beyond the slightest peradventure, by the public, thorough education of its labor.

It is not alone demanded in the interest of a greater production, but also to secure a more just and uniform distribution of wealth. The more highly educated, industrially, the workman is, the firmer and apter resistance will he offer to the aggressions of capital or competing labor ; the higher will become his necessary wages, the more reasonable his remuneration. It is the poor man's share of wealth which, after all (while we respect the rights of capital for its own sake no more than for the welfare of labor), is the object of humane science and legislation. To rob the rich, or to make them objects of invidious enactments, is not to help the poor ; it is only to make their misery complete and hopeless : but, while wealth is sacred and luxury is unrebuked, to elevate and strengthen the humbler classes by all moral and educational influences, — this is to bring comfort and leisure to every cottage, frugality and temperance to every home, to attain the perfection of the industrial state, almost to realize the dreams of Locke and Sidney.

CHAPTER X.

IV. REPRODUCTIVE CONSUMPTION — ITS CHARACTER AND ORIGIN.

REPRODUCTIVE consumption is the use of wealth as capital. Only a portion of the wealth of the world is applied to the office of creating new wealth. That portion is called "capital:" that application is reproductive consumption.

It has been shown that mankind are continually wearing out their wealth; indeed, that it wears out by natural causes, independently of use; and that therefore, if men would not become destitute, they must make constant, unceasing efforts after fresh production.

But it is a principle of our nature to do what we have to do with as little labor as possible; that is, with as much help as possible. Now, it is found true, that, by employing present wealth, production is easier and larger, even after the amount so used has been replaced. For this reason, men take freely of what they have, and destroy it to-day that they may get a greater good to-morrow. This is the only reason why capital is used. The first capital was created without capital. Why should not all succeeding creations be brought about likewise? Because it is found to save human labor and multiply human enjoyments to devote the present to the future.

But this application of capital presupposes the constancy of nature. Men would not put grain into the ground unless they had the assurance of a return. Every act of this kind requires faith, — is an act of faith.

But even yet we have not secured reproductive consumption. Every article of value, either in itself, or in that it will exchange for other things, is fitted to gratify some craving of the human appetites, tastes, or passions; and, if nothing withstands these, they will certainly prevail. Here is an object of value. A positive force operates on the possessor to consume it at once; and he will do so as surely as a hungry lion will tear his prey, unless something more than brutal instinct of immediate self-gratification is found in the man. What is that which can stand up against the craving of immediate wants, and keep them away from wealth, that it may be devoted to other uses? It is not necessarily a high moral quality. It may be purely selfish. It may look on to the gratification of personal desires only. It may entertain no benevolent designs, nor be capable of any sacrifice for others. All its denial may be in its own interest. Yet we say that it is wise and brave and commendable. It is the principle of frugality. Only as this is found can the reproduction of wealth be secured. Here, then, we have the conditions complete. The process is as follows: —

1st, The certainty that present wealth will fail in time.

2d, The willingness to anticipate such destitution by labor.

3d, The fact that capital can greatly assist labor in this matter.

4th, Such a constancy in nature as secures the return of capital.

5th, Such a capacity of self-denial as will resist the impulse of immediate gratification, and devote wealth to reproduction.

But we find we have omitted one condition. Here is wealth. If nothing intervenes, it will certainly be devoted to luxurious consumption, because the desires of man in that direction are a positive and constantly operating force. Frugality comes in with wise forecast and strong restraint, and wrests a share from the grasp of the appetites. Seemingly all that is necessary has been attained. But it is yet to be decided whether this share shall go into the province of mistaken, or into that of reproductive consumption. There is a very considerable chance yet before it. We have not, however, regarded this as of great practical importance, inasmuch as it is generally admitted that the intelligence of mankind is, on the whole, sufficient to direct its own industry; and that this intelligence resides not in the major will of the mass, but in each individual, or voluntary association. It has often been proposed to take wealth away from luxurious consumption, by force of law, for the good of the whole; but legislators and philosophers have usually agreed to leave it to the intelligence and self-interests of capitalists and laborers how the wealth so saved from luxury shall be applied. To be sure, we have found in certain specific matters, and under the confusion of political forms, that laws have been enacted to instruct industry as to its own wants and behoofs; but such can never be reasonably defended on general grounds, and have to hide themselves under pleas of state policy, or find "protection" under the banners of party. It will not be necessary to discuss, as a principle, the superiority of government over individual and associated intelligence and interest in the direction of labor.

We have now shown how it is that wealth becomes capital; for what reasons and by what forces it is taken out of the province of enjoyment or of waste, and devoted to the office of reproduction.

I. What amount of reproductive consumption is necessary?

What should be the proportion of capital to the entire mass of wealth, to secure the industrial well-being of any people? This question will be best answered by an examination of the several offices which capital is to perform.

1st, Capital must support labor.

To all industry there is an entrance fee. Not only must the child be supported through years of helplessness until he becomes an able-bodied laborer; but even then every day's work requires a previous supply of food, clothing, and shelter. These form, at the least, no inconsiderable share of capital, though varying greatly with climates and habits.

A country which turns its crops three or four times a year will not need so large a stock of provisions for the maintenance of its labor as one that has a short season, and is locked up in frost and ice the rest of the time. The same diversity exists in respect to shelter and clothing. All degrees of difference will be found among the countries of the world.

Here, then, is the first duty of capital. It must support labor. Out of its products enough must be regularly laid by to subsist the laborers and those dependent on them till the next yield. The necessity is so plain and absolute as to be generally recognized. Few, indeed, are the peoples or persons who have not forethought enough to prepare for their bodily maintenance from year to year; while, yet, there are found individuals in every community, and even large communities are found in the world, which make so scanty provision, that, at the least accident or delay of the coming crop, they are caught in great physical distress, and are often reduced to suffering and beggary. What a light Alkman throws on early economy when he calls spring "the season of short fare"!

2d, Capital must provide for the increase of population. This is not because capital wants population to increase, but because population decides so. It is elsewhere shown what causes operate in limitation. But, so far as this increase takes place, capital evidently must furnish support either in pauperism or in labor. It is needless to say that the latter is the cheapest and best, under any condition, for capital. And this may be continued until the limits of capital are filled. If subsistence can be had, propagation will naturally go forward. This, of course, increasing the industrial power, tends, in a healthy state, to augment capital; and so, by mutual interaction, an advancing condition of society is secured. It is only by false and vicious laws that misery and crime are multiplied in this way, rather than power and happiness.

3d, Capital must supply its own waste.

Nothing else will. Labor only wears out capital. Whatever is wanted to renew and keep up the present stock of machinery and material, must be got out of wealth.

4th, Capital must keep up with economic improvements. Individuals and communities are affected in this respect just as they are by the introduction of new implements of war. All were on a level before; but, if new and deadlier arts are introduced into one, all others are at once forced to adopt them, or be at a disadvantage. So while a people might be getting along very well, and feel no need of any discovery to shorten or supplement its labor, yet, if such a discovery is made, it must use it, or be thrown out in the competitions of commerce. The operations of this cause may sometimes soon reduce the amount of capital required for a specific purpose; but, generally, its effect is, while multiplying prodigiously the results of labor, to increase the actual amount of tools and materials which labor employs. Irrespective of this, a great deal is also wasted by falling out of fashion and use, in the change of business, or of location.

5th, Capital must support government.

This is not the place to show the economical merits of government, or to dwell on its necessity. It does and will exist, and capital will be charged with its maintenance. At the last resort, and after all the complaints capital may make of the burden, it would never consent to be deprived of the protection of the public force. Capital can only live under law, and for law it must pay, — no matter what the price.

II. What amount of reproductive consumption is desirable?

We have been able to develop with precision those absolute necessities which take wealth off to capital. Wealth *must* support population, provide for its increase, furnish labor with tools and material, and meet the demands of government. In this it has no liberty. It must do so, or cease to be. But when these first gross demands have been met, shall wealth go further in the direction of reproduction. Shall the energies of the people still be bent on acquisition? shall greater wealth be set always in front, as the goal of universal effort? Shall the products of the past be scrupulously employed as the seed of still more abounding harvests? or shall the energies relax, when nature is satisfied in her simplest wants? Shall leisure or culture or pleasure now become the objects of life? Shall the fruit of to-day be enjoyed in itself, and the passing hour be spent in its own duties and amusements?

It cannot be denied that these are vital questions, and that as they are answered will the economical character of each people be taken on. But we here enter rather the field of the statesman, the moralist, and the philosopher, than of the economist. The science of wealth, of course, cannot reasonably object to the pursuit and acquisition of wealth in any degree; yet it may also recognize that, as man has other than economical relations, so he may have other obligations, and may rightfully yield to them. These, while it does not discuss, it respects. It is for the philosopher, the moralist, the statesman, to decide, if they can, how far the public or individual welfare, looking at all interests and duties, will be subserved by the increasing production of wealth, by heaping stone on stone, gathered from the bounty of nature; by pushing up the fabric of industry to its mightiest proportions; or, on the other hand, by resting satisfied with a moderate and primitive competence, and working for quite other objects than wealth.

So that we have no great occasion here to discuss these questions, while yet two or three observations may set them in their proper relation to our science.

(1) In a normal and healthful condition of society, there will be as little reason to ask such questions, for practical purposes, as to inquire how much centrifugal or centripetal force the universe needs. All that is determined in the constitution of things. The desire to gain and the desire to

spend are both manifestly in the original appointment of our minds; constant, abiding forces; and no more benefit can be derived from destroying or weakening either, than from loosening or tightening the bands of the universe. It is just right as it is. The two forces, by their antagonism, bring out the best order.

But human institutions and human actions can affect these forces in wealth. The course of things may be such that the possession of property shall be made undesirable by violence; or the springs of industry fail, in the loss of ambition and hope; or bodily and mental vigor be sapped by vice or self-indulgence. On the other hand, the tendencies of personal character and social condition may bring out the desires of gain in such a degree as no moralist, no lover of his kind, can approve; all arts, all interests, all duties, may be forgotten in the universal haste to be rich; avarice may grow into a passion, may spring into crimes; all that is good or holy, all benevolent ministries, all noble aspirations, may be drowned in the fast-rising waters of greed.

These are the limits, on the one hand and the other, of our economical condition. It will not be denied that the subject has all the interest that belongs to human welfare. But, we repeat, this is the province of other sciences than that of wealth. Let the statesman, the moralist, the religious teacher, instruct and persuade men to the true wisdom of life. Political economy can only regard them as the producers of wealth.

(2) We may be permitted to remark, however, that the degree of reproductive consumption which is desirable will be determined somewhat by the geographical position and political relations of a people. A nation that has, or aspires to have, international power and influence, has need of greater resources than one which is content with the simple pursuits of internal comfort and tranquillity. There is a marked difference in the degrees of wealth necessary, as a people thrusts itself into the arena where commercial advan-

tages, colonial acquisition, territorial conquests, military glory, and continental supremacy, are contended for; or retires to the development of its own soil, and the care of its domestic happiness.

But, still further, we find that one controlling reason for production, even in the least ambitious nations, has been the general and distant apprehension that it may at some time be called on to defend itself. The world over, statesmen, in all ages, have felt the necessity of securing economical power as the means of national security. Here, again, we see that as a country is isolated or open to attack, is naturally fortified or easy to be overrun, so the reasons for obtaining a large production will be less or more urgent. Many such considerations will influence the founder or governor of a state, in determining whether the reproductive agencies shall be pressed to their extreme, and the influence of law be thrown on the side of acquisition and accumulation, or all shall be left to individual taste or caprice.

(3) It is unquestionably true, that, all other things equal, the desires to spend or to gain will be differently developed in different people, according to the individual genius. Peace and liberty will not inspire some races with a high economical ambition; nor can the utmost violence of persecution, disorder, and corruption wholly suppress the mighty instincts of acquisition in others. And between these extremes every degree will be met. Just as some plants are born for beauty, grace, and fragrance; others with homely virtues and for unromantic uses, — so men bring with them impulses, ideal or practical, that determine them to their several courses, all the way from the serenest speculations in ontology to the maddest speculations in oil.

CHAPTER XI.

POPULATION.

THE question of population has been invested, by the treatment of British writers, with a great mystery and terror. The glut, famine, and death theories of Malthus have done much to impress upon political economy the shape it has to-day in the world's estimation. Rightly enough, if they are correct, is it called a dismal science. Malthus exhausted the direct horrors of the subject; but the effect was greatly heightened by the benevolent efforts of many subsequent writers to provide some way of escape from this fatal conclusion, — efforts which, as they resulted in palpable failure, only made the outlook of humanity more dreary and hopeless.

The fact is, all this British philosophy of population is perverted and diseased from its root. It comes out of social wrongs and false political institutions. It strives to apply, as a universal condition of human being, the miserable results of local misrule. Prior to all consideration of such arguments, there is reason to suspect theories of subsistence and population that come from an island where holdings of land are only as one to six hundred or seven hundred inhabitants.

These principles are intended to apply to the entire surface of the earth, and have no merit unless capable of such extension; but, to give them their most favorable conditions, we will first consider a single district of limited area, — say, England itself.

The two postulates of Malthus are, — 1st, That subsistence is stationary or retrogressive; 2d, That propagation is a constantly operating force, enlarging population in some assignable ratio. The inference is, that the relation of these two must bring out destitution and famine.

There are here three fallacies: 1st, That subsistence is not progressive; 2d, That population necessarily increases; 3d, That, even if these were granted, there would exist between them any such melancholy relation as is assumed.

1st, Subsistence.—The fertility of the earth, instead of diminishing, is, under intelligent culture and with the aids of science and machinery, constantly increasing. The advance of industrial power, in commerce and manufactures, not only furnishes direct assistance in agriculture, but releases, if required, a great amount of labor for the latter pursuit. As is the amount of labor applied to land, so is the yield, the world over. The England of to-day is vastly more fertile than that of the Heptarchy, the Norman conquests, or the civil wars. Nor are all its capacities of production exhausted. It has now millions of acres unreclaimed, which are susceptible of cultivation. It is no answer to this to say that they will not pay for reclaiming. That merely shows that English labor has now a more profitable employment. We are discussing only the absolute capabilities of the soil. With the known laws of agriculture, prudently followed, the produce of any country should advance in a certain and considerable ratio. Besides, we know not what new agents of fertilization may be discovered, or what shorter methods may be devised for applying power. Certainly, the mechanical and chemical discoveries of the last fifty years justify almost any degree of expectation.

2d, Propagation.—The rule of geometric increase is a favorite weapon in the defence of certain theories; but it is wonderfully far from the truth of nature. Boys have frequently exhibited, on the blackboard, the immense wealth they could acquire if they should lay by a penny a day, at interest, for so many years; and the result seems very alarming, as if that particular school would eventually become the owners of by far the greater part of the earth's surface. So much for mathematics. But, in fact, some days the boys don't earn their pennies, and some days they don't lay them by, and some of the boys die; and perhaps the bank unfortunately breaks, or, after a few months of continence, a juvenile rush is made upon it, and all hopes of fortune disappear in a saturnalia of candy and ginger-pop. The illustration is plain and humble; but it involves all the elements that limit the theoretic advance of wealth or population.

To argue from abstract and individual possibilities of propagation to the future actual increase of the race, would be like a philosopher's predicting an infinite flight for his arrow, because of his ascertained law of impulse and continued motion, disregarding the opposition of the atmosphere and the constant subtraction of gravitation.

Indeed, contemplating certain positive unquestionable facts in history, great instances of depopulation, ages of decline, the slow advances of reviving production, we may fairly begin to doubt whether propagation is a permanent force irrespective of conditions. We may not unreasonably inquire whether it ever appears without *a special reason in the case;* whether the rule is not the other way; viz., not that population does not proceed in spite of adverse influences, but that it is never called out except by physical circumstances, which, in all their contradiction and bewilderment to us, really form the condition precedent of human reproduction. Why not? We do not say, that individual *growth*, either vegetable or animal, is a constantly operating force, irrespective of circumstances. We recognize the necessity of heat, moisture, and special properties of soil to educe the latent powers of expansion. Similar, though more remote and perplexed, are the influences which bring out *reproduction* in the animal or vegetable. It is therefore more correct to say, that population, instead of being limited by adverse, is only developed by favorable, conditions. We are deceived in this matter, because propagation acts almost universally. That happens simply because the favorable conditions are almost universal.

This argument is not affected by exhibiting a great deal of misery, the result of want. The laws of reproduction are not responsible for subsequent mismanagement and abuse. Nor does this obstruction to propagation, coming out of circumstances, operate to the degree of preventing deformity or suffering. But it does apply its check before the limits of destruction are reached. Speaking generally, nothing is born where it cannot live.

In reference to general use, however, we shall speak of adverse circumstances limiting population.

This whole matter may be perfectly exhibited by an illustration from vegetable life. The forests have a constant tendency to enlarge their bounds, and thicken their growth. The rate of individual increase is prodigious in the family of trees. And so forests may, when there is no opposing force, spread over all adjacent country, and may grow closer and closer till the perfectness and beauty of the solitary oak are lost in the maze of interlacing boughs. But just as it would be absurd to suppose that the trees would ever grow so thickly as to require the woodman's axe or a vegetable pestilence, so it is unphilosophical to anticipate an increase of population which will require war or plague to reduce it to the limits of food. The shoots of human life will no more crowd their soil than will the children of the forest. As well might a benevolent botanist, lamenting the natural logical increase of the trees, predict internecine arborial war or sylvan infanticide, as Malthus, from abstract principles of human increase, possible in individual cases, forecast his dreadful tables of starvation and crime. The spread of the human race, as of the sylvan, limits itself by the chemical resources of the soil, the fostering influences of the air, the superficial capacities of the ground. The agencies of animal as of floral propagation are possessed of a delicate discrimination, a prudent forecast, and a virtuous continence, which shame the most cautious calculations of the reason. They may err somewhat, and that, too, within limits which allow much deterioration of the species, and much local misery; but their conditions restrict them within the bounds of life.

What these circumstances are which control the increase of population, we shall not discuss at this point.

3d, The third fallacy we detect is, that, granted the two postulates of stationary subsistence and advancing population in any country, there is any necessary relation of distress and deterioration between them. Such a view puts commerce out of the question. In the present state of the world, the only matter of interest to determine in regard to the supply of any people is, whether they are able to produce values sufficient to command in exchange the commodities they must consume. It is of no consequence whether Manchester or Birmingham can raise their own breadstuffs within their corporate limits, if they can create values which will lay all the markets of the world under contribution. Labor, if law does not hinder, is self-supporting. The powers of industry are commensurate with their wants. But, if legal and social institutions interrupt or burden exchanges, in one way or another, distress will result. There is no fault in human propagation, but in what is subsequent. To illustrate: thirty years ago, there was great suffering among the poor of England. This gave rise to the very theory of population we are considering. It became a matter of common belief, that starvation was inevitable in human society.

Now it used to be a generally accepted principle of physics, that "nature abhors a vacuum;" and much machinery was constructed on that principle. On one occasion, an experimenter happened to apply it to a tube longer than usual, when it failed to work. Rushing in great excitement to the office of a distinguished philosopher, he announced the catastrophe. "Perhaps," was the quiet response, — "perhaps nature does not abhor a vacuum higher than thirty-four feet."

Just such a discovery was made at this time in England. The corn-laws were repealed, and half the misery of the laboring class sank out of sight for ever. This it was which first led men to suspect that "nature did not abhor a vacuum higher than thirty-four feet;" that is, to drop the anecdote, that nature creates no human labor to be starved out of existence, but that whatever misery and suffering there is, comes of man's folly and sin.

In England, bad laws, passed by class legislation; oppressive institutions, the relics of feudalism; onerous taxation, incurred by the senseless war system; and unjust monopolies, created for selfish purposes,—have combined to cause the ignorance, poverty, and degradation of the people, and to make the beneficent agencies of reproduction a partial curse. The laborers of England suffer for the commonest necessaries of life, while England is the richest nation on the face of the globe. Unquestionably, the value of the total production of English industry amounts to five times the value of the simple necessaries of life for her whole population. Now, if labor starves, is it the fault of nature? The density of population has nothing to do with it. It is because the common people have so little influence on the government; because the land is held for the pleasures and dignity of the lordly few; and because the national majority is borne down by a powerful, selfish, and grasping aristocracy. Though the people suffer, it is because of nothing in the extent or fertility of their soil. But for a complicated, legalized system of robbery and wrong, every man, woman, and child in the United Kingdom might be as well fed, clothed, and educated, as are the inhabitants of the United States, and as much more so as England is to-day richer. Any man and any people that can create value can command subsistence in God's way.

If now we extend our inquiry from England to the whole industrial world, we shall bring another element into the calculation, not to increase the chances of distress by overpopulation, but to diminish them. Whatever may be true of individual peoples at any particular time, the general advance of population all over the earth has not been very clearly proved. But, whether it has taken place from century to century or not, it certainly has not progressed in the last five centuries at so rapid a rate as the means of subsistence; nor is there any ground for believing, that the present advance will, the world over, continue when the means of subsistence shall become stationary. There never has occurred a case of starvation in the history of the world which resulted solely from a deficiency in the natural means of procuring food; and there is no reason to believe that there ever will be one. There have been countless millions of deaths from hunger occasioned by the destructiveness, envy, or heedlessness of man, through war, commercial restrictions, or personal neglect.

We have spoken of the forces which limit population. We shall not assume to express them all, or to give an exact measurement of them; yet we shall be able to state enough to show what is the course of nature in this matter.

1st, Subsistence. — We do not mean any thing so commonplace as that there can be no more population than there is subsistence to maintain in life. That, of course, could not be. But it might be avoided in two ways, — by death operating on population, or prevention operating on propagation. We mean that the ultimate bounds of food are the bounds also of reproduction. At the last resort, and after its own extreme limit has been reached, subsistence limits growth. This, however, is only because to the impulse of the latter is opposed an unyielding prohibition in the former; and even this may only be effected (so far as the operation of this principle is concerned), the springs of population may only finally be dried, after a long and painful process: after the comfort and health of the laboring classes have been greatly, it may be permanently, reduced by continuous privation and hardship. So long as population can, so to speak, induce subsistence to increase, so long it may itself increase; and it is only when the latter returns a positive refusal that the former begins to check itself. In the interval of adapting itself, *i.e.* before it can hold up, there may result much misery and crime. So long as the increase of capital, *i.e.* food, clothes, and shelter, for the laboring class, is possible, the natural advance in the wants of the community, coming out of growing numbers, will determine a still larger share to reproductive consumption; will call off more and more from play to work. The causes that increase population, all other things being propitious, are positive and powerful, and will not yield to any feeble or distant objection from subsistence. So long as more capital *can* be taken up, they will continue to operate, and wealth must conform itself accordingly. But, when capital can go no further, propagation must stop, or population will starve. The former will be found to occur. It does not matter by what degrees of cold, hunger, feebleness, over-work, this is effected. Nature secures the result. We are no more bound to show how it is brought about than how it is that lions and elephants are not found on islands. Nature has discrimination and proportion in her work, and it takes all the recklessness and folly of man to bring about the least degree of distortion.

Destitution is, of course, a relative term. Perhaps, as a general condition, it is found mainly among savage tribes, which subsist on spontaneous productions or the captures of the chase. This is the limited state, and here the increase of population is very slow. Such has been the case with the North-American Indians, who, as we are told by Dr. Robertson and others, rear seldom more than two children to a family, and often none. We must not confound individual with general destitution. It is not claimed, that the former, when abruptly occasioned, is sufficient to check propagation. That would be against nature and reason. Such is the first gross cause which limits population.

It only applies to peoples in the lowest condition of life and of the least moral endowment. Upon those of a higher scale of being other influences will be found to operate.

2d, The second cause which we shall cite is directly the reverse of the first. It is luxury. How any one could ever have held the view that the forces of propagation are constantly operative, in the face of the experience of the Roman state, extending over many generations, destroying even the name of nearly all its great families, calling for the earnest remonstrances of its rulers, censors and emperors alike, and forming the subject of repeated legislation both in premiums and penalties, we cannot understand.

Luxury commences when trade and arts have been carried to a considerable degree of perfection. It is even a stronger check on population than destitution, though acting on a smaller class. Its artificial habits, its irregular occupations, its indolence, its self-indulgence, all combine to weaken the forces of reproduction. Rarely indeed would patents of nobility and entailed estates fall in, if committed to the inhabitants of the cottage rather than of the castle.

3d, We have that class of influences which are found in vicious habits and unwholesome occupations. The sure results of these are to check propagation, a most beneficent provision of nature. In a marked degree is this true of those occupations which, by heated air, by poisonous exhalations, by cramping postures or excessive labor, dwarf and distort the functions of the body. The same causes most mercifully defeat the powers of reproduction. It is well that it should be so; that, if these places must be filled, fresh life may be poured into them from the hillsides, rather than that the course of health and strength should be downward without relief, falling faster every generation. For the effects of vicious courses, we need only cite those savage nations which, in every quarter of the globe, are disappearing so fast, not more by the pressure of civilization than by their own destructive habits.

4th, We have also that class of influences which come from misgovernment and war. These serve to retard the progress of population, though not necessarily to throw it backward. France under the old regime, England through her most sanguinary civil conflicts, still held on their way in wealth and numbers; but Campania by excessive taxation, Belgium by religious persecution, Germany in the Thirty Years' War, Prussia under the great struggles of Frederick, fell off widely in both respects. It really seems too bad to quote, but many writers have ventured to suppose that war was God's own method of restraining population! The money spent in any war would, ten times over, support all the men killed in it; if, indeed, the destruction of the able-bodied could be supposed to take any thing from the difficulty of subsistence, especially when their helpless dependants remain. How the war-system affects population may be shown in an instance. Nearly half a million of young men in France are required to serve in the army from the ages of eighteen to twenty-five. This embraces the period at which the occupations of life are usually chosen, marriage contracted, and domestic habits formed. At the end of their service, they are thrown out on society with the vices of the camp and the restlessness of military life, with no position in life secured, and no occupation learned. The results have been plainly visible in diminishing from year to year the ratio of increase in population.

5th, The fifth cause which we shall notice is altogether different in its origin and character. The others have all been on the brutal side of man, operating by misery and want. This works in alliance with the nobler part of his being, and is of a kind with reason. It is self-restraint. In a degree, indeed, a great part of the world exercises this. The Chinaman will rear as many children as he can find vermin for as food; but the Hindoo, through his religious faith, stops short of all animal food, and limits population by vegetable subsistence. And so almost all nations have a point of decency below which they will not go. But the self-restraint of which we speak is of a higher kind, and begins to operate before the senses revolt in disgust or pinch in hunger. It is found wherever there is self-respect and social consideration. Hence the moderate increase of many countries where population maintains a just proportion to the general wealth, taste, and customs. As this is a subject to which belongs illustration rather than analysis, we give at length a remarkable example, which will also enable us to set in contrast the operation of the other causes. We take the State of Massachusetts, of which, let it be observed, only a very small class is influenced by luxury, and a smaller class even affected by destitution. Vice, war, and misgovernment certainly work as little injury here as in any portion of the world.

The annual registration, made with much care, shows the following result in regard to births among the native and foreign population in 1860: —

Native population, whole number of persons	970,952
Foreign " " " "	260,114*
Number of births in native population	16,672
" " foreign "	16,138

The number of births in the native population, to be in proportion to the foreign, should have been 60,239, or nearly four times the actual number. The difference is very striking and suggestive. It may be accounted for in part by the following considerations: —

(1) A very considerable share of the foreign population consists of those under fifty years of age, and so generally able to contribute to the increase of population. How far this fact is operative may be seen in the statement, that, if all persons above fifty were removed from the native population, it would be diminished somewhat over one-sixth; that is, brought so much nearer the numbers of the foreign.

* Of these, 185,434 are from Ireland.

(2) The foreign population is engaged somewhat less than the native at in-door and sedentary employments, and in so far are likely to be more vigorous.

(3) But the grand cause for the remarkable difference we have observed is found in the fact, that the foreign population are far less influenced by prudential considerations and social restraint. They therefore enter the marriage state with less regard to their ability to support a family respectably. Destitution, in the sense which restricts propagation, hardly exists among them. Indeed, it may be said that they are actually richer, according to the standard of living they were accustomed to at home, than are our native population. Consequently, they do not for a moment hesitate to marry from any fear of want or of losing caste by poverty.

On the other hand, the resistance to marriage from a more costly style of living, is constantly increasing with the native population, among whom the standard of family expenditures rises rapidly with the finer culture, the more elegant arts, and the greater social vivacity of each new year. The foreign population can get food, shelter, and clothing of some kind. That is their idea of life. Why, then, should they not marry, and rear families? To show how this cause operates to produce marriage among them, we refer to the same statistics: —

American marriages	7,381
Foreign "	4,057
One party foreign	,943
Nativity not stated	,447
Total	12,828*

* Of deaths in Massachusetts the same year, we find that the whole number was . . . 23,068

Of which were American	19,404	
Foreign	3,381	
Nativity not stated	283	
		23,068

Here we see that the mortality of the native population exceeds that of the foreign, comparing their respective numbers. So that, while we attribute

According to population, the purely American marriages should have been about 18,000, or considerably more than twice the actual number. Here we find the force of social restraint acting on the native population.

Such, then, are the principal causes which limit population. The course of propagation, as affected by subsistence alone, may be described as follows: From a given point destitution will bear it down by the most painful pressure, involving social and individual misery and degradation. Under a scant and difficult livelihood it will bear upward by its inherent forces, but slowly and with constant opposition. Competence gives it an assured and regular course; relieving from all considerations of physical maintenance, but substituting therefor healthful and harmonious restraints, hardly less powerful. Under these influences, society gains in wealth, leisure, and comfort, and is able to organize, educate, and control its population. Every child born into this condition may be born to health and happiness, and to be a strength and ornament to the state. Luxury may now enter as an element (though luxury, in the degree to affect population, is not a necessary concomitant of wealth and culture), and, as such, will either reduce the rate of increase from that of a condition of competence, or, by becoming excessive, it may bring population down with great rapidity. We have, then, these three grand conditions which limit the propagation of the race, of which two can only operate, by debasing and perverting the bodily powers of man; the third adds to his dignity, secures his physical well-being, promotes industrial activity, and establishes the state. There can be no question towards which the effort of the moralist and teacher, or the sanctions of the statesman and jurist, should be directed.

to the latter a greater proportion of marriages and births, we find them falling off in mortality. And what is true of Massachusetts probably holds true throughout the United States. Of course, this diminished mortality is in part accounted for by the fact before remarked upon, that their aged and feeble members were left at home when the emigration took place.

We have thus far spoken of the reproductive forces without recognizing the differences originating in diversities of climate and ethnical stock. These unquestionably exist, and greatly modify the facts of propagation; but, as they are local and peculiar, we shall enter upon no discussion of them.

CHAPTER XII.

IMPORTANCE OF A RIGHT CONSUMPTION.

THIS has been already shown by the light of our definition of consumption. It has all the importance which belongs to the science itself.

Consumption makes use of the wealth which production has brought about with all the world's industrial energy. It determines how each appreciable atom shall be applied: whether to degrade, or to elevate; whether, like fruitful seed, to re-appear in harvest, or, like a virulent acid, to destroy the very vessel in which it is placed; whether to set forth the humble household of the laborer, or to gleam a moment in the halls of revelry; whether to feed a thousand workmen on the temple of national industry, or to melt out of sight, like Cleopatra's jewel, in wanton luxury.

All the moral and social interest that belongs to wealth, belongs to its use; for as that is right or wrong, healthful or hurtful, so wealth itself is a blessing or a curse; so science should strive after it with earnest efforts, or guard against with the same wise precaution and thorough research which keep out the plague.

There is a right consumption of wealth that would bring comfort, health, and education within the reach of every human being not born incapable of receiving them; that would make poverty impossible on the earth; that would dispense with half the inducements to crime; that would beautify every home, and lighten every work. It may not be wise to expect the quick attainment of such a result, or worth while to prepare our robes for such an ascension of humanity; but just as far as the consumption of wealth can be affected by human laws, or customs and agreements, in so far may this end be approached in every day of time. It is only one part of this possibility at which the poet looked, when he said: —

> "Were half the power that fills the world with terror,
> Were half the wealth bestowed on camps and courts,
> Given to redeem the human mind from error,
> There were no need of arsenals and forts."

The mind can hardly lift itself to see —

> "What might be done, if men were wise."

Yet political economy is a "dismal science," indeed, if we cannot look on to the gradual amelioration of our human condition, not by miracle from the earth or the air, but by a wiser use of wealth, for kind purposes created and bestowed, —

> "All slavery, warfare, lies and wrongs,
> All vice and crime might die together;
> And wine and corn,
> To each man born,
> Be free as warmth in summer weather."

Not only does all the advantage of present or accumulated wealth depend on the use made of it in consumption, but the very existence of future wealth is decided on the same ground.

We have said that wealth has its generations. The life of man is brief, but he outlives property. A few articles of value may endure for centuries; but, in the average, their term is very short. Simply by wear and tear, the earth would be left destitute in a few years, if no provision were made for reproduction. Our kind is placed on the verge of such a chance, and can never go away from it. The dreary desolation of many nations illustrates the tremendous possibilities that lie in the *use* made of wealth.

We are accustomed to things as they have been. It is difficult to appreciate even that which we know might be. There is no economical reason why every people on the face of the earth should not be rich, prosperous, and independent; every person free, comfortable, ambitious, with plenty at hand, and every thing to hope for. As it is, the homes of competence or decency are, the world over, hardly more than islands struggling up from the ocean; a few spots redeemed from misery and ruin.

This advance towards economic good is not a piece of work to be paid for only when finished. If the grand result seems hopelessly distant, every step towards it does yet receive its reward; every effort brings something of fruition. No government or individual conforms, for a single act, to right principles of consumption; but the community gains palpably by it: perhaps the "last straw" of taxation is removed, or a capitalist offers employment to a starving workman.

There have been efforts to restrict political economy, so that it should have no occasion to ask these questions; to cut off all that view which looks out on the field of reproduction; to shut up our inquiries to the immediate, present creation of wealth, its exchange, distribution, and consumption, without regard to ultimate effects, and considering one article of value as equally commendable with any for which it will exchange. Such a mode of treatment practically detaches the department of consumption from the science.

A sagacious and generally correct writer* has even gone so far as to announce, "if a laborer is willing to work all day for a quart of whiskey to get drunk upon, political economy does not question his wisdom."

It is, of course, within the discretion of any author to

* Mr. Newcombe, in his "Financial Policy."

confine his inquiries so narrowly, and to erect them into a consistent system; but such a system will have little of that interest which attaches to a scheme that considers the industrial interests of man as a whole, and for all time. It may be *a* science of political economy, but not the science, as we choose to regard it.

If the laborer expends his day's earnings on a quart of whiskey, he will, most likely, be disabled one day after. The account with society will stand, at the close of the second day, as follows: one day's work done, of which the employer, and consequently society, has the advantage; no wages laid up; something taken off the health of the laborer, and the order of the community. But if the earnings are spent on tools or the education of self and family, or on personal support, the account will read quite otherwise: two days' work done, of which the employer and society obtain the advantage; two days' wages in the hands of the laborer, to be applied to the rearing of a useful and self-respecting family, to the maintenance of government, to the increase or perfection of tools, or to wholesome enjoyment and culture.

It is not, of course, possible, that, from a moral standpoint, there can be any question as to the importance of a right consumption; but does not the same interest attach to it in the light of political economy, considered merely as seeking to effect the largest production, and the most beneficent distribution of wealth? We do not ask whether such inquiries cannot properly be received into the science, but whether any scheme can be respectably complete which does not embrace them. It must not, of course, look at any question in a purely moral light. Yet the two interests will not be found widely and permanently apart. Political economy has for its end the economic good of society on the whole, and in the long-run. It does not limit itself to taking a *section* of the trunk. It is content with nothing but the *whole* tree, and *alive* at that.

We have used a phrase which explains itself, and which has already received various illustrations in what has gone before. But it may be worth while to fix and detain in positive shape the general impression we have of it.

WHAT IS THE ECONOMIC GOOD?

It is that application of the industrial faculties to the agencies of matter which will bring out, easiest and fullest, the satisfaction of those desires which are healthful and harmonious in the nature of man.

Does this imply the satisfaction of the greatest amount of desires, if, indeed, they can be thus spoken of in aggregation? Not necessarily, by the terms of our definition; yet practically we believe it is true, that, taking in all of life and the whole of society, a *greater* satisfaction will be obtained by ministering to those desires which are natural and reasonable, than by catering to artificial tastes, depraved appetites, and violent passions.

Does it imply the greatest possible creation of values?

Again we say, not necessarily; and yet it is undoubtedly true, that there is no surer way of securing the *best* satisfaction of the greatest amount of desires, than by striving for the accumulation of the largest possible wealth. There may be, will certainly be, a portion of such wealth that does not tend to improve its possessor, either as to character or condition; there will be a portion that will not receive its best application, either morally or economically, just as the nourishing rain falls not less on the streams that do not need it, and on the stony ground that will not profit by it, than upon the grass and the grains that are thirsty for it, and will repay it in a plentiful harvest. But this is the way of earth. If human laws and institutions do not interfere to prevent, the natural order of things will be sure to bring out the best physical condition of mankind, through the *greatest creation* of values.

It will be observed, that this definition of the economic good requires an equitable distribution of wealth, since the desires of one can be but poorly satisfied out of the possessions of another. We should therefore regard with more complacency a certain amount of values, fairly divided, than a much greater amount heaped in wasteful and unjust aggregations, or bestowed on those that can neither employ nor enjoy it. But this, again, we leave to the operation of natural laws, when undisturbed by legislation and prescription, confident that a better state of things will result than can be brought about by man's wisdom.

To sum up, then: Although much may be produced that does not satisfy any wholesome or lawful desire of man's being; although much inequality and injustice may take place in distribution, which shall so far neutralize the bounty of nature, and the industry of man; and although the greatest wealth is not logically coincident with the highest economic good, — we can yet accept the former as the end and aim of our science, satisfied it is in this shape that the latter is to come to us.

INDEX.

INDEX.

THE END.

Cambridge: Stereotyped and Printed by John Wilson and Son.